CREATIVE CONSTRUCTION

"Modern capitalism is a system of such concentrated economic and political power that its opponents often feel helpless when they consider how it might be replaced. *Creative Construction* helps to address this issue by exploring varied approaches to the democratization of critical social institutions – and the challenges involved in this process of democratization – to empower those seeking to challenge capitalism while developing creative solutions to the multiple, overlapping crises capitalist systems have created."
Grace Blakeley, author of *Vulture Capitalism*

"This is a brilliant and inspiring book about visions and the urge to imagine and create a socially and ecologically just and viable future. A refreshing exercise at a time of despair that pushes us to rethink democratic planning and how it can transform security and freedom into collective values. A must-read even – especially – for those that cannot avoid but thinking that planning is either authoritarian or doomed to failure."
Cecilia Rikap, University College London

"In the face of the climate emergency, war and financial crisis, a democratically planned economy is the only way to a more just and sustainable future. This book is an essential contribution to that project from some of its leading thinkers. Ranging from concrete models for organising production and reproduction, to pieces that address the challenges facing democratic planning, this is a must-read for activists, students and scholars alike."
Nick Srnicek, King's College London

Alternatives to Capitalism in the 21st Century

Series Editors: **Lara Monticelli**, University College London and **Torsten Geelan**, University of Bristol

---

Debates about the future of capitalism demonstrate the urgent need to envision and enact alternatives that can help tackle the multiple intertwined crises that societies are currently facing. This ground-breaking series advances the international, comparative and interdisciplinary study of capitalism and its alternatives in the 21st century.

Also available in the series:
- *A Desire for Equality* by Michel Lallement
- *Remaking Money for a Sustainable Future* by Ester Baringa Martín
- *Prefiguring Utopia* by Suryamayi Aswini Clarence-Smith
- *From Capital to Commons* by Hannes Gerhardt
- *Alternative Societies* by Luke Martell
- *Politics of the Gift* by Frank Adloff
- *The Future Is Now: An Introduction to Prefigurative Politics* edited by Lara Monticelli

Find out more at:
bristoluniversitypress.co.uk/alternatives-to-capitalism-in-the-21st-century

CREATIVE CONSTRUCTION

Democratic Planning in the
21st Century and Beyond

Edited by
Jan Groos and Christoph Sorg

With a Foreword by
Kohei Saito

First published in Great Britain in 2025 by

Bristol University Press
University of Bristol
1-9 Old Park Hill
Bristol
BS2 8BB
UK
t: +44 (0)117 374 6645
e: bup-info@bristol.ac.uk

Details of international sales and distribution partners are available at bristoluniversitypress.co.uk

© Bristol University Press 2025; Chapter 1 © Audrey Laurin-Lamothe, Frédéric Legault and Simon Tremblay-Pepin 2025

The digital PDF version of Chapter 1 is available open access and distributed under the terms of the Creative Commons Attribution-NonCommercial-NoDerivatives 4.0 International licence (https://creativecommons.org/licenses/by-nc-nd/4.0/) which permits reproduction and distribution for non commercial use without further permission provided the original work is attributed.

British Library Cataloguing in Publication Data
A catalogue record for this book is available from the British Library

ISBN 978-1-5292-3512-8 hardcover
ISBN 978-1-5292-3513-5 ePub
ISBN 978-1-5292-3514-2 ePdf

The right of Jan Groos and Christoph Sorg to be identified as editors of this work has been asserted by them in accordance with the Copyright, Designs and Patents Act 1988.

All rights reserved: no part of this publication may be reproduced, stored in a retrieval system, or transmitted in any form or by any means, electronic, mechanical, photocopying, recording, or otherwise without the prior permission of Bristol University Press.

Every reasonable effort has been made to obtain permission to reproduce copyrighted material. If, however, anyone knows of an oversight, please contact the publisher.

The statements and opinions contained within this publication are solely those of the editors and contributors and not of the University of Bristol or Bristol University Press. The University of Bristol and Bristol University Press disclaim responsibility for any injury to persons or property resulting from any material published in this publication.

Bristol University Press works to counter discrimination on grounds of gender, race, disability, age and sexuality.

Cover design: Liam Roberts Design
Front cover image: Assembly by Zualidro
Bristol University Press uses environmentally responsible print partners.
Printed and bound in Great Britain by CPI Group (UK) Ltd, Croydon, CR0 4YY

Contents

List of Figures and Tables	ix
List of Abbreviations	x
Notes on Contributors	xi
Acknowledgements	xvi
Foreword by Kohei Saito	xxi
Introduction	1
Jan Groos and Christoph Sorg	

PART I Blueprints of Desire

1	A Brief Sketch of Four Models of Democratic Economic Planning	21
	Audrey Laurin-Lamothe, Frédéric Legault and Simon Tremblay-Pepin	
2	Basic Problems of a Democratically Planned Economy	52
	Jakob Heyer	
3	Social Dividend Socialism: Labour Autonomy in a Participatory Planned Economy	68
	James Muldoon and Dougie Booth	
4	Distributed Commonist Planning	83
	Stefan Meretz and Simon Sutterlütti	
5	Counter-Planning the Polycrisis: For Biocommunism	98
	Nick Dyer-Witheford	
6	Planning as an Art of Government	115
	Jan Groos	
7	Discovery Beyond Competition	133
	Evgeny Morozov in conversation with Jan Groos	

PART II Building Bridges

8	(Re)imagining Housing as an Infrastructure for Social Reproduction	169
	Rabea Berfelde and Philipp Möller	

9	Democratic Planning in One Country? From the Anarchy of Public Planning to Negotiated Globalization *Christoph Sorg*	185
10	The Question of Transformation: Approaches to Economic Planning in Existing Policy Proposals *Samuel Decker*	201
11	Care Revolution: A Transformation Strategy for a Solidary Society *Gabriele Winker and Matthias Neumann*	218
12	Relational Revolutions *Eva von Redecker in conversation with Jan Groos*	230

PART III Non-Boundaries

13	Planned Degrowth: Macroeconomic Coordination for Sustainable Degrowth *Elena Hofferberth, Cédric Durand and Matthias Schmelzer*	247
14	Post-Sovereign Planning? Nature, Culture and Care in the New Socialist Calculation Debate *Samia Zahra Mohammed*	265
15	Democratizing the Forces of Re/Production: AI Planning as a Sensing Device for a Degrowth Economy *Simon Schaupp*	279
16	Embracing the Small Stuff: Caring for Children in a Liberated Society *Heide Lutosch*	294
17	Socialism, Planning and the Relativity of Dirt *Nancy Fraser in conversation with Christoph Sorg*	308

Conclusion 329
Jan Groos and Christoph Sorg

Index 334

List of Figures and Tables

Figures

1.1	Devine and Adaman's negotiated coordination annual planning diagram	26
1.2	Albert and Hahnel's participatory economics annual planning diagram	30
1.3	Cockshott and Cottrell's detailed central planning model	34
1.4	David Laibman's taxonomy of post-capitalist models	36
8.1	Illustration of the council structure as proposed by the campaign 'Expropriate Deutsche Wohnen & Co'	178
10.1	Planning in capitalism and post-capitalism	211
13.1	A visualization of the goals of planning provisioning systems within the doughnut	251
13.2	A fractal architecture of multilevel ecological planning beyond growth	257

Table

10.1	An integrated scheme of post-capitalist transformation	209

List of Abbreviations

CC	Communist Commonwealth
CPE	Centrally Planned Economy
GDP	Gross Domestic Product
IMF	International Monetary Fund
NUPES	Nouvelle Union Populaire Écologique et Sociale
PPE	Participatory Planned Economy
SASE	Society for the Advancement of Socio-Economics
SCD	Socialist Calculation Debate
SU	Soviet Union
UNCTAD	United Nations Conference on Trade and Development
WWII	World War Two

Notes on Contributors

Rabea Berfelde is a postdoctoral researcher at Humboldt University, Berlin. She is currently working on developing a social and political theory of socialization, asking how socialized means of production and reproduction can show ways towards a social-ecological transformation of societies.

Dougie Booth is a PhD Candidate at the University of Essex within the Department of Government. His research is concerned with the political economy of energy, contemporary governance of the ecological crisis and the role of economic planning in accelerating the green transition. His dissertation is titled *Transitional Inertia: A Comparative Analysis of Energy Transition Governance in China and the United States.*

Samuel Decker is an economist and activist based in Berlin, Germany. He works as scientific coordinator for the online platform Exploring Economics and is an active member of the movement for pluralism in economics.

Cédric Durand is Professor of Political Economy at the University of Geneva. His research focuses on the transformation of contemporary capitalism. Following the Marxist and the French Regulation School traditions, he studies unequal development in the context of globalization, the financialization of economies, processes of intellectual monopolization and the issue of planning and the eco-socialist bifurcation. He is the author of *Fictitious Capital. How Finance is Appropriating our Future* (Verso Books, 2017) and *How Silicon Valley Unleashed Techno-feudalism* (Verso, 2024). He is a regular contributor to the radical online journal *Contretemps* and the *New Left Review*.

Nick Dyer-Witheford is Professor in the Faculty of Information and Media Studies at the University of Western Ontario, author of *Cyber-Marx: Cycles and Circuits of Struggle in High Technology Capitalism* (University of Illinois Press, 1999) and *Cyber-Proletariat: Global Labour in the Digital Vortex* (Pluto Press, 2015), and has also written on the video and computer game industry, the uses of the internet by social movements and theories of technology. Two recent books are co-authorships: with Svitlana Matviyenko, *Cyberwar and Revolution: Digital Subterfuge in Global Capitalism* (University of Minnesota Press, 2019), and, with Atle Mikkola Kjøsen and James Steinhoff, *Inhuman Power: Artificial Intelligence and the Future of Capitalism* (Pluto Press, 2019).

Nancy Fraser is the Henry and Louise A. Loeb Professor of Philosophy and Politics at the New School for Social Research. She works on social and political theory, feminist theory, and contemporary French and German thought. Recent works are, together with Rahel Jaeggi, *Capitalism: A Conversation in Critical Theory* (Wiley, 2018) and *Cannibal Capitalism: How our System is Devouring Democracy, Care, and the Planet – and What We Can Do About It* (Verso, 2022).

Jan Groos is a researcher and podcaster. He studied fine arts at the Academy of Fine Arts Vienna and completed his PhD in sociology on 'Sociotechnical Imaginaries of Algorithmic Governance' at the Centre for Sociological Theory (Kiel University). He is part of the DFG funded project 'Governing Algorithms – A Sociology of the Algorithmic Art of Governing' and runs the podcast *Future Histories* as part of his research.

Jakob Heyer is currently writing his doctoral thesis on 'Basic Problems of a Postcapitalist Mode of Production' at the University of Jena, in which he analyses different historical and present approaches to a planned economy.

Elena Hofferberth is a postdoctoral researcher at the University of Lausanne, core researcher of the SNIS-funded project 'CliMacro: Alternative Macro-Financial Frameworks for Climate-Just and Post-Growth Futures' and member of the ERC-funded project 'REAL – A Post-Growth Deal'. She holds a PhD in economics from the University of Leeds. In her research, she analyses systemic drivers of ecological crisis and inequality and explores macroeconomic and political economy dimensions of a social-ecological transformation of the economy.

Audrey Laurin-Lamothe is Associate Professor in the Department of Social Science at York University, Canada. Her research programme is informed by the understanding that financialization is a driving force of economic transformation. In particular, she is conducting research on care and finance, extractivism and ecological transition. She is the author of *Financiarisation et élites économiques au Québec* (Presses de l'Université Laval, 2019), co-author of *Construire l'économie postcapitaliste* (Lux, 2023), and co-editor of *Business and Society: A Critical Introduction*, 2nd edn (Bloomsbury Academic, 2023).

Frédéric Legault is a teacher and has a PhD in sociology about post-capitalist economics. He lives in Montreal, also known as Tiohtià:ke.

Together with Audrey Laurin-Lamothe and Simon Tremblay-Pepin he co-authored *Construire l'économie postcapitaliste* (Lux, 2023).

Heide Lutosch is a literary scholar and feminist activist. Her book *Kinderhaben* (Having Children) was published by Matthes & Seitz Berlin in spring 2023. She works as a translator, editor and writing coach.

Stefan Meretz is an engineer, computer scientist, co-founder of the Commons Institute, co-founder of the interdisciplinary scientific project 'Society After Money', columnist at the Vienna magazine *Streifzüge* (Wanderings), and blogger on keimform.de. He provided contributions to books like *The Wealth of the Commons* (Levellers, 2012), *Perspectives on Commoning* (ZED, 2017), and *Society After Money* (Bloomsbury, 2019). Together with Simon Sutterlütti he is the author of *Make Capitalism History* (Palgrave Macmillan, 2023).

Samia Zahra Mohammed is part of the DFG Research Group Contradiction Studies at the University of Bremen. She studied Political Science and Literature at the University of Bielefeld and graduated in May 2022 with a thesis on the Socialist Planned Economy Debate. Her research interests lie particularly in the fields of critical theory, feminist theory, democratic theory, political economy and freedom theory. In her dissertation project she works towards an updating of a critical-theoretical concept of freedom, taking economic and ecological contradictions of the present as a starting point.

Philipp Möller is an urban sociologist researching social and municipal housing and regulation of the housing market. He works as a research assistant for the Left Party in the Berlin House of Representatives and as a freelance journalist. He is based in Berlin and is involved in the tenants Union Berliner MieterGemeinschaft as well as in the New Municipal Housing Construction Initiative.

Evgeny Morozov is an author, researcher and founder of The Syllabus. His writing on the politics of big tech has made him one of the most influential voices in contemporary critical thinking in the field of technopolitics. His articles, essays and reviews have appeared in *The New Yorker, The London Review of Books, The Economist, The Wall Street Journal* and *The New York Times* among many other publications. He is the author of two award-winning books: *The Net Delusion: The Dark Side of Internet Freedom* (Public Affairs, 2021) and *To Save Everything, Click Here: The Folly of Technological Solutionism* (Public Affairs, 2013).

James Muldoon is Senior Lecturer in Political Science at the University of Exeter and Head of Digital Research at the Autonomy think tank. He is the author of *Platform Socialism: How to Reclaim our Digital Future from Big Tech* (Pluto, 2022) and *Building Power to Change the World. The Political Thought of the German Council Movements* (OUP, 2020).

Matthias Neumann is a social scientist and care activist. At the centre of his engagement is the Netzwerk Care Revolution. For 25 years he acted as a sales assistant and as a member of works councils in the retail trade.

Eva von Redecker is a philosopher and non-fiction writer. She currently holds the Metropolitan writer residency in the Ruhr area. Her latest book *Bleibefreiheit* (The Freedom to Stay) pursues the idea of freedom in a temporal way – as enjoyment of fulfilled time. Her previous book, *Revolution for Life* (S. Fischer, 2020) – already translated into six languages – offers a unifying interpretation of contemporary anti-capitalist struggles. Eva hosts the talk series 'Eva and the Apple' at Cologne Theatre, and has a regular column in *Philosophy Magazine*, entitled 'Without Banisters'.

Simon Schaupp is a sociologist working at the University of Basel. He is researching the digitalization of work as well as current and historical social conflicts. Recent publications are *Algorithmic Integration and Precarious (Dis) Obedience: On the Co-Constitution of Migration Regime and Workplace Regime in Digitalised Manufacturing and Logistics* (Work, Employment and Society, 2021); *Cybernetic Proletarianization: Spirals of Devaluation and Conflict in Digitalized Production* (Capital & Class, 2021) and *Technopolitics from Below. A Framework for the Analysis of Digital Politics of Production* (NanoEthics, 2021).

Matthias Schmelzer is an economic historian, social theorist and Professor for Social-Ecological Transformation Research at the University of Flensburg. He has published *The Hegemony of Growth – The OECD and the Making of the Economic Growth Paradigm* (Cambridge University Press, 2016) and edited *Degrowth in Movement(s): Exploring Pathways for Transformation* (John Hunt Publishing, 2020).

Christoph Sorg is a social scientist at Humboldt University Berlin, with a broad interest in intersectional theories of capitalism and post-capitalism, social movements, globalization, digitalization, finance and debt. He is the author of the book *Social Movements and the Politics of Debt* (Amsterdam University Press, 2022), the article 'Failing to Plan is Planning to Fail – Towards an Expanded Notion of Democratically Planned Postcapitalism' (Critical Sociology, 2023) and the article 'Finance as a Form of Economic Planning' (Competition & Change, 2023).

Simon Sutterlütti is a sociologist and economist, blogger on keimform. de, active at the Commons Institute and the Utopia Network and works at the university project 'Society After Money'. Together with Stefan Meretz he is the author of *Make Capitalism History* (Palgrave Macmillan, 2023). Meretz and Sutterlütti are regularly invited to talks at left and eco-social conferences (degrowth, ecopsychology, future for all, etc.), sociology (great transformation), heterodox economics (evolutionary political economy) and podcasts (for example, *Future Histories* and *Dissens*).

Simon Tremblay-Pepin is a professor at Saint Paul University in Ottawa. He has written various publications on post-capitalist economics. Among them the co-authorship of *Construire l'économie postcapitaliste* (Lux, 2023), his article on 'Five Criteria to Evaluate Democratic Economic Planning Models' (2022) and his work within the collective Planning for Entropy (2022).

Gabriele Winker is a social scientist and care activist. She held a position as Professor for Work Science and Gender Studies at the TU Hamburg until 2019; she is co-founder of the Netzwerk Care Revolution. Her most recent book is *Solidarische Care Ökonomie. Revolutionäre Realpolitik für Care und Klima* (Solidary Care Economy. Revolutionary Realpolitik for Care and Climate) (transcript Verlag, 2021). It has been published by transcript.

Acknowledgements

The debate around questions of democratic economic planning is certainly not new. By now multiple generations of scholars have engaged with what is termed the socialist calculation debate, and we are deeply indebted to the rich body of work that grew out of this engagement. What is new, however, is a noticeable resurge in interest in the topic over the past few years. We are blessed to have been part of a wonderful group of people that has formed an (often, but not exclusively, academic) community with the declared intent to put democratic (economic) planning back on the mainstream agenda, and not only as a field of research, but as a veritable alternative to capitalist market economies. Not that planning has ever been away; it is an essential element of capitalism after all (albeit usually non-democratic and profit-oriented). But the ambition of those who have grouped around the notion of democratic (economic) planning in recent years, of course, goes well beyond that. We want to thank everybody involved in this small but rapidly growing planning community for the rich discussions, the intellectual curiosity so prevalent among them and the rewarding collaborations and enriching friendships that have formed over the time. We would also like to thank the editors at Bristol University Press – Paul Stevens, Ellen Pearce and Isobell Green – for their support throughout the whole process, the anonymous reviewers of the book, as well as the editors of the Alternatives to Capitalism series Torsten Geelan and Lara Monticelli.

Conferences and workshops have played a crucial role in forming an international community around this shared interest and we want to thank the organizers for their efforts in bringing together the right people at the right time. In this respect, 2022 was a busy year. The Max Weber multidisciplinary research workshop 'Socialist Futures – Past and Present Debates over Post-Capitalist Governance' at the European University Institute Florence, organized by Catherine Lefèvre, Marius S. Ostrowski, Troy Vettese, Morshed Mannan, Giacomo Vagni and Anna Dobrowolska, was an important connecting element that has resulted in several collaborations. The fact that Nick Dyer-Witheford has contributed to this volume is one such collaboration. Multiple episodes of *Future Histories*, a podcast run by one of the co-editors of this volume, are another. The workshop

ACKNOWLEDGEMENTS

'The Algorithmic Road to Socialism?' at Kiel University, organized by Marlon Lieber, was an important get-together in Germany. The workshop 'Biological Life and Political Cybernetics' at Vienna University's department of Philosophy was not directly concerned with democratic planning, but the audience was nonetheless kind enough to listen to Jan Groos's talk about 'Planning as an Art of Government'. Many thanks to the organizers Anna-Verena Nosthoff, Eugenia Stamboliev and Wessel Reijers for their interest in the topic. At the 2022 SASE conference we were lucky to organize a workshop ourselves, titled 'Creative Construction: Planned Economies in the 21st Century and Beyond'. Together with Rabea Berfelde and Simon Schaupp, two of the authors of this volume, we presented the first outlines of this book to the Alternatives to Capitalism network and the broader SASE community. A couple of months later Christoph Sorg introduced participants of the Bits&Trees (Bits&Bäume) conference to the planning debate and was (slightly) surprised to find overwhelming interest in the topic. Very importantly and also in 2022, the first symposium of the newly established German planning network took place. We want to thank the Rosa-Luxemburg Stiftung Berlin for kindly hosting the symposium and our special thanks go out to the organizers of the first symposium, Eva Völpel, Justus Henze, Samuel Decker and our own Christoph Sorg. Forming this network and coming together every year to deepen our ties has enormously positive effects for the German-speaking strand of the planning debate.

The year 2023 has brought a noticeable surge in media coverage of the topic within the German-speaking landscape, which was already a little familiar with the subject through the important edited volume *Die unsichtbare Hand des Plans* (Daum and Nuss, 2021). Due to the relentless efforts of the planning network (here, specifically, Eva Völpel, Justus Henze, Jakob Heyer, Samia Mohammed, Christoph Sorg, Rabea Berfelde and Samuel Decker) several special editions of German magazines and journals, such as *Prokla* and the magazine *Luxemburg*, were initiated. The year 2023 also saw the wonderful conference 'The Great Transition' in Tiohtià:ke/Montréal, organized by our Canadian comrades, who have formed around the collective Planning for Entropy. The Workshop 'CYBERPLAN: Does the Economy fit into a Matrix or Tensor? Interrogating Cybernetic Planning Proposals' was held at Informatik 2023, and the planning network had its second symposium at the Rosa-Luxemburg Stiftung Berlin. Last, but not least, the workshop 'Socialisation of the Social', organized by our wonderful colleagues Rabea Berfelde and Jacob Blumenfeld, saw a convergence of debates about socialization with debates about democratic planning – something we would love to see more of in the coming years.

We want to thank everybody involved in this vivid debate and want to send our warmest welcome to everybody interested to join the discussion. We have created a research platform that provides a good entry point for everybody who is interested in learning more. Find it at: www.creativeconstruction.online.

Additional acknowledgements by Jan Groos

I would like to thank my friends and family for going along with what, at times, amounts to a semi-obsessive passion. I would not have the energy to follow through with this were it not for you. I also like to thank the many brilliant guests of *Future Histories* with whom I had the pleasure of having in-depth conversations about democratic (economic) planning and related topics. It cannot be overstated how essential these conversations are for me and my work. Without them this book would not exist in its current form. Many thanks to (in chronological order of the corresponding *Future Histories* episodes): Benjamin Seibel, Jakob Kapeller, Frieder Vogelmann, Daniel Loick, Rouzbeh Taheri, Simon Schaupp, Jan Philipp Dapprich, Ines Schwerdtner, Joseph Vogl, Philipp Staab, Joanna Pope, Thorsten Thiel, Paul Feigelfeld, Daniel E. Saros, Aaron Sahr, Eva von Redecker, Ulrike Herrmann, Jens Schröter, Benjamin Bratton, Stefan Meretz, Sabine Nuss, Timo Daum, Kalle Kunkel, Michael Seemann, Silja Graupe, Jasper Bernes, Katharina Hoppe, Vincent August, Ute Tellmann, Thomas Biebricher, Isabella M. Weber, Aaron Benanav, James Muldoon, Friederike Habermann, Jakob Heyer, Drew Pendergrass, Troy Vettese, David Laibman, Trebor Scholz, Robin Hahnel, Nina Scholz, Gabriel Kuhn, Bini Adamczak, Nick Dyer-Withford, Marcus Meindel, Max, Lemon und Lukas von Communia, Thomas Swann, Heide Lutosch, Pat Devine, Thomas Lemke, Shintaro Miyazaki, Raul Zelik, Max Grünberg, Samia Mohammed, Evgeny Morozov, Felix von den Freundinnen und Freunden der klassenlosen Gesellschaft, Christian Fuchs, Matt Huber, Alex Demirović, Kohei Saito, Jenny Stupka, Søren Mau, Ulrich Brand, George Monbiot, Planning for Entropy (particularly Simon Tremblay-Pepin, Sophie Elias-Pinsonnault and Mathieu Perron-Dufour) and Tim Platenkamp. Two of these conversations, those with Eva von Redecker and Evgeny Morozov, have found their way into this book, for which I am absolutely grateful.

I would also like to thank Robert Seyfert, Alex Demirović, Jakob Heyer, Thomas Lemke, Christoph Sorg and the Colloquium of the Centre for Sociological Theory for their feedback on my chapter 'Planning as an Art of Government'. And I would also like to thank Christoph Sorg for our years-long, extremely enriching and enjoyable collaboration, which has spanned several projects and continues into our next endeavour. I am deeply grateful for Christoph's rich insights and continued enthusiasm. Furthermore, I want to thank the many people with whom I had the pleasure of discussing questions of democratic planning apart from *Future Histories*: Raphael Arar, Annika Beckmann, Simon Sutterlütti, Jacob Blumenfeld, Nils Rochowicz,

Houssam Hamade, Andreas Vondran, Maximilian Petras, Jakob Brossmann, Marlon Lieber, Niklas Stoll, Mario Taschwer, Tom O'Brien, Lukas Müller-Wünsch, Walther Zeug, Thomas Stölner, and the whole planning network. The research project 'Society After Money', led by Jens Schröter, with which I had the pleasure of interacting via *Future Histories* has to be mentioned as a unique facilitator for debate around utopian realism and democratic planning.

Lastly, but with the greatest possible emphasis and gratitude, I want to thank Robert Seyfert for providing me with the best entry into academia one could possibly imagine. After entering the field with a background in fine arts, I heard quite a few horror stories about the realities of academia. Over time, it became increasingly clear that the very pleasant interpersonal relationships, excellent working conditions, and stimulating intellectual exchange I was experiencing at Kiel University were far from guaranteed in the academic world. Robert demonstrated in his ever-present calmness that there *is* a way to do academia differently, a way that is supportive and full of trust, that provides stability, guidance and the freedom to pursue the peculiarities of one's own work. I am absolutely grateful to Robert that he has created such an enriching environment.

Additional acknowledgements by Christoph Sorg

I would first of all like to wholeheartedly thank every single participant in the new planning debate. Before this debate I was personally frustrated with the defeat of the square occupation and anti-austerity movements and the transnational rise of the far right. I was also disoriented by the failure and/or refusal of many contemporary movements to articulate clear alternatives to the status quo. The debate has cured several years of political depression and 36 years of internalized capitalist realism.

I developed an interest in the socialist calculation debate and in alternatives beyond Western capitalism and Eastern state socialism when reading Johanna Bockman's wonderful research on the history of neoliberalism, socialism and the non-aligned movement about a decade ago. However, it was not until Houssam Hamade convinced me to read *The People's Republic of Walmart*, Samuel Decker showed me Jan Groos's amazing podcast *Future Histories* during one of our lockdown walks, and Jakob Heyer later introduced me to older theories and models of democratic planning, that I decided to engage more with post-capitalist alternatives in general and democratic planning in particular. Special thanks to Jan Groos for his invaluable work on post-capitalist imaginaries and for the wonderful collaboration on this and other projects. It has been such a pleasure to work with someone so passionate, knowledgeable and kind.

I would like to thank the amazing (former and present) participants of our democratic planning reading group for countless interesting debates, insights, fun evenings and for helpful feedback on my work-in-progress texts. This includes Sophie-Marie Aß, Nina Bach Rabea Berfelde, Samuel Decker, Justus Henze, Theresa Klostermeier, Lukas Müller-Wunsch, Anna Neuhauss, Luca Vogel, – and special thanks to Samuel Decker for putting the whole thing together. Thanks also to Laura Horn, Louison Cahen-Fourot and the members of the research groups Economic Policy, Institutions and Change and The Socio-Economic Research Centre at Roskilde University for feedback on my work on planning in capitalism and post-capitalism. Special thanks to Sabrina Zajak and Laura Horn for academic support in a particularly precarious period of my (anti-)career.

I would also like to thank the numerous people who provided feedback, insights or any other kind of support during this project, among others David Bailey, Samuel Decker, Jan Groos, Sandra Sieron, Leo McCann, Yousaf Nishat-Botero, Matthew Thompson, Jacob Blumenfeld, Rabea Berfelde, Sabine Nuss, Philipp Staab, Bernd Bonfert, Donatella della Porta, Nancy Fraser, Sabrina Zajak, Carolina Vestena, Christian Scheper and Lisa Scholey. Special thanks to Heide Lutosch and Savvina Chowdhury for their work in rendering feminist blindspots of the planning debate more visible.

Finally, I would like to thank my child Malu for charging my emotional battery; and for refusing to nap anywhere but a moving pram for a couple of months and thus providing me with countless hours to think about the content of the book on long walks. Thanks to my friends Imke Rueben and Samuel Decker for emotional support during the period in which the book was edited. Most importantly, special thanks to my partner Wiebke for putting up with my (irrational) decision to stay in academia and my terrible time management, and for listening to my regular rants, frustrations and ramblings.

Reference

Daum, T. and Nuss, S. (2021) *Die unsichtbare Hand des Plans*. Berlin: Dietz Berlin.

Foreword: Planning in the Age of Polycrisis

Kohei Saito

'No is not enough' (Klein, 2017). This famous phrase from Naomi Klein is more compelling than ever today. We are heading to a planetary catastrophe at full speed. The experience of COVID-19 alone suffices to show how the current socio-economic system is incapable of adequately responding to a planetary crisis and protecting our lives. Rather, it threatens both civilization and ecosystems. In addition, the global pandemic is not the last crisis, but rather the beginning of a chronic emergency in the Anthropocene, a geological epoch, in which humans have become a 'geological force'. The chronic emergency consists of pandemic, war, inflation, and climate breakdown among others, each of which amplifies the polycrisis of democracy, the geopolitical tension, and economic inequality due to increasing natural disasters, food/water shortage, and refugees.

While the Anthropocene is characterized by this long-lasting multistranded crisis, its main cause is human-driven climate change as it brings about irreversible changes in the earth system. Considering the enormous scale of the current planetary crisis, all the previous attempts of decarbonization that pivot around the UN Paris Agreement turn out to be completely infinitesimal. After repeating failures of the COPs (conference of the parties) in the last three decades, today's inconvenient truth is that we can no longer achieve the 1.5 °C target. Unfortunately, this means that the situation will drastically worsen in the next decades, especially in the Global South where people are least responsible for the polycrisis. In this context, continuing 'business as usual' is simply irrational. Rather, it is necessary to abandon the outdated optimism of 'progress', 'rationality' and 'freedom' associated with the history of modern capitalism.

In this situation, the left needs to part from its traditional approach of 'merely' critiquing capitalism. In fact, critique alone is no longer effective. Everyone plainly knows today that neoliberalism is bad, capitalism is not sustainable, and war is destructive. The problem is not that people are trapped into some kind of 'false consciousness' and unable to see the real crisis, but rather that people are not mobilized and radicalized as they do not find any attractive and compelling alternative to capitalism in the left-wing discourses. If this is the case, it is necessary to abandon the '*Bilderverbot*' that prohibits thinking about what alternatives to capitalism might look like in concrete terms, and to positively present a concrete utopia.

In recent years, there have been various attempts to provide such a vision. In this context, democratic planning gains more attention. The experience of the COVID-19 pandemic demonstrated how the belief in market fundamentalism characteristic to neoliberal policies only worsened the crisis, although under the hegemony of neoliberalism and the collapse of actually existing socialism, the free market had been celebrated as the most efficient and rational system. The market produces only what is profitable, and not what is necessary to mitigate the crisis. Economic inequality increased even more, and the government had to intervene in the market to provide the necessary goods and services, through radical measures such as lockdown, free vaccination and cash payouts to households.

This experience of market failure marks the end of neoliberalism. At least, neoliberalism is already a 'zombie neoliberalism' in that it does not yet recognize that it is already dead. It is increasingly clear that free market competition is rather an obstacle in the moment of acute crisis. It is more necessary than ever to plan consciously in deciding what is essential and unnecessary. From this perspective, in *Marx in the Anthropocene* (2022) I demand the revival of communism.

Planning today must have an ecological dimension. Greta Thunberg rightly criticized 'fairy tales of eternal growth' (Thunberg, 2019). Since the absolute decoupling of economic growth and resource and energy use is unlikely to occur fast enough to achieve the climate target, further economic growth is an obstacle to establishing a sustainable society. The main drive for economic growth is obviously capitalism, whose insatiable desire for profits has constantly expanded its frontiers of exploitation of workers and extraction of natural resources. Without global capitalism, there would be no planetary ecological crisis. Since this system of endless growth is, from the very beginning, dependent upon fossil fuel, green capitalism is easy to imagine but hard to achieve in reality. Since capitalism as a system of infinite accumulation comes to be regarded as a root cause of climate breakdown, degrowth is gaining more attention as a radical alternative to the current irrational economic system.

Obviously, this requirement of reducing production from the perspective of ecosocialist degrowth requires careful planning. However, in contrast to the recent popularity of degrowth, planning remains marginalized due to the traumatic failure of Soviet socialism. Many people still believe that planning is *anti-democratic*. This situation needs to change, if a positive post-capitalist vision of the future society is to be concretized. This is why this book is of great importance today.

Of course, there are various problems that such new socialist attempts need to answer. Here are some questions that need to be addressed:

1. How would it be possible to plan at all when the existing world is experiencing increasing radical uncertainties due to the polycrisis. When the world is heading towards a climate breakdown, abnormalities become normal. How can ten-year planning take place in such a situation?
2. Democratic planning is an absolute precondition for a socialist politics to avoid the disaster of Soviet socialism. However, deliberation and participation take time. There is always the temptation for a more top-down transition to a new society, especially when the climate crisis is so acute. How could democratic planning guarantee the rapid transition that climate activists demand?
3. Democratic planning alone is not sufficient. It needs to plan *ecologically*. This means that the planned reduction of production is required in the Global North. How can 'ecological planning' take place in a democratic manner, when everyone today wants to continue consuming more.
4. Planning must not be limited to the factory. It needs to be expanded to households. However, reproductive labour is often excluded from the previous debates. How is it possible to quantify caring activities?
5. How is it possible to concretize the strategic transition to planned economy? Who will be the subject of this transformative change? What is the role of new information technologies in realizing a planned economy?

The answer to these questions is far from obvious. This is why more people from various disciplines should participate in thinking about the urgent issue of planning. In other words, a new socialist calculation debate in the age of polycrisis must take place now, and I hope that this book will be its beginning.

References

Klein, N. (2017) *No Is Not Enough: Resisting Trump's Shock Politics and Winning the World We Need*. Toronto: Knopf Canada.

Saito, K. (2022) *Marx in the Anthropocene: Towards the Idea of Degrowth Communism*. Cambridge/New York: Cambridge University Press.

Thunberg, G. (2019) Speech at the United Nations Climate Action Summit. [min 41:05–45:37]. https://www.youtube.com/watch?v=haewHZ8ubKA.

Introduction

Jan Groos and Christoph Sorg

Demystification, practiced alone, leads to a dead end.

(Dyer-Witheford, 1999)

The multiple crises of climate, reproduction and finance – among others – continuously remind us that far-reaching democracy, structural security and ecological sustainability cannot be achieved under capitalism. To reproduce itself capitalism needs to inhibit democracy within the economic realm to ensure that any societal surplus will be used to foster further accumulation instead of directly satisfying needs (Schweikart, 1993); 'cannibalize' (Fraser, this volume) our solidarity by exploiting the sphere of reproduction as unpaid work; and exploit nature as an extractive resource and waste sink (Malm, 2016). A rich and convincing body of work points out the many ways in which capitalism is unsustainable as a socio-metabolic regime (Moore, 2015; Saito, 2022) and as an 'institutionalized social order' (Fraser and Jaeggi, 2018). There are, in short, numerous well-crafted and insightful critiques of capitalism. This book, however, focuses on the construction, development and imagination of desirable alternatives to capitalism rather than the critique of existing conditions. It does so not to dismiss one for the other (not by a long shot), but simply because one – the *creative construction* of scalable alternatives – is dramatically underexplored compared to the plethora of rich critique.

Engaging in such creative construction of scalable alternatives to capitalism is all the more important at a time when the proposition of neoliberalism, as an ideology and as a regulatory regime, has lost some of its persuasive power in the eyes of the public. The massive interventions of central banks in the wake of the 2008 financial crisis and the coronavirus pandemic, large-scale state-led investment in the green transition accompanied by a renewed interest in the role of industrial policy (Mazzucato, 2021), the rise of financial capital and, with it, the rise of powerful asset managers (Braun, 2020) all point towards capitalism transitioning into a new, and yet to be defined, regulatory regime.

Such transitions are never seamless, and they suggest that – even from the perspective of those who had up to this point benefitted from its operations – the status quo cannot be upheld in its current form. It is then all the more important to not just analyse, comment on and speculate about what form capitalism will take next, but instead to actively develop viable alternatives to capitalism as a mode of (re-)production and an institutionalized social order.

Developing such alternatives is *constructive* not only because it aims to go beyond critique, but also crucially because the struggle for the alternative is always already a process of constructing different forms of social relations. It is *creative* because it understands this construction as a continuous process of democratic deliberation and coordination. Creative construction is not about having a plan, but about planning together. Creative construction means deliberate and collaborative forms of organizing society that contrast with the (ultimately not really creative) destruction that is a necessary aspect of submitting key decisions of life to impersonal market forces.

By engaging in the creative construction of alternatives this book contributes to new academic and popular debates about post-capitalist alternatives (Vrasti, 2016; Hahnel and Wright, 2017; Arruzza et al, 2019; Fraser, 2020; Adamczak, 2021; Fishwick and Kiersey, 2021; Lane, 2023). These range from propositions centred on degrowth (Kallis, 2018; Burkhart, Schmelzer and Treu, 2020; Saito, 2022), commoning/commonism (Federici and Linebaugh, 2018; Sutterlütti and Meretz, 2023; Gerhardt, 2023), prefiguration (Redecker, 2021; Monticelli, 2022) and different calls for a Green New Deal (Klein, 2019; Ajl, 2021; Riexinger et al, 2021), all the way to techno-optimistic calls for a fully automated, post-work and post-scarcity post-capitalism (Rifkin, 2014; Mason, 2015; Srnicek and Williams, 2015; Hester and Srnicek, 2018; Bastani, 2019). We highly appreciate this turn towards broader discussions of post-capitalist alternatives and think that it is of utmost importance to further engage in these debates by including an important issue that is not yet sufficiently addressed in these proposals: democratic economic planning.

While many still associate economic planning with Gosplan authoritarianism, we argue that democratic planning in the 21st century should be understood as a paradigm that goes beyond what is often framed as a dichotomy between central planning and market economies. Such democratic planning can be a fruitful carrier to overcome a merely defensive stance towards capitalism since it provides alternative modes of engaging with large-scale problems that can only be resolved through cooperation and collective coordination. This resonates with an intuitive assessment of how to approach problems like the ecological crisis, opening the gate for the creation of both concrete alternative praxis at scale as well as new collective imaginaries of possible futures.

Along these lines we would like to link new debates about post-capitalist alternatives to recent work about the feasibility of economic planning in the

21st century (Dyer-Witheford, 2013; Saros, 2014; Bratton, 2016, p 327ff; Morozov, 2019; Project Society After Money, 2019; Dapprich, 2020; Jones, 2020; Arboleda, 2021; Groos, 2021; Hahnel, 2021; Benanav, 2022; Planning for Entropy, 2022; Sorg, 2022; Vettese and Pendergrass, 2022; Mohammed, 2023; Sorg and Groos, 2025; Durand and Keucheyan, 2024; Hannah, 2025). A variety of authors has recently reminded us that economic planning actually features prominently in capitalism (Adler, 2019; Phillips and Rozworski, 2019; Alami and Dixon, 2024; Blakeley, 2024). Different divisions in corporations do not trade with one another (Mandel, 1986) but collaborate according to a plan, and large-scale distribution networks such as Amazon and Walmart coordinate supply chains across the globe, albeit in an authoritarian fashion and for profit (Jameson, 2009, p 420ff). A related body of literature interprets the further development of digital technologies, increasing computing power, artificial intelligence and big data as the technological foundation for new forms of non-capitalist economic planning and coordination (Bratton, 2016; Morozov, 2019), asking whether these new digital technologies have the potential to solve the socialist calculation problem, which occupied Austrian, neoclassical (non-socialist and socialist) and Marxist economists since the early 20th century. In response to Marxist proposals for moneyless socialist economies based on public ownership of the means of production and central planning in kind (Neurath, 1919), Austrian economists such as von Mises (1922) argued that there could be no rational socialist economic calculation since this would require prices and markets for the means of production. A variety of socialist proposals dispute the claim (Bockman et al, 2016), the most well-known of which is Lange and Lerner's (1938) model of a socialist economy in which central planners and factory managers determine prices via a trial-and-error method. Foreshadowing the recent return of the socialist calculation debate in the age of digitalization, Lange (1979) argues that computers can solve the complicated and numerous equations of the trial-and-error approach 'in less than a second' – the market may thus 'be considered as a computing device of the preelectronic age'.

Very much along the lines of this reasoning some more recent authors intend to harness increasing processing power for such central planning boards (Cockshott and Cottrell, 1993; Dapprich, 2020; Cockshott et al, 2023). Others seek to democratize and decentralize planning by making use of 'communist software agents' based on artificial intelligence that reduce the complexity of planning to make it more accessible for democratic debate (Dyer-Witheford, 2013). Still others ask whether the possibilities that new digital platforms and information and communication technologies offer can be used to instantaneously communicate needs to an interconnected network of producers who collaborate to fulfil those needs, all without the need for a central planner (Saros, 2014). Such visions for a democratic economy relate much less to Soviet authoritarianism than to Chile's brief 1971–1973

Project Cybersyn under the Allende administration that attempted a form of democratic economic planning with the help of a distributed system to connect factories and planners based on cybernetic principles (Medina, 2011).

However, any contemporary project engaged in the development of an alternative social order must keep in mind that social problems cannot be solved through technical means alone (Morozov, 2013; Rendueles, Simanowski and Cleary, 2017). While new technologies do indeed provide new spaces of possibility and thereby new ways of imagining and developing alternative futures, the issue of how these spaces of possibility are used and which alternative is being pursued is deeply political. As such, a call to engage with democratic planning in the 21st century is first and foremost a political call. Furthermore, as Bratton rightly points out, the data that are being harnessed under the imperatives of digital capitalism do not constitute the data that we need for democratic planning (Bratton and Groos, 2020), and contemporary technological infrastructure is deeply entangled with predatory practices of exploitation of human and non-human nature in multiple ways (Crawford, 2021). Accordingly, it is not adequate to simply appropriate the digital infrastructures of today's tech giants, but instead, we must engage in the development of alternative political projects that make use of technological infrastructure in alternative ways. This book thus suggests the need for democratic planning that is decisively political in nature and therefore non-technocratic, that is democratic and directed at human and non-human needs.

As such it not only builds on recent proposals for digital planning but also on the broader tradition of democratic economic planning (Devine, 1988; Albert and Hahnel, 1991; Laibman, 2002). Some have conceptualized democratic planning as a bottom-up, participatory process that establishes a balance between the demand that consumer councils identify and the supply that worker councils suggest (Albert and Hahnel, 1991). We can also think about planning as the negotiation of changes in productive capacity by those affected by the decision (Devine, 1988). Still another perspective would be to understand planning as a multilevel iterative process between production collectives with particular local knowledge and central regulating bodies that mediate between them (Laibman, 2002). All these varieties of democratic planning suggest different ways of linking the technical expertise of workers and workplaces to our multiple lived realities, needs and desires as citizens, workers, consumers and status groups.

The infamous and long-standing *Bilderverbot* within the left emphasizes the inherent danger of formulating concrete and tangible post-capitalist alternatives. It is argued that describing can all too quickly turn into prescribing, and theoretical discourses may quickly lock in mindsets or become deaf to the insights, dynamics and processes of experimentation from below. Furthermore, since we are all socialized within capitalism, there is an undeniable risk of extending undesirable aspects of capitalism into conceptions of the future. However, we argue that this does not mean that we should refrain from asking what non-capitalist futures might actually look like and how their inner logics might set them apart from capitalist laws of motion. On the contrary, we argue that it is of the utmost importance to collectively work towards convincing alternatives to capitalism and in the process provide concrete answers to fundamental questions such as those discussed in this book. Proposing a multiplicity of tangible approaches as possible elements of desirable alternatives opens up debate instead of closing it down (Adamczak, 2017). Furthermore, people have a justifiable interest in knowing the basic parameters of the alternatives being proposed. Since any desirable alternative will have to be based on mass movements, this justifiable interest in plausible explanations must be addressed. In addition, articulation renders practical problems that can get lost in abstraction legible. It is not enough to vaguely state that post-capitalism will need to be democratic, social and sustainable or that we will figure out post-capitalist institutions along the way. Postponing such discussions into a potentially dynamic and messy period of transformation not only generates risks but also lacks persuasive power in that it is based on a giant leap of faith. However, the experiences (and failures) of 20th-century socialism show that constructing non-capitalist alternatives is an extraordinarily difficult task and we must provide concrete ideas about the functioning of alternative social orders and remain open to a collective engagement and tinkering with the (re)shaping and constant evolvement of these models. This involvement can only be established via active debates taking place about these questions that inspire people to critically engage with them.

Thus, the main rationale of this book is: democratic planning is urgently necessary and feasible. A paradigm shift regarding the question of how the multiple crises of our time can be addressed on a fundamental basis is urgently needed. We argue that only comprehensive democratic planning can meet this challenge for a number of reasons. First, planning allows for conscious democratic decisions over the direction of economic development instead of submitting such pivotal questions to undemocratic and blind private investment decisions companies make (Devine, 1988). The possibility of capital strikes and capital flight (Lindblom, 1977; Block, 1987) will undermine any such attempt at democratically coordinating economic development *within* capitalism if such planning threatens the overall logic of capital.

Second, and closely related, the primacy of profitability drives the said overall logic, not social and ecological needs. This means that companies have a perpetual incentive to externalize what they perceive as (ecological and social) costs and circumvent related regulation, if any exists. In addition, not all sectors have equal potential to increase productivity via technological innovation. As a consequence, productive sectors, such as arms industries, automobiles and microelectronics, will always attract more investment than reproductive ones, such as child and eldercare, health and education, which depend on human interaction and care. Profitability is also reproduced in time and space, for example economically successful regions more easily attract investment, which produces core-periphery dynamics at various scales. In contrast to such impersonal market forces, democratic planning enables deliberate decisions to value ecological sustainability, social reproduction, public goods and regional equality.

Finally, planning allows for the coordination of interdependent actors before conducting (ex-ante) investment decisions (Devine, 1988). In market economies companies invest atomistically and compete for profits, the realization of which by some (but not all) allows for the transformation of productive capacity. While uncertainty about the future is a permanent (and indeed desirable) aspect of human existence, market economies produce particular forms of harmful 'subjective uncertainty' (Dobb, 1960, p 74ff). Decisions over changes in our productive and reproductive capacity (that is investment) are made by highly interdependent actors, but in isolation and thus in ignorance of one another. So, it is only after (ex-post) producers have committed resources in durable forms (for example, particular machines that cannot easily be repurposed) that they find out whether demand exists for their particular products vis-à-vis their competitors. Such lack of coordination necessarily produces cyclical crises, bottlenecks and under- or over-capacity (usually the last-mentioned in capitalism). This subsequently means that either some solvent desires remain unfulfilled (under-capacity), or that machines and factories have been built and/or workers employed and trained in vain (over-capacity).

New technologies have increased the possibilities of non-market forms of social coordination, but any transformation towards democratic planning remains chiefly a political project. The latter can only emerge from actually existing movements and must take note of the lessons learned from past experiments, shortcomings and failures. Learning from the past also means that if planning returns to the agenda of counter-hegemonic movements, it cannot do so in the form of orthodox economism, class reductionism or productivism but needs to be reinvented to face the social and ecological tasks of the 21st century and the full matrix of domination beyond class. Thus, decision-making should involve a range of groups and communities, and such planning must be consciously reparative of present injustices.

The first part of the book will discuss proposals for what 21st century democratic planning could look like and interrogate rationales of government that might inform these alternative political economies. Part II will ask how various current movements and propositions for a socio-ecological transformation fare with respect to democratic planning. The chapters thus link the planning debate to existing transformative movements and present experiences; a task the recent debate has so far failed to do. Finally, the third part will expand the agenda of planning by explicitly asking how social reproduction, ecology and politics can be organized to avoid reproducing capitalism's androcentrism, anthropocentrism, ethnocentrism and Eurocentrism. These issues have not been given enough attention in proposals for democratic planning but should be front and centre for any transformative project (Sorg, 2022). The following three sections will further elaborate the scope and underlying rationale of this volume's three parts.

Part I – Blueprints of Desire

The first part of the book goes beyond the idea of a communist *Bilderverbot* that prohibits engaging with the question of what alternatives to capitalism might look like in concrete terms. Instead, this part advocates for the need to work towards 'blueprints of desire' (Adamczak, 2017) that make fulfilling the desire for alternatives to capitalism conceivable. By engaging with a variety of proposals for organizing the reproduction of society democratically, and therefore necessarily in a non-capitalist way, the chapters in Part I provide a space for critical debate about how we want to live together differently in concrete terms. Proposing comprehensive models and concrete approaches of democratic economic planning and discussing them in a detailed and critical manner do not serve a prescriptive function. Radically different futures will neither fall from the sky nor can they be commanded in a top-down manner if they justly want to be called democratic. They will have to be developed collectively. Concrete proposals for democratic planning provide a necessary friction surface precisely for this collective development.

Furthermore, since the argument is not merely that alternatives to capitalism are possible, but that these alternatives are desirable, engagement with democratic planning is also a work of developing new imaginaries of attainable futures. Such work must successfully challenge deep-seated imaginaries of liberalism that have taken root in our minds and institutions alike. Focusing on the issue of democratic planning as the kernel of such alternative imaginaries provides a convincing framework for addressing the multiple crises that we collectively face. The renaissance of democratic planning has just begun and the chapters in Part I engage with concrete proposals to explore the full potential of this reawakening.

In Chapter 1 Audrey Laurin-Lamothe, Frédéric Legault and Simon Tremblay-Pepin introduce the reader to the following four canonical models of democratic economic planning: negotiated coordination, first developed by Devine (1988) and later developed further in collaboration with Adaman (Adaman and Devine, 1997), parecon, developed by Albert and Hahnel (1991), multilevel democratic iterative coordination, developed by Laibman

(2002) and Cockshott and Cottrell's (1993) model. Developed from the late 1980s onwards these models remain highly influential within the larger contemporary debate and provide a thorough entry point for questions regarding the feasibility of democratic economic planning. While the first chapter provides an overview of these models, Jakob Heyer uses the second chapter to distil basic problems that any model of democratically planned economy will have to face. Based on an overview of historical experiences with large-scale economic planning, theoretical debates around reform socialism (Kalecki, 2010; Brus, 2003) and the role of modern information technology, he identifies information and incentives as two such central problems. Categorizing the canonical models and enriching them with more recent work (Platenkamp, forthcoming) he identifies productive lines of conflict to work towards a synthesis of various models. Inspired by Devine's (1988) model of negotiated coordination in Chapter 3, James Muldoon and Dougie Booth propose what they call social dividend socialism. Going beyond Devine, they suggest replacing wage labour with a form of social dividend based on a communist principle of distribution. By doing so they address a central critique Sutterlütti and Meretz introduce in Chapter 4 against canonical socialist proposals, namely that they reproduce wage labour as a social relation. Quite distinct from these socialist approaches, Sutterlütti and Meretz (2023, English translation) propose a comprehensive picture of commonism in their 2018 book (and use the chapter to expand on the notion of planning in a commonist society). Based on a strong critique of what they consider to be a continuation of commodity production, wage labour, the money form and an inherent ignorance of care labour within socialist planning models, Sutterlütti and Meretz propose commoning as the central form of mediation within a free society. To circumvent the need for elements of central planning they propose polycentric distributed planning based on stigmergic signals and logics of inclusion. While certainly sympathetic to the idea of commonism, a concept he himself has coined (Dyer-Witheford, 2007), Nick Dyer-Witheford nonetheless argues in Chapter 5 that the contemporary polycrisis demands a multilayered approach in which bottom-up mobilization is as important as a decisive and comprehensive emergency mobilization of resources that, at least for the time being, can only be commanded by the state. He argues for a communist biopolitics that he calls biocommunism, a communism emerging from the catastrophes that capitalism inflicts throughout the bios, that is the realm of life itself. The chapter highlights how biocommunism would have to be able to navigate in times of explosive conflicts around disaster response, migration, ownership, consumption and work. In Chapter 6, in accordance with this Foucauldian-inspired approach, Jan Groos proposes to incorporate the analytical lens of arts of government into the planning debate. In reference to Foucault's (2008) famous claim that socialism lacks an intrinsically socialist governmentality, the chapter investigates how an expanded notion of a government of things (Lemke, 2021) might be useful for a constructive effort beyond the well-worn paths of the planning debate. In the final chapter of Part I Evgeny Morozov argues, in an interview with Jan Groos, that the debate's focus on developing alternative mechanisms for the production and allocation of use values for the satisfaction of needs is too narrow. Instead, he proposes to shift the debate's focus towards questions surrounding discovery and the production of the new, or what he calls planning in the realm of freedom.

Part II – Building Bridges

The contributions in Part II take us into the present of disruptive movements and prefigurative practices. How do such transformational politics relate to the contemporary debate about democratic planning? How could they be linked further? Although many of the concrete proposals mentioned in this part of the book could be implemented within the currently existing structures of social, political and economic life, they may eventually conflict with the structural necessities of capitalist accumulation, which is why they are in need of more far-reaching conceptions of alternatives. Yet, this applies in both directions, since planned economies of the 21st century cannot and should not appear out of nowhere but crucially have to be a product of extensive experiments in alternative practice in the here and now. In a prefigurative sense the alternative projects of today lay the groundwork for futures in which this alternative practice has become the new normal.

The chapters in Part II interrogate struggles concerning care work (Winker and Neumann), public housing (Berfelde and Möller) and public policy (Decker), asking where the inherent paradigms complement or contradict a transformation towards democratic planning. They provide in-depth knowledge of existing movements, their respective points of connection and points of suspicion or disagreement with the topic of planning. The authors of Part II – many of whom are part of the respective movements themselves – engage in building bridges between the contemporary discourse around democratic planning and the movements without which any vision of desirable futures would be mere sandbox games.

Rabea Berfelde and Philipp Möller elaborate the interesting case of 'Expropriate Deutsche Wohnen & Co', a successful referendum to expropriate the property of all private real estate companies that own more than 3,000 units in the city of Berlin. By discussing the expropriation movement's proposal for radical democratic planning of socialized infrastructure, the authors provide an important link between practical examples emerging from real-life struggles and the theoretical questions the new planning debate poses. In Chapter 9 Christoph Sorg departs from the observation that models of democratic planning seem to assume closed national economies, unaffected by the broader context of world economy and interstate system. He elaborates two issues that arise from taking a more global perspective, that is the short-term question of how to transform towards a democratically planned economy in a capitalist world system and the related longer-term question of how varieties of democratic planning relate to each other once such a transformation is successful on a worldwide scale. In Chapter 10, Samuel Decker presents a model of post-capitalist transformation that conceptually links redistribution, socialization and planning. Through this analytical framework he screens political programmes of left parties and election campaigns for components of capitalist and post-capitalist economic planning. In Chapter 11 Gabriele Winker and Matthias Neumann introduce a transformation strategy they call a 'care revolution' towards a caring, solidary society. This form of revolutionary realpolitik includes a reduction in working hours, individual and collective security that is independent of employment, socialization of central economic sectors and support for commons-based experiments. In the final chapter of Part II, Jan Groos interviews Eva von Redecker regarding how democratic planning can bring about alternative notions of freedom and security by always already considering reproduction to be the primary modus operandi of democratic planning. By linking democratic planning to such expanded notions of (re)production, Redecker dissolves dichotomies that have been reproduced within the planning debate for far too long, notably that between a sphere of production and a sphere of reproduction, with the latter having been notoriously ignored within much of the literature on democratic *economic* planning, a fact that Part III addresses head on.

Part III – Non-Boundaries

The new advocates of democratic planning have many interesting things to say about what post-capitalist economic laws of motion could look like in the age of digitalization. Unfortunately, however, they are frequently much less clear on what Nancy Fraser (2014) would call capitalism's social, ecological and political background conditions of possibility: social reproduction, non-human nature and political institutions (Sorg, 2022). These arose when the emergence of capitalism broke up feudalism's traditional livelihood practices and thus divorced production from reproduction, society from nature and economy from polity. Capitalist laws of motion render these background conditions invisible and treat them as infinite, but at the same time the system pivotally depends on them. The violence inscribed into these boundaries and their relation to the economic sphere derives not primarily from the exploitation of wage labour via commodity production but from the oppression, dispossession and destruction of women and sexual minorities, racialized/colonized groups and non-human nature (Mies, 1986; Robinson, 2000; Federici, 2004; Fraser, 2014; Patel and Moore, 2017; Virdee, 2019).

This perspective expands the issue of how to replace market society via democratic planning by integrating the additional issue of how to ensure that such a transformation empowers all groups that have never had equal access to the market to begin with – and adding non-human nature to the equation. Varieties of democratic planning that do not wish to perpetuate these exclusions and destructions thus also need to centre on 'the nurturing of people, the safeguarding of nature, and democratic self-rule as society's highest priorities' (Fraser, 2020, p 10). The contributions in Part III discuss how democratic planning can abolish the gendered division of labour and universalize care giving without reproducing the romanticization of 'housework' (Federici, 2004; Hester and Srnicek, 2018; 2022), moving beyond resource extraction, infinite growth and imperial modes of production and living (Klein, 2019; Brand and Wissen, 2021). In addition they explore political institutions of democratic self-rule to ensure that those affected by a decision have the right to participate in making it – thus transcending the status-based, colonial and imperial exclusions inherent within and among Westphalian nation-states (Amin, 2013; Muchhala, 2020).

In Chapter 13 Elena Hofferberth, Matthias Schmelzer and Cédric Durand argue that the idea of degrowth necessitates planning, although both bodies of literature have so far not sufficiently explored the synergies between them. The authors argue that the fact that degrowth refers to a planned contraction of economic activity aimed at increasing wellbeing and equality is a distinguishing feature of degrowth compared with a recession in a capitalist economy. To provide an idea of how such a planned contraction might be brought about, the authors develop a possible design for social-ecological transformation based on planning for degrowth. In Chapter 14 Samia Mohammed also poses ecological questions for planning, but through the lens of democratic and feminist theory. From this perspective she proposes a post-sovereign form of planning that goes beyond the widespread Prometheanism of the current planning debate. In doing so she questions some of the principles and core assumptions that can also be found within the canon of planning literature described in Part I. Her aim, however, is not to dismiss this body of work but to productively complicate and enrich it. In Chapter 15 Simon Schaupp investigates the role that technology could play for degrowth planning, arguing against a techno-deterministic understanding of technology, which is found both in techno-optimist and techno-pessimist camps. He stresses that degrowth not only requires planning but that the necessary planning will also be dependent on technologies, albeit assessed under the aspect of them having the potential of becoming forces of (re)production. A critical and non-deterministic interpretation of the concept of productive forces allows

Schaupp to develop an understanding of the forces of production as forces of re/production and potentiality. Along these lines he sees technologies of digital planning as a potential sensing apparatus for degrowth by design. Next, in Chapter 16, Heide Lutosch challenges not only the loud absence of questions of care work in literature on democratic economic planning but also the tendency to romanticize affective labour in the research that does not completely ignore the topic. Specifically, she explores how childcare could work in a free society that has moved past the nuclear family and properly centres on the needs of both parents and children. Finally, in Chapter 17, Christoph Sorg interviews Nancy Fraser on how to expand our notion of post-capitalism and democratic planning, creating visions of a better future that does not subjugate identity politics and political ecology to class politics or vice versa. The issues they discuss range from markets and planning to transformation, socialist care and the relativity of dirt.

The attentive reader will have noticed that each part of the book concludes with a conversation, Part I with Evgeny Morozov, Part II with Eva von Redecker and Part III with Nancy Fraser. The idea to include interviews as such an integral part of this volume arose from one of the co-editors, Jan Groos, having developed a peculiar research practice over the last years, namely podcasting as research. The vehicle for this praxis is the podcast *Future Histories*, which has, over the years, assembled a large number of conversations dedicated to the topics of this book. The dialogical, collective and public nature of this form of research is able to create its own qualities, which we wanted to include in this book. The conversations in Parts I and II were held by Jan Groos and are available in their entirety as *Future Histories* podcast episodes via links provided in the respective endnotes.[1] Christoph Sorg conducted the conversation with Nancy Fraser in Part III. In this case no audio version is available.

The book concludes with reflections by the editors on what it means to collectively engage in the *creative construction* of alternatives, including the inherent contradictions, the need to broaden the discussion and the promise of relief contained in democratic planning.

Note

[1] Find the extended audio version of Chapter 7 (Part I) here: https://www.future histories.today/episoden-blog/s02/e44-evgeny-morozov-on-discovery-beyond-competition/ and Part II (Chapter 12) here: https://www.futurehistories.today/episoden-blog/s02/e38-eva-von-redecker-zu-bleibefreiheit-und-demokratischer-planung/

Bibliography

Adaman, F. and Devine, P. (1997) 'On the economic theory of socialism', *New Left Review*, 1(221): 54–80.

Adamczak, B. (2017) *Communism for Kids*. Cumberland: MIT Press.

Adamczak, B. (2021) *Yesterday's Tomorrow: On the Loneliness of Communist Specters and the Reconstruction of the Future*. Cambridge: MIT Press.

Adler, P.S. (2019) *The 99 Percent Economy. How Democratic Socialism Can Overcome the Crises of Capitalism*. Oxford: Oxford University Press.

Ajl, M. (2021) *A People's Green New Deal*. London: Pluto Press.

Albert, M. and Hahnel, R. (1991) *The Political Economy of Participatory Economics*. Princeton, NJ: Princeton University Press.

Alami, I. and Dixon, A.D. (2024) *The Spectre of State Capitalism*. New York: Oxford University Press.

Amin, S. (2013) *The Implosion of Capitalism*. London: Pluto Press.

Arboleda, M. (2021) *Gobernar la Utopía. Sobre la planificación y el poder popular*. Buenos Aires: Caja Negra Editorial

Arruzza, C., Bhattacharya, T. and Fraser, N. (2019) *Feminism for the 99%: A Manifesto*. London, New York: Verso.

Bastani, A. (2019) *Fully Automated Luxury Communism: A Manifesto*. London, New York: Verso.

Benanav, A. (2022) 'Socialist investment, dynamic planning, and the politics of human need', *Rethinking Marxism*, 34(2): 193–204.

Blakeley, G. (2024) *Vulture Capitalism: Corporate Crimes, Backdoor Bailouts, and the Death of Freedom*. New York: Simon & Schuster.

Block, F. (1987) *Revising State Theory: Essays in Politics and Post-Industrialism*. Philadelphia, Baltimore, MD: Temple University Press; Project MUSE.

Bockman, J., Fischer, A. and Woodruff, D. (2016) '"Socialist Accounting" by Karl Polanyi: With preface "Socialism and the embedded economy"', *Theory and Society*, 45(5): 385–427. doi: 10.1007/s11186-016-9276-9.

Brand, U. and Wissen, M. (2021) *The Imperial Mode of Living: Everyday Life and the Ecological Crisis of Capitalism*. London, New York: Verso.

Bratton, B. (2016) *The Stack: On Software and Sovereignty*. Cambridge, MA: MIT Press.

Bratton, B. and Groos, J. (2020) 'S01E44 – Benjamin Bratton on synthetic catallaxies, platforms of platforms & red futurism', *Future Histories*. https://www.futurehistories.today/episoden-blog/s01/e44-benjamin-bratton-on-synthetic-catallaxies-platforms-of-platforms-red-futurism-part-1-2/

Braun, B. (2020) 'Asset manager capitalism as a corporate governance regime', *SocArXiv*, 18 June. doi: 10.31235/osf.io/v6gue.

Brus, W. (2003) *The Economics and Politics of Socialism: Collected Essays*. London: Routledge.

Burkhart, C., Schmelzer, M. and Treu, N. (2020) *Degrowth in Movement(s): Exploring Pathways for Transformation*. Winchester: Zero Books.

Cockshott, W.P. and Cottrell, A. (1993) *Towards a New Socialism*. Nottingham: Spokesman.

Cockshott, W.P., Cottrell, A. and Dapprich, J.P. (2022) *Economic Planning in an Age of Climate Crisis*. Independently published. https://publishup.uni-potsdam.de/frontdoor/index/index/docId/57647

Crawford, K. (2021) *Atlas of AI: Power, Politics, and the Planetary Costs of Artificial Intelligence*. New Haven: Yale University Press.

Dapprich, J.P. (2020) 'Rationality and distribution in the socialist economy', PhD Thesis. http://theses.gla.ac.uk/id/eprint/81793

Devine, P. (1988) *Democracy and Economic Planning: The Political Economy of a Self-Governing Society*. Cambridge: Polity Press.

Dobb, M. (1960) *An Essay on Economic Growth and Planning*. London: Routledge & Kegan Paul.

Durand, C. and Keucheyan, R. (2024) *Comment Bifurquer: Les Principes de la Planification Écologique*. New York: Zones.

Dyer-Witheford, N. (1999) *Cyber-Marx: Cycles and Circuits of Struggle in High-Technology Capitalism*. Urbana: University of Illinois Press.

Dyer-Witheford, N. (2007) 'Commonism. turbulence'. http://www.turbulence.org.uk/turbulence-1/commonism/index.html

Dyer-Witheford, N. (2013) 'Red Plenty Platforms', *Culture Machine*, (14): 1–17.

Federici, S.B. (2004) *Caliban and the Witch: Women, the Body and Primitive Accumulation*. New York: Autonomedia.

Federici, S.B. and Linebaugh, P. (2018) *Re-enchanting the World: Feminism and the Politics of the Commons*. Oakland, CA: PM Press.

Fishwick, A. and Kiersey, N. (2021) *Postcapitalist Futures: Political Economy Beyond Crisis and Hope*. London: Pluto Press.

Foucault, M. (2007) *Security, Territory, Population: Lectures at the Collège de France, 1977–78*. Edited by M. Senellart, F. Ewald, A. Fontana et al. Basingstoke/New York: Palgrave Macmillan.

Fraser, N. (2014) 'Behind Marx's hidden abode: for an expanded conception of capitalism', *New Left Review*, 86: 55–72.

Fraser, N. (2020) 'What should socialism mean in the twenty-first century?', *Socialist Register*, 56: 21–43.

Fraser, N. and Jaeggi, R. (2018) *Capitalism: A Conversation in Critical Theory*. Cambridge: Polity Press.

Gerhardt, H. (2023) *From Capital to Commons. Exploring the Promise of a World beyond Capitalism*. Bristol: Bristol University Press.

Groos, J. (2021) 'Distributed planned economies in the age of their technical feasibility', in J. Herder, F. Maschewski and A.-V. Nosthoff (eds) 'Futures of critique: theorising governmentality and power in the digital age', *Behemoth*, 14(2): 75–87.

Hahnel, R. (2021) *Democratic Economic Planning*. London: Routledge.

Hahnel, R. and Wright, E.O. (2017) *Alternatives to Capitalism: Proposals for a Democratic Economy*. London, New York: Verso.

Hannah, S. (2025) *Reclaiming the Future: A Beginner's Guide to Planning the Economy*. London: Pluto Press.

Hester, H. and Srnicek, N. (2018) 'The crisis of social reproduction and the end of work', in *The Age of Perplexity: Rethinking the World We Knew*, Barcelona: Fundacion BBVA.

Hester, H. and Srnicek, N. (2022) *AFTER WORK: The Fight for Free Time*. London: Verso.

Hozic, A.A. and True, J. (eds) (2016) *Scandalous Economics: Gender and the Politics of Financial Crises*. New York: Oxford University Press.

Jameson, F. (2009) *Archaeologies of the Future: The Desire Called Utopia and other Science Fictions*. London: Verso.

Jones, C. (2020) 'Introduction: the return of economic planning', *South Atlantic Quarterly*, 119(1): 1–10.

Kalecki, M. (2010) *Selected Essays on Economic Planning*. Cambridge: Cambridge University Press.

Kallis, G. (2018) *Degrowth*. Newcastle upon Tyne: Agenda Publishing.

Klein, N. (2019) *On Fire: The (Burning) Case for a Green New Deal*. New York: Simon & Schuster.

Laibman, D. (2002) 'Democratic coordination: towards a working socialism for the new century', *Science & Society*, 66(1): 116–129.

Lane, D. (2023) *Global Neoliberal Capitalism and the Alternatives: From Social Democracy to State Capitalisms*. Bristol: Bristol University Press.

Lange, O. and Taylor, F.M. (1938) *On the Economic Theory of Socialism*. Minneapolis: University of Minnesota Press.

Lange, O. (1979) *The Computer and the Market. Comparative Economic Systems Models and Cases*. New York: M.E. Sharpe.

Lemke, T. (2021) *The Government of Things: Foucault and the New Materialisms*. New York: NYU Press.

Lindblom, C.E. (1977) *Politics and Markets: The World's Political-Economic Systems*. New York: BasicBooks.

Mandel, E. (1986) 'In defence of socialist planning', *New Left Review*, 159(1): 5–22.

Mason, P. (2015) *Postcapitalism: A Guide to Our Future*. London: Allen Lane.

Malm, A. (2016) *Fossil Capital*. London: Verso Books.

Mazzucato, M. (2021) *Mission Economy. A Moonshot Guide to Changing Capitalism* London: Penguin Allen Lane.

Medina, E. (2011) *Cybernetic Revolutionaries: Technology and Politics in Allende's Chile*. Cambridge, MA: MIT Press.

Mises, L. (1922) *Die Gemeinwirtschaft – Untersuchungen über den Sozialismus*. Jena: Gustav Fischer.

Mohammed, S.Z. (2023) *Zukunft jenseits des Marktes. Demokratie und gesellschaftliche Naturverhältnisse in sozialistischen Utopien*. Baden-Baden: Nomos.

Moore, J.W. (2015) *Capitalism in the Web of Life: Ecology and the Accumulation of Capital*. London: Verso Books.

Morozov, E. (2013) *To Save Everything, Click Here: The Folly of Technological Solutionism*. New York: PublicAffairs.

Morozov, E. (2019) 'Digital socialism? The calculation debate in the age of big data', *New Left Review*, 116/117: 33–66.

Muchhala, B. (2020) 'Towards a decolonial and feminist global green new deal'. https://www.rosalux.de/en/news/id/42847/towards-a-decolonial-and-feminist-global-green-new-deal?cHash=2273743732e7578e67f560ff6c2e8663

Neurath, O. (1919) *Durch die Kriegswirtschaft zur Naturalwirtschaft*. München: Callwey.

Mies, M. (1998) *Patriarchy and Accumulation on a World Scale: Women in the International Division of Labour*. London: Palgrave Macmillan.

Monticelli, L. (ed) (2022) *The Future Is Now: An Introduction to Prefigurative Politics*. Bristol: Bristol University Press.

Patel, R. and Moore, J.W. (2017) *A History of the World in Seven Cheap Things: A Guide to Capitalism, Nature, and the Future of the Planet*. Oakland, CA: University of California Press.

Phillips, L. and Rozworski, M. (2019) *The People's Republic of Walmart: How the World's Biggest Corporations Are Laying the Foundation for Socialism*. London, New York: Verso.

Planning for Entropy (2022) 'Democratic economic planning, social metabolism and the environment', *Science & Society*, 86(2): 291–313. doi: 10.1521/siso.2022.86.2.291.

Platenkamp, T. (forthcoming) *The Constitution of Socialism*.

Project Society After Money (2019) *Society After Money: A Dialogue*. New York: Bloomsbury.

Rendueles, C., Simanowski, R. and Cleary, H. (2017) *Sociophobia: Political Change in the Digital Utopia*. New York: Columbia University Press.

Riexinger, B., Becker, L., Dahme, K. et al (2021) *A Left Green New Deal: An Internationalist Blueprint*. New York: Monthly Review Press.

Rifkin, J. (2014) *The Zero Marginal Cost Society: The Internet of Things, the Collaborative Commons, and the Eclipse of Capitalism*. New York: Palgrave Macmillan.

Robinson, C.J. (2000) *Black Marxism: The Making of the Black Radical Tradition*. Chapel Hill, NC: University of North Carolina Press.

Saito, K. (2022) *Marx in the Anthropocene: Towards the Idea of Degrowth Communism*. Cambridge, New York: Cambridge University Press.

Saros, D.E. (2014) *Information Technology and Socialist Construction: The End of Capital and the Transition to Socialism*. Hoboken: Taylor and Francis.

Schweikhart, D. (1993) *Against Capitalism*. Cambridge: Cambridge University Press.

Sorg, C. (2022) 'Failing to plan is planning to fail: toward an expanded notion of democratically planned postcapitalism', *Critical Sociology*, 48(4–5): 639–654.

Sorg, C. and Groos, J. (2025) 'Rethinking economic planning', *Competition & Change*, special issue. doi: 10.1177/10245294241273954.

Srnicek, N. and Williams, A. (2015) *Inventing the Future: Postcapitalism and a World Without Work*. London: Verso.

Sutterlütti, S. and Meretz, S. (2023) *Make Capitalism History: A Practical Framework for Utopia and the Transformation of Society*. Cham, Switzerland: Palgrave Macmillan.

Vettese, T. and Pendergrass, D. (2022) *Half-Earth Socialism: A Plan to Save the Future from Extinction, Climate Change, and Pandemics*. London; New York: Verso.

Virdee, S. (2019) 'Racialized capitalism: an account of its contested origins and consolidation', *The Sociological Review*, 67(1): 3–27.

von Redecker, E. (2021) *Praxis and Revolution. A Theory of Social Transformation*. Translated by Lucy Duggan. New York: Columbia University Press.

Vrasti, W. (2016) 'Self-reproducing movements and the enduring challenge of materialist feminism', in A.A. Hozic and J. True (eds) *Scandalous Economics: Gender and the Politics of Financial Crises*, New York: Oxford University Press, pp 248–265.

PART I

Blueprints of Desire

1

A Brief Sketch of Four Models of Democratic Economic Planning

Audrey Laurin-Lamothe, Frédéric Legault and Simon Tremblay-Pepin

Introduction

Getting out of capitalism implies finding desirable and functional alternatives to replace it. Although this might seem obvious, only a few proposals have been put forward on how a postcapitalist society could work. Among those proposals, democratic economic planning stands out in its attempts to reconcile the need for broad coordination and preserving local autonomy and self-determination. Our goal in this text is to lay out what we consider the four main models' functioning to give a quick overview of them to a broader public. Laying out these four models of democratic planning in a concise and structured manner will also allow us to discuss and criticize them in further writing.[1]

It is no coincidence that three of those models were published at the turn of the 1990s. The era was marked by the collapse of the Soviet regime and the end of the Cold War. Capitalism's ideological victory took a large part of the legitimacy of the socialist option in the countries of the West. Thus, these models are to be understood as a response to the failure of central planning under 'really existing socialisms' and monopolistic market coordination under capitalism.

Let us have a quick look at them.

Devine and Adaman's coordinated negotiation

In 1988, the English economist Pat Devine published *Democracy and Economic Planning*, in which he presented his model called 'negotiated coordination'. Later, he improved and discussed his project in articles written with the

Turkish economist Fikret Adaman who became his main co-writer on this matter. Two fundamental principles are institutionally embodied in negotiated coordination. First, it strives to maximize participation by everybody affected by a given economic process. Second, it supports a division between market exchanges and market forces.

Participation through representation

Negotiated coordination makes participation possible at various levels of society, and significant economic decisions should be taken according to the subsidiarity principle. Subsidiarity enables all the social owners' knowledge to be used so that those proportionately affected by decisions take them according to their preferences and interests (Devine, 2019, p 58). According to Devine, this principle promotes locally-based economic activity and shorter production circuits, thereby reducing ecological damage (Devine, 2017, p 43).

Devine keeps the idea of a representative government elected by the people and law-making within a representative assembly but with genuinely participatory political parties and a much more democratic electoral system (Devine, 1988, pp 189–190, 212–213). The equivalent of enterprises, what he calls production units, are owned collectively. Representatives from four sectors sit on the decision-making body of each production unit: the general interest (national, regional, and local planning commissions and negotiated coordination bodies); the interest of consumers, users, and suppliers (consumer associations, government and public services, production units that buy from or sell to the production unit and other negotiated coordination bodies related to the production unit); the interest of workers (workers of the production unit itself and their unions); and the interest of the community (interest groups and activist groups) (Devine, 1988, p 226). These representatives then agree on the most appropriate use of productive capacities through negotiation, considering each other's interests. These governing bodies decide on the general administrative orientation of the production unit, while workers organize the day-to-day operations through self-management (Devine, 1988, pp 227–228).

On economic issues, the representative assembly receives a series of national plans designed by a planning commission. These national plans establish national investment priorities, the resources (including money, goods, and services) offered for free to those who are not working (the young, the sick, the elderly), 'primary input prices' (wages, energy, natural resources), means and levels of 'taxation' and the public services offered by the 'social bodies' of the government directly to households (Devine, 1988, p 193).

A chamber of interests – a group of people representing different sections, causes, and interests of society – first reviews these plans and presents a report to the representative assembly on what elements civil society agrees or disagrees with. After extensive public debate, the representative assembly selects and adopts a single plan. Production units offer their goods and services on the market at a price that equals the production cost, which is the sum of the primary and intermediate inputs (supply, infrastructure, parts, repairs, and so on) (Devine, 1988, pp 197–203). This price does not vary directly according to demand but only indirectly 'when returns to scale are variable rather than constant' (Devine 1988, p 243).

Through self-management, workers will have, during their work life, the opportunity to do various tasks that are unskilled and repetitive, skilled, nurturing, creative, and related to organizational planning and management. According to Devine, this repartition will significantly reduce inequality in the social division of labour (Devine, 1988, pp 174–179). A central aspect of democratic economic planning is that workers control their own activity and society's general direction. In other words, formalizing a task rotation involves a redistribution of decision-making power to the workers, something that was previously captured by the economic and political elite in previous systems, whether capitalist or central planning.

Market exchanges and market forces

Although production units are self-managed, their decisional power is limited to the capacity of their existing infrastructures. They cannot choose to invest in new assets or close facilities by themselves. Here lies the difference between market exchanges and market forces, a central element of the negotiated coordination process. Market exchange gives consumers and entrepreneurs a means of transmitting valuable information (that is, preferences) through selling and buying at given prices. Negotiated coordination includes market exchange, and day-to-day production can adapt to market signals. However, negotiated coordination rejects what Devine calls market forces – making investment choices that follow the logic of value accumulation. In negotiated coordination, the capitalist class does not make investment decisions through an atomistic, ex-post coordinated process that aims for profit maximization. Instead, the social owners (all the affected parties) make investment decisions through an ex-ante negotiated coordination process seeking to fulfill collectively decided social objectives (Devine, 1988, p 236).

Indeed, when collectively owned self-managed production units want to change their productive capacity (like building a new facility or investing in new technology development), a demand must be made for the next planning cycle. In the following plan allocation process, the negotiated coordination body will review and approve them in light of what other production units are doing. Everyone affected by the sector sends a representative to the negotiated coordination body: production units of the industry, obviously, but also suppliers, consumers, government, and interest groups from civil society. Based on the national planning commission projections and the representative assembly's national priorities, the negotiated coordination body tries to establish the best investments for its sector after considering the demands of the various production units (Devine, 1988, pp 237–238).

The way negotiated coordination uses knowledge to involve workers and every other part of society affected by the planning process is essential for Devine and Adaman. It allows them to answer the Austrian argument about tacit knowledge in the socialist calculation debate.[2] Tacit knowledge is a form of knowledge that is practical, local, and not transmissible as quantitative information. Simply put, tacit knowledge comes from the fact that 'we can know more than we can tell' (Polanyi, 2009, p 4). The Austrian argument (Hayek, 1945) says that those who hold that local knowledge should make the economic decisions and that central planning cannot access this knowledge and, therefore, will always be inefficient. For Devine and Adaman (1996), putting representatives of those affected by the economical choice in the investment (negotiated coordination body) and the day-to-day (governing bodies) decision process puts their tacit knowledge back into the decision process without needing to transform it into quantitative information that is sent to a central planning bureau.

As mentioned earlier, in the negotiated coordination model, the means of production are owned collectively, except for very small-scale initiatives that can be privately owned. However, Devine proposes to collectivize them as soon as they grow (Devine, 1988, pp 112–130). Society, as a whole, therefore, owns the means of production and lends them to production units. The latter must make effective use of those means. Thus, the representative assembly, helped by the planning commission, sets a rate of return that infrastructure use should generate and transfer to the government. Production units should reach the set rate of return or otherwise justify that they should be 'subsidized' by the rest of the economy. To prioritize the best use of resources, the rate of return also guides the negotiated coordination bodies when deciding which production unit to invest in. The rate of return can differ from one production unit to another for three reasons: (1) reasons within the control of the production unit (like wage, prices, working conditions and work organization); (2) reasons beyond the control of the production unit (like location and fashion); or (3) reasons related to the macroeconomic situation that concerns a whole branch of production (like the fall or rise of demand for this type product, significant technological or social changes) (Devine, 1988, pp 245–248).

It is by no means certain that the negotiation process at the centre of the model will reach a successful conclusion every time. Pat Devine keeps insisting on this point: in time, people will learn to make sound economic decisions because failure will affect their lives. The repercussions might include inflation, a production unit having to shut down, or the exhaustion of specific resources at the local level (Devine, 1988, pp 201, 270–272). These dire consequences are similar to those encountered in capitalism. However, negotiated coordination would ensure that all individuals become aware of the results of their economic decisions and take responsibility for them. Devine claims that people would, in the longer term, change the way they operate accordingly.

Recent work from proponents of negotiated coordination focuses on how the model would take care of ecological considerations (Adaman, Devine and Ozkaynak, 2003; Adaman and Devine, 2017; Devine, 2017). For the authors, the institutions of negotiated coordination are re-embedding the economy into society and nature. They are making the economic process more self-conscious and subject to a variety of points of view, including those defending the environment (Adaman, Devine and Ozkaynak, 2003, pp 270–271; Devine, 2017, pp 45–47). Collective ex-ante coordination of major investments would then tie economic activity to human needs instead of profits. From an ecological perspective, here lies the main advantage of a democratically planned economy over capitalism. Since significant investments will be democratically planned, competition and growth incentives will presumably be inoperative; hence, the pressure on workers and ecosystems would be significantly lightened. Therefore, according to Devine and Adaman, negotiated coordination is well suited to respond to today's ecological concerns without needing critical institutional changes. Devine and Adaman's model is illustrated in Figure 1.1.

Albert and Hahnel's participatory economics

Three years after Pat Devine's book on negotiated coordination, in the United States, activist Michael Albert and economist Robin Hahnel published two books laying out the basic concepts of participatory economics: one for academics (1991a) and another for a wider audience (1991b). While participation through representation is at the centre of Devine and Adaman's model, Albert and Hahnel's focus is on a more directly democratic form of economic participation.

Iterative planning process

In participatory economics, all workplaces are managed by workers' councils. Contrary to what negotiated coordination proposes, only workers have the right to vote in these councils, but all do so directly at the local level, not through representatives (Albert and Hahnel, 1991a, pp 23–24). Though the basic production unit in participatory economics is the workplace, other democratic spaces form concentric circles around and inside it. All offices or workshops are assembled in a workplace; each workplace is part of a

CREATIVE CONSTRUCTION

Figure 1.1: Devine and Adaman's negotiated coordination annual planning diagram

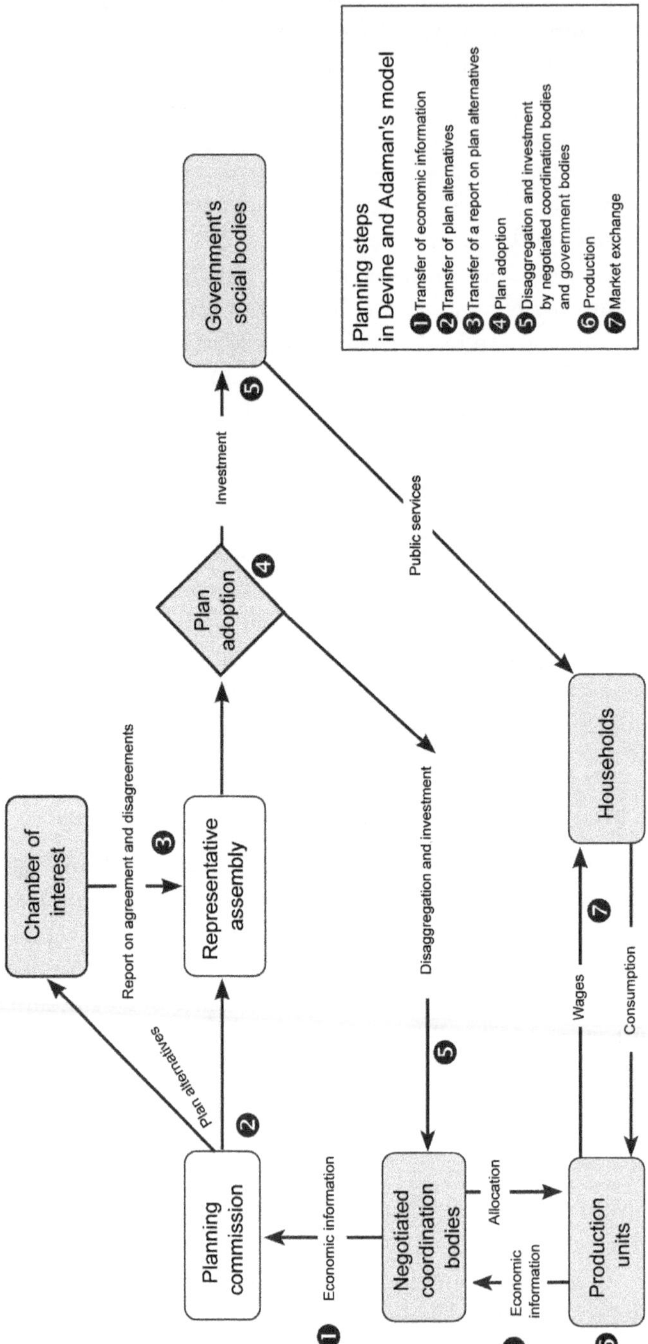

Planning steps in Devine and Adaman's model
① Transfer of economic information
② Transfer of plan alternatives
③ Transfer of a report on plan alternatives
④ Plan adoption
⑤ Disaggregation and investment by negotiated coordination bodies and government bodies
⑥ Production
⑦ Market exchange

Source: Laurin-Lamothe, Legault and Tremblay-Pepin, 2023, translated and modified by the authors.

federation that groups workplaces according to what they produce (Albert and Hahnel, 1991b, p 21). Each of these levels is organized through council-based direct democracy.

Participatory economics is also based on consumers' councils, similarly organized into concentric circles that range from households to large entities such as a country. Peers from other councils review each other's demands and decide if the lower body is making consumer decisions that affect other councils and, thus, should be treated at a higher level: 'The colour of my underwear concerns only me and my most intimate acquaintances. The shrubbery on my block concerns all who live on the block … The frequency and punctuality of buses and subways affect all in a city. The disposition of waste affects all States in a major watershed' (Albert and Hahnel, 1991a, pp 40–41). The idea is simple: those who are affected by a democratic decision should take part in it.

These two sets of councils (workers' and consumers') are at the centre of the planning process that Albert and Hahnel call 'participatory planning' (Albert and Hahnel, 1991a, pp 57–71; 1992; Albert, 2003, pp 219–227; Hahnel, 2005, pp 193–194; Hahnel, 2012, pp 89–104). Iteration facilitation boards (IFBs) support the councils' work. These boards are workplaces in charge of producing economic analyses and indicative prices based on workers' and consumers' desires, previous years' results, and the enormous amount of data shared during the planning process. After receiving prices and information from the IFB, each council writes a proposal for consumption or production. Each actor modifies its proposal through iterations before reaching a final proposal without any goods or services in excess demand or supply.

Let us dig deeper into this iterative process. IFBs start the process by releasing information: last year's production statistics coupled with the current social cost of all goods and services ('indicative prices' are similar to the production costs in Devine's model but directly influenced by supply and demand), labour costs, and qualitative information on goods and services. All actors have access to this information.

The IFBs then send their demographic, technological and economic forecasts. Considering all these factors, each council decides what changes they would like to make to their previous year's proposals: do they want to produce or consume more or less? Do they want to do it differently? What are the consequences of those changes on their inputs and outputs?

They then send their first proposal to the higher federative level, providing quantitative and qualitative information about their choices. These proposals are broad and do not go into the details of the options; they are general categories (for example, four clothing pieces rather than one pair of blue jeans, two sweaters and one jacket). The statistically predictable personal preferences are left to the care of the councils and federations, helped by the data from IFBs. It is always a committee of peers who approve the proposals of those who make them. Households that make up a neighbourhood council approve each other's consumption proposal. A neighbourhood council receives approval from other neighbourhood councils. It continues like that up to the largest circles, and the same is valid on the production side. The criteria for approving a consumption proposal is that it should not exceed the consumption rights acquired through work. Following the same logic, production proposals are approved because the level of social benefits produced by their outputs is equal to or higher than the social costs of the inputs they intend to use (Hahnel, 2012, pp 91–96).

Once every proposal is approved, the IFBs adjust indicative prices according to what goods and services are now in excess supply and demand. A new round starts with this new data: the councils can develop plans to consider these new prices. The iteration continues until no good or service in the economy is in excess supply or excess demand. According to the authors, this process can be greatly simplified by using computers. Albert and Hahnel also contend that this allocation process can lead to a Pareto optimum outcome[3] (Albert and Hahnel, 1991a, pp 73–106).

Workers' compensation

As we saw, the major constraint imposed on consumers' councils is through workers' compensation. Consumers can only get the amount of product equivalent to the effort and sacrifice they make through work. Participatory economics offers a decentralized mechanism for compensation based on the principle that payment equals effort and sacrifice. If we apply this 'distributive maxim' to today's world, those with the most taxing and tiring jobs would be entitled to higher remuneration. In contrast, the more exciting and least demanding jobs would receive lower pay. This remuneration scheme is the opposite of what many are experiencing today.

How does this work in participatory economics? Through what the authors call 'balanced job complexes'. This proposal differs both significantly and very little from the current work organization. It differs a lot because its starting point is that everyone should have a set of tasks with the best possible balance between them. It also varies very little because what we call a 'job' is, in fact, a blend of tasks whose aggregate is simply the result of other motives than the balancing of effort and sacrifice. With balanced job complexes, the tasks that best foster the individual's development will be balanced out by others that promote it less.

Workplaces can distribute tasks as they wish because they are democratic spaces. However, Michael Albert provides a relatively simple way to determine the 'sacrifice value' of each task. Each worker could grade each existing task in that environment on a scale of 1 to 20. The workplace council would then assemble all the grades and determine an average for each task. The tasks would then be distributed among workers according to their tastes and skill levels to come as close as possible to the workplace average (Albert, 2003, pp 105–106).

How is this linked to the planning process? The entire society sets the average sacrifice grade for each industry branch through delegate committees for each industry. It also sets a general average for the whole economy. This general average is the measurement standard for remuneration: giving less effort than average means getting paid less and vice versa. If they are far from the average, workers are encouraged to work in multiple workplaces to reach an equilibrium.

Hence, when workers' councils decide on their production choices, it directly impacts their compensation and consumption capacity. Likewise, a rise in prices affects the capacity of the consumption councils. By 'forcing' actors to find an equilibrium between what they want and what others want (expressed through price and compensation averages), 'this procedure "whittles down" overly ambitious proposals … about what they would like to do to a "feasible" plan where everything someone is expecting to be able to use will effectively be available' (Hahnel, 2012, pp 94–95).

In recent years, Robin Hahnel has proposed two evolutions of the model. First, he developed what he calls 'a pollution damage revealing mechanism', which gives participatory economics the possibility to evaluate the damage pollution is doing to different communities and integrate this damage into the indicative prices of goods in the form of a Pigouvian tax (Hahnel, 2005, pp 198–203; 2012, pp 123–132; 2017; 2021, pp 138–148). He also worked on investment and development planning to propose how participatory planning would function in the longer term and how these longer-term plans would interact with the annual planning procedure (Hahnel, 2005, pp 203–207; 2012, pp 115–122; 2021, pp 253–282; Hahnel and Kerkhoff, 2020). He also recently worked on organizing and rewarding reproductive labour in a democratically planned economy (Hahnel, 2021, pp 195–207; see also Bohmer, Chowdhury and Hahnel, 2020). Albert and Hahnel's model is illustrated in Figure 1.2.

Cockshott and Cottrell's computerized central planning

In 1993, the economist and computer scientist Paul Cockshott and the economist Allin Cottrell published *Towards a New Socialism*. This book summarized previous publications they wrote, separately and together, about the effect of the advancement of computer technology on the arguments presented in the socialist calculation debate. Instead of opting for a decentralized form of planning as the two models we just discussed did, they argue that a centralized but computerized form of planning was not only possible but a better option than market or non-market decentralization.

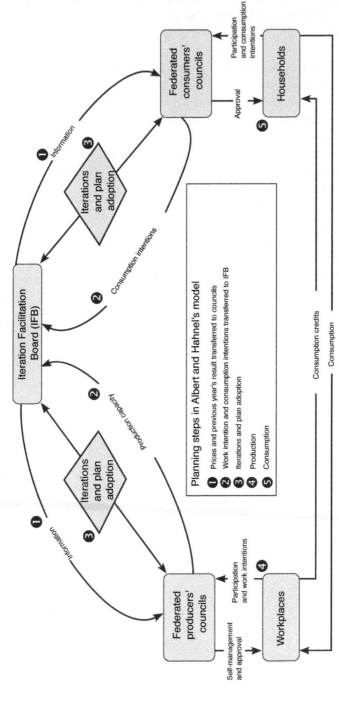

Figure 1.2: Albert and Hahnel's participatory economics annual planning diagram

Source: Laurin-Lamothe, Legault and Tremblay-Pepin, 2023, translated and modified by the authors.

A centralized planning bureau

At the heart of Cockshott and Cottrell's model lies one institution: a centralized planning bureau they often simply call planning. This bureau is responsible for producing various plans of three different sorts: macroeconomic plans, strategic plans and detailed plans (Cockshott and Cottrell, 1993, pp 58–59).

Macroeconomic plans are about balancing broad economic measures: levels of taxation, savings and investments for the whole economy (Cockshott and Cottrell, 1993, pp 89–102). Strategic plans say where the economy should go in the short, medium, and long term: what part of the industrial structure do we want to develop, which one do we want to leave aside, how do we want to adapt to new environmental or, say, demographic realities; by how much do we want to see our labour time increase or decrease (Cockshott and Cottrell, 1993, pp 61–72). The detailed plans make macroeconomic and strategic plans a concrete reality in a given year after considering available resources (Cockshott and Cottrell, 1993, pp 73–88).

Planners use two essential tools to prepare these plans: first, a network of computers with at least one station in every workplace where 'a local spreadsheet of its production capabilities and raw materials requirements' (Cockshott and Cottrell, 2008, p 12) is continuously and automatically updated; second, supercomputers that integrate this information into an algorithm designed to allocate raw materials and the labour force according to a set of desired outputs for the whole economy (Cockshott, 1990; Cockshott and Cottrell, 1993, pp 81–86). With these tools, planning can design various macroeconomic, strategic, and detailed plans with different total output results and workload inputs. These plans are then submitted to a political process – to which we will come back – for approval or rejection.

The basic unit of these plans is labour time. Cockshott and Cottrell argue that the labour theory of value is a solid economic proposition upon which to base the planning process (Cockshott and Cottrell, 1989; 1993, pp 41–52; 1997). The authors offered answers to a series of classical objections to labour value theory, for instance the complexity of taking skilled labour into account (Cockshott and Cottrell, 1993, pp 34–36), the integration of the value of time through a discount rate (pp 67–69) or the inclusion of the value of natural resources (pp 64–67). So, the planning bureau has access to a value for each good regarding labour time. To form a market-clearing price for each good, it adds a multiplier based on the ratio between the demand for the good and its value in labour time (Cockshott and Cottrell 1997, pp 347–348).

When adopted, the plans are implemented by 'projects' in which people work to create planned goods or services. These projects are not enterprises because they would have the economic right to 'own' specific means of production or resources or to 'pay' workers to do some work. Instead, they are being allocated a certain amount of work time from workers and using specific infrastructure and resources by planning.

This central bureau owns all the means of production, and every natural resource integrates all projects 'as [...] a capitalist company [integrates] the individual activities that it may be carrying out [...] projects are managerial or administrative rather than legal entities' (Cockshott and Cottrell, 1993, p 179). The workers are paid in labour tokens directly by planning. These labour tokens equal the labour time a worker has accomplished in a given period. Workers then exchange them for consumer goods. As soon as they do so, the tokens lose their value, like a theatre ticket (Cockshott and Cottrell, 1993, pp 24–25). The trends in token spending will give the central planning bureau the necessary information to establish market-clearing prices.

Innovation could be handled through an 'innovation budget' through which individuals and companies could apply for funding for their ideas and projects (Cockshott and Cottrell, 2008, p 90).

Democracy, planning and individual rights

At first sight, the Cockshott and Cottrell model may seem not only centralized but also quite hierarchical, with the central planning bureau commanding from the top and everyone underneath obeying. While they have not developed the political aspect of their model as much as the economic one, in their 1993 book and in a few articles, Cockshott and Cottrell proposed a direct democracy based on sortition, inspired by the Athenian classic democracy (Cockshott and Cottrell, 1993, pp 157–170). Hence, '[t]he various organs of public authority would be controlled by citizens' committees chosen by lot. The media, the health service, the planning and marketing agencies, the various industries would have their juries' (p 167). These committees could act as regulatory bodies, establishing norms, rules, and regulations, and economic bodies, being allocated production mandates and resources by the central planning bureau and ensuring they are fulfilled. They would be responsible for the day-to-day decision-making at the top of each organization and societal institution. It is noteworthy to mention that local democracy only intervenes ex post in Cockshott and Cottrell's model. It democratically organizes the decisions taken by the plan, written by the central planning bureau and adopted by referendum.

The macroeconomic plan and some aspects of the strategic plan would be submitted to citizens through annual referenda using electronic procedures (Cockshott and Cottrell, 2008, pp 11–12). The most important aspect of these votes is the level of taxation: the amount of work time that society should invest in goods and services available for free to all citizens. When the quantity of work time necessary for these public services is adopted democratically, a flat tax covering this exact amount is deducted from every working person's labour token (Cockshott and Cottrell, 1993, p 166).

This democratic system also offers rights to individuals: the right to earn a living (even if they are, for some reason, unable to work, in which case they receive essential goods without any obligation on their part) and the right to receive the total value of their labour and to dispose of this value as they see fit (Cockshott and Cottrell, 1993, p 175). 'In all cases, the people are the ultimate delegators of power. Either they vote to tax themselves and entrust a demarchic council with a budget to produce a free service, or they choose to purchase goods, in which case they are voting labor time to the production of those goods' (Cockshott and Cottrell, 2008, p 16).

Cockshott and Cottrell (2008) updated their argument in recent years by including the new technologies now available. Their vision has informed many contemporaries by demonstrating that democratically planned economies can take advantage of technological advances, including the ones used by the largest capitalist corporations that are deeply involved in planning massive economic networks (Durand and Keucheyan, 2019; Phillips and Rozworski, 2019). In a recent book Cockshot, Cottrell and Dapprich (2022) deepened the link between their postcapitalist proposal and the fight against climate change, while answering critiques about the tractability of planning and the use value in their model.

Thus, the authors propose a centralized, entirely computerized, and moneyless system that calculates and expresses all goods' value in working hours. Their contribution is crucial to understanding that democratic economic planning is technically feasible. Cockshott and Cottrell's model is illustrated in Figure 1.3.

Laibman's multilevel democratic iterative coordination

Economist David Laibman is Professor Emeritus at Brooklyn College and the City University of New York. Laibman played a leading role in the direction of the journal *Science and Society*. Since 1992, this journal helped rekindle the debate on alternative economic models to capitalism as the Soviet Union collapsed. In many contributions (Laibman, 2001; 2011; 2015; 2022) but none taking the form of a book strictly about his model, he presents a model named multilevel democratic iterative coordination (MDIC).

The central contribution of MDIC is to offer an operational model of a socialist economy that combines decentralized and centralized aspects, as well as qualitative and quantitative modes of regulation. In particular, the model focuses on performance measurement for production units, reward mechanisms for ambition around the economic plan, and for its realization.

Figure 1.3: Cockshott and Cottrell's detailed central planning model

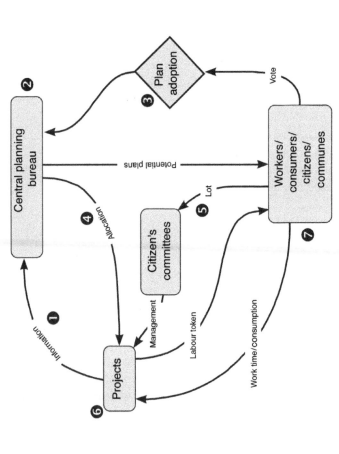

Source: Laurin-Lamothe, Legault and Tremblay-Pepin, 2023, translated and modified by the authors.

A synthesis

Having been at the centre of the debate around postcapitalist economics, David Laibman knows well and for a long time the models we have presented earlier in this chapter. He started working on his own proposal to produce a synthesis of those models (and others), arguing that, without that synthesis, they are not integrating in a functional way two fundamental dimensions common to all of them. Those dimensions are spectra, on which Laibman orders the different options for a postcapitalist economy. The first dimension, organization 'traverses a spectrum running from *central* to *decentral,* with highly concentrated decision-making, at one end, and extreme dispersal of decision-making, at the other' (Laibman, 2022, p 227). The second dimension, regulation, is about the methods used to make decisions, either quantitative (numbers, data) or qualitative (arguments, words). For him, previous models did not productively integrate those two dimensions, often focusing only on one side of the spectra. The continuous interactivity he proposes is one element that gives Laibman's model its balance on those spectra. Figure 1.4 is a slightly adapted version of a figure produced by Laibman (2015, p 329) that gives a good idea of the usage he makes of those two dimensions and where he locates his models compared to the models presented in this chapter and others.

What does 'iterative' mean?

The noun 'iterative' in the name of the model refers to the constant exchange of information between different levels and production units and the balance between local initiative and centralized coordination. These levels include, on the one hand, a central planning authority (also called the 'centre') and, on the other, different levels of production units. Production units are sometimes called 'enterprises', but they should not be confused with capitalist corporations focused on profit creation and accumulation. Iteration allows production units to retain their autonomy and nurture the creative spirit and innovation that emerge locally while framing them by a centralized coordination mechanism that ensures social optimization (Laibman, 2015, p 312).

Each production unit prepares its own plan, developed from the profile of the local workforce, the physical environment, available materials, and so on. Production is also codetermined within the production unit by a consumer council, ensuring that decisions about the types of goods and services correspond to the community's needs. The production unit is socialized: it belongs to a community that determines its economic, political, social and environmental impact.

Contracts between production units are always possible, but the centre must be informed. The 'production units/centre' iterations balance the inputs and

Figure 1.4: David Laibman's taxonomy of post-capitalist models

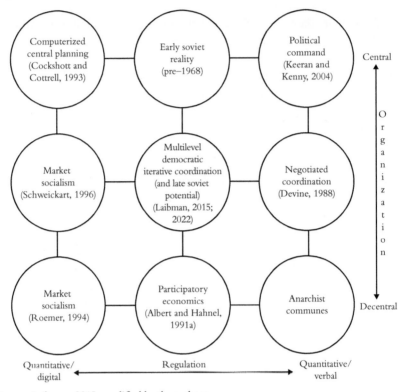

Source: Laibman, 2015, modified by the authors.

outputs of all units and aggregate supply and demand. The centre, therefore, resolves supply issues and checks the correspondence of production unit plans against broader criteria such as environmental impacts, available energy resources, the built environment, residential development, and resources demanded by hospitals and schools, among others (Laibman, 2022, p 237), and then, if necessary, requests adjustments from the production units.

Think, for example, of limited timber resources that several production units would require in large quantities simultaneously. Without the centre's intervention, the ecological limits of forest preservation and regeneration could not be ensured. The same applies to highly skilled workers, whom the centre could send to certain localities at critical times to meet more urgent needs before returning to their home localities to perform tasks with longer-term benefits. The development and adjustment of plans are simultaneous and continuous, thanks to a systematized digital data exchange accessible via a computer network. The plan is not imposed from the top down. The planning activity takes place as production units formulate the implementation of their objectives. We can see here how Laibman's model balances the organization dimension between centralized and decentralized decision-making processes.

Prices and measuring production unit activities

Measuring the activities of production units plays a significant role in the multilevel democratic iterative coordination model. In capitalist economies, this measurement often boils down to one primary indicator, usually the rate of profit. Instead, Laibman proposes an indicator that condenses all quantitative information on production and combines qualitative data on each unit's objectives. Moreover, the leading indicator of the activities of production units is different from the 'rate of return on investment' or the 'rate of profit' as calculated in a capitalist economy (Laibman, 2015, pp 317–320) because it does not consider wages as a cost. It measures the income the production unit generates once expenditure on non-human resources (capital) has been disbursed. These resources, internalized in the model, include elements that capitalist companies tend to externalize when calculating their profitability, which are nonetheless essential: the education system, social protection, domestic work, and so on.

Costs are determined by a pricing system that considers available resources and environmental factors, which Laibman calls social reproduction prices (SRP) (Laibman, 1992, pp 316–333). Those prices are profoundly different from prices in a capitalist setting. They 'generate a uniform social rate of return to all production activities, where this rate measures the value-creating effect of each activity using the entire income stream generated by it [...], and by identifying and calculating the entire set of social resource stocks (capital) used by enterprises' (Laibman, 2022, p 239). It enables broader societal objectives to be attained, unattainable through spontaneous market organization. Those prices account for the social stocks (public buildings, education, health) needed to support and make possible the work of production. In our current economy, these elements are regarded as externalities, but are taken into account when calculating SRPs.

Measuring social indicators: a key factor in evaluating production units

Production units are evaluated using conventional quantitative performance criteria – based on historical data, the average rate of return in the sector, or a combination of the two – and qualitative criteria – a measure of ecological, solidarity, and community objectives that Laibman names a 'social indicator measure' (Laibman, 2015, pp 318–320). Suppose a production unit aims to increase the number of its workers from diverse backgrounds, reduce the environmental impact of its activities, or assist another less-favoured region by providing technical tools and transferring knowledge. In that case, the performance indicator will include achieving each objective.

A committee of representatives from the production unit, industry, trade unions, NGOs, and environmental activists determines the number of objectives, content, and evaluation (Laibman, 2015, p 321) based on the different groups of people affected by the production unit's activities.

Superior performance enables the production unit to distribute surpluses such as wages, solidarity funds for the community, aid funds for other production units, and so on. On the other hand, if a production unit underperforms, it has severe consequences for its ability to compensate for its monetary and social deficit. Following Laibman's logic – even though this is never clearly mentioned – such a situation would lead to remedial measures imposed by the centre or the community. Because of how the evaluation of their activities functions, production units have every interest in achieving the goals they have set themselves and broadening the spectrum of their activities to benefit the community as a whole (Laibman, 2015, p 324). This evaluation mode is Laibman's strategy to balance quantitative measures (rate of return) and qualitative ones (social indicators).

Laibman wanted to address the issues of incentives and motivation that he saw as central to planning models. In his view, the search for best practices and solutions by work units and their communities are powerful tools for achieving high-performance, sophisticated technical and social quality with a level of motivation, freedom and responsibility that is highly rewarding for workers (Laibman, 2001). The ambitious nature of the plan is also part of the performance assessment, leading to a higher reward if it is achieved (Laibman, 2015, p 326). Thus, a production unit has no incentive to propose a lazy or unrealistic plan. In this way, planning relies on individuals' critical capacity and knowledge, enabling them to develop goals and strategies autonomously and creatively while meeting broader social norms. Participatory coordination thus ensures constant production and allocation of resources, allowing 'the progressive creation of consensus and shared vision: a sense of intentionality and control over the social process' (Laibman, 2001, p 90).

Conclusion

These proposals are imperfect and would benefit from further improvement and greater detail. Several nuances and distinctions are absent from this text. Nevertheless, these imperfections should not prevent us from starting to reflect now on the possible configurations of a postcapitalist economy. We also omitted in these brief sketches the critiques formulated by previous readers of these models and the ones we could have proposed. Instead, our goal was to lay out the models' functioning simply and clearly so that a broader public could discuss and criticise them elsewhere.

Getting out of capitalism implies finding desirable and functional alternatives to replace it. It is necessary to continue analysing and criticizing the world as it presents itself to us, and it is just as imperative to question the nature of the world we want to build. We should consider these two tasks as two sides of the same coin.

Glossary

Devine and Adaman's coordinated negotiation

Chamber of interests

The chamber of interests is a consultative body representing interest groups and cause groups. There are chambers of interests at the three levels of Devine's model (national, regional and local). The chamber of interests brings together all interest groups and cause groups representatives to debate and ideally agree on the plan's content to be adopted. When they have reached an agreement or have decided that such an agreement is not attainable, they then send a report to the representative assembly presenting their agreements and disagreements. Based on this report, the assembly will discuss and adopt the plan (Devine, 1988, p 194).

Functional services or functional activities

Functional services or functional activities are the terms Pat Devine uses to designate the equivalent of today's public services in most advanced capitalist countries: health, education, environmental protection, etc. Social bodies are tax-funded and offer these services (Devine, 1988, p 213).

Interest groups and cause groups

Interest groups are self-organized citizens interested in a specific question: professional bodies and unions, organizers of recreational activities (cultural, sports, and so on). Cause groups can broadly be understood as social movements. All these groups function through the logic of election and representation. Their representatives meet in the chamber of interest to defend their respective groups' interests in elaborating the plan (Devine, 1988, p 153).

Market exchange

Market exchange consists of an act of sale/purchase between a production unit and another or between a production unit and an individual as long as the sale does not significantly affect production capacity and requires major investment. Negotiated coordination keeps market exchanges (Devine, 1988, p 24).

Market forces

Market forces refer to how changes in production capacity (like major investments) occur. Under capitalism, big corporations coordinate these investments ex-post in an atomistic way. Under negotiated coordination, a democratic and negotiated coordination process replaces market forces (Adaman and Devine, 1996, p 534).

Negotiated coordination bodies

The negotiated coordination bodies are responsible for economic coordination within a production sector. These bodies make the major investment decisions regarding an industry. This body comprises elected representatives of the same sector's production units, main customers, major suppliers, relevant planning commissions and interest groups. The main objective of this institution is to coordinate economic activities in the same sector. Issues relating to the main changes in production capacities, achieving targets and managing production gaps between the same sector's production units are addressed here (Devine, 1988, p 231).

Planning commissions

The planning commissions have two primary purposes. Its first is to elaborate plans. Based on the negotiated coordination bodies' economic information, the planning commission members elaborate and submit various plans to the representative assembly, where one plan will be adopted. Planning commissions consist of members of the concerned governments, production units, negotiated coordination bodies, and interest and cause groups. The second purpose of the planning commission is related to the plan's implementation. They are responsible for economic coordination between the different authorities at a geographic scale (national, regional, and local). After receiving the version of the representative assembly's plan, planning commissions allocate the principal investments to the various production units through the appropriate negotiated coordination body. There are planning commissions at the local, regional and national levels (Devine, 1988, pp 190, 213).

Prices and wages

The production units determine prices and correspond to the social costs of production. Production costs are divided into two types: primary inputs and secondary inputs. The cost of primary inputs (natural resources, energy, and capital) is determined at the national level since they affect all production units. An income policy is adopted at the national level, but local production units establish wage levels while respecting the policy's parameters. With this data and adding the depreciation for the equipment and building, each production unit can set its prices by adding up production costs (Devine, 1988, pp 197–198).

Production units

Production units (roughly equivalent to enterprises) produce goods and services and provide them to consumers. Representatives from four sectors sit on the decision-making body of the production unit: the general interest (through national, regional, and local planning commissions and negotiated coordination body), the interests of consumers, users and suppliers (through consumer associations, government and public services, production units that buy from or sell to the production unit and other industry development councils related to the production unit), the interest of workers (in the form of the workers of the production unit itself and their unions) and the interests of the community (through interest groups and cause groups). These representatives then agree on the most appropriate use of productive capacities through negotiation, considering each other's interests. They are also responsible for making small local investments. Within this framework, the production unit is self-managed by its workers.

Representative assemblies

Representative assemblies are political decision-making bodies composed of all the people's representatives elected by universal suffrage. Political parties assemble different representatives on an ideological basis. The party whose representatives form the majority constitutes the executive power, while the legislative power includes opposition parties. Their primary economic purpose is to adopt the plan. Based on the planning commission's various plans and considering the report from the chamber of interest, the elected members of the representative assembly deliberate and adopt the plan's final version. This final version will then be sent back to negotiated coordination bodies for implementation. Representative assemblies are at the three levels of the negotiated coordination model: local, regional and national (Devine, 1988, pp 142, 254).

Small-scale activity

Self-employed individuals or small coops carry out what the model calls small-scale activities (repairs, art, personal growth, massage therapy, graphic designers, and so on). Workers in these sectors could be grouped in 'centres'. Like co-working spaces, these centres would provide workspace and resources for these workers. The centres would be self-managed within guidelines decided by the local planning commission. If their activity level extends outside their initial locality, this activity would have to register as a production unit and have its own governing body (Devine, 1988, p 230).

Social bodies

Social bodies are the government's agencies that provide the functional services (the equivalent of public services in this model): health, education, environmental protection, and so on. Social bodies are decentralized, present at the model's three levels (national, regional and local), and are financed by taxation (Devine, 1988, p 213).

Social ownership

Social property is a dynamic form of ownership of the means of production that is adapted to the needs of the communities that are concerned by a decision. It is not equivalent to state ownership as it means control by society. There are two conditions for social ownership: the people most affected by using specific means of production should take part in decisions concerning them, and these decisions should be coherently integrated into a broader plan decided by society as a whole.

The adequate governing bodies of the production units, planning commissions, and the negotiated coordination bodies coordinate the implementation of this form of ownership (Devine, 1988, p 223).

Subsidiarity

The principle of subsidiarity favours decision-making being done in the utmost decentralized way possible. This principle implies that decisions should be made primarily by those proportionally affected by it (Devine, 2002, p 75).

Taxes

The government collects two kinds of taxes: one on production units and one on wages. The tax on production units equals the renting out resources and the return on assets employed. Depending on the amount produced by this tax on production units, it could be complemented by a wage tax. These taxes are the government's source of revenue and finance the government's social bodies providing functional services. Local and regional governments would also collect taxes. The taxes on production units would be set at a rate that would leave production units with a surplus for minor investments (Devine, 1988, p 216).

Albert and Hahnel's participatory economics
Balanced job complex

In participatory economics, jobs would be divided into tasks and reorganized to create a balanced set of tasks. This redistribution aims to equalize desirable and undesirable tasks across workers in the same workplace and workplaces. It involves reviewing the division of labour to balance the work content between planning and execution tasks as much as possible. Participatory economics, therefore, does not seek to 'abolish' the division of labour. Instead, it aims to review the division of labour to redistribute burdensome and empowering tasks equitably. It aims to give decision-making time and power back to workers while letting them stay in contact with the production sphere (Hahnel, 2012, pp 55–56).

Complementary holism

Complementary holism is the general theory underpinning participatory economics, which sees society as divided into several spheres containing social institutions responding to human needs and desires. These institutions shape human wants and human needs, just like institutions are shaped in return by those desires and needs. It aims to describe society by integrating and going beyond four social theories described as monistic: nationalism, feminism, Marxism and anarchism. These social theories are monistic as they do not offer a perspective that subtly understands the complexity of society (Albert et al, 1986, p 80).

Consumers' councils

Consumers' councils are in charge of consumption in the planning process. Like workers' councils, consumers' councils are organized according to the federal principle, but on a geographic basis instead of a sectoral basis. They are nested in each other from the individual household to the national council (Albert, 2003, p 93).

Iteration facilitation board

The primary role of the IFB is to facilitate and coordinate the planning process. This body collects all the proposals for production and consumption, compares them, and sends alternative suggestions back to the various councils. Its function is strictly perfunctory. It is a technical workplace like many others, and it does not hold any extraordinary political power. It assists workplaces and households by integrating the participatory planning process through information (Albert and Hahnel, 1991a, p 62).

Prices

The IFB calculates prices. They are cost-based and influenced by supply and demand. In the iterative planning process, IFBs emit prices that are then affected by supply and demand as expressed by workers' and consumers' councils. A new round starts by taking into account these new prices. Prices provide helpful information about the social costs and the social benefits of goods and services (Hahnel, 2012, pp 91–92).

Remuneration

Workers' councils set remuneration according to effort and determine the level of effort for each task. The objective of linking wages to effort is to ensure that everyone is compensated according to their effort, the only thing that workers have a clear impact on. Remuneration is distributed through consumption credits that customers can use to get consumption goods. Workplaces do not keep these credits after the transaction and are not used in production (Albert, 2003, p 112; Hahnel, 2012, p 59).

Workers' councils

Workers' councils are the self-management body of workplaces producing goods and services. Only workers are members of those councils. All workers of a workplace take part in the workers' council decisions. They do so directly in their local councils. Workers' councils are in charge of the day-to-day management of their local workplace, are federated by sectors, and manage the entire productive economy through this process. They are nested in each other, from the small working team to the national council. These councils are where workers express how many hours they wish to work, what they wish to produce, how they want to organize their workplace, and so on (Albert, 2003, p 92).

Cockshott and Cottrell's computerized central planning

Central planning bureau

The central planning bureau is the central institution of Cockshott and Cottrell's model. It is often simply called 'planning' by the authors. It comprises experts (economists, technicians, computer scientists, and engineers). The central planning bureau's main task is to produce alternative plans. Planning makes three kinds of plans: macroeconomic, strategic and detailed. Those plans are proposed to the population by electronic referendum and adopted (Cockshott and Cottrell, 1993, p 179).

Citizen's committees

The state would be maintained, but not as we know it. It would be an 'acephalous state' in that it would have no legislative power, and its role would be limited to implementing the decisions made by its constitutive committees. These committees would be composed of citizens chosen by lot from among their users and workers. All public bodies and each industrial sector would be governed this way (health, education, water, electricity, transport, and so on) (Cockshott and Cottrell, 1993, p 167).

Commune

Communes are non-mandatory living spaces that Cockshott and Cottrell think would be more efficient and adapted to their model. They should offer one room per individual within a collective habitat and be designed with an architecture suited for this new domestic lifestyle. Communes would collectively realize four economic activities: housing, childcare, certain leisure activities and assistance to the elderly. The pooling of these activities would allow for significant economies of scale (Cockshott and Cottrell, 1993, p 150).

Detailed plan

The detailed plan contains the concrete allocation of resources within the framework established by the macroeconomic and strategic plans. If the strategic plan invests, for example, a certain amount of national revenue in a specific sector, the detailed plan will specify the concrete amount of resources needed in each project to meet this goal (Cockshott and Cottrell, 1993, p 73).

Macroeconomic plan

The macroeconomic plan establishes general parameters that aim to frame economic development in the long term. It contains investment levels for the economy as a whole, the level of taxation and savings (Cockshott and Cottrell, 1993, p 89).

Prices

The value of goods and services would be expressed in hours of work socially necessary for their production. However, prices would not necessarily correspond to value. The central planning bureau would make adjustments according to demand. Thus, if a commodity is in high demand, prices would be adjusted to meet this demand adequately. Concretely, two numbers would be displayed at the time of purchase: the 'value' (the number of hours of work socially required to produce it) and the price adjusted according to demand. Thus, labour value would be a milestone to curb price elasticity (Cockshott and Cottrell, 1997, pp 347–348).

Projects

Projects resemble business in capitalist society and are where production occurs. Projects have no formal legal existence; they are only administrative units that belong to the community through planning. The link between the central planning bureau and projects is similar to the one between a single company's and its executive's different divisions. Projects and the central planning bureau mostly communicate through digital data. Each project has a computer dedicated to planning connected to an information network dedicated to this task (Cockshott and Cottrell, 2008, p 9). Each project is self-managed by its workers (Cockshott and Cottrell, 1993, p 179).

Strategic plan

The strategic plan concerns the evolution of the economy's structure in the short, medium, and long term. The strategic plan presents which sector to develop and which to compress, the economy's environmental dimension, and the total working time (Cockshott and Cottrell, 1993, p 61).

Taxes

Income tax, land rent, and consumption tax pay for the services offered to the population free of direct charge. Since the income distribution would be roughly equal, there would be no reason to introduce a differentiated tax. The authors propose introducing a 'flat tax', the amount of which would be decided annually by democratic means. The second source of government revenue is land rent. Land ownership would be a public monopoly. Like natural resources, land would be safeguarded by an international environmental agency. A national organization would serve as an intermediary to coordinate such an agency's activities. Thus, when someone buys a house, she owns the materials but rents the land through a rent to the state. A consumption tax would be introduced for socially and ecologically undesirable goods and services. This tax would make it possible to limit the use of these goods and services. For instance, specific taxes could target products such as oil, tobacco, and alcohol to adjust consumer behaviour (Cockshott and Cottrell, 1993, pp 70, 99, 211).

Value

The labour theory of value is the foundation of Cockshott and Cottrell's model. Hours worked are the basic unit used in the whole model. Hence, wages, prices, and plans are all expressed in work hours equivalent (Cockshott and Cottrell, 1993, p 41).

Wages

Wages are differentiated according to productivity and paid in labour tokens. According to the authors, associating productivity with wages makes it possible to recognize disparities in the effort invested in work and remunerate workers according to their effort, measured in output. The authors suggest three productivity levels: A, B, and C; A being highly productive, and C being less productive. This rating would not be related to the worker's training or education level but strictly to their productivity. It would be a way of recognizing each worker's contribution at their actual height. When people contribute more to society, they receive proportionally more, and vice versa. In the case of a labour shortage in a particular sector, Cockshott and Cottrell consider the possibility of increasing wages as an incentive. The central planning bureau pays the wages in labour tokens, not the projects. Those tokens can be used only by the person they were given to. When the tokens are used, they are destroyed, just like theatre tickets (Cockshott and Cottrell, 1993, p 34).

Laibman's multilevel democratic iterative coordination
Centre

The centre is a decision-making space where democratic economic planning is coordinated at a large level. Enterprises constitute and report to that centre. 'A visual metaphor might refer to "higher" and "lower" levels, so long as we avoid smuggling in invidious implications (thinking of "higher" as somehow "better" or "privileged"); an alternative might use an inner-outer conception' (Laibman, 2015, p 309).

Enterprises

Local units of production (Laibman, 2015, p 309).

Iterative

> 'Iterative' refers to repeated, sequential flows of data and proposals between the center and the enterprises, and (where appropriate)

constraining orders from the center to the enterprises. Each enterprise prepares its plan and, in so doing, incorporates specific local knowledge: the peculiarities of its workforce, the physical environment, equipment, history, etc. The 'upward' (or 'inward') flow of these plans to the center involves aggregation; coordination for consistency of supplies and demands, inputs and outputs; establishing optimal solutions to problems involving choice (where relevant); and vetting the emerging aggregate plan against wider criteria. (Laibman, 2015, p 309)

Measure of enterprise activity

The measure of enterprise activity is a quantitative and qualitative measurement of how production units perform, 'which is the object of planning, the means of evaluation, and the basis for forming enterprise income' (Laibman, 2015, p 317). The quantitative aspect is based on a rate of return, and the qualitative one is based on a social indicator measure (see below).

Organization

Organization is a dimension of every postcapitalist model about how centralized or decentralized the decision-making process of this model is. '"Organization" traverses a spectrum running from *central* to *decentral*, with highly concentrated decision-making, at one end, and extreme dispersal of decision-making, at the other' (Laibman, 2022, p 227).

Rate of return

> In MDIC socialism, we can also envision a single rate of return, which will concentrate all of the quantitative aspects of activity measurement. […] The return can be related to a wider set of assets, including those held outside of the enterprise; meaningful social time horizons can be applied in the evaluation of investment, product design and development; and fully appropriate accounting prices […] can be used for purposes of evaluation. (Laibman, 2015, p 317)

Regulation

Regulation is a dimension of every postcapitalist model about the type of information on which decision-making is based. '"Regulation" refers to a different dimension of choice: between *quantitative* methods at one extreme; and *qualitative*, or verbal, or political, methods at the other' (Laibman, 2022, pp 227–228).

Social indicator measure

The social indicator measure is the qualitative part of the measure of enterprise activity.

> From a socialist standpoint, the enterprise's work is measured not just by the products or services it provides, but by its achievements in a number of social areas. To illustrate, we might posit four areas: ecology, community, solidarity, and industry. 'Ecology' is a measure of the enterprise's contribution toward sustainability, meeting social goals regarding carbon emissions, use of alternative fuels, waste disposal, etc. 'Community' refers to its connection to the surrounding community — its work with schools, its help in developing residential sites, providing recreational resources, and so forth. 'Solidarity' measures the enterprise's efforts to address still-existing oppressive divisions within the workforce and the wider working community: racism, sexism, heterosexism and heteronormativity, and national or ethnic exclusion. This category could also include international solidarity work. Finally, 'industry' measures the enterprise's industry-wide relations, perhaps its sharing of resources with less-developed enterprises and participation in industry- or sector-wide planning. [...] Teams of evaluators, drawn from 'stakeholders' in each area, will develop *ratings* of the enterprise's activity, each in the area of its special concern. These are then aggregated, and added to the measure based on the socialist rate of return. (Laibman, 2022, p 243)

Social reproduction prices

> [A] set of benchmark prices organized by a core principle for defining and calculating a uniform rate of return, or profit, and a uniquely inclusive method of defining and measuring the relevant resource ('capital') stocks involved in each sector of production. These prices are a 'classical' price system, along the lines of the Sraffa or other modern linear production-price models, but oriented toward socialist rather than capitalist ownership, in consideration of both what constitutes the 'income' or 'surplus' accruing from production, and what stocks of social resources are the appropriate base on which to compare that surplus when computing a rate of return. (Laimban, 2015, p 311)

Notes

[1] This chapter was first published in 2021 as a research note of the Research Center on Social Innovations and Transformations (CRITS), but it focused only the three first

models. We added Laibman's model at the request of the editors of this volume, translating and modifying parts of a chapter from our book published in French in 2023: *Construire l'économie postcapitaliste*. This chapter draws on research supported by Canada's Social Sciences and Humanities Research Council.

2   The debate was about the technical possibility of planning a complex modern economy. The debate was between two camps. The first, composed of economists from the Austrian school (mainly Friedrich Hayek and Ludwig von Mises), rejected the possibility of rationally calculating economic activity through central planning. The second camp, composed of socialist economists, defended this possibility. See Devine and Adaman (1996) for further readings.

3   A Pareto optimum outcome is an economic state where it is not possible to improve the situation of one individual without degrading the situation of at least one other.

Bibliography

Adaman, F. and Devine, P. (1996) 'The economics calculation debate: lessons for socialists', *Cambridge Journal of Economics*, 20(5): 523–537.

Adaman, F. and Devine, P. (2017) 'Democracy, participation and social planning', in C.L. Spash (ed) *Routledge Handbook of Ecological Economics*, London: Routledge, pp 517–524.

Adaman, F., Devine, P. and Ozkaynak, B. (2003) 'Reinstituting the economic process: (re)embedding the economy in society and nature', *International Review of Sociology – Revue Internationale de Sociologie*, 13(2): 357–374.

Albert, M. (2003) *Parecon: Life After Capitalism*. London: Verso Books.

Albert, M. et al. (1986) *Liberating Theory*. Boston: South End Press.

Albert, M. and Hahnel, R. (1991a) *The Political Economy of Participatory Economics*. Princeton: Princeton University Press.

Albert, M. and Hahnel, R. (1991b) *Looking Forward: Participatory Economics for the Twenty-First Century*. Boston: South End Press.

Albert, M. and Hahnel, R. (1992) 'Participatory planning', *Science & Society*, 56(1): 39–59.

Bohmer, P., Savvina, C. and Hahnel, R. (2020) 'Reproductive labor in a participatory socialist society', *Review of Radical Political Economics*, 52(4): 755–771.

Cockshott, W.P. (1990) 'Application of artificial intelligence techniques to economic planning', *Future Computing System*, 2(4): 429–443.

Cockshott, W.P. and Cottrell, A. (1989) 'Labour value and socialist economic calculation', *Economy and Society*, 18(1): 71–99.

Cockshott, W.P. and Cottrell, A. (1993) *Towards a New Socialism*. Nottingham: Russell Press Ltd.

Cockshott, W.P. and Cottrell, A. (1997) 'Value, markets and socialism', *Science & Society*, 61(3): 330–357.

Cockshott, W.P. and Cottrell, A. (2008) 'Computers and economic democracy', *Revista de Economía Institucional*, 1: 161–205.

Cockshott, W.P., Cottrell, A. and Dapprich, J.P. (2022) *Economic Planning in an Age of Climate Crisis*. Independently published.

Devine, P. (1988) *Democracy and Economic Planning. The Political Economy of a Self-Governing Society*. Boulder: Westview Press.

Devine, P. (2017). 'Ecosocialism for a new era', in R. Westra, R. Albritton and S. Jeong *Varieties of Alternative Economic Systems Practical Utopias for an Age of Global Crisis and Austerity*, New York: Routledge, pp 33–51.

Devine, P. (2019) 'Marx, la démocratie et la planification économique', *Actuel Marx*, 65(1): 54–66.

Devine, P. (2002) 'Participatory planning through negotiated coordination', *Science & Society*, 66(1): 72–85.

Durand, C. and Keucheyan, R. (2019) 'Planifier à l'âge des algorithmes', *Actuel Marx*, 65(1): 81–102.

Hahnel, R. (2005) *Economic Justice and Democracy: From Competition to Cooperation*. New York: Routledge.

Hahnel, R. (2012) *Of the People, By the People: The Case for a Participatory Economy*. Oakland: Soapbox Press.

Hahnel, R. (2017) 'Wanted: a pollution damage revealing mechanism', *Review of Radical Political Economics*, 49(2): 233–246.

Hahnel, R. (2021) *Democratic Economic Planning*. London: Routledge.

Hahnel, R. and Kerkhoff, A. (2020) 'Integrating investment and annual planning', *Review of Radical Political Economics*, 52(2): 1–17.

Hayek, F.A. (1945) 'The use of knowledge in society', *American Economic Review*, 35(4): 519–530.

Laibman, D. (1992) *Value, Technical Change, and Crisis: Explorations in Marxist Economic Theory*. Armonk: M.E. Sharpe.

Laibman, D. (2001) 'Contours of the maturing socialist economy', *Historical Materialism*, 9(1): 85–110.

Laibman, D. (2011) 'Incentive design, iterative planning and local knowledge in a maturing socialist economy', *International Critical Thought*, 1(1): 35–56.

Laibman, D. (2015) 'Multilevel democratic iterative coordination: an entry in the "envisioning socialism" models competition', 마르크스주의연구 [*Marxism*], 12(1): 307–345.

Laibman, D. (2022) 'Systemic socialism: a model of the models', *Science & Society*, 86(2): 225–247.

Laurin-Lamothe, A., Legault, F. and Tremblay-Pepin S. (2023) *Construire l'économie postcapitaliste*. Montreal: Lux.

Phillips, L. and Rozworski, M. (2019) *The People's Republic of Walmart: How the World's Biggest Corporations are Laying the Foundation for Socialism*. London: Verso.

Polanyi, M. (2009) *The Tacit Dimension*. Chicago: The University of Chicago Press.

Roemer, J. (1994) *A Future for Socialism*. Cambridge, MA: Harvard University Press.

Schweickart, D. (1996) *Against Capitalism*. Boulder, CO: Westview Press.

2

Basic Problems of a Democratically Planned Economy

Jakob Heyer

Introduction

To assess recent debates on and models of a democratically planned economy, it is reasonable to distil and discuss some important preconditions, basic problems and categories beforehand. On this basis productive areas of conflict can be identified in an attempt to advance the debate.

This chapter begins by considering two important preconditions – major historical experiences and theoretical debates – before arguing that information and incentives, as basic problems, can be distilled out. Recent proposals for solving those problems are then discussed and brief suggestions are proposed for basic categories and how they can help to classify models. Finally, while discussing the models, productive areas of conflict are identified in a critique of essential details, first in relation to more classical models and then two more recent models. Combined, this analysis can aid in providing a synthesis for overall discussion and advancing the debate.

Preconditions

Historical experience (and beyond)

To this day the historical experience of actually existing socialism in the 20th century has compromised the idea of a post-capitalist economy. Planned economies, in particular, are associated with problems such as over-centralization, authoritarianism and inefficiency. This chapter will briefly touch on the 'traditional model' of the centrally planned economy (CPE), an economic system that is historically associated with socialism and communism and was best exemplified in the Soviet Union, before going on to discuss the reform socialism that emerged within actually existing socialism from the 1960s onwards and that was never fully implemented in practice. These models transcend historical experience as both remain the subject of theoretical debate and continue to evolve, with more recent models building on them.

Major lessons can be drawn from the failures of CPE. Experts on the Soviet economy, such as Ellman (2014), emphasized that comprehensive, centrally determined, physical output targets[1] and input allocation for local production units – which were the essence of Soviet top-down planning – are wasteful and dysfunctional in a complex economy in the long run. Nonetheless, central planning limited to specific sectors or tasks, stripped of the Soviet Union's authoritarian distortions and organized democratically, can make sense; for example, in terms of natural monopolies, broad infrastructure or large structural change and major investments in key sectors (Kalecki, 2010; Allen, 2011). However, history shows that CPE, as a model for the economy as a whole, is destined to fail, at latest with the transition from extensive to intensive growth. And that is without considering the often accompanying undesirable authoritarian political structures.

Cockshott and Cottrell (1993) argued that underdeveloped information technology (IT) in the Soviet era and the nation's inability to collect and process sufficiently detailed data, rather than provide only aggregate output targets, thwarted the success of CPE. However, substantial information and incentive problems represent a much more general problem for CPE, even in contemporary conditions. Economies of sufficient size are complex systems and must inevitably address uncertainty and local, tacit knowledge, which CPE is woefully ill-equipped to do due to a significant contradiction between central and decentral levels. Central planning authorities are plagued by considerable ignorance of economic realities on the ground, and their production commands subsequently lead to largely arbitrary decisions and inconsistencies in local plans. Subordinate agents exhibit apathy toward the planning process since they have no real influence over it and instead apply their local knowledge to their own narrow and often opposing interests, resulting in perverse incentives and wasteful strategic behaviour, like distorting production to match narrow production targets, concealing reserves and deliberately providing misinformation on output potential and input requirements. This approach leads to an enormous waste of resources and systemic inertia while severely undermining the planning system in the long term (Ellman, 2014). Therefore, any modern approach to a planned economy must incorporate substantial local autonomy for socialized enterprises from the outset, even without considering workplace democracy, which is an equally important factor in decentralization.

Reform socialism, a historical strand of socialist economic thought, contains many important, mainly theoretical, insights that address these very issues (Brus, 2003; Kalecki, 2010)[2] and had its beginnings in the analysis of practical experiences and problems within CPE. These insights were never fully applied in the Soviet Union, Hungary or the German Democratic Republic, where top-down systems largely remained in place. More recent authors have taken up these insights, and can be regarded as modern adepts of this strand (Laibman, 2001; Devine, 2010; Platenkamp, forthcoming). The general approach taken in this chapter and the subsequent description are heavily influenced by these authors.

The basic reasoning of reform socialist thought has argued that different levels in a planning system should be given their proper place and function. In a two-level model comprising only one central (planning bureau) and one decentral (enterprise) level, specific functions are assigned to each level (Laibman, 2002b). The central level should encompass participatory democratic determination of macroeconomic and strategic plans, including broad priorities, the level and direction of growth,[3] macroeconomic tradeoffs, such as consumption versus investment, income differentiation and the level and structure of public spending such as universal basic services (infrastructure, housing, food, education, healthcare and care). Natural monopolies, broad infrastructure and major investment projects should be centrally planned, but with democratic control and disaggregation.[4] Today, to ensure a reasonable standard of living within planetary boundaries, other aspects that should also be determined centrally are absolute caps and priorities concerning resource use related to biophysical limits;[5] however, centralization should be limited to this point. Beyond that, at the central level, there should be primarily comprehensive parametric control of the framework within which local units plan and operate, using prices and incentive schemes, such as cost and efficiency indices that provide rational decision-making criteria as the basis for accounting and planning at both levels. This approach should allow local units to make decisions that are consistent with societal needs locally and self-responsibly. This modus operandi implies central price control. The decentral level, that is democratically controlled enterprises, conduct their own detailed planning of outputs, inputs, technology and minor investments, including responsibility for implementing their plans. This approach also implies horizontal links between enterprises, such as customers and suppliers. The aim is to achieve full integration of local knowledge, autonomy and responsibility – and thus the vested interest of local units in passing reliable information upwards – into a comprehensive planning system that enables stable macro control. Contradictions between central and decentral levels and between local units must still be addressed, just as the decisions and actions of myriad local units must be mediated throughout the planning system and reconciled with social goals. Addressing these issues can be done, for example, by maintaining comprehensive openness and a continuous flow of all relevant information, and ongoing iterative coordination between levels

(Laibman, 2001). Local units must plan with respect to broad priorities set in macro plans and based on their specific local conditions. The central level must then aggregate local plans, identify inconsistencies that require correction and provide forecasts, optimization proposals and input–output tables indicating broad proportions (in physical and accounting terms), not as top-down production instructions, but as a '"baseline" set of outputs for industries and enterprises, [...], a point of departure' (Laibman, 2001, p 92). In this way local units are provided with a reasonable information framework that allows them to continuously and self-responsibly adapt their plans and behaviour to central aggregates and broad trajectories. The central level adjusts parameters or prices (metrics to account for cost, scarcity and utility), performance indicators and incentive schemes that determine rewards and penalties to harness the emergent behaviour arising from the interaction of relatively autonomous local units within the planning system and align this macro-behaviour with democratically determined goals. Due to the incentive system local units have a vested interest in consciously coordinating their activities with each other and with regard to social priorities. The result could well be a truly cybernetic planning system, where local autonomy is built into the planning system from the outset and that operates through continuous feedback loops, iterative communication and coordination between levels and units, where macro control is primarily achieved through parametric means, and planning and activity are highly adaptive (Beer, 1994).

Socialist calculation debate

Central themes in the socialist calculation debate include the question of the unit of account under socialism and the theorem of local, tacit knowledge (Hayek, 1945). The latter theme was mentioned earlier in the critique of CPE, while the former will be further addressed later. Here, developments in complexity theory and cybernetics, an area of debate that has recently drawn the attention of Austrian scholars, are briefly discussed (Moreno-Casas, Espinosa and Wang, 2022). Computational complexity does not seem to be a major obstacle to socialist computation,[6] but mastering the dynamic complexity and emergent behaviour of a socialist system that must be conceived as cybernetic control of a complex system clearly appears to be what represents a fundamental challenge for a modern socialist economy. Conceptualizing democratic control of a vastly complex system requires referencing some of the following ideas: emergent complex behaviour based on simple rules for agents; harnessing this emergent behaviour by manipulating those rules (Pitt, 2021); and combining attenuating complexity with amplifying regulatory complexity through dynamic subsystem self-regulation and continuous, real-time feedback loops between levels, filtering information for relevance (Beer, 1994) and the law of requisite variety, which indicates the need for a sufficiently complex model as a precondition for control. It seems that the development of modern IT within contemporary capitalism – interconnected computer networks, modern computing power, cloud computing, big data, artificial intelligence and cybernetic feedback infrastructure – and the advancement of data-driven management and planning technologies within capitalist firms, makes meeting precisely these requirements a realistic goal (Schaupp, 2018; Morozov, 2019; Phillips and Rozworski, 2019; Grünberg, 2023).

Basic problems

The discussion of the preconditions thus far has identified two basic problems: information and incentives. Proposals for addressing these problems will next be tentatively discussed and related, somewhat anticipatorily, to more complete models, just as more scattered, but no less important, contributions will be examined. Specific models will then be considered, first by briefly outlining and reviewing basic categories, and then by identifying productive areas of conflict within the debate.

Information

The strand of the socialist calculation debate that concerns socialist accounting and its corresponding unit is particularly important under conditions of resource constraints and strong local autonomy within the framework of cybernetic socialism. In this context, local units must be able to independently assess the social and environmental consequences of their actions and compare the relative costs and benefits of various uses of limited resources. In line with the reform socialist tradition, rational decision-making criteria (possibly provided through an objective price system)[7] and an elaborate incentive structure must be in place.

If the discussion on a socialist unit of account is to move forward, it should not focus solely on the choice between the options of in-kind, labour time (or monetary) units. Rather, it should explore the various dimensions that must be considered in socialist calculation and accounting.

In light of the ecological crisis, a growing need has emerged for a socialist accounting system to incorporate ecological costs. The research collective Planning for Entropy (2022) proposed integrating modern ecological accounting techniques into planning, such as life cycle analysis, which is a sophisticated method for accounting for myriad biophysical indicators that represents material throughput along the entire life cycle of goods. Life cycle analysis is a cradle-to-grave approach that includes a sophisticated input–output model and extensive databases encompassing nearly all production processes that not only expands the perspective on social metabolism but also considers natural resource scarcity from the outset.

In addition to ecological costs, a socialist accounting mechanism should also include measures of broader social costs, including the social impacts of various production methods.[8] Further advancements in life cycle sustainability assessment incorporate ecological, economic and broader social factors that are sufficiently holistic to potentially serve as the foundation for germinating an accounting and pricing framework for an eco-socialist planned economy that approximates internalizing the externalities (Zeug, Bezama and Thrän, 2023). But socialist accounting must also consider more narrow, vertically integrated labour costs[9] to be able to democratically control the social surplus product, in other words Marx's 'common funds' (Marx and Engels, 1987). Furthermore, in addition to a cost price there should be a clearing price (Cockshott and Cottrell, 1993; Campbell, 2002; Dapprich, 2022a) to account for scarcity due to fluctuations in supply and demand and for utility, quality and preferences, as expressed in real demand recorded by payment in consumer tokens, perhaps in addition to more explicit information on demand through online reviewing and rating (Morozov, 2019).

With regard to the various dimensions of a socialist accounting mechanism mentioned, it may be worthwhile to consider the fundamental scepticism on commensurability that Neurath (1973) initially introduced (see O'Neill, 2002) initially introduced. Would it be reasonable to conflate these dimensions into a single scalar? This is similar to discussions on synthetic indicators in reformist socialist thought. Why would that even be necessary? Because it attenuates complexity, making it better possible to cope with it in planning, accounting and budgeting by enabling commensurability between outputs and inputs, costs and performance of myriad different goods, production techniques and enterprises, which in a social mode of production will always require a degree of abstraction (Platenkamp, forthcoming). It would be necessary to not unconsciously conflate all complex factors as in the market, where labour-time costs and supply and solvent demand relationships, excluding major externalities, are condensed into a single monetary price through the act of sale. Yes, treating unequal things as equal is possibly reductionist or unjust, but this can be consciously dealt with as this commensurability would not be established by value through market exchange, as in capitalism, but would result from a conscious planning process. The important difference is that disaggregation is possible and desirable, for example to enable multiple-criteria decision-making, and the underlying categories and rules used in combination and aggregation are fully known and accessible. This comes close to the kind of conscious and differentiated, but still complexity-reducing, socialist price system that must be envisaged.

Arguably the various dimensions described earlier can be quantified and combined into an aggregate unit of account, which life cycle sustainability assessment suggests, just as it has developed sophisticated methods for weighting and aggregating myriad economic, ecological and social indicators, vertically and horizontally, making it possible to condense all this differentiated information into a doughnut[10] or spider web chart, or even into a single scalar.

But, while a unified framework is necessary, some basic dimensions should be viewed as accounting dimensions sui generis, to be considered separately like labour costs or specific environmental constraints. Also, some distinctions within units of account should be maintained, such as that between cost and clearing price, since ecological and social costs and resource scarcity can be known ex ante and independent of scarcity due to ex-post fluctuations in supply and demand. Regarding the fear of an intruding universal equivalent, another important separation between producer accounting units and consumer tokens will be discussed later.

Incentives

What should the content and measure of socialist incentives be? For enterprises, Laibman's (2012) socialist incentive design, and in particular his collective morale function, which incentivizes ambitious and realistic detailed planning by local units, seems to present a reasonable solution. Laibman combined narrower economic performance indicators with broader social and environmental performance indicators (a socialist common good matrix) to which local units must ambitiously and realistically aspire. Both types of indicators can be condensed into single scalars, though stakeholders would directly assess social and environmental performance. But, according to Platenkamp (forthcoming), historical experience has demonstrated the detrimental effects of overemphasizing political performance indicators in enterprises' operation and evaluation. Hence, additional solutions should be employed that ensure that micro plans are consistent with and adapted to macro plans, including environmental and social objectives, for example considering absolute resource constraints and the humanization of work. Therefore, enterprises should first be rewarded for planning consistently. In other words, detailed enterprise plans must be consistent with, contribute to and adapt to macro plans to make them consistent with societal vertical demand, which must be mediated with the horizontal customer demand in day-to-day operations. This is still similar to Laibman's proposal, but the issue can be shifted in a more parametric direction, where planned producer budgets form the basis for evaluating and rewarding coherence between macro and micro plans, as opposed to directly evaluating environmental and social performance. For instance, regional and sectoral environmental constraints, such as greenhouse gas emissions, could be reflected in centrally allocated emissions budgets, with associated penalties for non-compliance.[11] Second, to encourage ambitious planning, local units should be rewarded for planning for high net output that considers the difference between output and input (or surplus in terms of planned accounting prices) and thus provides incentives to meet demand at low cost, that is economic efficiency, and clear output (by adapting to customer demand). The objective of local plans should also be linked to compliance with industry norms for average production costs. Third, firms should be rewarded for realistic planning, as measured by the deviation of planned from actual outcomes. Producer budgets used to acquire inputs (via the token system) should be determined algorithmically by universal rules to avoid soft budget constraints (Kornai, 1980). Producer budgets should be related to current plans (output and input requirements) and past performance (coherent, ambitious and realistic planning).

Basic categories

Establishing some basic classification categories is helpful for discussing the proposed models of a democratically planned economy. According to Laibman (2022) two crucial dimensions allow the classification of models, each of which comprises a pair of categories representing opposite extremes on a spectrum. Laibman (2022) called the first dimension organization, which includes central and decentral poles, and the second regulation, which includes verbal/qualitative and digital/quantitative poles. The latter poles can also be called political/personal and parametric/technical.

Having already addressed the central–decentral dimension in this chapter, a remark must be made about the regulation dimension. While this chapter emphasizes the parametric aspects of a democratic planning system, it is crucial to avoid giving the impression that an exclusively algorithmically regulated economy devoid of participatory structures is desirable. To reiterate, comprehensive democratization of both the economy and society is a necessary condition for the effective functioning of a planned economy. All the various social entities, such as enterprises, industrial associations, investment councils, territorial citizens' groups and representative assemblies, should be subject to democratic governance and deliberative decision-making processes that involve relevant stakeholders at all levels (while respecting the enterprises' local autonomy and accountability). However, the importance of the parametric dimension is its ability to optimize rather than maximize democratic participation (Laibman, 2002a).

Productive areas of conflict

These preliminary considerations relate to productive lines of conflict that can be identified in the discussion of specific models of a democratically planned economy, but it is beyond the scope of this chapter to summarize them. Instead, a few selected critical remarks will be made concerning some essential details of more classical, and two more recent, models.[12]

In accordance with Laibman, a balance must be struck within the two dimensions of basic categories mentioned earlier. On this basis, the four most prominent models that have been discussed since the 1990s can be roughly categorized and evaluated. The Cockshott and Cottrell (1993) model is too centralized and merely algorithmic,[13] whereas Hahnel's (2021) model is exceedingly decentralized and overly reliant on purely parametric coordination between councils. Devine's (2010) model struck a better balance between central and decentral levels, but ultimately excessively relies on a political process of negotiated coordination, a view with which Laibman (2022) also concurs. Laibman's model achieved the most adequate balance between these poles and represents an advanced synthesis of the other models. Nonetheless, this section will argue that Laibman's model can also be criticized and expanded upon, though not before briefly discussing the central planning and neoclassical/libertarian strands in a bit more detail. A short discussion of Platenkamp's (forthcoming) model will then shed light on the modern reform socialist strand.

As mentioned above, the computerized central planning model, as embodied, for example, by Cockshott and Cottrell (1993) and Dapprich (2022a), is considered inadequate. This is the case because an old-fashioned conception of central planning basically provides the underlying foundation of many useful remarks on modern technical and mathematical possibilities for a new type of planned economy. Computerized central planning involves comprehensive and centrally determined physical output targets and input allocations for local units, while largely rejecting the notion of enterprises' autonomy to draw up their own plans for these (besides setting technical coefficients, which is too limited and no different from Soviet-type planning whatsoever). The CPE model is rendered infeasible not only due to its level of detail and data-processing capabilities but also due to its inability to cope with substantial problems concerning information and incentives that have been identified based on historical experience and theoretical reflection and that advances in modern IT have not eliminated.

By ignoring these, Cockshott and Cottrell (1993) and Dapprich (2022a) contradict the tradition they claim to follow – referring to optimal planners like Kantorovich, who have argued that optimal planning is not identical to optimal computation; that is, the idea of running an optimization algorithm for the whole economy that produces a detailed plan of physical output targets and input allocations for each local unit (Ellman, 1968). According to Soviet mathematical economists like Kantorovich, optimal planning can be achieved by introducing optimal parameters and sufficient decentralization to allow 'taking decisions maximally consistent with the interests of the national economy *locally*' (Kantorovich cited in Ellman, 1968, p 117, emphasis added).[14] Inventively mediating substantial macro control and local self-organization is also an essential characteristic of any cybernetic notion of a planned economy. In cybernetics language, the computerized central planning model can be seen as an extreme form of mere complexity reduction, contrary to the cybernetic vision of combining attenuating complexity with amplifying regulatory complexity (Beer, 1994). An argument against this strand is that modern IT should not be applied to aid the implementation of mere central planning but rather to advance the truly cybernetic vision of a planned economy that has developed, inter alia, within the reformist socialist tradition – a comprehensively planned economy that incorporates local autonomy and horizontal links from the outset and achieves macro control, inter alia, through parameters set at the central level and feedback loops between levels with the help of the immense technological potentialities that are developing within 'cybernetic capitalism' (Schaupp, 2018).

The other types of models that are considered inadequate can be categorized as a form of neoclassical or libertarian socialism. Although often not explicitly stated, these models draw heavily on neoclassical theory (and very little on historical experience), which is criticized by heterodox economic schools for its serious flaws in grasping even some of the most basic aspects of the capitalist mode of production. This abstractness is carried over into its radical post-capitalist strands. For example, the essential mechanism of Hahnel's (2021) model was aptly described as a Walrasian process – ultimately a completely atomistic process whose degree of rigidity surpasses even the inflexibility of the Soviet system. It involves completely unrealistic wish lists in which detailed consumption wishes for long periods of time must be explicitly stated ex ante as the basis for a tatonnement-like process of approximating socialist equilibrium prices (Laibman, 2014; Grünberg, 2023).

Saros's (2014) model presented an even more libertarian form of neoclassical socialism of the Parecon type. Saros also started with explicitly ex-ante detailed preference scales of consumer goods in the form of wish lists to be drawn up by individuals. His allocation mechanism then solely concentrated on the distribution of productive resources in proportion to these explicitly stated preferences through a form of points rationing similar to the Borda count voting rule (Cox, 2013; Pitt, 2021). Decision-making proceeds entirely atomistically, and there is no political deliberation on macro plans, not to mention a democratically controlled planning centre. The investment fund is determined completely arbitrarily, and the model does not consider the information and incentive problems that historical experience reveals. For example, objective cost considerations have no explicit influence on the allocation mechanism. Similarly, no mechanisms are in place for monitoring and comparing enterprises' efficiency.

Saros's model does, however, have some advantages that may explain its appeal in recent debates. Even if the model is rather crude, the idea that the distribution of productive resources must be proportional to consumers' preference scales, and that the allocation mechanism must consider resource scarcity, is significant and must be addressed in any serious model. Another advantage is that the model embodied a harder stance towards categories of the capitalist mode of production, because market exchange, the circulation of money and the profit motive did not exist. The units of account and distribution for production goods (production points) are completely separate from and not interchangeable with those for consumption goods (consumer tokens). To some extent production points circulate between producers of production goods but they are not a universal equivalent. Consumer tokens are non-circulating units of account that are used solely for the purpose of budget constraints and to record the satisfaction of consumer needs through consumer goods transfers. Hence, sales are not accrued as income and a portion of sales as profit, either for reinvestment or as individual income for workers or managers of the enterprise in question. Thus, any function similar to that of profitability under capitalism is abolished from the outset.

Saros's harder stance was particularly striking when compared with modern adepts of the reformist socialist tradition, such as Devine (2010) and Laibman (2001), who have generally developed more advanced models; however, their imprudence concerning categories such as money, profit and market relations have been a major source of scepticism within the debate critical of capitalism. This seems to prevent their notable achievements from being addressed, although I agree that these categories have taken on a different meaning in their models than they do under capitalism. It is suggested here that if market enthusiasm is removed from the historical reform socialists, and this imprudence from their modern adepts, they can be pushed beyond themselves. With an idea like Saros's[15] separation of accounting units, a harder stance can be combined with the reform socialist recognition of the need for budget constraints and rational criteria to account for the relative costs of resources and compare enterprise performance.

Platenkamp's forthcoming book argues along lines that are similar to Devine (2010) and Laibman (2001) but takes the debate further. Platenkamp's proposal, which is based on many of the same preconditions, basic problems and categories discussed here, can be considered as an advanced synthesis of some of the recent models discussed. In the following, brief comments will be introduced regarding some of the details of his economic proposal that will serve to move the debate forward. Like Devine's model, and especially Laibman's, Platenkamp's model aims at a comprehensive cybernetic planning system that reasonably mediates central and decentral levels and combines sectoral central planning, macro planning and macro control by means of various parameters, with enterprises' self-responsible micro planning and dynamic self-regulation. Major investments, infrastructure, cost metrics, performance indicators and incentive schemes for parametric control are centrally determined. In terms of incentive design for a socialist system, an explicit reference is made to Laibman's (2012) collective moral function.

However, Platenkamp (forthcoming) presents significant advances compared with Laibman's model, overcoming the use of money, profit and markets in the model, inter alia, by using producer accounting units and consumer tokens, which is similar to Saros's (2014) approach of separating units of account (without explicit reference to this model). Used for planning and accounting and the assessment of costs and scarcity, producer accounting units are also employed to calculate net output to determine and compare how ambitious plans are. They are not, however, transferred when the transfer of goods occurs. At exactly this point, net output does not equal profitability because, again, sales are not accrued as income or profit. Saros's model raised the issue of how, despite abandoning profitability, the model can still ensure that productive resources are allocated to their most efficient uses,[16] while Platenkamp's model ensures this through net output as a performance criterion, which differs from profitability.

Used for individual and productive consumption, consumer tokens may reflect the same information on costs and scarcity of goods, but they are not exchangeable to producer accounting units. These tokens are allocated for the sole purpose of budget constraints and to record the transfer of goods to verify that needs have been satisfied and plans are realistic and adapted to demand. Consumer tokens are transferred when the transfer of goods occurs but are personalized and deleted after use. Hence, tokens do not circulate and do not constitute a universal equivalent. This approach, which essentially amounts to taking Marx's theatre ticket argument seriously, represents a reasonable way to address the universal equivalent issue that is evident in Devine and Laibman's models (Cockshott and Cottrell, 1993; Marx and Engels, 2008, p 109; Saros, 2014; Dapprich, 2022b; Platenkamp, forthcoming).

This separation of units runs in both directions. On the one hand, the consumer tokens that enterprises acquire when clearing output cannot be used to buy producer inputs. On the other hand, producer budgets in productive consumption tokens allocated to enterprises in relation to plans and performance are not the source of income in consumer tokens for individuals, whether they are workers or managers of the enterprise in question (their income only indirectly depends on the enterprise's performance based on a scheme of labour incentives through moderate income differentiation that is democratically determined at the central level). Thus, for example, when a production unit produces high quality goods that are in high demand, it is not more profitable and reinvests income acquired through higher sales. It simply adjusts its plans to account for the higher demand for its products, as recorded by the higher number of tokens spent on them. Hence aiming for higher output, the unit is entitled to a higher producer budget (based on algorithmic rules). Notably Platenkamp does not elaborate on the substance of the accounting units; therefore, the earlier reflections on information and socialist accounting and its various dimensions can enrich his model.

Also in contrast to Laibman's model, the central level does not intervene when major inconsistencies occur as this would undermine enterprise autonomy and hence incentives. Realistic planning is in the interest of the enterprise itself, as implemented in the incentive structure. A functioning incentive system is ensured when a consistent parametrical framework, full local responsibility and production unit accountability are operational. However, no constant fear is present regarding bankruptcy or unemployment (the indisputable aspects of socialism are a genuine social safety net and a job guarantee; the failure of enterprises to achieve at least average performance leads to conscious contraction). Thus, this model contains a workable socialist emulation of hard budget constraints within a system of comprehensive planning that does not amount to market socialism.

Conclusion

To conclude, given a complexity science-based perspective (Foley, 2020) and Wright's (2005) social architecture of capitalism, which is an agent-based model of the capitalist social relations of production, it seems essential to design a contemporary agent-based model that embodies the social architecture of cybernetic socialism. A radical transformation of the kind envisaged in this chapter will inevitably represent a leap into the unknown, although reflection on historical and current experience of planning can mitigate uncertainty. Modern advances in computer simulation mean that testing and further elaboration of the models are already possible, which is why an important next step is to conduct computer simulations and comparisons of theoretical models derived from Marxist and reform socialist traditions.

Notes

[1] Although physical output targets were predominant, aggregated criteria in prices such as gross output were also wasteful.

[2] In historical reform socialism, profound knowledge of the problems of the centrally planned economy was often countered by a naïve idealization of the market' (Wemheuer, 2021), including an overly uncritical view of capitalist criteria such as profitability and a universal equivalent. Brus (2003) and Kalecki's (2010) models must nevertheless be distinguished from market socialism, as they envisaged comprehensively planned economies. Brus later switched to a radically market-orientated form of market socialism.

[3] Today, this should include contractions and qualitative changes at a steady state in resource use.

[4] For example, investment councils comprising stakeholders (Devine, 2010).

5. Cf Durand, Hofferberth and Schmelzer in this anthology.
6. The theoretical arguments here are unconvincing, just as practice has demonstrated (Cockshott and Cottrell, 1993; Grünberg, 2023).
7. This does not imply capitalist 'value' or 'exchange value'. Further considerations concerning this type of price system are discussed later.
8. See Zeug et al's (2023) development of life cycle analysis into 'holistic integrated life cycle sustainability assessment'.
9. Considering vertically integrated energy costs is also conceivable.
10. Cf Durand, Hofferberth and Schmelzer in this anthology.
11. Optimization methods can facilitate this (Vettese and Pendergrass, 2022). In agreement with Vettese and Pendergrass (2022), the assumption is that biophysical limits must be addressed on a planetary scale and that optimization methods such as linear programming can help determine broad proportions in land use, energy mix and use, and emissions constraints. Furthermore in accordance with the aforementioned authors, this must essentially form the basis for a nested structure of optimization and planning efforts at each descending level, giving sufficient scope for decision making at each level by running a global optimization algorithm for biophysical limits in aggregated terms only to determine proportions in descending order and allocate budgets for regions and sectors, down to individual units that must take matters into their own hands from there on.
12. Notably, although some of this criticism seems rather harsh, all the models discussed have merit and can be learned from, and their input is highly appreciated.
13. Tremblay-Pepin's (2022) description of the model as 'computerized central planning' was correct.
14. Another reasonable approach to optimization is to determine the threshold at which the gains from top-down production instructions from central optimization are outweighed by the losses from disregarding local knowledge with respect to the specific productive activity and level under consideration (Laibman, 2015).
15. Note that similar ideas are also already presented in other models.
16. Capitalism is indifferent to the distinction between the internal and external causes of high profitability – whether the causes are good performance or completely arbitrary factors (Kalecki, 2010). In an analogous case in socialism, this distinction regarding net output is crucial because special treatment for internal factors would imply undesirable, soft budget constraints.

Bibliography

Allen, R.C. (2011) *Global Economic History: A Very Short Introduction*. Oxford/New York: Oxford University Press.

Beer, S. (1994) *Designing Freedom*. Chichester/New York: Wiley.

Brus, W. (2003) *The Economics and Politics of Socialism: Collected Essays*. London: Routledge.

Campbell, A. (2002) 'Democratic planned socialism: feasible economic procedures', *Science & Society*, 66(1): 29–49.

Cockshott, W.P. and Cottrell, A. (1993) *Towards a New Socialism*. Nottingham: Spokesman.

Cox, S. (2013) *Any Way You Slice It: The Past, Present, and Future of Rationing*. New York: New Press.

Dapprich, J.P. (2022a) 'Optimal planning with consumer feedback: a simulation of a socialist economy', *Review of Political Economy*, 35(4): 1136–1156. doi: 10.1080/09538259.2021.2005367.

Dapprich, J.P. (2022b) 'Tokens make the world go round: socialist tokens as an alternative to money', *Review of Evolutionary Political Economy*, 4(3): 497–513: doi: 10.1007/s43253-022-00091-6.

Devine, P.J. (2010) *Democracy and Economic Planning: The Political Economy of a Self-Governing Society*. Cambridge: Polity Press.

Ellman, M. (1968) 'Optimal planning: a review article [*Soviet Studies*. Edited by V. A. Volkonsky]', 20(1): 112–136.

Ellman, M. (2014) *Socialist Planning*. Cambridge: Cambridge University Press.

Foley, D.K. (2020) 'Socialist alternatives to capitalism II: Vienna to Santa Fe', *Review of Evolutionary Political Economy*, 1(3): 313–328. doi: 10.1007/s43253-020-00013-4.

Grünberg, M. (2023) 'The planning daemon: future desire and communal production', *Historical Materialism*, 31(4): 1–45. doi: 10.1163/1569206x-bja10001.

Hahnel, R. (2021) *Democratic Economic Planning*. London: Routledge.

Hayek, F.A. (1945) 'The use of knowledge in society', *The American Economic Review*, 35(4): 519–530.

Kalecki, M. (2010) *Selected Essays on Economic Planning*. Cambridge: Cambridge University Press.

Kornai, J. (1980) *Economics of Shortage*. Amsterdam/New York: North-Holland Pub. Co.

Laibman, D. (2001) 'Contours of the maturing socialist economy', *Historical Materialism*, 9(1): 85–110. doi: 10.1163/156920601760039195.

Laibman, D. (2002a) 'Comment', *Science & Society*, 66(1): 86–93. doi: 10.1521/siso.66.1.86.21010.

Laibman, D. (2002b) 'Democratic coordination: towards a working socialism for the new century', *Science & Society*, 66(1): 116–136.

Laibman, D. (2012) *Political Economy After Economics: Scientific Method and Radical Imagination*. Abingdon/New York: Routledge.

Laibman, D. (2014) 'Horizontalism and idealism in socialist imagination: an appraisal of the participatory economy', *Science & Society*, 78(2): 207–234. doi: 10.1521/siso.2014.78.2.207.

Laibman, D. (2015) 'Multilevel democratic iterative coordination: an entry in the "envisioning socialism" models competition', *MARXISM 21*, 12(1): 307–345. doi: 10.26587/MARX.12.1.201502.011.

Laibman, D. (2022) 'Systemic socialism: a model of the models', *Science & Society*, 86(2): 225–247. doi: 10.1521/siso.2022.86.2.225.

Marx, K. and Engels, F. (1987) *Werke. 19: März 1875 bis Mai 1883*. 9. Aufl. Berlin: Dietz.

Marx, K. and Engels, F. (2008) *Werke. 23: Das Kapital, Bd. 1*. 23. Aufl. Berlin: Dietz.

Moreno-Casas, V., Espinosa, V.I. and Wang, W.H. (2022) 'The political economy of complexity: the case of cyber-communism', *Journal of Economic Behavior & Organization*, 204: 566–580. doi: 10.1016/j.jebo.2022.10.042.

Morozov, E. (2019) 'Digital socialism?', *New Left Review*, 116/117: 33–67.

Neurath, O. (ed) (1973) *Empiricism and Sociology: With a Selection of Biographical and Autobiographical Sketches*. Dordrecht: Reidel (Vienna Circle collection, 1).

O'Neill, J. (2002) 'Socialist calculation and environmental valuation: money, markets and ecology', *Science & Society*, 66(1): 137–151. doi: 10.1521/siso.66.1.137.21006.

Phillips, L. and Rozworski, M. (2019) *The People's Republic of Walmart: How the World's Biggest Corporations Are Laying the Foundation for Socialism*. London/New York: Verso.

Pitt, J. (2021) *Self-Organising Multi-Agent Systems: Algorithmic Foundations of Cyber-Anarcho-Socialism*. London/Hackensack: World Scientific.

Planning for Entropy (2022) 'Democratic economic planning, social metabolism and the environment', *Science & Society*, 86(2): 291–313. doi: 10.1521/siso.2022.86.2.291.

Platenkamp, T. (forthcoming) *The Constitution of Socialism*.

Saros, D.E. (2014) *Information Technology and Socialist Construction: The End of Capital and the Transition to Socialism*. New York: Routledge, Taylor & Francis Group.

Schaupp, S. (2018) 'Vergessene Horizonte. Der kybernetische Kapitalismus und seine Alternativen', in *Kybernetik, Kapitalismus, Revolutionen. Emanzipatorische Perspektiven im technologischen Wandel*. Münster: UNRAST Verlag, pp 51–73.

Tremblay-Pepin, S. (2022) 'Five criteria to evaluate democratic economic planning models', *Review of Radical Political Economics*, 54(3): 265–280. doi: 10.1177/04866134221093747.

Vettese, T. and Pendergrass, D. (2022) *Half-Earth Socialism: A Plan to Save the Future from Extinction, Climate Change, and Pandemics*. London/New York: Verso.

Wemheuer, F. (ed) (2021) *Marktsozialismus: Eine kontroverse Debatte*. Wien: Promedia.

Wright, I. (2005) 'The social architecture of capitalism', *Physica A: Statistical Mechanics and its Applications*, 346(3–4): 589–620. doi: 10.1016/j.physa.2004.08.006.

Zeug, W., Bezama, A. and Thrän, D. (2023) 'Life cycle sustainability assessment for sustainable bioeconomy, societal-ecological transformation and beyond', in F. Hesser et al (eds) *Progress in Life Cycle Assessment 2021. Sustainable Production, Life Cycle Engineering and Management*, Cham: Springer, pp 131–159.

3

Social Dividend Socialism: Labour Autonomy in a Participatory Planned Economy

James Muldoon and Dougie Booth

Introduction

In this chapter, we propose an alteration to Pat Devine's model of participatory planned economics in which socialist wage labour is replaced by a system of a social dividend. The challenge for any model of democratic economic planning is to sufficiently balance democratic control, economic feasibility and labour autonomy. In an era of climate emergency and global supply chain challenges, any effectively planned economy has to simultaneously meet consumer preferences, radically reduce and ration our consumption of limited resources and maintain a steady output of essential goods and services. To do this while realizing the socialist commitments to democratic control and the autonomy of labour is an immense problem. In our evaluation, Devine's model of participatory planning has, thus far, come the closest to realizing this balance. However, we hold that, as it is currently formulated, it does not sufficiently realize labour autonomy. We argue that the relation of wage labour necessitates a regime of labour control, which undermines the possibility of having a sufficient degree of labour autonomy. As such, we argue that wage labour must be removed from the model and replaced by an alternative means of distribution: a social dividend that is disconnected from participation in the workplace but based on a communist principle of distribution.

We begin the chapter by situating Devine's participatory planning model within the existing planning literature and showing that it is preferable to two alternatives we refer to as 'algorithmic planning' and 'utopian decentralized planning'. We argue that the algorithmic approaches to planning do not provide sufficient means for democratic control over production and suffer from issues of incommensurability between different values. We also argue that utopian decentralized models lack a rigorous institutional basis for coordination. In contrast to these approaches, Devine offers a participatory model that embraces decentralization while maintaining a clear institutional structure for democratic decision-making suited to dealing with technical complexities. We then outline how the model's reliance upon generalized wage labour as its means of distribution undermines the realization of its goals.

A social dividend scheme would enable the transformation of workplaces from labour-employing firms that act as overseers of labour into true free associations of producers working towards the realization of a democratic plan. Here we draw on Cole's conception of a social dividend (or basic income), in which society provides sufficient funds to every individual to cover their material necessities. This would allow society to realize the communist distributive principle of 'from each according to their ability, to each according to their needs'. We outline that this fits naturally into a process of negotiated coordination, wherein additional funds could be allocated to meet differing needs that arise on the basis of natural, historic and social conditions through democratic deliberation. While we push for a maximalist approach to the social dividend and labour autonomy, pushing for the abolition of wage labour, we acknowledge that there could be problems. We argue that the complete decoupling of contribution and consumption, if possible, would require a period of transition wherein pocket-money wage labour would be maintained as society adjusted to the dividend. In our final section, we defend our proposal from two objections. First, we address the concern that, without wage labour, there would be labour shortages, especially in less desirable workplaces. Second, we address the accusation that, without a mechanism of discipline or incentives, workplaces will shirk their responsibilities and consistently fail to meet the responsibilities allocated to them by the democratic plan. In our conclusion, we highlight that social dividend socialism, while specifically presented as an engagement with Devine's model, holds relevance for proponents of other models of planned economics when considering the question of distribution.

Three approaches to economic planning

The existing planning literature can broadly be divided into three categories: algorithmic planning, utopian decentralized planning and participatory planning. While these are not fixed categories and models can incorporate overlapping elements, we argue here that participatory planning is the most promising starting point and that this approach finds its strongest representation in Devine's model of negotiated coordination.

Paul Cockshott and Allin Cottrell (1993) put forward the most notable example of algorithmic planning in their model of cybersocialism.[1] Utilizing developments in the field of cybernetics, they propose a model of planned economics that would be responsive to shifting consumer demands. Labour would be compensated via non-circulating labour money that, when spent, would provide information about supply and demand to planners. Shifts in supply and demand would then cause adjustments in the price of goods on the basis of the labour values required to produce them. This would enable an algorithmic calculation that would optimally assign limited resources to production to satisfy demand in accordance with labour values.

A major sticking point for algorithmic planning has been concerns around the commensurability of values, drawn from Austrian philosopher and economist Otto Neurath's contribution to the socialist calculation debate (Neurath, 1925a; 1925b). Neurath rejected the claim that monetary calculation is a rational method for decision-making and considered that multiple criteria would need to be considered simultaneously. This would require democratic deliberation, rather than simple calculation, as these criteria could not be flattened into one numerical value. Fikret Adaman and Pat Devine (2022) have utilized this insight to argue for the insufficiency of the algorithmic approach, arguing that a multitude of competing values need to be articulated and negotiated in a political process. Any system that merely optimizes distribution based on a single unit of calculation would be blind to the multifaceted nature of our needs and values, which can only come to the surface through a process of democratic deliberation.

This incommensurability problem becomes prescient when considering the ecological crisis and how a system built around labour values and supply and demand would not sufficiently incorporate these considerations. Notably, Jan Philipp Dapprich (2021) has attempted to reformulate the cybersocialist model to be compatible with the addition of external, deliberate, constraints on the algorithmic calculation. However, being capable of placing numerical constraints in the form of a carbon budget does not get us closer to addressing how we should allocate such a budget in a just manner. An algorithmic approach might tell us how to maximize the satisfaction of demand within carbon constraints, but this is insufficient; humanity needs to consciously determine where the remaining investment of our budget should be allocated.

On the other end of the spectrum lies utopian decentralized models of planning. Examples of models we place within this category include the Commonism of Stefan Meretz and Simon Sutterlütti (2022; in this volume) and other anarchist gift economies (Nelson, 2022; Leahy, 2023). In these models, production and distribution are undertaken on an entirely free and voluntary basis. People labour within voluntary associations towards the production of goods that they then freely distribute to those in need, often favouring a model of localism or confederation of small-scale communities. Mediation between associations is handled on a case-by-case basis in which producers of goods negotiate and decide who they will prioritize to receive their goods. It is presumed that an emergent order will arise based on maximizing inclusion and generous behaviour between associations, creating overlapping webs of gift exchange, with requests for aid stimulating the development of new associations and distributive flows.

Whilst utopian decentralized planning promises to maximize the freedom of labour and empower the self-direction of associations, the theory does not provide a rigorous institutional basis for establishing an economically feasible production process. The climate crisis requires that we deliberate upon how to distribute our remaining resources within a fixed ecological budget to improve the conditions of the globally dispossessed (Hofferberth/Schmelzer/Durand, in this volume). In the following decades, this will require a radical overhaul of our energy systems and careful planning of complex networks of clean energy production, storage and integration. These models often embrace a model of degrowth and seek to minimize the usage of rare earth materials and fossil fuels. However, decisions will need to be made about questions such as how to distribute the remaining carbon budget or how to prioritize the usage of lithium batteries and silicon chips. The decentralized approach places the decision-making power in producer associations, giving them extraordinary negotiating power within the common web of mutual associations. Those who become dissatisfied with distributive decisions have one choice: disassociate and seek alternative sources of goods. Simply put, this is an unfeasible model for running a global economy, as it creates an imbalanced power structure that threatens to disrupt crucial supply chains, because negotiations between voluntary associations are liable to break down. Economic collaboration cannot be left to spontaneous, overlapping and impermanent mutual associations. There needs to be established protocols to ensure equitable rights of participation and control and to establish environmental protections.

In contrast, participatory approaches to planning create institutionalized bodies wherein affected parties can engage in negotiation, making investment and allocation decisions based on qualitative judgment. As such, participatory planning is built upon an acknowledgement of the incommensurability of values and the political nature of needs. However, unlike utopian decentralized approaches, they maintain fixed democratic institutions that balance power, create procedures to structure negotiation and ensure that continued cooperation is achieved. Though there are other models of participatory planning (Albert and Hahnel, 1991; O'Neill, 2020), we hold that it is presently best articulated in Devine's (1988) model of a participatory planned economy. The model was first articulated by Devine in 1988, though it has received further elaborations and evolutions, especially in collaboration with Adaman (2017; 2022). For simplicity, we will refer to it as Devine's model or a participatory planned economy (PPE).

A PPE would socialize the means of production and democratize the process of investment. Unable to simply calculate the optimal distribution of goods, made impossible by the incommensurable nature of our values, Adaman and Devine (2022) argue that there needs to be a repoliticization of the allocation of resources and our economic priorities. This entails a widespread democratization of economic decision-making, which would encourage robust engagement from all affected parties. Society's prioritization of resource distribution and goods production would be negotiated via a plurality of federative and interwoven democratic organizations, with decision-making operating under a principle of self-government and decentralization where possible. General, community, worker, consumer and supplier interests would each find themselves represented by a democratic association that partakes in economic governing bodies (Devine, 1988, p 226).

In Devine's model, the distribution of goods is still left to market exchange, wherein productive units produce goods for sale in a marketplace. However, they argue that their model does not constitute market socialism (neither Langean nor Illyrian) because the dynamics of the system are driven by conscious decisions rather than market forces. The flow of investment would not be determined according to a profit-maximizing logic. Instead, democratic decision-making would determine how funds were distributed and the prioritization of their usage. By removing market forces and leaving decisions to democratic deliberation, conscious control can be maintained that fully reflects our ecological commitments alongside other values. This provides a framework in which to handle the difficult decision-making required in addressing the climate crisis.

Devine's approach to labour autonomy in a participatory planned economy

A common question about planned economies is how to ensure that individuals retain autonomy even when economic activity is directed by a common social plan. Devine's model outlines multiple avenues through which labour will be able to influence the planning process. The first is through workers electing officials to the national government and planning commissions and partaking in trade unions, consumer and civic organizations and negotiated coordination bodies (Devine, 1988, p 199). This represents a democratic vision of autonomy, drawn explicitly from Held (1987), wherein autonomy is understood as the ability to participate and collectively shape the direction of social life and human development.

Adaman and Devine (2022) are aware that democratic coordination alone would not sufficiently protect the autonomy of labour. Hence, they argue a second important consideration is that workplaces themselves need to be democratized. In practice, this would have every workplace acting as a democratic firm. Workers would vote directly on the firm's operations, giving them autonomy about how they meet the requirements of the negotiated plan.

A third remaining concern regarding autonomy is that wage labour would still compel workers to work. Devine (1988, p 160) acknowledges this problem, arguing that there can be no compulsion to work if we are to realize autonomy. Instead, individuals need to be self-activating subjects who are driven by a self-acknowledged motivation. Only with self-activation would labour be properly autonomous, even if the compelled work was democratically organized. Devine's solution to this problem is less developed than other parts of the model. However, he indicates (Devine, 1988, p 206) that it could be resolved through the introduction of a basic income scheme. By providing a guaranteed source of income to fall back on, workers could opt out of the production process. It is on this third and final point where the main antagonism of Devine's model lies. The inclusion of wage labour emerges from his commitment to maintaining market exchange as the mechanism of distribution of consumer goods. It is clear, despite the limited provision of a basic income, that Devine envisages workers' income to be primarily awarded through their wages. We argue that Devine does not completely consider how the wage relation limits the autonomy of labour.

In the exchange of labour power for a monetary wage, workers place themselves under the social control of the firm. In Devine's model, this means placing oneself under the control of a decentralized and participatory democratic organization. This does not constitute a form of domination, as it is defined in the republican literature (Pettit, 1999; Muldoon, 2019; O'Shea, 2020). The structure of labour control is non-arbitrary in so far as it is democratic, contestatory and participatory. Nonetheless, it is a system of labour control, meaning a practice by which labour is observed, directed and evaluated by an overseer (whether that figure is fixed management or a body of co-workers) to ensure that productivity is sufficient to entitle labourers to their compensation. This becomes necessary when utilizing the wage relation to ensure that wages are not being fraudulently paid out to non-contributing employees. We might think that in a PPE this could be a fairly innocuous process of verification to prevent the fraudulent claiming of wages.

However, we argue that, even within a PPE, labour control would substantially undermine labour autonomy because it reinforces the social division of labour, which Devine seeks to abolish (1988, p 138). If people's consumption is tied to their employment in a firm and the continual verification of their presence within its production process, then this will undermine the ability of labour to participate in the full range of labouring activity. For somebody to maintain a certain level of consumption, they would be incentivized to remain working within one workplace. To move freely between forms of labour would be disincentivized by the risk it would impose on one's living standards. How many would explore different professions, knowing it would destabilize their economic prospects?

The purpose of maintaining wage labour is to have a system of incentives for particular jobs and encourage a disciplined approach to work. However, if there is not a strict regime for the regulation of labour participation and controlling its expenditure, then it will become easier for large swathes of the population to make fraudulent claims about their contribution to the labour process. This might be difficult for an individual, but it will be possible, as seen in 'actually existing socialism', for firms to falsify information to gain access to greater funds than they would otherwise have been entitled to. If we maintain the wage labour regime, we have to abandon a maximalist conception of labour autonomy and the abolition of the division of labour.

A social dividend as a principle of distribution

We propose that maintaining a maximalist conception of the autonomy of labour, built upon the abolition of the division of labour, requires the abolition of wage labour. Secondly, we propose that this is possible within Devine's model by embracing the distribution of a social dividend according to a communist principle. In this section, we will outline what changes this entails for a PPE, before addressing possible concerns with our proposal in the following section.

To abolish wage labour, workplaces will have to stop paying wages, simply put. In the absence of working for a wage, labour will be organized through free association. Through complete self-activation, workers will voluntarily decide which workplaces they wish to contribute towards without entering into an employment contract for a monetary wage. This would remove the necessity of a regime of labour control and maximize the autonomy of labour. Furthermore, it would remove any perverse incentives within the workplace, making the decisions made about labour expenditure into free choices, which should create better conditions throughout production.

The immediate question becomes: if wages are not going to be paid in exchange for labour, how will goods be distributed? Devine's model relies upon markets for consumer goods, in which prices will be set in accordance with the costs of production. Society's prioritization of the creation of certain types of goods will thus be partially determined by individuals' consumption choices in accordance with their monetary budget. A PPE presumes that people's budgets will be based on their contribution towards the labouring process, receiving wages in accordance with a negotiated rate.

The challenge is how to maintain this system of distribution if workplaces will not be paying wages.

We propose that, in the place of wage labour, we fully embrace a scheme of a social dividend, reversing Devine's presumption that most people would be receiving wages and a slim minority on a basic income so that everybody was in the reception of a social dividend. We are drawing on the proposals of guild socialist G.D.H. Cole in his work on economic planning (Cole, 1935). Cole proposed that income should mostly be received as direct payments from the state in the form of a social dividend. These payments were to be 'a recognition of each citizen's claim as a consumer to share in the common heritage of productive power' (Cole, 1935, p 235). The benefit of this is that we would draw closer to the communist principle of distribution of 'from each according to their ability, to each according to their needs' even without the abolition of money (Marx and Engels, 1870).

Cole argued that the social dividend should be distributed according to a principle of need. It would be set at a level in which every recipient would be able to meet their basic needs and live comfortably by virtue of being a citizen. In a reversal of Devine's distributive scheme, Cole proposed that the vast majority of people's income would consist of the social dividend rather than wages (Cole, 1935, p 236). Under guild socialism, one's wages would be far less important, treated more as pocket-money with which to purchase additional luxuries. Wages would be set to the minimal level required to incentivize people to partake in each position, dramatically reducing the labour costs of firms. To prevent distributive divides, Cole proposed a wage-cap set at an equal level to the social dividend, meaning that the largest wealth gap would be 2:1 for somebody working an exceptionally in-demand job.

Cole held that, in the medium term, it would be necessary to preserve the system of pocket-money wages to incentivize participation in difficult industries. However, he acknowledged that, in the long term, incomes could eventually be entirely provided by the social dividend and wages could be done away with (1935, 318). In accordance with our view that we should push for the maximization of labour autonomy, we argue that the displacements of wages and the reliance upon the social dividend should be pushed as far as possible. While this push should be given a sense of immediacy, feasibility remains a crucial point and thus we acknowledge that a transitional period of pocket-money wages would be necessary.

Cole argued that a dividend should only be paid if an individual had demonstrated a willingness to participate in the common tasks of society (1935, p 252). However, he struggles to articulate what would be the appropriate treatment for non-contributors, leaving his solution ambiguous. We believe that the social dividend should be unconditional. Without resorting to an outright call for the right to be lazy (Lafargue, 1883), it is likely that complete non-contribution, in a PPE, will be exceedingly rare. To do nothing socially beneficial at all for a sustained period of time, like Bartleby the Scrivener, would surely be the result of a personal crisis that ought not to be punished by deprivation. Furthermore, introducing conditionality would require the introduction of an intrusive system of observation upon recipients.

Cole proposed that the dividend's rate would apply universally, with increased allowances for those with children and a lower rate paid out to teenagers. In terms of how the social dividend's rate would be set, Cole claimed that this would be the concern of the entire community, channelled through planning authorities and handled finally by national governments (1935, p 315). This would naturally work within a PPE, wherein the level of dividend payments could be negotiated through democratic planning bodies. While Cole proposed a flat rate, there would be room to introduce higher rates of payments for those with additional needs. Through democratic deliberation, additional support could be provided for those with disabilities and other conditions, placing them above the baseline in accordance with their additional needs. Once established, individuals would be able to apply for recognition that they are covered by certain criteria and receive additional levels of payment. We also propose that there could be additional dividend funds assigned to community organizations to flexibly provide additional support to those whose needs have yet to be officially recognized.

In a global PPE, there would be room for adjusting the social dividend based not only on individual circumstances but also on regional and national differentials. Negotiations could occur to provide a more generous dividend to those who live in areas affected by climate change or historical underdevelopment. This would not only allow for the partial rectification of previous injustices but also enable for distribution of resources that are responsive to different levels of needs based on historical conditions. Our scheme is even more preferable for realizing this than a negotiated scheme of differing regional wage levels because it is not reliant upon there being sufficient economic activity within a region for people to fully benefit from the policy's implementation.

Of course, the relevance of the social dividend scheme would be dependent on how many goods in society were provided on a free basis or via marketized distribution. We suggest that, where possible, goods should be distributed on a free basis. Essential life services and infrastructure will be distributed freely with priority based on need. Healthcare, public transport and utilities will always be free to use. However, where a consistent surplus of certain consumer goods is easy to achieve, we believe those should also be distributed freely. If it was possible to continually expand the realm of free distribution, this would transform the social dividend increasingly into a policy for distributing and accessing scarce goods only. We are also open to the prospect of democratic bodies determining that certain scarce goods should be distributed by non-market mechanisms, through some form of rationing.

A social dividend scheme might encounter problems regarding disagreements over levels of consumption. However, we argue that this is inevitable. Even with a system of wage labour, there would be disagreements about remuneration for workers in particular industries or regions. At least with a social dividend there would be a common interest in ensuring it was sufficient to maintain a proper standard of living. To relieve some of the problems of democratic negotiation, we would advocate for an institutional system of independent safeguards, such that minority groups will have an external avenue to seek resolution if they find themselves subject to democratic discrimination (Booth and Muldoon, 2022).

Returning to the workplace once more, with wage labour replaced by a social dividend scheme, we reiterate that participation would be purely voluntary and driven by self-activating individuals. Movement between workplaces, aiding in the abolition of the division of labour, would be made smoother as there would be no need to sign an employment contract to contribute to the association's endeavours. If one wished to move between focusing on community cleanup, providing care work, contributing to the rewilding effort or assisting in the steel mill, they would be free to do so without concern for how it would affect their budget. However, free association with workplaces would not be purely spontaneous and without requirements. A steel mill cannot function without knowing how many trained people will be turning up to run it each day. People would sign up for commitments to aid in certain workplaces, creating obligations towards them for a period of time, but these would not be tied to remuneration, merely being an accounting measure so that workplaces could track their expected labour force. When workplaces see an absence of signups, they would begin to advertise, requesting more participants or make adjustments to their production setup. Workplaces would likely seek oversubscription of labour participants for every period, to ensure there was a reserve if people went absent. This would be possible because there would be no labour budget.

The replacement of wages with a social dividend would also change the relationship of labour to the social plan and the dynamics regarding how to organize labour within the workplace. The former can be seen in the simple point that economic activity would no longer be hoarded to benefit particular hubs of activity – a transformation in economic dynamics that will be essential to fighting climate change. Scaling back the oil industry will produce far less friction when people's incomes in key extractive regions will be guaranteed to remain the same via the social dividend. The latter point regarding workplace dynamics becomes apparent when considering that the division of labour would no longer have the option to determine wage differentials, meaning that tasks might be assigned more freely, rather than competed over. This would help to organically produce balanced workplaces without resorting to Albert and Hahnel's imposition of balanced job complexes (1991).

Overall, we hold that the social dividend provides a more robust integration of labour autonomy within a PPE. The democratic notion of autonomy within the social plan remains unaltered, aside from the negotiation of distribution being moved from industrial negotiation to social negotiation about consumption levels. Autonomous decision-making within the workplace becomes enhanced under the dividend because it removes the necessity of labour control, making it so that internal competition nor compulsion to work motivates the choices taken. Lastly, the ability to opt out of the labour process becomes more rigorous by making income entirely dependent on the social dividend. Not only does this make dropping-out fall under less social pressure but it also creates more freedom about moving between forms of labour. We hold this would substantially aid in abolishing the division of labour and creating a more complete notion of labour autonomy that remains compatible with a comprehensive plan.

A mechanism without a spring?

In his critical evaluation of the Soviet planned economy, Christopher J. Arthur, drawing on Hillel Ticktin, produces the metaphor of a mechanism without a spring (2004, 208). He describes the Soviet model as a dysfunctional non-mode of production in which capitalist accumulation was emulated by planning decrees that lacked the mechanisms of economic discipline to effect its realization (Arthur, 2004, 210). Without market forces and threats of unemployment and bankruptcy, dysfunction ruled throughout the economy. A concern for any model of planned socialism is how to ensure that there is a functioning mechanism to ensure the realization of the plan.

Devine's mechanism is that workers directly benefit from the performance of their firms, hold democratic control over the production of social benefits and that underperforming workplaces could be disciplined by being denied investment, subsidies or losing existing credit (1988, p 208). Individuals are directly incentivized to turn up to work and perform well, while the collective workplace has clear incentives to act efficiently. A concern regarding social dividend socialism is that it removes the spring from the economic mechanism. By replacing wage labour with guaranteed income, there is a concern that labour shortages will arise as people refuse to take on certain arduous tasks. Furthermore, even when people turn up to work, they might simply underperform and collectively shirk responsibilities assigned to them by the economic plan. Without wages at risk, the threat of losing the firm's funding would not invoke the same pressure to produce according to the indicative plan's targets. Workers would always have their needs secured by the social dividend and universal provision of basic goods and services.

On the point of labour shortages, we argue they are not inevitable. Undesirable tasks can be divided up into smaller tasks, which a far greater population will be able to partake in because doing so will not affect their income. It is more feasible that vast numbers of volunteers will take on occasional six-hour chunks of undesirable labour, compared to expecting a full-time retinue of volunteers doing 35 hours weekly. Should spontaneous volunteering be insufficient, we propose that society could organize a volunteer labour army to act as a reserve supply of labour. An internationalist organization, it would be composed of work brigades responsible for training and sending labourers to rectify shortages. Participants would rotate between multiple workplaces and job roles alongside their team to avoid burnout. The organization would build interpersonal comradery, mutual development, cultural exchange and internationalist solidarity through cooperation. The incentives to join the army would be the ability to travel globally, develop skills, personally develop and find fulfilment through service.

One might baulk at the formulation of a 'labour army' as reminiscent of the regimes of compelled labour in service of the nation-state under early 20th-century socialism. However, enrollment would remain strictly voluntary and encouraged through the benefits it would bring for its participants and the social good. Beyond the incentives already described, it is also possible that service within the labour army could be associated with rewards, such as priority over accessing international travel opportunities or an increase in social dividend payments. If voluntarism proves unsustainable, there is still room for the reintroduction of supplementary wages into social dividend socialism. Pocket-money wages could be reintroduced solely for workplaces with dire labour shortages. By limiting their application, regimes of labour control would only exist in specific areas rather than being generalized. This would prevent the generalization of labour control's negative effects on autonomy and help maintain the abolition of the division of labour.

Concerning the shirking of responsibility by workplaces, we argue this will not be a problem for two main reasons. First, in a PPE, productive units will be responsible for registering their productive capacity based on tacit knowledge. This means if workplaces believe themselves incapable of meeting indicative targets, they will be capable of reporting a lowered production capacity for future plan iterations. We do not believe this will lead to endemic underreporting of productive capacity, as with the Soviet model. Managers will not be rewarded for underreporting capacity and beating lowered production targets. The incentive for accurate incentive reporting is to ensure that there is enough fulfilling work to be shared out and prevent idle hands. As such, workplaces will rarely be assigned overly burdensome outputs, meaning underperformance will most likely be the result of unforeseen consequences, not responsibility shirking.

Second, democratic control over investment and production orientated towards needs will transform people's relationship with planning directives. Participation in the formulation of the social plan will create a sense of collective investment in the plan's realization. With society's economic surplus under democratic control, the realization of people's collective desires shall be dependent upon mass participation in the economic process. This will produce common stakeholdership, wherein even those not presently being directly benefited from the democratic investment decisions will have a stake in the plan's realization, as future investment will only be freed up for their own desired ends once the present round has been completed.

Conclusion

This chapter has outlined how Devine's model of participatory planning can better realize labour autonomy through the implementation of a social dividend scheme. We have shown that only through the abolition of wage labour and regimes of labour control can the division of labour be dismantled. We have argued this is made feasible through the social dividend. By disentangling consumption and contribution, there will be greater freedom to explore labour forms and we will draw closer to the communist principle of distribution. In our penultimate section, we have addressed two feasibility concerns around the absence of direct monetary incentives, showing that new motivational states, differing stakeholdership and organizational possibilities allow these concerns to be overcome. Though this chapter is framed as a direct engagement with Devine's model, we argue that the insights are applicable to other models of planned socialism. We push that all proponents of planned socialism need to reevaluate the inclusion of wage labour within their models if they are committed to realizing labour autonomy. As we have shown via the social dividend, wage labour is not a necessary condition of a feasible model of socialism, in fact, it is a direct hindrance to the emancipation of labour and realizing the communist principle of distribution.

Note

[1] For other recent developments in algorithmic planning models, see also: Phillips and Rozworski (2019), Samothrakis (2021), Härdin (2021) and Grünberg (2023).

Bibliography

Adaman, F. and Devine, P. (2017) 'Democracy, participation and social planning', in Clive L. Spash (ed) *Routledge Handbook of Ecological Economics*, London: Routledge, pp 517–525.

Adaman, F. and Devine, P. (2022) 'Revisiting the calculation debate: a call for a multiscale approach', *Rethinking Marxism*, 34(2): 162–192.

Albert, M. and Hahnel, R. (1991) *The Political Economy of Participatory Economics*. Princeton, NJ: Princeton University Press.

Arthur, C. (2004) *The New Dialectic and Marx's Capital*. Leiden: Brill.

Booth, D. and Muldoon, J. (2022) 'Socialist democracy: Rosa Luxemburg's challenge to democratic theory', *Philosophy and Social Criticism,* 0(0). https://doi.org/10.1177/01914537221107403.

Cockshott, W.P. and Cottrell, A. (1993) *Towards a New Socialism*. Nottingham: Spokesman Books.

Cole, G.D.H. (1935) *Principles of Economic Planning*. London: Macmillan and Co.

Dapprich, J.P. (2021) 'Optimal planning with consumer feedback: a simulation of a socialist economy', *Review of Political Economy*. doi: 10.1080/09538259.2021.2005367.

Devine, P. (1988) *Democracy and Economic Planning: The Political Economy of a Self-governing Society*. Cambridge: Polity Press.

Grünberg, M. (2023) 'The planning daemon: future desire and communal production', *Historical Materialism*, 31(4): 115–159. doi: 10.1163/1569206x-bja10001.

Härdin, T. (2021) 'Planning complexity for model economies'. https://www.xn--hrdin-gra.se/blog/2021/02/24/planning-complexity-for-model-economies/

Held, D. (1987) *Models of Democracy*. Cambridge: Polity Press.

Lafargue, P. (1883) 'The right to be lazy'. https://www.marxists.org/archive/lafargue/1883/lazy/

Leahy, T. (2023) '4. Pathways out of capitalism: the gift economy'. https://www.researchgate.net/publication/368874969_4_Pathways_out_of_Capitalism_The_Gift_Economy

Marx, K. and Engels, F. (1870) 'Critique of the Gotha Program', *Marx & Engels Selected Works, Volume Three,* Moscow: Progress Publishers, pp 13–30.

Meretz, S. and Sutterlütti, S. (2022) *Make Capitalism History: A Practical Framework for Utopia and the Transformation of Society*. Cham: Palgrave Macmillan.

Muldoon, J. (2019) 'A socialist republican theory of freedom and government', *European Journal of Political Theory,* 21(1): 47–67.

Nelson, A. (2022) *Beyond Money: A Postcapitalist Strategy*. London: Pluto Press.

Neurath, O. (1925a) 'Economic plan and calculation in kind', in Thomas E. Uebel and Robert S. Cohen (eds) *Otto Neurath: Economic Writing Selections: 1904–1945,* London: Kluwer Academic Publishers, pp 405–465.

Neurath, O. (1925b) 'Socialist utility calculation and capitalist profit calculation', in Thomas E. Uebel and Robert S. Cohen (eds) *Otto Neurath: Economic Writing Selections: 1904–1945,* London: Kluwer Academic Publishers, pp 446–472.

O'Neill, M. (2020) 'Social justice and economic systems: on Rawls, democratic socialism, and alternatives to capitalism', *Philosophical Topics*, 48(2): 159–202.

O'Shea, T. (2020) 'What is economic liberty?', *Philosophical Topics*, 48(2): 203–222.

Pettit, P. (1999) *Republicanism: A Theory of Freedom and Government*. Oxford: Oxford University Press.

Phillips, L. and Rozworski, M. (2019) *The People's Republic of Walmart: How the World's Biggest Corporations are Laying the Foundation for Socialism*. London: Verso Books.

Samothrakis, S. (2021) 'Artificial intelligence inspired methods for the allocation of common goods and services', *Plos One*, 16(9): 1–16.

4

Distributed Commonist Planning

Stefan Meretz and Simon Sutterlütti
Translated from German by Manfred Renken

Introduction

The 20th century can perhaps teach us that the socialist transitional society bears more than just a few birthmarks (Marx, 1970) from capitalism, and both also share a common basis: commodity production, wage labour, splitting off care labour, money, externalization and the logic of exclusion. The great promise of societal planning, liberation from private property and the rational development of productive forces, was bound to fail (Kurz, 1991; Ellman, 2014). Many of these birthmarks continue to appear in the diverse alternative concepts that are currently circulating, ranging from more market-based to more state-socialist approaches. With commonism, we sketch a society that adopts multiple impulses from the commons – as today's re/productive practice beyond market and state (Ostrom, 2010) – and generalizes them on a societal scale. The authors' 2023 book, *Make Capitalism History* examined this, as does this chapter, which focuses on addressing a three-pronged question about planning.

In commonism, where some produce what others need, the mediation of production and the satisfaction of needs takes place through commoning, which is the self-organized planning and coordination of what must occur to achieve a goal in a commons (for example, a cooperative or a commune). Currently already being adopted and its patterns of action an object of study (Bollier and Helfrich, 2019), the relational model of commoning exists interpersonally (direct agreement) and transpersonally (mediated agreement). Participation is voluntary in all necessary processes and work is not compulsory since any form of compulsion erodes motivation. Critical psychology has demonstrated (Holzkamp, 1983) that, if the necessary conditions for activities are available and participants can freely agree on their implementation, then they are taken on in a motivated manner or even out of pressing necessity. Coercing people to work – through personal or structural pressure (he who does not work shall not eat) – is considered to be an inhumane artefact of commodity-producing societies that are shaped by the market or state. If central means of power and coercion, such as property ownership and structural violence, are abolished and the disposal of the necessary means (including production) is in collective hands, then goals can only be achieved if the conditions for implementation (for instance, in the workplace) are so inviting and collaborative that enough people wish to participate. This wish is based on productive needs (Holzkamp, 1983). People do not necessarily feel satisfied and secure just because their sensual-vital needs are provided for (possibly externally), but driven by their productive needs they want to participate in the societal process of the precautionary creation of the conditions necessary to satisfy sensual-vital needs in the long term (Holzkamp, 1983); only then does a sense of security arise that is impossible to achieve under capitalism because the vast majority are excluded from the disposal of societal conditions.[1] Commonism suggests cooperative action, producing a logic of reciprocal inclusion – rather than the logic of exclusion that capitalist competition produces. Our thesis is: only a society based on radical freedom is able to maximize cooperation and subsequently produce security and long-term stability for all. The key challenge is to build anonymous transpersonal mediation on the aforementioned foundations in such a way that even highly collaborative activity processes interlock coherently. The following will expand on a transpersonal planning process.

Mediation

Almost every creative activity comprises two parts – intention and activity – which can also be interpreted as planning and implementation. What is true for individual activities is valid for collective endeavours. Until a mature intention or plan is determined, there is an additional need for coordination or, based on our terminology, mediation between participants' different needs, goals and implementation ideas. Although this mediation can occur interpersonally in direct communication, societally it is a matter of transpersonal mediation between anonymous participants.

The exchange of information is the most essential aspect in mediation, where distinctions can be made between mediation in the production sector, planning and coordination (allocation) and mediation between production, distribution and consumption. Planning is done to prepare for production, and coordination is necessary to implement what has been planned. In addition to information that ensues from production and its preconditions, planning requires information from distribution (such as demand). Moreover, planning is an adaptive and dynamic process that involves assembling and providing all relevant information that is necessary for the ability to produce on the ground. The following three issues arise in this regard, each of which must be addressed separately: the *information* that is needed on the ground and where it originates; how the *planning process* (accumulation and provision of information) is organized; and how the *distribution process* is structured, as well as how information enters the planning process as feedback.

In the following, production concerns interpersonally organized households and the communal production occurring in the immediate vicinity[2] but also transpersonally organized and collective production activities that take place in society. This way of viewing production is based on the idea that all necessary living conditions (material, symbolic and social caring), including the people themselves, are produced and/or provided for at a specific place in society. Production, which is also always reproduction, is comprehensively understood in this sense. Therefore, necessary activities are generally spoken of and not labour specifically (see Sutterlütti and Meretz, 2023).

Information

Qualitative and quantitative information are required to ensure societal mediation in production planning and the distribution of its results, namely, what kind of goods (including services) and how many. This is the case for goods that are for the direct sensual-vital satisfaction of needs and for goods that enter into the production of goods as intermediate products and means of production.

The concepts of mediation in kind and mediation by value are useful for describing the provision of the required information.[3] In the first concept, the goods themselves are used as carriers of information for mediation, meaning that only the quantity of the goods is missing. The goods speak for themselves since they have an inherent constitutive logic and embody the underlying societal processes of production and use. The utilization needs they can satisfy (qualities) are clear, as are what is required to be produced, that is the processes that have to be planned and how to produce the desired product in the desired amount (quantities). Quantities such as amount of material, energy and activity time to produce a certain product are inherently related to qualities, while distribution results from the practice of extraction, either directly as consumption of final products or indirectly as the use of preliminary products and means of production in a production chain. The goods to be produced remain carriers of qualitative (use) and quantitative (quantity) information. Planning and distribution occur in situ and ex ante in that they move in the same information space and occur before and after production. Thus, mediation in kind[4] transpires as a qualitative and quantitative mediation with and through the thing itself.

The situation differs with the second concept of mediation by value because monetization takes over the function of information in capitalism. As a general unit of account (UoA), societally, mediation by value exerts every effort to produce goods that are comparable and calculable. Production and distribution inform each other through a common measure: price. In the process, qualitative and quantitative information are separated based on usefulness and mediatability (in capitalism: use value and value) but actually doubled. Usefulness, which refers to sensual-vital needs, results from the concrete form of a product, which also has qualitative and quantitative aspects. Usefulness plays a central role in the immediate act of production and consumption. Distribution, however, is realized ex situ and ex post via an independent cycle structured by the downstream UoA of production as mediation by value creating two cycles. As in consumption, production is about the thing itself and its qualitative and quantitative properties, which refer – directly or in the case of intermediate products indirectly – to the sensual-vital needs that the good can satisfy concerning the logic of use value or the logic of need. The cycle of distribution revolves around the value or, in informational terms, the price, which represents the societal effort to produce the good: logic of exchange or logic of value. Marx (1976, p 132) attributed this doubling to the dual nature of a commodity's ability to represent use value (usefulness), on the one hand, and value (mediatability), on the other, which he considered, 'crucial to an understanding of political economy'. The commodity is thus a particular social and informational form of planning, producing and distributing goods, wherein mediation, and thus the logic of value, takes primacy.

The doubling of cycles simultaneously includes their coupling. Without the disposal of the societal incarnation of a general UoA, money, participation in production and distribution – thus the preservation of one's own existence – is impossible.[5] In societies that are dependent on mediation by value, this pressure is distilled in production as a compulsion towards competition-driven growth and in distribution as a labour compulsion.

Another consequence of the doubling of cycles is a polar division of societally necessary activities. The results of any and all activities that can be represented, evaluated and mediated by means of the UoA can enter the mediation by value cycle, and whether this occurs depends on specific conditions (in capitalism, for example, whether profit can be extracted from them). Those activities that cannot (yet) be represented by means of the UoA or that are no longer profitable, such as essential aspects of caring for children, the elderly and people with disabilities, are relegated to the interpersonal sphere of household production or organized by the state. The societal division of spheres is based on gender due to its intersection with the patriarchy that historically preceded the division (Scholz, 2000).

Planning

Mediation in kind and mediation by value systems differ considerably in planning. Notably no society with highly collective labour has yet to exist that has embraced mediation in kind. Any historical examples have been based on the low development of productive power with low vertical integration (Widlok, 2017), while mediation by value exists in capitalist (or has existed in socialist) commodity production (Marx, 1976; Kurz, 1991). More recent studies have combined aspects of mediation in kind and mediation by value systems (Adaman and Devine, 2022; Dapprich, 2022).

One of the challenges for mediation in kind systems is transporting and using the multidimensionality of information as automatically processable data in a qualitatively unreduced manner.[6] Due to the low bandwidth of earlier communications systems (such as letters, telegraphs, telephones and faxes) addressing that challenge was not possible for a long time. Reducing a few key figures inevitably led to distortions in economic coordination, which is known as tonne ideology in real socialism (Ellman, 2014). Modern information and communication technology now makes transporting unreduced data possible, meaning that mediation in kind systems with centralized and decentralized distributed planning are now conceptually conceivable.[7] As a result planning can ex ante integrate three fields of production conditions: the concrete production prerequisites (materials, energy, intermediate products, knowledge and activities); the consequences of production implementation and its treatment (filtering, processing and recycling); and the conditions and consequences of the production of materials, energy and intermediate products that others provide. The prerequisite for this type of mediation is general information transparency and access to automatically condensed information on all aspects of the production chain. Consequently, planning becomes an exploration of options for realizing the satisfaction of societal needs, including the associated consequences. The relationship between the sensual-vital and the productive satisfaction of needs and their consequences then becomes accessible to conscious shaping. In sum, people place themselves (again) in a position of finding their humanity in the more than human world (Abram, 1996).

Generally speaking, mediation by value has historically served as a solution to the societal information paradox (Hayek, 1945), which purported that increasing societalization meant that more and more information was available for a conscious overall societal shaping of human–world relation. But there was no instrument available to translate this abundance of information into a societal and local ability to act (for example, planning ability). According to Hayek:

> The peculiar character of the problem of a rational economic order is determined precisely by the fact that the knowledge of the circumstances of which we must make use never exists in concentrated or integrated form, but solely as the dispersed bits of incomplete and frequently contradictory knowledge which all the separate individuals possess. (Hayek, 1945, p 519)

The obvious solution was the radical reduction of the abundance of information to a one-dimensional quantity of price, since only a price system that self-organizes via the market could provide the necessary knowledge for decisions. However, due to radically reduced information content and the ex-post character of distribution, any commodity production planning by separate individuals always contains a certain degree of speculation about whether the commodities can ultimately be sold.

Since all market participants basically plan for themselves in a capitalist system, no integration across the entire production chain takes place. The final producers have no insight into suppliers' production conditions for raw materials and intermediate products. The upstream and final producers or the contractual partners generally only comply with elementary human rights and environmental protection requirements under the threat of punishment by the state.[8] The structural ex-post character of mediation by value systems is thus evident from not only the perspective of individual companies but also the state vis-à-vis the economy as a whole.

Planning in commonism

Commonism generalizes the concept of the commons towards the societal level and embedded planning plays a central role. The underlying societal structure of mediation is described next for the sake of clarity.

Commonism is a conceptual concretization of a polycentric mediation in kind system with distributed planning. Societal mediation (planning, coordination and distribution) takes place in situ and the societal production system can be represented as a global network. The nodes are the commons, which, depending on the societal location, can be enterprises, institutions, communities or households, while the edges are the material and informational connections between the nodes. Informational connections, which are based on standardized protocols, are created when two nodes enter into an agreement on a cooperation, for instance establishing a delivery connection. Agreements are part of the protocol, involve steps that both sides must confirm, and gain their stability from basic information transparency as well as consensus about and confidence in their viability. One aspect of the protocol is that nodes have access to information about past and present cooperation results (for example, deliveries) of the federated partner nodes at any time. This creates trust. The inclusion logic of transpersonal commoning is at work here, in which enterprises strive for reliability vis-à-vis their cooperation partners since they also want to rely on the partner enterprises upon which they depend. Conversely, unreliable enterprises are less likely to achieve their goals as partner enterprises might not accept their unreliability and turn to other enterprises. Cooperatives basically make decisions autonomously, but their ability to act depends on their cooperativeness and the reliability of third parties; they are semi-autonomous (Carlisle and Gruby, 2019). The decisions that cooperatives make externally result from commoning within cooperatives. Collective disposal of cooperatives is the prerequisite of their semi-autonomy.

Mutual acceptance of cooperation depends on more than just reliability and includes other factors that are often externalized under capitalist conditions of utilization, such as working conditions, environmental pollution and energy consumption, which most people consider important and that can be implemented at the protocol level. As a result, such conditions are incorporated into standard routines of public transparency and when drawing up agreements, including the resulting cooperative relationships.

Protocols are thus of great importance and represent societally agreed upon consensuses concerning how to cooperate. Moreover, they potentially represent an abundance of different information and agreements, including activity time, emissions, energy consumption and material efficiency. As a result, cooperatives can recognize the externalities that are embodied in the means of production and intermediate products, choosing their partners accordingly. These ideas represent suggestions for concrete action on the ground. While the logic of money and the market suggests earning profit by undercutting the competition at the expense of people and the environment, semi-autonomy, information transparency and protocol agreements imply that cooperation should be reciprocal and inclusive, the former type creating a logic of exclusion and the latter a logic of inclusion. Neither of these approaches determines action; however, the achievement of respective goals and ultimately the subsequent safeguarding of livelihoods is closely linked to an orientation towards these approaches. Asserting oneself at the expense of others and the more-than-human world is functional in capitalism; including them in cooperation is functional in commonism.

Inclusion also extends to household and communal production. Although the term 'production' may sound technocratic in the context of household and communal activities, it illustrates that the creations derived from being human in interpersonal close relationships, which are both emotional and material, are the foundation of human existence in general, for everything really. Although interpersonal care conducted in proximity cannot be expressed in terms of value in capitalism, it must still be carried out and is still primarily delegated to women (Winker, 2021). In commonism, interpersonal care is an essential and recognized aspect of societal provision, a special place that is inseparable from the economy. This is also the case in capitalism, which has difficulty extracting profit from these apparently worthless activities. Regardless the very first production remains the creation of a human being.[9] At the same time, the difference in the transpersonal precautionary production of living conditions should not be levelled since the familiar near household and the communal arrangement completely depend on the functioning of the anonymous far household of society as a whole. In antiquity, the ancient Greek philosophers called household production *oikonomia*, but capitalism has disqualified the place where human life is created and turned economy into an 'automatic subject' (Marx, 1976, p 255), a megamachine (Scheidler, 2020) that inserts itself into every corner of the earth in pursuit of multiplying profits.

In commonism, the more-than-human world and human beings find themselves in a restored relatedness to each other. Humans are a unique kind of nature, but nature nevertheless. In capitalism, the subject–object separation tore this relationship apart, legally establishing it as property-based material domination (Redecker, 2020). This reflects the abstraction that the machine of exploitation performs on people and their world. Only quantifiable aspects matter, and everything becomes an external object to be dominated, even the subjects who are subjugated by force or who conform themselves and submit to the external material constraint.

The self-referential economic logic of capitalism that rules over people as an automatic subject is overcome, allowing the relational social logic of commonism to unfold. In the latter form of logic, needs are the primary driver of enjoyment and activity. As shown, every need has two aspects – that of the sensual-vital immediate preservation of existence and that of the precautionary productive creation of the conditions for satisfying existential needs. In capitalism, sensual-vital and productive needs are separated into different spheres and over shaped in a process by which the sensual-vital satisfaction of needs takes place in the private sphere in the form of commodity consumption and unpaid care work. In addition to occurring solely in the economy, the productive satisfaction of needs chiefly comprises joyless wage labour (or its exploitation). Commonism abolishes this separation and over shaping. The sensual-vital aspects of producing–providing activities are just as important as productive–creative aspects of the caring activities in the interpersonal environment and vice versa. Provision becomes care and the other way around. Both aspects constitute quality of life, with no area forced to compensate for another since collective disposal and, consequently, creatability underpin all areas, including the weakest members of society who are not yet or are no longer able to contribute. Since provision and care are free of exchange logic and thus unconditional no one is excluded.

Only autonomous (disembedded) privileged subjects have freedom of choice in capitalism, while voluntariness in commonism has the character of semi-autonomous connectedness. Individuals do not separately engage in free decision-making but it is reciprocally and inclusively related to other people, situations and environments. Voluntariness, which is inseparable from responsibility, is not the opposite of necessity but a component of it.

Planning and coordination

The planning of societal production is not separate from its implementation, for example of a separate planning authority, but a component of production. Like embedded planning, it is oriented towards the size of the task to be achieved. Participants can plan smaller projects alone, while meta-commons can take over intercooperation planning and coordination for larger projects, such as commons alliances. This approach can be compared to the planning and control that planning offices execute in capitalist companies or consortia. The difference is, however, that the companies or consortiums' boundaries mark the planning range, just as all decisions are made separately from workers and the general public and are oriented towards third reasons (profit). Thus, unsurprisingly, state policy must represent the general interests of society alongside the partial interest of those entities in capitalism. In commonism, on the other hand, the split between economy and politics/state is abolished, with the planning and coordination of societal affairs transpiring in the same structures. This embedded, distributed planning is where the concept of political economy first realizes its full meaning because economy and politics are reconciled in the Hegelian sense.

The concrete design of the governance structure depends solely on the specific task to be executed and the people involved. Thus, the governance structures in areas as diverse as research, production, care, education, media, health and energy are likely to differ significantly. The people involved semi-autonomously determine the contents and set the goals in cooperation with the other areas they depend on. The differentiation does not take place along different logics (profit vs common good), but with the same (inclusive) logic along different contents. Planning and coordination are special tasks within the societal division of activities, just like bridge-building and nursing.

Commonism also eliminates the division of spheres that have been structured based on gender between transpersonal-societal and interpersonal close production in capitalism. Nevertheless, households and local authorities are located at the end of societal production chains, which means that everything that is not provided by society but needed must be provided in the household or by local authorities. Society can, in fact, provide many necessary goods and services but by no means all. Determining the activities that are societalized and thus transpersonalized is an empirical issue that cannot be addressed in advance. In any case, in principle consciously making this decision is possible since various places of production have no structural barriers between them.

Various studies (Ellman, 2014; Vettese and Pendergrass, 2022) have rightly considered the assertiveness of planning authorities to be essential, which also aligns with this chapter's repeated insistence that completed planning cannot be imposed by command but must be adopted from the sensible proposals of producers (Sutterlütti and Meretz, 2023, p 158). The notion of the separateness of planning and implementation, of politics and economics, also resonates in this regard. Although planning and implementation are qualitatively different activities, they do not run side by side ex situ in separate spheres but are closely related to one another in situ. The size of planning, and thus the distance between planning and implementation, depends solely on the size of the task. Large tasks, like converting global production chains due to the climate crisis, do not necessarily also require big planning structures, as a central proposal can break down the requirements top down as increasingly concrete subplans. Comparatively small commons can also plan large tasks by defining parameters that flow into production regionally or locally as framework conditions (such as not exceeding an emissions budget). Other tasks, such as the construction of a new factory to manufacture microelectronic components, also require big plans to explicitly define what individual partner companies in the network must achieve. The overall prerequisite is that all network partners have publicly declared that they will contribute to the collaborative project (see earlier). These two examples of big tasks show that it is possible to distinguish between target and operational planning, and the latter is only possible when all (partial) goals have been set. Building a chip factory not only requires the decision to achieve the primary goal but also that other goals are simultaneously internalized, such as meeting emissions budgets.[10]

But how do decisions like the construction of a resource-intensive chip factory or setting a universally binding emissions budget occur? Is it necessary to have political decision-making structures that are separate from production?

Framework goals, decisions and conflicts

Framework goals are generally valid societal goals[11] and are part of the protocols that structure the connections between cooperating entities (commons). New framework goals emerge when people, due to expertise, affectedness or reach, research certain overarching issues, bringing them to bear on local, regional, continental or global living conditions in terms of their relevance. A present-day example is the UN Intergovernmental Panel on Climate Change, which not only describes situations and scenarios, but also provides recommendations for action that the climate commons can concretize to the corresponding geographical and thematic conditions. Such a hierarchical commons system could develop correspondingly adapted proposals that are implemented as framework goals through protocols and incorporated into operational goal planning.

On the ground, decisions are unproblematic when all the conditions for the steps to be taken to achieve a goal are in place. If the underlying conditions are not in place, decisions can raise conflict, with manifold sources of conflict emerging, like resource limitations, lack of participation, contradictory framework goals and goals that are incompatible due to differing prioritization of needs. In this case, operational planning cannot be carried out but must be interrupted in favour of conflict management. Conflict loops like this can be understood as collective learning loops (Holzkamp, 1993, p 183) in which the people involved explore, evaluate and prioritize all aspects of the conflict and collectively endeavour to propose a solution that is then mirrored to the participating cooperations and accepted or rejected via the respective local decision-making procedures (consensual, consentual,[12] majority democratic and council democratic). If accepted, the commitment to participate is assessed at the protocol level to ensure that the entire production chain (and also the public) is aware of who will participate under the new conditions. If the solution is rejected, either a new conflict loop commences or cooperators decide to leave the production chain and look for a new one. The option to leave a cooperation procedure is an essential regulatory feature of free cooperation (in contrast to forced cooperation, cf Spehr, 2003), allowing parties to have the option of withdrawing from a cooperation procedure, which is a provision that applies to both interpersonal and interinstitutional cooperation.

Looking at the big picture, it becomes clear that three conflict dimensions unfold a regulative dynamic. First, for example, if a local production unit wants to begin taking steps to achieve its own goals, it may be unable or unwilling to accept all the conditions others set. Second, corresponding constellations that supply intermediate products or receive products that the unit under consideration has requirements for or from which it receives requirements also exist in local production units. Third, given production conditions (processes and machines), general societal targets may contradict the unit's own targets and neglecting the general targets may make partial targets seem easier to achieve. This contradiction triangle is not specific to commonism, but gaining a better understanding of its dynamics can be accomplished by examining how it is managed in capitalism.

First, under capitalism, a company can only produce if the right framework conditions exist. Second, preliminary products, energy and labour must be purchased at a reasonable price or at least at one in which the profit margin does not fall below the level of self-preservation. Conversely, the price of the company's own products must be oriented to the general market level. Third, externalization offers obvious cost-cutting options, such as environmental destruction or labour disintegration due to poor working conditions. The logic of exclusion clearly has driving (excluding competition) and destructive (externalizing costs) effects.

In commonism, the framework conditions must also be met before production can commence. Pre-products, energy and qualified people must be available. Second, suppliers and local producers must make sure that their requirements are met – for instance, the extent to which their products are processed further in such a way that, from the upstream producers' perspective, the desired criteria or goals (which ultimately represent needs) are realized, or from local workers' perspective, working conditions are provided that correspond to their own desire for productive fulfilment of needs. Third, societally determined criteria create pressure to organize production to meet the targets set. Failing to comply with targets draws attention and makes them open to criticism from partner enterprises and the general public, putting pressure on producers to remedy deficiencies, particularly in the production chain. If this does not help, misaligned cooperations will ultimately be replaced by partner cooperations that act more suitably. This is the only effective and indirect sanction mechanism available since successful cooperation is the only way for enterprises to realize their own needs and goals. The logic of inclusion thus works in two directions to create inclusive reciprocity, where both sides strive to consider the criteria and goals, that is the needs of the respective partners, just as they want to see their own needs considered.

Semi-autonomous networking clearly ensures that enterprises have a much stronger mutual influence than that in capitalism, where each enterprise largely isolates itself from others and only interacts through market relations. There is no influence on the use of one's own products, working conditions or production consequences since the state is responsible for this kind of regulation.[13] Instead of production chain control ex post, production chain design largely occurs ex ante in commonism.

Households and local authorities play a special role since they are at the end of the goods production chain and use products whose free extraction is an upstream signal for production. Moreover, their cooperative influence on production is weaker than that of cooperations within production chains. All material, symbolic and socially caring preconditions for a satisfying life that are not provided for through general provisioning must be created locally in households and local interpersonal contexts. It is precisely this collective disposal of spatially, socially and emotionally close living conditions that is explicitly desired. Conversely, the need may arise to create and make certain social infrastructure generally available. In capitalism, unprofitable and psychophysical care activities are allocated to isolated households, assigning them a cleaning-up function that addresses the failure of destructive commodity production that classist, sexist and racist segregation impose on the most vulnerable people who have little choice.

Conclusion

Commonism does not have a functional barrier between household/communal and societal production, since all productively active people can decide whether their activities are in the interpersonal (near) field for specific individuals or in transpersonal production for anonymous others (or a combination of both). Every activity that produces results that are needed and satisfy needs is societally necessary, which includes redundancy. Activities that are particularly essential to maintaining people's existence can also be secured with large buffers to cope with any failures. In capitalism, however, redundancies merely figure as costs that disappear in the next round of rationalization. With commonism, a new historical form of truth production that reaches beyond the market – which is supposedly always right – and essentialism, where entities must come into their own also asserts itself, where the truth of needs assures itself of its historicity.

Notes

[1] An artefact of capitalism is the division of unavailable production and available consumption (monetarily) of goods, the former referencing labour that tends to lack satisfaction and the latter implying enjoyment that closely resembles satisfaction. Thus, assigning burden to production activities, even in a free (socialist or otherwise) society, and pleasure to consumption activities, as done by Dapprich (2020), naturalizes capitalism. Whether an activity is perceived as a burden, pleasure or a mixture of the two varies from individual to individual; the more decisive factor is whether the activity is forced or voluntary, that is, motivated.

[2] A household is understood in a broad sense and not solely as a domestic unit, while communal production refers to the provision of means of satisfaction in close proximity but beyond the household, such as neighbourhoods and districts.

[3] The subsequent analysis is based on the concept of stigmergy (Sutterlütti and Meretz, 2023, p 160).

[4] Calculation in kind and calculation in natura are commonly discussed but purely consider quantitative aspects, which fails to address the qualitative issue of which needs are to be satisfied.

[5] If the UoA were to be distributed as universal income irrespective of performance, the labour compulsion would have to be established in a different form.

[6] This implies that a quantitative size always refers to its quality, for example where a quantity of material X is of Y quality, or a quantity of activity A is a qualification of B. A general UoA abstracts from quality, cuts the context and becomes mere quantity.

[7] Neurath (1919) developed *Naturalwirtschaft mit Vollsozialisierung* (natural economy with full socialization), which is the historical model of a central mediation in such a system.

[8] One example is the (mostly inadequate) supply chain laws of some European countries (Paasch and Seitz, 2021).

9. Rather than introducing wages for domestic work, which cyber socialists also propose (Dapprich, 2022), the aim is to remove wages from production and make people's own existence unconditional.
10. Internalization is thus the material side of the logic of inclusion.
11. Topical examples are the UN Human Rights Charter and the Paris Agreement on Climate Change.
12. While consensus requires everyone to agree, consent is achieved when there are no serious objections.
13. The supply chain laws enacted in some European countries, most of which are completely inadequate, are an example of current efforts.

Bibliography

Abram, D. (1996) *The Spell of the Sensuous. Perception and Language in a More-Than-Human World*. New York: Vintage.

Adaman, F. and Devine P. (2022) 'Revisiting the calculation debate: a call for a multiscale approach', *Rethinking Marxism*, 34(2): 162–192.

Bollier, D. and Helfrich, S. (2019) *Free, Fair and Alive. The Insurgent Power of the Commons*. Gabriola Island: New Society.

Carlisle K. and Gruby, R.L. (2019) Polycentric systems of governance: a theoretical model for the commons. *Policy Studies Journal*, 47(4): 927–952.

Dapprich, J.P. (2022) 'Tokens make the world go round: socialist tokens as an alternative to money', *Review of Evolutionary Political Economy*, 4: 497–513.

Ellman, M. (2014) *Socialist Planning*. Cambridge: Cambridge University Press.

Hayek, F.A. (1945) 'The use of knowledge in society', *The American Economic Review*, 35(4): 519–530.

Holzkamp, K. (1983) *Grundlegung der Psychologie*. Frankfurt/Main: Campus.

Holzkamp, K. (1993) *Lernen. Subjektwissenschaftliche Grundlegung*. Frankfurt/Main: Campus.

Kurz, R. (1991) *Der Kollaps der Modernisierung – Vom Zusammenbruch des Kasernensozialismus zur Krise der Weltökonomie*. Frankfurt/Main: Eichborn.

Marx, K. (1970) 'Critique of the Gotha Programme', in *Marx/Engels Selected Works, Volume 3*, Moscow: Progress, pp 13–30.

Marx, K. (1976) *Capital. A Critique of Political Economy, Volume 1*. London: Penguin.

Neurath, O. (1919) 'Character and course of socialisation', in M. Neurath and R.S. Cohen (eds) (1973) *Empiricism and Sociology*, Dordrecht: Reidel, pp 135–150.

Ostrom, E. (2010) 'Beyond markets and states: polycentric governance of complex economic systems', *The American Economic Review*, 100(3): 641–672.

Paasch, A. and Seitz, K. (2021) 'Lieferkettengesetz: Aufstand der Lobbyisten'. www.misereor.de/fileadmin/publikationen/briefing-lieferkettengesetz-aufstand-der-lobbyisten-2021.pdf

Redecker, E. von (2020) *Revolution für das Leben. Philosophie der neuen Protestformen*. Frankfurt/Main: S. Fischer.

Scheidler, F. (2020) *The End of the Megamachine. A Brief History of a Failing Civilisation*. Alresford: Zero Books.

Scholz, R. (2000) *Das Geschlecht des Kapitalismus. Feministische Theorie und die postmoderne Metamorphose des Patriarchats*. Bad Honnef: Horlemann.

Spehr, Ch. (2003) *Gleicher als andere. Eine Grundlegung der freien Kooperation*. Berlin: Dietz.

Sutterlütti, S. and Meretz, S. (2023). *Make Capitalism History. A Practical Framework for Utopia and the Transformation of Society*. Cham: Palgrave Macmillan.

Vettese, T. and Pendergrass, D. (2022) *Half-Earth Socialism: A Plan to Save the Future from Extinction, Climate Change and Pandemics*. New York: Verso.

Widlok, T. (2017) *Anthropology and the Economy of Sharing*. New York: Routledge.

Winker, G. (2021) *Solidarische Care-Ökonomie. Revolutionäre Realpolitik für Care und Klima*. Bielefeld: transcript.

5

Counter-Planning the Polycrisis: For Biocommunism

Nick Dyer-Witheford

Introduction: Polycrisis prospects

In his famous diagnosis of capitalism's current condition, Adam Tooze (2021, p 6) describes a contemporary 'polycrisis' of 'overlapping political, economic and environmental conflagrations'. He regards this as an aberration from world-market normality. Others, however, see the start of an ongoing, intractable condition. Alex Callinicos (2022) posits a 'new age of catastrophe' in which competitive accumulation culminates in a 'multidimensional crisis' with four elements: (1) biological, with global warming, accompanied by symptoms such as zoonotic pandemics; (2) economic, as problems of stagnancy, inequality and financial instability persist; (3) geopolitical, with great power struggles for global hegemony; (4) political, as the 'extreme centre' of neoliberalism grapples with populist eruptions. 'Disaster capitalism' (Klein, 2008) normalizes, manages, provokes and instrumentalizes catastrophe. Yet if a mode of social reproduction beyond capitalism is to emerge, it too will arise from polycrisis. What follows, therefore, maps the contours of a potential collectivist system – biocommunism, a communism emerging from the catastrophes capital inflicts throughout the *bios*, the realm of life itself – appearing in the midst of intensifying turmoil. The temporal horizon of this speculation is a near-future when, while the abyss of full-scale nuclear war is avoided, successful governance is increasingly defined by the sustenance of populations under mounting ecological, economic and geopolitical stress. The sketch is oriented towards conditions in the OECD countries, the rich zone of the world market. It does not assess China's polycrisis policies, and touches on the uneven and combined nature of global disaster only via issues of migration and refuge. Yet despite these inadequacies, it hopes to suggest broad possibilities within polycrisis for the inception of a new social system. After a summary of theoretical premises, it presents five elements of biocommunism: disaster relief; opening borders; expropriation of industries; rationing consumption; and labour mobilization. It then concludes by discussing this agenda in relation to planning and 'counter-planning'.

Theoretical premises

'Biocommunism' makes a rendezvous between Marx's communist thought and Michel Foucault's (2007; 2008) proposition of 'biopower' as the governance of 'life itself'. Foucault conceives such governmentality not solely in terms of state power but in more capillary form, involving a range of institutions and organizations in a 'mesh of power' (Foucault, 2012). This 'mesh' is politically ambivalent. It can clearly be an insidious, implacable disciplinary apparatus. Yet there is an inverse concept, in which the disaggregated and distributed nature of power becomes the occasion to reverse its hierarchical organization, diffusing and distributing it to communal organization.

Thus, Michael Hardt and Antonio Negri (2000) and Tiziana Terranova (2009), writing within the tradition of autonomist Marxism, propose biopower exercised from above can be countered by an insurgent biopolitics arising from below. This thesis was taken up in a somewhat different political register by Alberto Toscano (2016; 2020) and debated by Panagiotis Sotiris (2020a; 2020b) and Gareth Dale (2021) in a pandemic context. However, Hardt and Negri's version of biopolitics, and my own previous work on biocommunism and 'red plenty' planning (Dyer-Witheford, 2010; 2014), were shaped by a Promethean techno-logic. The centrality of ecological catastrophe to today's polycrisis demands revision. Of particular importance to my rethinking of the concept has been Emanuele Leonardi's (2021) articulation of Marxist biopolitics with 'degrowth' ecology.

Biocommunism may thus seem to simply replicate the problematic of 'eco-socialism', already the topic of a large body of important literature (Foster, 2000; Moore, 2015). But it rephrases the issue, because the ecological crisis has entered a new phase in which the time for averting disaster has expired, and battles are now fought out on already-catastrophized ground, demanding new measures of mitigation and adaptation. It also disputes the hyphen of eco-socialism, which, while bringing the ecological and social together in left thought, also continues to conceptually separate them. Biopower, biopolitics and biocommunism are terms proper to a moment where 'ecological' and 'governmental' processes relentlessly loop around in mutual reconfiguration.

The biocommunism sketched here triangulates 'solar communism' (Schwartzman, 1996), 'war communism' (Malm and the Zetkin Collective,

2021) and 'disaster communism' (Out of the Woods, 2020). It makes a qualified affirmation of the potential of a new, plenitudinous mode of species reproduction drawing on renewable energy sources, but holds this will only be created under conditions of disaster, rescue, repair and restoration. This situation will require the emergency mobilization of resources that can only currently be commanded through the state apparatus (Malm and the Zetkin Collective, 2021), but also requires forces beyond that apparatus, including forms of autonomous organization and mutual aid (Out of the Woods, 2020). Biocommunism is thus an 'in-against-and-beyond the state' (Angel, 2017), pressing towards the crisis-driven reconstruction of social governance, what Marx and Engel termed a 'vast association' (1848), components of which we will now examine.

Vital systems

As capitalism's forces of production turn against it, biocommunist organization starts at the point of destruction, among populations struck by pandemics, fires, floods, super-storms, droughts, heatwaves and war. The multiplication of these terrifying events, and the threatened collapse of hospitals, medical aid, burial services, the food and water supply, transportation, energy grids and communication networks demonstrate the failure of the existing order direction; the rescue and protection of the endangered becomes a touchstone of any alternative hegemony.

In advanced capitalism the 'ready-to-hand toolkit for administering emergencies' is the apparatus of 'vital systems security' (Collier and Lakoff, 2015, p 19). This comprises special centralized organizations, such as the US Federal Emergency Management Administration or Center for Disease Control, but also regional and municipal networks coordinating rescue, policing, medical care, hospitalization, shelter and sustenance of displaced populations and reconstruction of damaged areas. These are institutions of 'reflexive biopolitics', managing risks arising from within the capitalist modernity they defend, designed to control civil disorders, suppress diseases of urban poverty, or prepare for conventional or nuclear war (Collier and Lakoff, 2015, p 19).

Today, however, biopolitical reflexivity takes another turn; crisis services are undermined by the accumulative logic they protect. Neoliberal austerity and just-in-time logistics have depleted vital systems, dismantling supply depots, dissolving organizational centres and outsourcing operations. Aspects of the system remaining intact are geared to protection of property and the circulation of capital, riddled with authoritarianism and discrimination, manifesting in racialized policing of disaster-struck cities and repeated failures to protect low-income communities.

In the COVID-19 pandemic, liberal democracies' response to a long-predicted pathogen crisis was contradictory and confused. Policies oscillated between protecting social reproduction (shutdown) and capitalist accumulation (business as usual). Decades of underfunding, deregulation and privatization of healthcare systems created a 'chokepoint' of potential hospital collapse, which then had to be managed by broad restrictions on public behaviour (Roth, 2022). In rich countries, unemployment benefits were available for some sections of labour. But others had to fight for 'quarantine wages', while 'frontline' workers toiled on, often without even proper sick leave provisions.

These real failures were all avidly exploited by the far right, misrepresenting a scene of disarrayed disciplinarity as a sinister, seamless conspiracy of elite control. Neo-fascists seized on Agamben's (2020) portrayal of lockdowns and vaccine mandates as totalitarian biopolitics to repudiate any social solidarity and promote ideologies of individual sovereignty or race war. The task of biocommunism is not to ratify such occult theories, but, while criticizing the insufficiencies of capital's disaster relief, to build a 'politics of care' (Fraser, 2016).

This would entail refunding vital systems degraded by neoliberal neglect and rethinking their operation with special focus on the most vulnerable social strata. It would include the normalization of replacement income for lost work, the rebuilding of destroyed homes, and the reconstruction of disrupted livelihoods, including trauma treatment, relocation and retraining for disaster victims. It should, centrally, train cadres of catastrophe communicators to relay criticism and counter-proposals from varied social groups to emergency planners, fighting for scientifically sound and socially just measures without repression of dissenting opinion.

Vital care systems should not be purely state led but should embrace and be integrated with mutual aid practices that emerge in catastrophes, such as Occupy Wall Street relief operations after Hurricane Sandy (Dawson, 2017), community movements after Mexican earthquakes (Cleaver, 2005), volunteer pandemic activism in Milan (Commune, 2020) and aid for the war-devastated by Ukrainian anarchist organizations (assembly.org.ua, 2023) . It is overly romantic to think mutual aid could today entirely replace state systems in marshalling technologies, supplies, personnel, and expertise; but combinations of state provision and self-organization, still alive in Cuba (Fitz, 2022) as offshoot of a 'revolutionary war' tradition, are a real possibility. None of this can prevent disaster relief from being painful and contentious, but such measures would pit communal power against capitalocene calamity, rather than dividing society further in the face of disaster.

Dissolving borders

Issues of migration and refuge are central to the polycrisis. Poverty, ecological devastation, war and oppression combine to displace millions. This 'loss of habitat' (Sassen, 2016) is and will be concentrated in tropics where global warming is most severe, and malign legacies of colonialism and imperialism deeply mark social order. Flight often takes local routes, from one poor and disadvantaged country to another, but also moves towards the rich world, across the Mediterranean, the US–Mexico border and other frontiers where migrants face exclusion, detention, deportation, criminalization, abandonment and death.

In 'border struggles' (Mezzadra and Neilson, 2013) migrant communities self-organize, repudiating sovereign powers regulating movement, with slogans such as 'the border is closed but we will pass' or 'no one is illegal', and initiating a new 'politics of movement' (Heller et al, 2019). This chapter will not adjudicate debates between advocates of 'open borders' – relaxing state regulation on migration – and 'no frontiers' – abolishing states – but a broad 'debordering' orientation is crucial to biocommunism, building the infrastructures, policies and social practices to allow expanded flows of movement and settlement.

This requires that biocommunism internalize what are today the oppositional activities of movements supporting so-called illegal migration. Thomas Nail (2019) categorizes these practices: 'sanctuary' – refusing cooperation with (or dismantling) state agencies seeking to arrest and deport migrants; 'solidarity' – providing access to medicine, housing, learning and communication; and 'status' – recognition as a full member of a new community. However, biocommunism cannot just be an expansion of liberal immigration programmes. It must recognize the specifically proletarian nature of global migration and dismantle the ways capital exploits migration. Thus, *sanctuary* would become the protection of migrants not only from racist persecution, but also from human trafficking, workplace exploitation, and slave labour. Solidarity would also be *labour* solidarity, connecting migrants with unions and other worker organizations, preventing division and insecurity in the workforce. And *status* would comprehend new rights of livelihood for all detached from a competitive wage market.

Migrancy is also an issue of international cooperation, involving out-flow as well as in-flow regions. Writing of Honduras and the USA, Joseph Nevins (2019) makes the case for 'migration as reparations', whereby populations deprived of the 'right to stay' in home regions wracked by destructive colonialisms and climate change gain a 'right to move' and participate in the remittance economy. This is a compelling argument, but has to be balanced against the dangers of regarding out-migration regions as sacrifice zones fated to become unlivable. The rich world's offshoring of refugee camps, exporting migrant detentions, should be reversed in the subsidy of mitigation, together with the adaption of climate change in the areas of its most severe onset, the termination of migration-causing military interventions, such as those in Afghanistan, Iraq, Libya, and the cessation of extractive ventures creating ecological and social chaos in the Global South, all set within a long-term framework of the approximate equalization of global living standards.

Migration is a politically fraught issue, fraught with racism and the field on which, in the era of global warming, 'fossil fascism' will fight with notions of ethno-nationalist eco-sustainability (Malm and the Zetkin Collective, 2021). As Stefan Wróbel (2020, p 311) observes 'the task of biocommunism is to fight ... above all, the racist cut of life' (2020, p 310). The European and North American response to Ukrainian refugees from Russian invasion demonstrates the humanitarian generosity migration can inspire, but also, in contrast to treatment of refugees from other parts of the world, how selective benevolence can be. Yet the costs, dangers and futility of fortification against migration, combined with the labour shortages of zones with ageing populations and low birth rates, tell against the far right. Slavoj Zizek (2015) says that the migration crisis demands humankind 'get ready to live in a more "plastic" and nomadic way'; biocommunism will make that reinvention favour the 'workers of the world'.

Expropriators expropriated

Socialized ownership of the means of production is a basic tenet of communism; but, for biocommunism, while socialization will sometimes be required to expand production, it will at other times be necessary to shut it down. Two examples indicate this dual case for expropriation of crisis-critical capitalism.

One is the 'no profit from pandemic' campaign against Big Pharma's intellectual property rights (Gebrekidan and Apuzzo, 2021). The development of COVID-19 vaccines at record speeds by companies such as Pfizer and Moderna was an outcome of state–capital cooperation. Governments in the USA, UK and EU partnered with drug-makers, pouring billions of dollars into raw materials, clinical trials and retrofitted vaccine factories. They then spent billions more to buy the finished product. But this rich-world success created stark global inequities; 'vaccine apartheid' allowed continued pandemic spread, encouraging vaccine-resistant variants. At the World Trade Organization, India and South Africa argued to temporarily suspend intellectual property rights to vaccines and other COVID-related medical supplies (Melimopoulos, 2021). Worldwide pressure forced the USA to shift from opposition to partial support; but, after frantic lobbying by Big Pharma, the proposal was eventually 'stymied and watered down by negotiators from rich countries', leaving the full scope of vaccination segregation untouched (Horti, Furlong and Aarup, 2022).

The second example is ending 'fossil capital' (Malm, 2016 and 2020). Drastically reducing fossil fuel use is paramount for ending the climate emergency. 'Leave It In the Ground' has therefore become a major slogan of ecological movements. It is supported by planning for the conversion of fossil capital enterprises to public utilities in order to shut them down. Holly Jean Buck's (2021) reflections on 'ending things' includes a five-step fossil fuel phaseout, moving through moratoria on prospecting, subsidy withdrawal, capping and ramp-down of production and 'nationalization to exit', with a final stage of 'reverse engineering' carbon capture and sequestration (CCS) that may eventually offer prospects of climate remediation (see also Gowan, 2018; Renzy, Skandier and Paul, 2020).

A major share of global oil production is, in fact, undertaken by state-owned companies, such as Saudi Aramco. The biocommunist socialization of resources cannot, therefore, be simply nationalization but must entail a larger decommodification of production, replacing management cadres and reorienting existing public utilities away from the world market. The major aim would be to terminate carbon emissions, but there are other reasons for communal repossession of both private and state-owned fossil capital, including the adequate retraining, pensioning, and re-employing of fossil industry workers (a process crucial to disarm opposition to an energy transition) and ensuring public control of CCS technologies, rather than leaving them in the hands of fossil capital to protract its activities.

These two cases illustrate the double-sided case – expansionary for vaccines, terminatory for fossil fuels – for capital expropriation in the age of catastrophe. Stressing 'expropriation' qualifies a term widely used in discussion of collective resource control: 'commons'. This term has been crucial to new models of communal ownership, more varied and inventive than bureaucratized nationalization: trusts, cooperatives, open-source production and peer-to-peer networks. The common must, of course, be central to any communism. But 'commonist' (Dyer-Witheford, 2007) discourse can suggest a supersession of capital by a sheer proliferation of commons – say, the creation of open-source software or the establishment of worker cooperatives. As these examples suggest, capitalism can accommodate a multiplication of commons, foster their initiation and certainly reap their fruits. The coexistence of commons and capital is feasible, always to the latter's advantage: commons move towards communism only when they diminish capital.

Universal provisions

In the age of catastrophe, the obverse of socialized production may be rationed consumption. Rationing is not a topic favoured by Marxisms; a confidence in the expanding forces of production steers away from discussion of scarcity. Even eco-socialists, rightly critical of corporations shifting responsibility for climate disaster to individual eco-footprints, fights shy of rationing discourse. Yet in polycrisis, rationing repeatedly rears its head, either as the immediate response to shortages of oil, gas or food caused by wartime disruptions and corporate opportunism, or, on a longer-term horizon, as an emergency fallback if carbon taxes, carbon trading and other market mechanisms fail to halt global warming. Biocommunism must therefore revisit the ration question, in both ecological and equalitarian aspects. While the topic summons the binary of 'despotic state versus free market', it also prompts recognition of markets as systems of rationing by price. Focusing on use-values rather than exchange-values, rationing foregrounds the material effects of capitalism's patterns of production and consumption on bodies and ecosystems with specific metabolic limits and tipping points, rather than endorsing the illusion of infinite fungibility implicit in monetary general equivalence.

Stan Cox's (2013) environmentalist account of rationing shows: (1) the ration was basic to many pre-capitalist societies; (2) socialist societies have used governmental rationing as a means of social equalization; (3) within capitalism, non-market rationing is regularly deployed to allocate necessities such as food, fuel, or water when escalating inequities threaten social order. In authoritarian regimes, such as contemporary Egypt, a food ration for the poor, coexisting with markets for the better-off, is stabilizing and upholds vertiginous inequalities – unless the ration is reduced, which is an occasion for riots. However, the comprehensive rationing of food and other supplies may, in crisis situations, not only enjoy broad popular support, but also model wider social equalization, as Britain's war-time rationing prefigured the creation of a welfare state.

Though the ruling class's major contribution to ecological crisis is investment in production, consumption is an aspect of this larger situation. Carbon emissions rise with wealth, along a curve steepening dramatically for billionaires with multiple mansions, giant yachts and private jets (Chancel and Picketty, 2015; Gore, 2020; Roston, Kaufman and Warren, 2022). Redistributive measures – increasing wages and welfare at the expense of profits or setting both minimum and maximum incomes – would eliminate such extravagance. Conversely, the rationing of specific ecologically damaging goods, such as airline flights, would restrain consumption in ways reducing both ecological destruction and social inequalities. Aaron Benanav's (2020) axiom 'abundance is a social relationship' suggests such measures would contribute both to a more equal and more ecologically frugal society.

Rationing is, however, not just limit but guarantee, prohibition but also promise, and security as well a scarcity. The long-running debate about universal basic income as an initiative is, in a way, a discussion about a ration, but confirms the norm of commodity exchange. More promising is the proposition of universal basic services (Portes et al, 2017), in which all members or residents of a community, region, or country receive unconditional access to some mix of shelter, sustenance, healthcare, education and legal aid. However, this proposal is too conceived in the welfare state model, as a subordinate, palliative addition to a market system – a dole of use-values.

A salutary reversal of this logic is George Monbiot's (2020) 'public luxury, private sufficiency' principle. This envisages major social investment in urban environments, public services, collective housing projects and mass transport systems, combined with rotated chances for everyone to occasionally enjoy extraordinary holidays and cultural events, alongside modest, ecologically sustainable levels of personal consumption. Monbiot shrinks from calling for the decapitation of capital, sticking to a familiar green trope of 'neither communism nor capitalism'. But his model actually implies dislodging for-profit accumulation from its direction of everyday life. It points to the organization of society around the universal provision of a limited but assured and broadly equalitarian 'basket of goods'; such biocommunist guarantees may become increasingly attractive as world-market chaos intensifies.

Essential workers

Biocommunism will not be a post-work utopia but a radical recomposition of labour. In the context of the COVID-19 crisis, Sandro Mezzadra (2020) proposes as a central figure 'the essential worker' whose labour is required under crisis conditions. In conditions of entropic ecological degradation, essential work escalates. Cory Doctorow (2020), criticizing Aaron Bastani's (2019) 'fully automated luxury communism', suggests: 'Remediating climate change will involve unimaginably labour-intensive tasks, like relocating every coastal city in the world kilometres inland, building high-speed rail links to replace aviation links, caring for hundreds of millions of traumatized, displaced people, and treating runaway zoontoic and insect borne pandemics.' To this list can be added emergency firefighters, mass tree planters, rewilding land clearers, solar panel installers, housing insulators, coders of climate-sensing software, gigafactory workers, and many more.

Under capital, much of this essential work will, because unprofitable, not be considered essential at all, and remain undone as habitat degradation intensifies. Labour necessary to maintain public order will be performed by threadbare state agencies. More lucrative developments will fall to a growing commercial or private–public climate adaption and mitigation sector. Essential work will be performed under conditions maximizing absolute and relative exploitation, with core teams of technical expertise surrounded by penumbras of precarious work, shielding enterprises from financially volatile conditions but providing workers minimal protections from mounting environmental risk.

In biocommunism, however, catastrophe-remediating work – in vital security systems, constructing and running refugia and sanctuaries, operating communal utilities, providing universal rations and services, and in planning all the above – would indeed be essential. So too would all the household activities of social reproduction. Large portions of these labours would be conducted by organs of communal governance as public works – a belated fulfilment of plans for 'a million climate jobs' or a Green New Deal. Unfortunately, these initiatives are being implemented not in proactive anticipation of a crisis, but amid increasingly chaotic conditions of biospheric deterioration.

Jameson's (2016) proposal for a 'universal army of labour' can serve as starting point of left biopolitics, with obligatory enrolment of all capable persons, performing assigned public tasks – 'essential work' – for four hours a day (or an equivalent period calculated weekly, monthly, annually). Jameson's 'army' is a deliberate provocation to left anti-statism, but its heresy is self-deconstructive, for this 'army' conducts tasks across the entire economy, auto-dissolving its military vocation. Not only would such an 'army' internalize within itself the disaggregated and contradictory nature of contemporary state functions, but a state apparatus mobilizing this 'army' would become indistinct from the larger society it governs.

Such an idea – the extreme development of the 'government job guarantee' attached to versions of a Green New Deal (Huber, 2022) – may invoke totalitarian nightmares. It can, however, be alternatively conceived as a communized decision-making process rich in contradiction, contention, and social ferment. This decision-making should be understood not as top-down command, but rather in terms of contemporary mission-oriented tactics (*Auftragstaktik*), in which the execution of broad objectives is devolved to on-the-scene units, and 'insubordinate' directive violations are expected or even fostered. Biocommunist essential workers can be imagined as having their own organizations, combining features of both worker cooperatives and unions with a say on rations, services, health and safety, task assignment and execution. These will be engaged in projects, such as greening cities, or localization of food supply, protecting, rebuilding and reconfiguring communities of which they may themselves be members, and whose survival and flourishing will be an object of pride. And these communities too will have their own councils and assemblies, which can both contest the work-teams' decisions and practices and collaborate with them to make interventions and adjustments at higher levels of the project. Seen in this light, Jameson's universal army, with half its day dedicated to labour in the realm of necessity and the other half liberated for the realm of freedom, comes to resemble the mix of anarchism and central planning imagined in Ursula Le Guin's (1974) sci-fi depiction of the communized planet Anarres. The essential worker becomes 'essential' not only in protecting vital social and species functions but also as a crucial agent in a sequence of collective planning activities, to which we now turn.

Planning and counter-planning

Although Marx used the terms 'socialism' and 'communism' interchangeably (Hudis, 2018), it is generally held that 'socialism' refers to an initial stage of human emancipation that still contends with poverty, material shortages, and other residues of capitalism, while 'communism' designates a later phase where, with forces of production freed from archaic restraints, society is organized according to the principle of 'from each according to their abilities, to each according to their needs' (Marx, 1970). However, in an age of extinctions – both human extinctions of other species and risks of human auto-extinction – this relation should be rethought.

Socialism could be understood as a progressive amassing of 'biopower' to regulate not only human populations but their environment, with its vast non-human populations of flora, fauna and other life-forms. Communism – or biocommunism – might then be a moment at which, for still-anthropocentric reasons of self-preservation, biopower is subjected to a social limitation to avoid eradicating the ecological 'web of life' (Moore, 2015) in which humanity is enmeshed. 'To each according to their need' is reinterpreted by the recognition that human need includes, materially and psychologically, the need for flourishing non-human species and populations.

This volume documents the revival of socialist and communist planning traditions, and biocommunism participates in this endeavour. It would be a social system steering between a ceiling of environmental sustainability and a floor of equalized social development. The basis for such planning exists in the 'boundary model' advanced by environmental authors (Raworth, 2017) but hijacked by corporate green-washers to legitimize ongoing economic extraction (Barca, 2020). Biocommunist planning would be a version weaponized to fight through to the abolition of capital, where the options offered by shifting ecological and economic boundaries could be assessed without presuppositions of the 'growth' imperative.

Such planning would not necessarily supply the highly variegated complex consumerism characteristic of advanced capitalist economies. Although digital, networked and algorithmic planning hold possibilities for solving historically intractable 'calculation problems' characteristic of such economies, it should not be presumed that a high-intensity consumption society would be the biocommunist *summum bonum*. It could have different goals, trading off high consumerism for free time, environmental plenitude, social solidarity, existential adventure and species survival. The struggle towards such a goal is truly radical but may come to seem pragmatic in the midst of vast market breakdowns, in which capital initiates its own spontaneous, barbaric 'degrowth'.

What a biocommunist optic should perhaps add to affine planning perspectives, however, is the concept of 'counter-planning'. This term comes from the lexicon of autonomist Marxism, in contexts of industrial shop-floor militancy (Watson, 1971), feminist struggles over social reproduction (Cox and Federici, 1975; Federici and Jones, 2020), and the defence of land commons (Benjamin and Turner, 1992). Counter-planning asserts that planning for a society beyond capital is necessarily adversarial and conflictual. Biocommunism follows this logic.

For capital has its own polycrisis plans. The social control and relief expenditures instituted in the pandemic lockdowns, the funding for a green capitalist energy transition, the rationings and nationalizations of energy supply enacted or considered in Europe because of the Ukraine war, all indicate that both the 'crisis state' and 'the planner state ' (Negri, 1988) are back, in a new, combined form. Whether one considers this the death or metamorphosis of neoliberalism, such planning clearly intended to save, not subvert, capitalism. The wager of biocommunism is that capitalist planning will not meet the basic requirements of social and ecological reproduction in the midst of polycrisis; steadily rising CO_2 emissions are only one index of this failure. Such failures create the possibility of responses to polycrisis 'from below' (Feltrin and Leonardi, 2023).

Biocommunism is one version of such a response; another is a neofascist ethno-nationalist authoritarianism. In such a context, all planning is counter-planning, planning against the plans of opponents. It is a project for the recomposition of social antagonisms, and a synthesis of anti-capitalists movements, bringing together ecological and equalitarian militancy, convening the forces of 'blockade' and 'riot' (Clover, 2019), but expanding and modulating them across multiple different registers, from sabotage to street action to elections (Nunes, 2021). Both the very notion of planning, and its implementation – the setting of goals, the determination of beneficiaries – will be contested. No diagram, however elegant, will be immune from the dissensus.

Conclusion

Planning post-capitalist transition is planning the crossing of a river of fire. The planning opportunities this chapter has sketched are also a series of explosive conflicts, over disaster response, migration, ownership, consumption and work. It is from the outcome of these jagged and dispersed collisions that any apparatus for communal planning must emerge – and such conflicts will continue within that apparatus once it is created. To face this is to rethink the politics of planning 'as a kind of planning for conflict', understanding it 'in terms of the persistence rather than the obliteration of antagonism' (Mandarini and Toscano, 2020, pp 13, 17). Biocommunism is predicated on Marx's assertion that cooperative planning is a – perhaps *the* – crucial attribute of human species-being. Christopher Sorg's (2023) application to post-capitalist thinking of the saying 'failing to plan is planning to fail' should be endorsed. Biocommunist thinking would, however, add to this another more stringent maxim, a reminder of conflict, contingency and stratagem, the friction and fog of class war: 'No plan survives first contact with the enemy' (Clausewitz, 1984).

Bibliography

Agamben, G. (2020) 'The invention of an epidemic', *American Studies Centre*, 26 January. https://www.asc.uw.edu.pl/wp-content/uploads/2022/03/Giorgio-Agamben-Invention-of-an-Epidemic.pdf

Angel, J. (2017) 'Towards an energy politics in against-and-beyond the state: Berlin's struggle for energy democracy', *Antipode*, 49: 557–576.

assembly.org.ua (2023) 'The war has become a daily routine', *Libcom*, 24 March. https://libcom.org/article/war-has-become-daily-routine-two-conversations-kharkov-underground-journal

Barca, S. (2020) *Forces of Reproduction: Notes for a Counter-Hegemonic Anthropocene*. Cambridge: Cambridge University Press.

Bastani, A. (2019) *Fully Automated Luxury Communism: A Manifesto*. London/New York: Verso.

Benanav, A. (2020) *Automation and the Future of Work*. London: Verso.

Benjamin, S. and Turner, T. (1992) 'Counterplanning from the commons', *Labour, Capital and Society*, 25(2): 218–248.

Buck, H.J. (2021) *Ending Fossil Fuels: Why Net Zero is Not Enough*. London: Verso.

Callinicos, A. (2022) 'The new age of catastrophe', *YouTube*, 23 April. https://www.youtube.com/watch?v=C-DTifOGfM4

Chancel, L. and Piketty, T. (2015) 'Carbon and inequality: from Kyoto to Paris', *World Inequality Database*. https://wid.world/document/chancel-l-piketty-t-carbon-and-inequality-from-kyoto-to-paris-wid-world-working-paper-2015-7/

Clausewitz, Carl von. (1984). *On War*. Edited and translated by Michael Howard and Peter Paret. Princeton: Princeton University Press.

Cleaver, H. (2005) 'The uses of an earthquake', *Libcom*, 10 August. https://libcom.org/article/uses-earthquake-harry-cleaver

Clover, J. (2019) *Riot. Strike. Riot: The New Era of Uprisings*. New York: Verso.

Collier, S. and Lakoff, A. (2015) 'Vital systems security: reflexive biopolitics and the government of emergency', *Theory, Culture & Society*, 32(2): 19–51.

Commune (2020) 'It's time to build the brigades', *Commune Magazine*, 27 March. https://communemag.com/its-time-to-build-the-brigades/

Cox, S. (2013) *Any Way You Slice It: The Past, Present and Future of Rationing*. New York: New Press.

Cox, N. and Federici, S. (1975) *Counter-Planning from the Kitchen*. New York: Falling Wall.

Dale, G. (2021) 'Lockdown politics: a response to panagiotis sotiris', *Historical Materialism*, 29(1): 247–262.

Dawson, A. (2017) *Extreme Cities: The Perils and Promise of Urban Life in the Age of Climate Change*. London: Verso.

Doctorow, C. (2020) 'Full employment', *Locus Magazine*, 6 July. https://locusmag.com/2020/07/cory-doctorow-full-employment/

Dyer-Witheford, N. (2007) 'Commonism', *Turbulence*, 1. http://www.turbulence.org.uk/turbulence-1/commonism/index.html

Dyer-Witheford, N. (2010) 'Digital labour, species-becoming and the global worker', *Ephemera: Theory in Politics and Organization*, 10(3/4): 484–503.

Dyer-Witheford, N. (2014) 'Red plenty platforms', *Culture Machine*, 13: 1–26.

Federici, S. and Jones, C. (2020) 'Counterplanning in the crisis of social reproduction', *South Atlantic Quarterly*, 119(1): 153–165.

Feltrin, L. and Leonardi, E (2023) 'Working-class environmentalism and climate justice', *PPPR*. https://projectpppr.org/populisms/working-class-environmentalism-and-climate-justice-the-challenge-of-convergence-todaynbsp

Fitz, D. (2022) 'Cuba prepares for disaster', *The Bullet*, 4 April. https://socialistproject.ca/2022/04/cuba-prepares-for-disaster/#more

Foster, J.B. (2000) *Marx's Ecology: Materialism and Nature*. New York: Monthly Review Press.

Foucault, M. (2007) *Security, Territory, Population: Lectures at the Collège de France, 1977–78*. Edited by M. Senellart, F. Ewald, A. Fontana et al. Basingstoke/New York: Palgrave Macmillan.

Foucault, M. (2008) *The Birth of Biopolitics: Lectures at the Collège de France, 1978–79. Lectures at the Collège de France*. Edited by M. Senellart. Basingstoke/New York: Palgrave Macmillan.

Foucault, M. (2012) 'The Mesh of Power', *Viewpoint Magazine*, 12 September. https://viewpointmag.com/2012/09/12/towards-a-socialist-art-of-government-michel-foucaults-the-mesh-of-power/

Fraser, N. (2016) 'Contradictions of capital and care', *New Left Review*, 100: 99–117.

Gebrekidan, S. and Apuzzo, M. (2021) 'Rich countries signed away a chance to vaccinate the world', *New York Times*, 10 November. https://www.nytimes.com/2021/03/21/world/vaccine-patents-us-eu.html

Gore, T. (2020) 'Confronting carbon inequality', *Oxfam International*, 21 September. https://www.oxfam.org/en/research/confronting-carbon-inequality

Gowan, S. (2018) 'A plan to nationalize fossil-fuel companies', *Jacobin*, 26 March. https://www.jacobinmag.com/2018/03/nationalize-fossil-fuel-companies-climate-change

Hardt, M. and Negri, A. (2000) *Empire*. Cambridge, MA: Harvard University Press.

Heller, C., Pezzani, L. and Stierl, M. (2019) 'Towards a politics of freedom of movement' in R. Jones (ed) *Open Borders: In Defense of Free Movement*, Athens, GA: University of Georgia, pp 51–76.

Horti, S., Furlong, A. and Aarup, A. (2022) 'Who killed the vaccine waiver?', *Bureau of Investigative Journalism,* 10 November. https://www.thebureauinvestigates.com/stories/2022-11-10/who-killed-the-vaccine-waiver

Huber, M. (2022) *Climate Change as Class War: Building Socialism on a Warming Planet*. London: Verso.

Hudis, P. (2019) 'Marx's concept of socialism', in M. Vidal et al (eds), *The Oxford Handbook of Karl Marx*, Oxford Handbooks (online edn), Oxford Academic. https://doi.org/10.1093/oxfordhb/9780190695545.013.50

Jameson, F. (2016) 'An American utopia', in S. Zizek (ed) *An American Utopia: Dual Power and the Universal Army*, London: Verso, pp 1–96.

Jones, R. (2019) 'In defense of free movement', in R. Jones (ed) *Open Borders: In Defense of Free Movement*, Athens, GA: University of Georgia, pp 264–272.

Klein, N. (2008) *The Shock Doctrine: The Rise of Disaster Capitalism*. New York: Picador.

Le Guin, U.K. (1974). *The Dispossessed. An Ambiguous Utopia*. New York: Harper & Row.

Leonardi, E. (2021) 'Autonomist Marxism and world-ecology', *Platforms, Populisms, Pandemics and Riots*. https://projectpppr.org/pandemics/autonomist-marxism-and-world-ecology-for-a-political-theory-of-the-ecological-crisis

Malm, A. (2016) *Fossil Capital: The Rise of Steam Power and the Roots of Global Warming*. London: Verso.

Malm, A. (2020) *Corona, Climate, Chronic Emergency: War Communism in the Twenty-First Century*. London: Verso.

Malm, A. and the Zetkin Collective (2021) *White Skin, Black Fuel: On the Danger of Fossil Fascism*. London: Verso.

Marx, K. (1970) 'Critique of the Gotha Programme', in *Marx/Engels Selected Works, Volume 3*, Moscow: Progress, pp 13–30.

Marx, K. and Engels, F. (1848) *Manifesto of the Communist Party*, Marxists Internet Archive. https://www.marxists.org/archive/marx/works/1848/communist-manifesto/index.htm

Mandarini, M. and Toscano, A. (2020) 'A critique of the proletariat as a revolutionary subject: Marx, Engels, and the critique of political economy', *South Atlantic Quarterly*, 119(1): 11–30.

Melimopoulos, E. (2021) 'What are patent waivers for COVID vaccines?', *Al Jazeera*, 29 June. https://www.aljazeera.com/news/2021/6/29/explainer-what-are-covid-vaccine-patent-waivers

Mezzadra, S. (2020) 'The capitalist virus: mutations of capitalism in the pandemic conjuncture', *YouTube*. https://www.youtube.com/watch?v=ApKGU9uWuKc

Mezzadra, S. and Neilson, B. (2013) *Border as Method, or The Multiplication of Labor*. Durham, NC: Duke University Press.

Monbiot, G. (2020) 'Private sufficiency, public luxury: land is the key to the transformation of society', *Schumacher Centre for New Economics*, 25 October. https://centerforneweconomics.org/publications/private-sufficiency-public-luxury-land-is-the-key-to-the-transformation-of-society/

Moore, J. (2015) *Capitalism in the Web of Life: Ecology and the Accumulation of Capital*. London: Verso.

Nail, T. (2019) 'Sanctuary, solidarity, status!', in R. Jones (ed) *Open Borders: In Defense of Free Movement*, Athens, GA: University of Georgia, pp 23–33.

Negri, T. (1988) *Revolution Retrieved: Selected Writings on Marx, Keynes, Capitalist Crisis and New Social Subjects*. New York: Left Bank Books.

Nevins, J. (2019) 'Migration as reparations', in R. Jones (ed) *Open Borders: In Defense of Free Movement*, Athens, GA: University of Georgia, pp 129–140.

Nunes, R. (2021) *Neither Vertical nor Horizontal: A Theory of Political Organization*. New York: Verso.

Out of the Woods (2020) *Hope Against Hope: Writings on Ecological Crisis*. New York: Common Notions.

Portes, J., Reed, H. and Percy, A. (2017) 'Social prosperity for the future: a proposal for Universal Basic Services', *Institute for Global Prosperity*. https://www.ucl.ac.uk/bartlett/igp/sites/bartlett/files/universal_basic_services_-_the_institute_for_global_prosperity_.pdf

Raworth, K. (2017) *Doughnut Economics: Seven Ways to Think Like a 21st Century Economist*. Vermont: Chelsea Green.

Renzy, R., Skandier, C.S. and Paul, M. (2020) 'Out of time: the case for nationalizing the fossil fuel industry', *People's Policy Project*, 20 June. https://www.peoplespolicyproject.org/wp-content/uploads/2020/06/OutofTime.pdf

Roston, E., Kaufman, L., and Warren, H. (2022) 'How the world's richest people are driving global warming', *Bloomberg News*, 24 March. https://www.bloomberg.com/graphics/2022-wealth-carbon-emissions-inequality-powers-world-climate/

Roth, K.H. (2022) 'The great fear of 2020', *Endnotes*. https://endnotes.org.uk/other_texts/en/karl-heinz-roth-the-great-fear-of-2020

Sassen, S. (2016) 'A massive loss of habitat: new drivers for migration', *Sociology of Development*, 22: 204–233.

Schwartzman, D. (1996) 'Solar communism', *Science & Society*, 60(3): 307–331.

Sorg, C. (2023) 'Failing to plan is planning to fail: toward an expanded notion of democratically planned postcapitalism', *Critical Sociology*, 49(3): 475–493.

Sotiris, P. (2020a) 'Against Agamben: is a democratic biopolitics possible?', *Critical Legal Thinking,* 14 March. https://criticallegalthinking.com/2020/05/25/democratic-biopolitics-revisited-a-response-to-a-critique/

Sotiris, P. (2020b) 'Thinking beyond the lockdown: on the possibility of a democratic biopolitics', *Historical Materialism,* 28(3): 3–38.

Terranova, T. (2009) 'Another life: the nature of political economy in Foucault's genealogy of biopolitics', *Theory, Culture & Society,* 26(6): 234–65.

Tooze, A. (2021) *Shutdown: How Covid Shook the World Economy.* New York: Viking.

Toscano, A. (2016) 'After October, before February: figures of dual power', in S. Zizek (ed) *An American Utopia: Dual Power and the Universal Army,* London: Verso, pp 211–242.

Toscano, A. (2020) 'Last resorts: jottings on the pandemic state', *Crisis & Critique,* 7(3): 387–397.

Watson, B. (1971) 'Counter-planning on the shop floor', *Radical America,* 5(3): 77–85.

Wróbel, S. (2020) 'Biocommunism and its role as it overcomes biopolitics', *Polish Sociological Review,* 211: 301–321.

Zizek, S. (2015) 'We can't address the EU refugee crisis without confronting global capitalism', *In These Times,* 9 September. https://inthesetimes.com/article/slavoj-zizek-european-refugee-crisis-and-global-capitalism

6

Planning as an Art of Government

Jan Groos

What governmentality is possible as a strictly, intrinsically, and autonomously socialist governmentality? In any case, we know only that if there is a really socialist governmentality, then it is not hidden within socialism and its texts. It cannot be deduced from them. It must be invented.

(Foucault, 2008, p 94)

Introduction

This chapter proposes to incorporate the analytical lens of 'arts of government' (Foucault, 2008, pp 27–50; Lemke, 2012, p 102ff; Dean, 2010, p 96) into the contemporary debate around democratic economic planning in order to interrogate some of the grounding upon which the debate itself is taking place and hopefully provide new pathways for its further development. After an introduction, the first part, 'Harbinger of truth', demonstrates the analytical usefulness of the approach by carving out a crucial omission in the way the planning debate[1] attends to one of its central themes: the market. The second part, 'A government of things', then highlights the usefulness for a constructive effort beyond the well-worn paths of the debate by providing possible starting points that might serve as fruitful ground for a collective development around planning as an art of government.

Why planning as an art of government?

By proposing an engagement with the debate around democratic economic planning as an art of government this chapter leaves the narrow corridor that the debate around comprehensive models of economic planning confines itself to in order to provide a perspective from which the debate itself can be critically examined. This critical engagement does not aim to prove individual positions as wrong and is not written against works that stay within the canonical corridor, the bread and butter of the debate, so to speak. It argues, however, that if one wants to provide comprehensive alternatives to capitalism and (neo)liberal governmentality, and this should be an underlying goal, a decisive broadening of scope as well as a critical inspection of foundational assumptions is needed in order to come to a position from which the role of democratic (economic) planning for a socialist governmentality (Foucault, 2008, p 94) can be discussed.

For this broadening of perspective the chapter draws on Foucault's 1978 and 1979 lectures on governmentality at the Collège de France (Foucault, 2007, 2008) and the rich body of work that has flourished around it (Tellmann, 2009; Terranova, 2009; Dean, 2010; Bröckling, Krasmann and Lemke, 2011; Lemke, 2012, 2021; Biebricher, 2019). In these lectures, Foucault engages intensely with the development of liberal governmentality from the mid-18th century onwards and its evolution into neoliberal governmentality in the 20th century. He describes this governmentality as an 'ensemble formed by institutions, procedures, analyses and reflections, calculations, and tactics that allow the exercise of this very specific, albeit very complex, power that has the population as its target, political economy as its major form of knowledge, and apparatuses of security as its essential technical instrument' (Foucault, 2007, p 108). Here, already, the mentioning of political economy as the major form of knowledge of (neo)liberal governmentality should make everyone interested in the planning debate prick up their ears. For it is no coincidence that socialists were challenged in the infamous socialist calculation debate to prove their worthiness in the field of truth-telling that is commonly called economics. Contrary to other forms in the exercise of power, (neo)liberal governmentality functions not primarily through discipline or sovereignty – which, as Foucault emphasizes, most definitely continue to exist in parallel (Foucault, 2007, p 107ff), but through the (biopolitical) government of populations (p 105). The knowledge produced within the field of political economy plays a crucial role in providing an indicator of measure and thereby also a limiting function for this specific form of government. With the advent of political economy as an art of government in the 18th century those who did not respect the supposedly natural qualities of the economy now ran the risk of being seen as a 'clumsy, inadequate, government that does not do the proper thing' (Foucault, 2008, p 10). The proper thing, as the physiocrat Quesnay marks it as one of the first, was a government as 'economic government' (Foucault, 2007, p 95; see also Quesnay, 1767). It might be one of the original tragedies of the debate that the socialist contenders that took part in the initial socialist calculation debate apparently likewise did not want to be seen as clumsy in the eyes of this divine judge – the economy – and therefore marched on proudly proclaiming 'We can do it!', without critically inspecting the ground they were marching on. The long history of neoclassical socialist economics (Lange and Taylor, 1938; Hahnel, 2021) is just one result of this mismatched rivalry.

When proposing to incorporate a perspective of planning as an art of government, it is important to note that the Foucauldian notion of government is to be understood in a broad sense. It goes beyond a definition that places the power to govern exclusively within the sphere of *the* government in terms of the state and its institutions. Instead, government refers broadly to all social fields, technologies and individual forms of action that serve the (self-)government of people by themselves and others. Such government includes 'a variety of techniques and forms of knowledge, that seeks to shape conduct by working through desires, aspirations, interests and beliefs, for definite but shifting ends' (Dean, 2010, p 267). As will be elaborated on in the closing part of this chapter the notion of a 'government of things' (Lemke, 2021) allows to expand this definition of government to include a relational materialist perspective that takes into account the more-than-human in a non-anthropocentric way, a project worth pursuing given the notorious anthropocentrism the planning debate suffers from (Mohammed, in this volume).

Incorporating a perspective of arts of government into the planning debate, then, means to examine the rationales that are brought forward to justify the use of certain techniques and practices over others, to investigate the knowledge formations they rely on, which truth claims they assert, which modes of government and technologies (of power) they propose in order to govern their subjects and, finally, how they conceptualize these subjects (Bröckling, 2017, p 45ff). Such a process of reflection around planning as an art of government is all the more important, since the history of state socialism has shown that there is indeed the possibility within nominally socialist countries to engage in a liaison with state administration in the form of a police state as well as to produce socialisms that are connected up with liberal governmentality (Foucault, 2008, p 91ff). This observation, contemporary at the time, led Foucault to claim that socialism does not yet provide an intrinsically socialist governmentality – as quoted at the start of this chapter –a claim that he doubled down on with the provocative statement: '[W]hat socialism lacks is not so much a theory of the state as a governmental reason, the definition of what a governmental rationality would be in socialism, that is to say, a reasonable and calculable measure of the extent, modes, and objectives of governmental action' (p 91).

There is a strong argument to make that Foucault's statement exaggerates this lack and that there is instead a rich residuum of prefigurative practices, historical experiences and experimental politics in general that might serve as a place of origin for the development of alternative socialist governmentalities. However, looking at the current debate around democratic economic planning through the lens of alternative arts of government shows that Foucault's provocative assertion is not without basis.

Harbinger of truth

Since a comprehensive comparative analysis of different models is well beyond the scope of this chapter, the usefulness of the proposed analytical lens of planning as an art of government will be illustrated by example of a central theme within the debate: the market.

Even though the rejection of market socialism and the insistence that market forces need to be overcome can be seen as one of the constituting elements of the debate around democratic economic planning, crucial functions of markets within (neo)liberal governmentality (Terranova, 2009; Tellmann, 2017; Biebricher, 2019) are still not sufficiently taken into account within the debate at large. When it comes to the role of markets, many approaches reference the Hayekian information problem (Hayek, 1945) and describe markets primarily as a distributed mechanism of information processing,[2] followed by an appeal to develop alternative mechanisms that would be able to provide this function for a socialist economy. While some approaches then emphasize the role of technological developments to do the job (Saros, 2014; Dapprich, 2022; Grünberg, 2023), others point towards the need for partial local autonomy in order to address the Hayekian 'information problem' (Adaman and Devine, 1997; Heyer, in this volume; Platenkamp forthcoming). However, while this aspect of markets certainly should be taken into account, it would nonetheless be a crucial mistake to think that this would constitute the most difficult part in overcoming 'the market' as a central mechanism of societal organization.

Using the analytical lens of alternative arts of government highlights a very different challenge for any approach that seeks to provide comprehensive alternatives to the market, namely its role as a 'site of veridiction' and production of truth (Foucault, 2008, p 32). In neoliberal governmentality, the market not only restricts sovereign power by defining a realm of exchange in which the government should not intervene – this demarcation would be its central function in liberal governmentality – but instead implements (market) competition as a structuring principle not only of the economy, but of society as a whole (Foucault, 2008, p 101ff). This includes an inversion of the market–state relation with regard to who evaluates whom. In neoliberalism, the market becomes a locus of truth about what constitutes good or bad government, thereby creating 'a state under the supervision of the market rather than a market supervised by the state' (Foucault, 2008, p 116). Looking at the market as 'a regime of truth and a technology of power' (Terranova, 2009) in such a way brings up very different challenges for anyone interested in providing comprehensive alternatives to its functions. It shifts the debate from discussing a problem of production and distribution and its derivatives, information and calculation, to the question of the production of truth as part of a rationale of government. This is where the self-immunizing, quasi-divine nucleus at the heart of neoliberal ideology comes into sight (Brown, 2016; 2017). It is simply not possible to refute the market in its function as a producer of truth 'through revealing it as a lie, a cover-up, or hypocrisy' (Brown, 2016, p 16), since, for neoliberals, it is precisely the fact that the truth of the market escapes human judgement that makes markets such a supreme mechanism in the first place. Otherwise, we could have had democratic economic planning from the start. The important question then becomes: Does the debate around democratic economic planning succeed in providing alternative rationales of government on this level of abstraction? What are the alternatives to the market *as a site of veridiction*?

At first glance the answer seems simple. Is it not obvious that it should be the democratic will of the people that takes the place of the market as a site of veridiction? Why all the fuss? We are talking about *democratic* planned economies after all. That of course is true, but simply stating 'we will do it democratically' is not a sufficient answer when faced with what might, in reference to the information problem, be called the veridiction problem. For if we 'do it democratically' the question arises: based on what? And this question 'Based on what?' is not so much geared towards the practical design of the democratic process, which in itself is its own huge field of inquiry, but it instead asks for the points of reference of such processes themselves. If 'the market' currently serves as a reference point for politicians of all kinds of persuasion to say 'no' to the demands of the populus, what then are the reference points within models for democratic planned economies to say 'no' (the 'yes' is obviously the easy part)?[3] What are the 'signals of truth' in a democratic planned economy, if market prices are not supposed to provide this function? Here, two important elements come into sight that form the double Achilles' heel of the planning debate: first, the notoriously difficult field of (e)valuation[4] and limitation and, second, the equally difficult question of subject. It is the somewhat daring assertion of this chapter that the canonical core of the planning debate (see the Introduction of this volume; also Sorg and Groos, 2025) does not yet provide an intrinsic alternative logic for the former[5] – a socialist governmental rationality if you will – and, therefore, frequently falls back to problematic notions of the latter to cover up this gap.

In the following, two examples from the planning debate will serve to make this argument more comprehensible. When focusing the following critique on aspects within the models developed by Laibman and Devine/Adaman it is because they can be seen as some of the most advanced models within the field (Heyer, in this volume). It is because they *do not* rely on neoclassical economics and *do* reflect on the need for multicriteria assessment based on qualitative *and* quantitative data within decisively *political* processes, that they are absolutely worth engaging with for further development.

In this spirit of comradery critique, let us first turn to an example in which elements of evaluation, limitation and subject come together to form a core concept within David Laibman's model of 'multilevel democratic iterative coordination' (MDIC). This core concept is called the 'collective morale function' (Laibman, 2011; 2020) and it is Laibman's attempt to solve a notorious problem around truth-telling distilled from historical experiences of centralized planning in the Soviet Union, including the internal reform processes starting in the 1960s (Ellman, 2014). For even though the question of markets as sites of veridiction is generally neglected within the debate, the relationship between truth and government is nothing new to the literature on socialist planning. On the contrary it is the history of failed government–truth relations in the form of so-called perverse incentives that stipulates a continuous engagement with incentive design literature within the debate (Laibman, 2011; Hahnel, 2021, p 141ff) with substantial consequences for the way in which many of the authors think about the fundamental design of the models they propose. And even though this specific government–truth relation does not operate on the same layer as the notion of markets as sites of veridiction,[6] it can nonetheless serve as a carrier to carve out a crucial omission within the planning debate when it comes to providing a rationale of government that is able to produce alternative *relations* within this triangle of subjects, government and truth.

The problem the 'collective morale function' seeks to solve is brought about through a specific constellation. Based on the correct assertion, that centralized planning will not be able to produce the normative goal of (partial) worker autonomy nor effectively address the 'information problem' brought forward by Hayek (1945), Laibman proposes a form of planning that is neither fully centralized nor fully decentralized (Laibman, 2002). In this multilevel planning, only broad indicators are set centrally so that the socialist enterprises have significant freedom to fill in the plans in a more decentralized bottom-up manner through a process of repeated coordination that flows up as well as down in an iterative manner – hence the name 'multilevel democratic iterative coordination'. Now, the problems arise with the specific way in which Laibman goes on to conceptualize the relation between collective interests embodied through a democratic centre and the more narrow interests of the local enterprises. Derived from the analysis of historical experiences in the context of authoritarian central planning, Laibman points out a specific tension between these layers. This tension manifested in so-called perverse incentives, subsequent hoarding of resources and widespread misinformation, both when it comes to truthfully reporting capacities from the enterprises upward as well as regarding realistic targets issued by the central planning bureau (Ellman, 2014). This leads

Laibman to the assumption that the problem at hand is one of installing correct incentive structures so that the enterprises communicate truthful information and strive for a maximum outcome in efficiency. For Laibman both of these goals – truthful information and maximum ambition regarding production capacity – are to be achieved without resorting to authoritarian force – neither authoritarian planning nor market forces (which are also authoritarian, even though indirectly). The solution he then proposes exemplifies central contradictions in the way democratic economic planning is thought of within the canonical corridor of the planning debate and is therefore illustrative of the need to step out of this corridor in order to question the ground upon which the debate currently takes place.

Laibman proposes a multifactorial measure of enterprise success, a 'socialist rate of return' (Laibman, 2020, p 519), that is in part based on quantitative data of productivity and efficiency, but crucially also on qualitative data in the form of evaluations by teams of various stakeholders that assess the enterprise with regard to ecological effects, cooperation with other enterprises, internal solidarity and so on. He then introduces incentives in the form of bonuses that are paid out on top of a base income for those enterprises that (1) plan ambitiously along the lines of the 'socialist rate of return', and (2) are subsequently able to fulfil these ambitious plans. The goal that enterprises should plan as ambitiously as possible is central to Laibman's concept, since he generally commits to the challenge on the grounds of efficiency as posed in the initial social calculation debate. He wants to show that socialist economies can be as *efficient* as capitalist ones, with the addition that what they should be efficient in is defined along the lines of the 'socialist rate of return' and not along the lines of mere profit defined as surplus value in the form of capital. This is precisely where the argument runs into problems, which Laibman can only escape from with a considerable amount of mental gymnastics and the accompanying bag of assumptions. The crux is that the monetary incentives in the form of bonuses that Laibman proposes are tied to successfully fulfilling a *self-defined* hypothetical possible maximum. However, if the enterprise itself determines what counts as the most ambitious plan, how is it then guaranteed that this actually corresponds to a possible maximum instead of a lower target that can be fulfilled easily in order to get the bonus without much effort? Laibman himself recognizes this as a problem: '[I]f enterprises are assumed to have unlimited capacity to falsify information about their local resources and possibilities, they would be able to claim any level of achievement, […] and this would undermine the entire effort to create a system of evaluation and reward within multilevel planning' (p 524). It is easy to see that performance-based bonuses and self-determined targets do not correspond well with one another. What then does Laibman propose to get out of this trap? Tight surveillance of the workforce and detailed tracking of every resource, coupled to target goals oriented towards averages within a given sector?[7] Competition based on hard constraints – a euphemism for going bankrupt when competing in a market place? Mutual effort ratings within the enterprise, conducted by your work mates to ensure everybody is giving his/her/their best, as proposed in Parecon? Fortunately, it is none of the previously mentioned, since they are all horrible in their own way. However, unfortunately Laibman's approach is no more convincing either, even though it rests on much more desirable imaginaries than, for example, ideas of comprehensive control through surveillance.

First of all, Laibman states that the preconditions for the successful implementation of his model do not (yet) exist, while simultaneously *not* engaging with the question of how they can be brought about: 'The extent to which a system of central–decentral planning (MDIC) can work now, without succumbing to the distortions imposed by unprincipled self-interest [...] may be regarded as an open question' (p 526). Ignoring this 'open question', he continues by simply assuming that the preconditions for the model 'are sufficiently present' (p 526). What follows is the use of graphics, formulas, and tables to make a simple point: The workers will give their absolute best, because they will want to give their absolute best, because everything else would be frustrating. Or, in Laibman's words: 'This [the MDIC] is a world in which morale matters' (p 526). It is important to highlight the inherent contradiction built into this constellation: The 'collective morale function' *simultaneously* assumes that one would need monetary incentives to motivate the subjects taking part, but that these subjects would not be incentivized to report falsely by these monetary incentives, because reporting falsely about one's capacities would undermine the collective morale within the enterprise (p 533). Reporting correctly about the maximum possible performance, so goes the assumption, is so motivating that this is an effective constraint against both overshooting in the form of unattainable goals as well as setting goals that are too low. The circular logic behind this 'principled optimizing behaviour' (p 529) asserts that self-interest will no longer be a problem. However, and this is a crucial detail, the reason for why it will not be a problem anymore is not that self-interest has vanished, but that it will supposedly be in the intrinsic self-interest of the worker collective to push for the maximum. In Laibman's 'collective morale function', self-interest and optimality are one and the same. Curiously, however, this is *not* because of the monetary incentive, since the bonuses would – under 'unprincipled' conditions, meaning every person not living up to this moral standard – incentivize to report lower goals in order to reach the goal more easily (and this would lead to distortions as experienced in the Soviet Union). The reason the 'collective morale function' assumes for why people push for the maximum is: *out of principle*. Hence the name 'principled optimizing behavior'. A certain separation of thought and a specific temporal chronology are crucial here, since the whole concept collapses if not imagined in the proper order. Workers will *first* have to become 'principled' in order to *then* still report truthfully even though monetary incentives are in place that would incentivize subjects suffering from 'unprincipled self-interest' to do otherwise. This truly is 'a world in which morale matters' (p 526).

Now, my argument is not that Laibman is necessarily too optimistic about the general potential of humans to act 'principled', but that the way in which the model is set up is inconsistent in bringing about the right circumstances for such behaviour. Arguably it is precisely the elaborate continuation of reform-socialist thought – a thought still deeply rooted in narrow questions of economic efficiency – that leads into the contradictory constellation that Laibman proposes. It is a constellation that reproduces (a socialist form of) wage labour as a fundamental social relation and that still relies on economic incentives to steer the behaviour of its subjects while at the same time expecting these subjects to behave in their truth-telling as well as with regard to their work motivation as if the underlying coercive element of this relation would not exist. It is this inherent contradiction that is insightful with regard to the rationales of government that might inform a socialist governmentality. If socialists want to overcome economic power in the form of mute compulsion (Mau, 2023) by providing everybody with unconditional access to everything that is needed for a good life, any economically incentivized scheme of mechanism design quickly loses its potency. Since the threat of a miserable existence is not within the toolkit of socialism – otherwise it would not be socialism – a socialist governmentality would have to provide alternative rationales of government as a basis for the mobilization of structured human activity towards collectively decided ends. For the planning debate this means that it will have to go beyond reform-socialist thought that still governs with carrots and sticks in the name of efficiency and instead ask how a mode of (re)production would need to be set up in order to bring about the *alternative relations* that are able to carry this weight in the absence of coercion.

The distinction between principled and unprincipled self-interest and the inherent assumption about the need for a specific type of human material in order to make one's model work is not unique to Laibman's approach. While Laibman mostly refrains from directly addressing the question of subject, but instead talks about certain qualities a worker collective should have, Pat Devine frequently refers to the layer of subject in his work. 'Participatory Planning Through Negotiated Coordination', the model initially proposed by Devine (1988) and later developed further in tandem with his collaborator Fikret Adaman (Adaman and Devine, 1997), extensively highlights the need for widespread participation and the involvement of as many affected actors as possible. At first glance this model seems to allow for a high variety of actors to be integrated into the planning process. Yet, on the level of subjects the plurality of the model collapses into an implicit imperative to become a specific subject that Devine imagines to be 'autonomous, self-activating and self-governing' (Devine, 1988, p 208). This normative grounding creates statements that might equally stem from a self-help book for future CEOs: 'The challenge of having to take responsibility for decisions that make a difference is at the same time an opportunity for personal development. It is part of the process of becoming fully human' (Devine, 1988, p 158).

Arguably, this normative grounding in which only the active and autonomous, those who successfully govern themselves and take responsibility for decisions, are thought of as on the right track, or becoming 'fully human', should not be the unquestioned grounding on which to base further development around democratic planning (Lutosch, in this volume; Mohammed, in this volume). The demand to be an active, autonomous, participating subject has been pushed upon us by neoliberal governmentality for at least 30–40 years now (Bröckling, 2015) and an uncritical relapse to notions of a 'society made up of autonomous, self-activating subjects' (Devine, 1988, p 248) does not sufficiently step out of this already omnipresent way of governing subjects today.

While a certain strategic pragmatism concerning real-life politics is called for when it comes to demands in the here and now, the *theoretical* strand of the planning debate should not allow itself to ignore such questions around its own grounding. As this volume demonstrates, there are many legitimate requests knocking at the doors of the canonical models, from the inclusion of the sphere of reproduction (Lutosch, in this volume; Sorg, 2023), incorporating degrowth perspectives (Hofferberth, Durand and Schmelzer, in this volume) to planning beyond nature/culture dichotomies and ideas of human sovereignty over nature (Mohammed, in this volume). When picking up on these requests, it is insufficient to think that one can simply attach these matters to the existing models of democratic economic planning without first examining the underlying assumptions that are built into these models and ask whether they can adequately accommodate the matters one intends to integrate. Turned into a positive, one might say that the debate at large has matured up to a point at which it should leave the confines of its canonical corridor. In order to do so, the debate needs to develop frameworks that not only move beyond productivist races from the past, but shift the outlook of what it is we should focus on when engaging with the question of how to organize the reproduction of societies in a desirable way. This task, however, is not appropriately framed by the label socialist *calculation* debate anymore. Not, because it would not involve calculation, which it surely will, but because calculation ultimately is not the central issue at stake. The central issue at stake is to develop modes of (re)production that allow us to *relate* differently and the canonical models run the risk of falling short precisely with regard to this central task when not being confronted with their implicit rationales of government. There is a need for a decisive broadening of the debate to include a reflection not only of the techniques and practices proposed in comprehensive models of democratic planning, but also of the underlying knowledge formations, implicit subject positions and truth claims they assert. Herein, a perspective of planning as an art of government can be a useful tool of analysis, but it can also be developed into a constructive framework for thinking about possible alternative pathways. The following closing section will outline some tentative starting points for such a creative construction around planning as an art of government. At this point these can only be hinted towards in a cursory way and will have to be further investigated elsewhere for a better understanding of their capacity.

Outlook: towards a government of things as sociometabolic planning

When engaging with the question of what a constructive approach towards planning as an art of government might look like, a relational materialist interpretation of a 'government of things' (Lemke, 2021; Lemke and Groos, 2022) might serve as a fruitful starting point. It provides useful elements for the development of environmental forms of government that go beyond the inherent anthropocentrism of the planning debate and allow to address the nexus between truth, agency and relationality that will have to be reworked in order to eventually come to alternative rationales of government based on alternative modes of veridiction and production of truth.

As Lemke (2021, p 85ff) points out, there are two different notions commonly associated with the government of things. First, there is the notion of 'things' inscribed in Auguste Comte's idea of 'replacing the government of persons by the administration of things' (Comte, cited by Kafka, 2012, np).[8] This idea originated from a desire to rationalize political decision-making in order to guard against authoritarian and arbitrary forms of rule, and it served as a technocratic utopian vision in which, if one was to govern according to evidence derived from the 'nature of things' (Foucault, 2007, p 49), it would be things themselves that govern, instead of 'men'. This implies an underlying naturalized truth that would have to be respected in order to produce good government. Notably, for Comte, the notion of 'things' was a broad one that superseded mere objects, but included nature, customs and culture, as well as the relations between these 'things' and men (Lemke, 2021, p 87; Kafka, 2012, np). This broad notion was based on the idea of things as the *subjects* of government with 'things' governing human affairs and not vice versa (Lemke, 2021, p 87).

Second, there is the famous Marxist notion of the 'administration of things' (Engels, 2011, p 79) that turned this relation on its head, making 'things' the *objects* of government (Lemke, 2021, p 88; Kafka, 2012, np). Crucially, this implies a change in the underlying notion of truth as well. It is no longer an assumed nature of things that has to be respected in order to provide an 'economic government' (Foucault, 2007, p 33), but it is the 'universal awareness' of the human subjects that would result in a conscious management of 'things' (Foucault, 2014, p 15; Lemke, 2021, p 88). Not only has this notion of things, brought forward in 20th-century Marxism, a much more narrow horizon than the more encompassing thingness of Comte (Lemke, 2021, p 88), but it also implies an assumed possibility of full intelligibility and control in the relation between things and 'men' as well as a depoliticized notion of a supposedly only functional rule over 'things'. Historically, within economic planning in statist Marxism of the 20th century, this notion of 'administration of things' has given rise to extractivist and productivist relations towards nature, seen as a disposable object and resource (Bahro, 1978).

Planning as an art of government, however, should neither base itself on technocratic ideas of quasi-objective control along the lines of an assumed 'natural' truth, nor should it try to reinstantiate the sovereign individual as the locus of truth through 'universal awareness' and ideas of full intelligibility. Instead, a relational materialist approach towards a *government of things* allows to approach planning as an art of government in a way that combines a broad notion of 'thingness' with a focus on relations – between humans and the more-than-human alike – without losing sight of the *political* nature of these relations, nor succumbing to scientific positivism as an ultimate grounding. Such an alternative governmentality would no longer have the population as its main target, but the *modes and quality* of relations itself, would rely on political ecology as its major form of knowledge, and indeed make heavy use of 'apparatuses of security as its essential technical instrument', albeit understood as unconditional and broad infrastructures of existential security and public luxury (Monbiot, 2023) that are accessible and free of charge for everybody. In this, a relational materialism is also a materialist relationalism (Lemke, 2021, p 192), since the desired alternative relationality can only come about on the basis of unconditional material security for all.

Instead of starting with an assumption of scarcity in the face of competing ends followed by a narrow focus on questions of efficiency and ending up with an assumed need to discipline its subjects[9] through incentive mechanisms and use of economic power, such an alternative governmentality would start with the question of what is needed in order to provide for *qualitatively different relations* – between humans as well as between humans and more-than-human nature – and develop alternative notions of democratic planning going from there. Such a focus that puts the quality of 'Beziehungsweisen' (modes of relation) (Adamczak, 2017)[10] first helps to avoid the theoretical trap of overemphasizing the individual or the collective and brings into sight an alternative mode of government that is decisively *environmental*.

Lemke describes a more-than-human form of government that he calls 'environmentality' (2021, pp 168–190) in which 'nonhuman organisms, geological forces, and technological artifacts are neither marginalized and ignored nor conceived of as passive and inert; rather, their "doings" are actively co-opted and captured for a diverse set of political, ecological, and economic strategies' (p 143). This is a crucial shift in the way a government *of* things is thought of as a government *through* things, seen as part of larger ecologies that span the 'natural' and the technological alike (p 177). As the phrase 'actively co-opted' indicates, currently the quality of relations enacted in this environmentality is largely determined by the specific ways in which it is employed as part of neoliberal governmentality. Herein the capacities and potentials of more-than-human nature are recognized and utilized, both as non-human labourers and something through which government can be exercised, yet they remain within a framework of objectification of nature and processes of profit driven valorization in the form of 'natural capital' (p 186). Planning as an art of government, then, would bring forward a critique of these normative inscriptions of a *neoliberal* environmentality without rejecting modes of environmental government altogether. Developing such an alternative environmentality would, again, attend to the *quality* of the underlying relations when including the 'doings' of 'nonhuman organisms, geological forces, and technological artifacts'. This includes being conscious of the different dimensions of the metabolic rift produced by the capitalist mode of production (Saitō, 2023), namely its disruption of material flows, its spacial and temporal dimensions (p 27), and to avoid reproducing the metabolic shifts (p 29) capitalism produces by trying to escape the destructive consequences that the metabolic rift brings about.

Furthermore, developing an alternative notion of environmentality is useful, since the concept of environmentality undermines the traditional distinction between *eco-logy* and *eco-nomy*, for example by bringing into sight the role that non-human labour plays within our economies today (Lemke, 2021, p 185). Overcoming this distinction, in which the economic is seen as separate from the ecological, is crucial for the development of planning as an alternative art of government. Such an approach is highly compatible with recent work around the integration of sociometabolic research into models of democratic economic planning (Planning for Entropy, 2022; Beaucaire, Saey-Volckrick and Tremblay-Pepin, 2023; Zeug et al, 2023; Heyer in this volume). The aim is to 'allow for a multidimensional analysis of interactions between nature, society, and economy by including systemic, biophysical, and politico-institutional dimensions and a diversity of accounting indicators' (Beaucaire, Saey-Volckrick and Tremblay-Pepin, 2023) thereby creating forms of response-ability (Haraway, 2016) current planning models are lacking. Including sociometabolic indicators into democratic planning would allow to address questions of scale of overall biophysical throughput (Planning for Entropy, 2022), but crucially also provide multifactorial sets of indicators that allow semi-decentralized actors to relate their actions to an overall societal and ultimately planetary context (Heyer, in this volume). While such a transparency of the material and energy use and overall biophysical throughput does not automatically lead to a change in our underlying social metabolism with nature (after all, there is plenty of life cycle analysis going on in capitalism already) and should equally not be misunderstood as indicating a 'natural truth', it does open up the possibility of mediating our social relation with nature along different lines (Zeug, 2023). However, as has been argued in this chapter, it is not enough to incorporate these expanded indicators of sociometabolic planning into the existing canon of models without at the same time addressing the need for a change in the underlying qualitative dimension of our modes of relating. The success of the former is premised on the implementation of the latter. If, for instance, forms of wage labour relations continue to exist, then conspicuous consumption will probably continue to have its place as a form of compensatory mechanism as well. If the underlying subject of democratic processes continues to be narrowly idealized along the lines of an active and autonomous self-government as a normative expectation, then the flip side of such an unquestioned subjectivization – its historically male coding, its connotation of sovereign control, implicit hierarchization and subjugation of everything that is *other* – will at some point also make itself felt.

Given the history and present of technocratic strands within the planning debate, it cannot be stressed enough that alternative environmental modes of government would have to be fundamentally distinct from notions of planning that are based on ideas of sovereign control and linear command in that they are not out for full intelligibility and deterministic control. Instead, they attend to 'qualitative properties, structural patterns, and complex relationalities' (Lemke, 2021, p 176) as carriers of a governmental practice that is not focused on targeting individual behaviour (for example, through elaborated incentive schemes). Planning as an environmental art of government would instead aim to produce the socio-techno-ecological environments that provide the concrete material conditions under which alternative forms of relation can flourish. This does not mean to erase the human from the picture. It does, however, mean to start from a perspective in which the human is always already entangled in multiple ways within ecologies that span the human, more-than-human nature and technologies alike (Hörl, 2017, pp 1–74) and to politicize these relations. Given this entanglement, simply reverting back to the autonomous subject as the nucleus of democratic planning, as the canon of comprehensive models of democratic planning currently does, is not only insufficient, but arguably blocks the development of ways of organizing the social metabolism in a *qualitatively* different manner.

Conclusion

This chapter has proposed to incorporate the analytical lens of 'arts of government' (Foucault, 2008, pp 27–50) into the contemporary debate around democratic economic planning. In this, it has highlighted the 'politics of truth' (Foucault, 2007) inscribed in the field of political economy as something that should be of central concern to those involved in the debate but that has been neglected so far. The 'collective morale function', a central building block in one of the most advanced models for democratic planning, MDIC developed by David Laibman, has served to illustrate how an analytics of arts of government can carve out crucial omissions within the way comprehensive models of democratic economic planning are currently set up. In order not to simply stop at criticism, a tentative outlook has used a relational materialist approach towards a government of things to point towards possible starting points for further work on planning as an art of government.

Notes

[1] For reasons of simplification the generic formula 'the planning debate' is used to refer to a debate broadly concerned with what has come to be known as the 'socialist calculation debate' and related questions regarding the feasibility of democratic economic planning, both in its historical as well as contemporary form.

[2] Which in itself is a misinterpretation of Hayek's position, as Morozov points out (Morozov, 2019, p 44ff).

[3] Note that this question equally applies to any form of 'self-governance' and is not at all tied to a split between some who govern and some who are governed.

[4] It is beyond the scope of this chapter to go into the ongoing discussions around value form theory that obviously relate to the question of (e)valuation. See for example: Murray, 2016.

[5] Note that this does not mean that there are not any proposals for how to address the question of valuation, but that these (labour time as 'objective' measure, opportunity costs, effort ratings and so on) fall short in terms of providing an intrinsic alternative logic.

[6] One merely addresses a game of cat and mouse derived from the 'principal agent' problem (Adaman and Devine, 1997), the other asks for collective processes for the production of truth.

[7] How would comparison based on averages come about? It would either have to rely on high degrees of standardization, which is not necessarily desirable and somewhat puts the wagon before the horse, or it would, ironically, imply a form of perfect competition for each and every use value to allow for the comparison between socialist enterprises. Furthermore, since there would probably be organized institutional bodies for different sectors, such incentive structures would incentivize cartel-like collusion between producers.

[8] While often attributed to Saint-Simon, Kafka (2012, np) points towards Auguste Comte as the originator.

[9] Including the disciplining through freedom in a realm of deliberately produced insecurity, as done in liberalism (Foucault, 2007, p 48).

[10] The use of the concept of 'Beziehungsweisen' in the context of arts of government is not part of Adamczak's body of theory. On the contrary, Adamczak is sceptical about the broadened understanding and use of the word 'government' in emancipatory contexts (Adamczak and Groos, 2022).

Bibliography

Adaman, F. and Devine, P. (1997) 'On the economic theory of socialism', *New Left Review*, 221: 54–80.

Adamczak, B. (2017) *Beziehungsweise Revolution: 1917, 1968 und kommende*. Berlin: Suhrkamp.

Adamczak, B. and Groos, J. (2022) 'S02E25 – Bini Adamczak zu Beziehungsweisen', *Future Histories*. https://www.futurehistories.today/episoden-blog/s02/e25-bini-adamczak-zu-beziehungsweisen/

Bahro, R. (1978) *The Alternative in Eastern Europe*. London: NLB.

Beaucaire, K., Saey-Volckrick, J. and Tremblay-Pepin, S. (2023) 'Integration of approaches to social metabolism into democratic economic planning models', *Studies in Political Economy*, 104(2): 73–92. doi: 10.1080/07078552.2023.2234753.

Biebricher, T. (2019) *The Political Theory of Neoliberalism*. Stanford: Stanford University Press.

Bröckling, U. (2015) *The Entrepreneurial Self: Fabricating a New Type of Subject*. Los Angeles: SAGE.

Bröckling, U. (2017) *Gute Hirten führen sanft: über Menschenregierungskünste*. Suhrkamp Taschenbuch Wissenschaft 2217. Erste Auflage, Originalausgabe. Berlin: Suhrkamp.

Bröckling, U., Krasmann, S. and Lemke, T. (eds) (2011) *Governmentality: Current Issues and Future Challenges*. London: Routledge.

Brown, W. (2016) *Neoliberalism in Marxist and Foucauldian Frames*. http://www.sussex.ac.uk/sussexasiacentre/newsandevents/events/pastevents?id=37928

Brown, W. (2017) *Undoing the Demos: Neoliberalism's Stealth Revolution*. New York: Zone Books.

Dapprich, J.P. (2020) 'Rationality and distribution in the socialist economy', PhD Thesis. http://theses.gla.ac.uk/id/eprint/81793

Dapprich, J.P. (2022) 'Optimal planning with consumer feedback: a simulation of a socialist economy', *Review of Political Economy*, 35(4): 1–21. doi: 10.1080/09538259.2021.2005367.

Dean, M. (2010) *Governmentality: Power and Rule in Modern Society*. London/Thousand Oaks, CA: SAGE.

Devine, P. (1988) *Democracy and Economic Planning: The Political Economy of a Self-governing Society*. Cambridge: Polity Press.

Ellman, M. (2014) *Socialist Planning* (3rd edn). Cambridge: Cambridge University Press. doi: 10.1017/CBO9781139871341.

Engels, F. (2011 [1880]) 'Socialism: utopian and scientific.', in N. Capaldi and G. Lloyd (eds) *The Two Narratives of Political Economy*, Hoboken, NJ: John Wiley & Sons, Inc, pp 447–465. doi: 10.1002/9781118011690.ch25.

Foucault, M. (2007) *Security, Territory, Population: Lectures at the Collège de France, 1977–78*. Edited by M. Senellart, F. Ewald, A. Fontana et al. Basingstoke/New York: Palgrave Macmillan.

Foucault, M. (2008) *The Birth of Biopolitics: Lectures at the Collège de France, 1978–79. Lectures at the Collège de France*. Edited by M. Senellart. Basingstoke/New York: Palgrave Macmillan.

Foucault, M. (2014) *On the Government of the Living: Lectures at the Collège de France, 1979–80*. Edited by M. Senellart. Basingstoke/New York: Palgrave Macmillan.

Foucault, M., Lotringer, S. and Hochroth, L. (2007) *The Politics of Truth*. Semiotext(e) foreign agents series. Los Angeles, CA: Semiotext(e).

Grünberg, M. (2023) 'The planning daemon: future desire and communal production', *Historical Materialism*, 31(4): 1–45. doi: 10.1163/1569206x-bja10001.

Hahnel, R. (2021) *Democratic Economic Planning*. Routledge Frontiers of Political Economy. London: Routledge.

Haraway, D.J. (2016) *Staying with the Trouble: Making Kin in the Chthulucene*. Durham, NC: Duke University Press.

Hayek, F.A. (1945) 'The use of knowledge in society', *The American Economic Review*, 35(4): 519–530.

Hörl, E. and Burton, J. (eds) (2017) *General Ecology: The New Ecological Paradigm*. London: Bloomsbury.

Kafka, B. (2012) 'The administration of things: a genealogy', *West 86th*. https://www.west86th.bgc.bard.edu/articles/the-administration-of-things-a-genealogy/

Laibman, D. (2002) 'Democratic coordination: towards a working socialism for the new century', *Science & Society*, 66(1): 116–129. doi: 10.1521/siso.66.1.116.21016.

Laibman, D. (2011) 'Incentive design, iterative planning and local knowledge in a maturing socialist economy', *International Critical Thought*, 1(1): 35–56. doi: 10.1080/21598282.2011.566039.

Laibman, D. (2020) 'Incentives, optimization, and democratic planning: a socialist primer', *Science & Society*, 84(4): 510–535. doi: 10.1521/siso.2020.84.4.510.

Lange, O. and Taylor, F.M. (1938) *On the Economic Theory of Socialism*. Edited by B.E. Lippincott. Minneapolis: University of Minnesota Press.

Lemke, T. (2012) *Foucault, Governmentality, and Critique*. New York: Routledge.

Lemke, T. (2021) *The Government of Things: Foucault and the New Materialism's*. New York: NYU Press.

Lemke, T. and Groos, J. (2022) 'S02E36 – Thomas Lemke zum Regieren der Dinge', *Future Histories*. https://www.futurehistories.today/episoden-blog/s02/e36-thomas-lemke-zum-regieren-der-dinge/

Mau, S. (2023) *Mute Compulsion: A Marxist Theory of the Economic Power of Capital*. London: Verso Books.

Monbiot, G. (2023) 'Private Suffizienz – Öffentlicher Luxus', in Communia and BUNDjugend (eds) *Öffentlicher Luxus*, Berlin: Karl Dietz Verlag, pp 40–51.

Morozov, E. (2019) 'Digital socialism? The calculation debate in the age of big data', *New Left Review*, 116/117: 33–67.

Murray, P. (2016) *The Mismeasure of Wealth: Essays on Marx and Social Form*. Historical materialism book series 126. Leiden/Boston: Brill.

Planning for Entropy (2022) 'Democratic economic planning, social metabolism and the environment', *Science & Society*, 86(2): 291–313. doi: 10.1521/siso.2022.86.2.291.

Quesnay, F. (1767) *Maximes Générales du Gouvernement Économique d'un Royaume Agricole*. Edited by D. Diderot and J. le Rond d'Alembert, Briasson, pp 271–276.

Saitō, K. (2023) *Marx in the Anthropocene Towards the Idea of Degrowth Communism*. Cambridge: Cambridge University Press.

Saros, D.E. (2014) *Information Technology and Socialist Construction: The End of Capital and the Transition to Socialism*. London/New York: Routledge.

Sorg, C. (2023) 'Failing to plan is planning to fail: toward an expanded notion of democratically planned postcapitalism', *Critical Sociology*, 49(3): 475–493. doi: 10.1177/08969205221081058.

Sorg, C. and Groos, J. (2025) 'Rethinking economic planning', *Competition & Change*, special issue. doi: 10.1177/10245294241273954.

Tellmann, U. (2009) 'Foucault and the invisible economy', *Foucault Studies*, 6: 5–24. doi: 10.22439/fs.v0i0.2487.

Tellmann, U. (2017) *Life and Money: The Genealogy of the Liberal Economy and the Displacement of Politics*. New York: Columbia University Press.

Terranova, T. (2009) 'Another life: the nature of political economy in Foucault's genealogy of biopolitics', *Theory, Culture & Society*, 26(6): 234–262. doi: 10.1177/0263276409352193.

Zeug, W., Bezama, A., Thrän, D., Raquel, K. and Gan, K. (2023) 'Holistic and integrated life cycle sustainability assessment: background, methods and results from two case studies'. doi: 10.13140/RG.2.2.21800.75526.

7

Discovery Beyond Competition

Evgeny Morozov in conversation with Jan Groos

Introduction

The following is an edited transcript of an episode of the *Future Histories* podcast, run by Jan Groos.[1] Jan pursues *Future Histories* as a form of research practice and has, since starting the podcast in 2019, recorded a variety of episodes related to the topic of this book. The conversation with Evgeny Morozov is one of those. With his influential article 'Digital socialism? The calculation debate in the age of big data' (Morozov, 2019). Evgeny Morozov has played a major role in reviving the debate around questions of democratic economic planning. In the following conversation he looks beyond the often quite narrow corridor of the socialist calculation debate and stresses the importance of thinking about alternative forms of discovery and the production of the new.

The extended audio version of the conversation can be accessed through the link provided in the endnote.

Evgeny Morozov in conversation with Jan Groos

Jan Groos: There's a lecture you gave at Berkeley (Morozov, 2021) in which you state that the left has a problem with making sense of its own project and specifically that there is an 'inability of the left to make sense of digital technologies and what to do with them'. Related to that you ask: 'what should their [the left's] future be other than just defending the welfare state and insisting that they can humanize capitalism'?
I'm very much interested in both of these tasks, making sense of a possible broader project of

the left as well as making sense of the role of digital technologies for such a project. What are the main challenges surrounding both of these tasks and how are they related to each other?

Evgeny Morozov: Let's first tackle some of the problems of the left and then we can talk about technology, because I think ultimately the reason why the left has not been able to come up with a more exciting plan for how to use technology is because it got stuck in a certain intellectual and political trap. I don't think that any forward thinking about technology can emerge, before we get it out of that trap. Traditionally, the left, or at least the radical left that's not liberal Keynesianism, has inherited this idea that its task is to figure out how to deploy the tools of planning and all the associated knowledge, techniques and repertoires in order to show that the market does a suboptimal job at allocating resources. So the project of the more hardcore left has been essentially to show that you can build alternative rationalities of allocating goods and resources that would beat the rationality of the market. And to some extent it has been done with various success in places like the Soviet Union, by relying on all sorts of techniques like input-output methods and so on (Heyer, in this volume). The temptation within that tradition, of course, is to think that now that we have more tools and techniques of organizing knowledge, including those of big data and artificial intelligence, we should essentially try to recover that focus on allocating goods and resources and turbocharge it with these new techniques. And the objective is to show the neoliberals, who have shifted this debate into this knowledge-intensive dimension thanks to people like Hayek (1945) and before him Mises (1922), that they got it wrong, that the market is suboptimal and that there is a better way to do it, that we can have a better allocative rationality. This is what some of the most tech-friendly leftists imagine the task of the left to be.

I, for one, remain sceptical that this task should retain the focus that it has retained within that cohort. I don't even think that it's a mainstream focus of the left, to be honest. I think that the left that has not opted for Keynesianism has opted for some kind of Hayekian view that markets are better at organizing knowledge and that maybe we should just focus on somehow cleaning up afterwards. And the left that is still thinking about something that goes beyond the market or some kind of Keynesian multiplier is trying to recover, improve and turbocharge the toolkit of Soviet planning. The conclusion I have reached after thinking about these issues for quite a few years now is that there is so much more for the left to do with these technologies if it slightly tweaks the initial question with which it starts this operation. And the question with which it starts this operation now, I think, is still primarily focused on how to satisfy human basic needs like housing, food security and so on. There is, of course, a huge debate on the left around these questions. How do you count needs? How do you quantify them? How do you qualify them? Are they transhistorical? Are they permanent? Do they change? That's a whole debate of its own and I don't want to take any position in that debate in this conversation. But ultimately, I think as long as you retain your focus within this needs paradigm, if you will, you are not going to ask truly exciting questions that will allow you as a leftist to win over the neoliberal camp and their vision of the market. Because the neoliberal vision of the market is no longer about the allocation of goods as it was at the beginning of this debate, the so-called socialist calculation debate, where the discussion was primarily about which of the two systems does a better job of satisfying the needs of the populace, whether it's the market or whether it's the plan. I don't think that the neoliberals are still arguing about needs, even though the leftists still are. For neoliberals of the more sophisticated kind, the market became something else entirely. To them it is a way of organizing the journey into the unknown, it's a way of assuming and allowing more complexity into our social affairs. For someone like James Buchanan (1975), it's even an instrument of becoming and allowing people to discover who they really are and who they want to be. So the market is no longer about satisfying basic needs. This, I would argue, is what accounts for the buy-in and legitimacy of the market as a tool of organizing society. For the more sophisticated end of the neoliberal debate, markets are not tools of organizing economies, they are infrastructures of organizing civilization. As long as the left doesn't present an equally powerful vision of its infrastructure for organizing civilization and not just allocating raincoats and beds, it will never be able to defeat neoliberalism, at least ideationally. This is the background. Any of these points could be their own discussion, of course, but this is a brief summary of my position, without yet giving you any hint as to what this alternative project of the left might be.

I think that the fight that the left is fighting has no opponent, because the neoliberals have moved on and so probably has the general public. Much of this discussion about how you can satisfy basic needs using AI and Walmart and Amazon-like planning is a debate that the sophisticated neoliberals who have engaged with socialist calculation debate don't even need to hear. If you read somebody like Buchanan, for example, writing about computers in the early 1990s, then he will tell you point blank that computers can maybe arrive at a perfectly planned economy, but that computers will still not give you the possibility of exploring who you truly are, of providing this element of becoming and discovery like the market does. This is their argument as to why socialism cannot win. And what I'm saying is that the answer of the left with regards to big tech, AI, cloud computing and infrastructures has to provide an answer to that critique.

Jan Groos: Let us try to pick this apart a bit. I am wondering to what extent we are discussing a successful myth, a neoliberal narrative so to speak, and to what extent we are talking about an actual ability to bring about something new. Depending on what we are discussing, different solutions have to be considered and to a certain degree I'm wondering why we should accept this Hayekian myth as a starting point in the first place. It is so extremely narrow and easily disproved by pointing towards the many inventions that are not really based on monetary incentives and market competition. And when it comes to the public imaginary, it seems to me that non-market based discovery is firmly being recognized within a broader public imagination as well. The stereotypical inventor in novels, films, comics and so on, used to be more of an intrinsically motivated nerd figure and not the business type who primarily seeks profit. In this case the business type only comes into the picture afterwards, when the invention has to be brought to the market. But if this is the case and discovery is not actually the problem, because there are these intrinsically motivated nerd types, then this would mean that what we need most are alternative modes of allocating funds and democratizing investment, in order to then effectively bring about this huge potential for the new, which seems to be a somewhat inherent feature of human potential. I would argue that, on a worldwide scale, this potential is extremely untapped, not the least because venture capital, for example, has an extreme bias with regard to flowing money to their own kind regardless of actual ability and talent.

So, do you think it is a narrative that we are combating, or is it an actual ability of market competition to really bring about the new?

Evgeny Morozov: I think you are framing it in a certain way, and I'm not sure that these are the only options. I understand what you're saying, but I don't think that the focus on invention is necessarily the correct one, because the whole point of linking it to becoming is that you can also account for the consumer side of things and not just for the inventor side of things. For the consumer side neoliberals would make the argument that having the market as the infrastructure of modernity is precisely what allows you to discover what you really want, to express and eventually satisfy your needs in a way that has not been done before, because these needs were not even in your head. So you can, of course, argue that there are all sorts of ways to do it differently and, of course, there are. I'm just saying that it's not just the story of the Schumpeterian entrepreneur (Schumpeter, 1976) inventing something in the garage. I mean, there are bigger things at stake here. I think with regards to the story told by neoliberals, if you account for the consumption side and the production side and if you also account for a very important element of it, which is scale, you get a better picture. Because ultimately the story that somebody like Hayek would tell you is that, sure, you can have solidarity and altruism in a small community or in a village where everybody knows each other, but as you start scaling things up and you have urbanization and modernization, it becomes very hard to scale these mechanisms of solidarity as well. So the additional factor in the neoliberal story, of course, is the process of modernization. Now you have the cash nexus that penetrates and intermediates everything in a way that wasn't there before. It provides certain benefits of which the ability to live in a modern world, where things are discovered and where new things are produced by the behaviour of both consumers and entrepreneurs, is one. Do I think this story is partly accurate? Yes. Do I think that this is the only way in which you can account for discovery or do I think there are different possibilities of discovery, becoming and scaling up the process of modernization in a way that bypasses the market? Of course, I think it's possible to do it differently. I think the way we should approach this neoliberal story is to historicize it rather than dismiss it.

During the Cold War the central state was set up as the neoliberal punching bag alongside Keynesianism, and the neoliberals treated it as if everybody involved in government spending was more or less one step away from slipping into communism and turning into the Soviet Union. But this is, of course, a false premise. Why are these the only options? You need to go beyond this narrow frame. Then a more complex and sophisticated vision of society becomes possible, where you can have more social coordination among people, actors and institutions that were not previously in touch with each other. And these mechanisms do not require any mediation by the price mechanism and the price system. The neoliberal argument is instead that the price system is a necessary intermediary to coordinate goods and needs. The coordination I am talking about, however, can be done directly and without the aid of any market. It is done all the time, for example within the family. Parents don't set up an auction or create a market to decide who picks up the children from school. A simple exchange of information via Messenger is sufficient. It happens all the time and that should prompt some questions in our mind. What are the prerequisites and possibilities for scaling this up? How can we make these forms of coordination richer? How can we make sure that things that have previously been mediated through the market can now be mediated through other types of social coordination? Maybe they need funding and infrastructures and the kind of risk-free environments in which to develop.

Essentially the argument should not be that the market doesn't work, because it does, rather it should be that the market produces massive costs which are partially unaccounted for, even by neoliberals. And the organizing religious myth at the core of neoliberalism is that you only have two options, the market and the state, and there is nothing else in between, and if you don't use the market, you'll eventually end up with a Gulag. This, of course, is not true, but I also think the story told by neoliberals is partly correct. What is correct is that you can have a bunch of small entrepreneurs who can treat everything as a black box, because the market system and the price system allows them to. They don't need to know why there is an earthquake in Sri Lanka or why there are suddenly a bunch of refugees driving up the prices of shelter accommodation. They don't care why, they just need to know where the price will be moving and, since the price will be moving, they can take action and other counterparts can take other action. And yes, you can run society as a black box, and by running it as a black box you can essentially coordinate effectively with all sorts of, to use a term from neoclassical economics, externalities. Now the question is if we really need markets to do that or if there can be alternative infrastructures of social coordination, discovery and becoming to do the job? Once you pose the question that way, then your programme should be to develop a good answer to this aspect of the neoliberal programme and not the question of satisfying basic needs by giving everybody a coat and a bed.

Jan Groos: What are the mechanisms and infrastructures that we need to bring about in order to provide for this type of alternative coordination that is able to deliver at the level of abstraction that you are describing?

Evgeny Morozov: The question should be: why? Why do you want to do that? What is the goal? There are multiple ways to answer this question.

One goal might be that you want to generate alternative ways of generating value, right? A kind of socialist value that is not capitalist. This would mean to have people engage in social coordination with each other, whose social being, if you will, is productive in a non-capitalist way, in order to create something that can then be valorized by society as such. This would also be used for satisfying the very basic human needs that are currently satisfied through the market. This answer would point towards a more, I don't want to say economistic, but a very, let's say, social reproduction-like rationale, right?

Another goal might be that we think that, by facilitating all these ways of engagement, collaboration, coordination, and so forth, we are advancing society forward. That we think that it will result in a society that will be many steps above where it was before because, for example, you would be able to cure cancer or avoid the next COVID, and so forth.

Yet another argument could be that people should be able to form all sorts of groups and communities, pursue whatever lifestyle they want at any scale and society should facilitate that by providing infrastructures and opportunities to do so. This would obviously require a slightly different set of interventions. In neoliberal thought the market serves all these functions. It is an allocative device and an infrastructure of seeking and allowing for greater complexity of social interaction, and it's a device which, for better or worse, allows people to withdraw and form their own communities and live as they want, with all sorts of constraints and restraints. There are probably many other functions, and I think that when people on the left are posing this question, they need to understand what part of it they are trying to address. Maybe they want to address all three or four, but I'm not going to give you an answer that from the get-go is going to solve all these problems. All I can tell you is that it seems obvious to me that the basic story accepted by the neoliberals, but also by many people on the left, that the choice between more market or more state is incorrect. There are already plenty of ways we coordinate differently. If you look at a basic school, there is a lot of complexity because there are a lot of students and teachers and rooms and activities. That problem of complexity is solved with a very simple device called the timetable, which, as far as I'm concerned, is neither an example of the market nor an example of the state. Essentially it is a part of tech infrastructure that greatly reduces complexity and allows for social coordination when none was possible before. We have hundreds of such devices in everyday life, and we have maybe even thousands of them, and the question then is can we have more? Yes. Can they be more advanced? Yes. Would our life be more complex, more interesting, more sophisticated, and not depend on the market if we had more and if they were more advanced? Yes. Once you answer 'yes' to all of that, then you can start asking questions about what our broader tech infrastructure should look like. What legal facets should it have? What property regime should govern it? How much money should be put into it? These are the kinds of questions I would be asking. In my opinion, asking the question of what should replace it in the abstract doesn't make a lot of sense without first posing the questions about why, for whom, and with what purpose.

Jan Groos: You already mentioned different functions of what markets supposedly can do. What are the functions that you think should be replaced? You suggested that maybe all of them could be replaced, but what are the ones that we should pick up first? And what then are the concrete infrastructures, the concrete modes of engagement that we can develop in order to bring about these alternative mechanisms?

	Maybe you could give examples that exceed the timetable and are scalable in different forms in order to provide modes of engagement that are able to replace certain functions of the market.
Evgeny Morozov:	From the three functions of the market I've outlined and mentioned, it's obvious to me that I am completely opposed to making the market the overall infrastructure of modernity, if you will. So I don't want the market to be the tool through which we move and advance forward. I think it's a completely mad bet to do it this way. So clearly, markets should not be instruments of reducing complexity, of organizing different types of coordination among social groups, of allowing new things to be discovered in a structured way. Now, am I against markets as allocative devices in certain limited cases? No, I'm not. I think markets, once they are well-designed and once they are supervised, controlled, and monitored, can deliver. Once you know what to expect of them and if you monitor how well they're functioning, you can have them all you want within this very limited focus, this very limited agenda. Now, beyond that, I don't have a great technocratic vision, because I don't think that vision should be technocratic. I think that vision should be managerial.

There is another dimension that I didn't really make clear in my previous essays, which I will make clear in the book I'm currently working on. If I think of traditional socialists in the European sense, the social democratic movement, the workers movement and communism as well, I think of them as movements that seek simplicity in the economic sphere. And planning is one way to get at it. You make sure that things are under control and that you know what goes where and control and monitor the inputs and outputs. It's a system that you might think is complex, but you're trying to make it simple. And you're using all sorts of tools, technologies, techniques of knowledge and so forth to arrive at that simplicity. Capitalists, even Keynesians, do not share this view, this approach towards complexity. They accept by and large that the system is complex. And they think that you can find ways to strive in its complexity. In big corporations complexity is dealt with by hiring managers who possess a skill set which allows them to handle the complexity of the given situation. It is not dealt with by trying to make it simple by reducing it to chunks that your system can digest, which I think is the socialist default temptation. Therefore, I would suggest building a system with a more managerial outlook rather than insisting on simplicity. This means that the infrastructures we need would have to make it easier to manage things. Managers try to anticipate the world as complex as it is without making it simpler, therefore infrastructures of prediction, modelling, simulation, and so on, are needed. I would argue that socialists have to go even further than that. They have to deliberately make it more complex. They have to take it upon themselves to make sure that the world is messier, more chaotic and crazier than it was before they started working. I mean, many socialists succeed in that just because of bad management, but I would argue that that has to be done structurally. And this is what socialism is about, allowing for this complexity. It's about allowing people to live in ways that they want outside of the market, outside of whatever mentality and subjectivity is imposed on them by this invisible Leviathan, as some people call the market. We want to have all this immense variety of behaviours, lifestyles, forms of lives, however you want to call it. The task is to allow for this complexity while at the same time making sure that the ship doesn't sink and making sure that the ship doesn't sink is what really makes it complex. Here is really where technology, big data and everything else can help, but not help by planning in the old sense of the word, but predicting and managing and then delegating the functions further down the line so that you don't have to centralize all the management in the hands of the Politburo. Now, this is how it works in the abstract. I'm not naive enough to think that in today's geopolitical milieu, you can have as much decentralization as I would wish personally, because even developing all these infrastructures of prediction, anticipation and management would require the pursuit of a far more autonomous technology and science policy than the hegemonic powers of today would be happy with. So it will be a trade-off. So I'm not naively proposing that we just have a bunch of communes interrelated with each other through a giant network, but I think as a kind of a horizon of where we want to be, that's not a bad vision.

Jan Groos: When it comes to the way in which you frame your overall argument it is interesting to me that you emphasize the aspect of discovery so much. To be honest, specifically with regard to a broader public, my guess would be that questions of existential security and also the ecological question would probably be much higher on the list. And when it comes to the question of discovery one could easily argue for a form of discovery through existential security since, if you simply bring people into the position where they do not have to hustle the whole day in order just to get through, then there's a huge potential of creativity that would be set free.

Evgeny Morozov: I understand what you're saying. And a lot of people have made that case with regards to the welfare state. But I just think that ultimately it's a much bigger battle than a battle between neoliberalism and whatever succeeds those who win the socialist calculation debate. Essentially, it's a debate about action. I would argue that you have more or less the same theory of action underpinning both neoclassical and

Austrian economics and to some extent also much of social science in the form of rational choice. And this is a very simplistic theory of action. It starts with Weber (1930), who partly borrows it from Menger (1981) and a bunch of other economists of the first-generation Austrian school and it goes something like this: we are all rational, we have goals, then we find the most rational ways of fulfilling them. That's basically it. And if we find a more efficient way of fulfilling these goals, then this is innovation. And the person who does that is an entrepreneur, which basically means to always be on the lookout for more efficient means of pursuing given ends. And that's a theory of action that I would argue, and I'm not the only one making that case, underpins most of the theories of socialism in the actual praxis in the Soviet Union and elsewhere, as well. If you look at Lange (Lange and Taylor, 1938) and everybody else, that's how they think about action. But this is wrong. It is wrong, because it doesn't account for people changing goals along the way. And it doesn't account for much of the stuff that happens in everyday life. I start doing something, I do it, then I understand I need to do something else. Then I realize it's all wrong, I need to do something else entirely. This is what human action is like. Unless you build a political system that accounts for these changes, you're going to end up wasting 90 per cent of human potential and human creativity, which is what really makes us humans as opposed to automatons and algorithms. Currently our social system is not optimized to take advantage of the sparks of creativity that really drive us and that make us human, because it has no alternative to channelling our desires and incentives into the price system. If we were to build an alternative system that would actually account for how humans really are, it would require very different theories of action, maybe informed by pragmatism, maybe informed by something else. There are many alternatives out there. Once you build an appropriate social system for that, I think the effects and benefits you're going to harvest will far exceed what the current welfare state could accomplish through universal basic income. That's what I'm talking about, but I don't think we are there, yet, in the sense that I don't think that people on the left are even interested in this question. Do you disagree? Tell me. Maybe there are some underground circles that I'm not aware of.

Jan Groos: I think that people are interested in so far as I think there's a similarity between the way that you pose the problem and a certain sense of frustration, at least on my part, with the way in which the debate around democratic economic planning is currently framed (Groos, in this volume). Because in my view, even though I'm obviously very much interested in the debate, I do think that the scope of the planning debate is far too narrow. So I think there is an interest in moving beyond this fixation on markets as information processes, at least on my part. The way that I try to approach this is through the lens of alternative arts of government (Groos, in this volume), which is a way for me to ask different questions towards this complex of problems. This, for example, leads to questions of markets as sites of veridiction and production of truth and so on and it provides a very different set of questions and a different set of problems that we need to engage with and bring up alternative ways to approach it. So I would say there is an interest in thinking about these things in different ways. At the same time I think I do maybe have a different timeline. I would say the first thing would be to provide some form of universal basic service and existential security. And then, on top of that, we should build these different kinds of infrastructures of discovery, so to speak, because I think that they can only be harnessed if the

Evgeny Morozov:

Jan Groos:
Evgeny Morozov:

material basis is given for the people, who will basically have to have time in order to engage with it. So this might be a slightly different kind of timeline.

I think it's not just the timeline. I really think that the social theory accepted in mainstream leftist circles is broken. It's broken because the theory of action underpinning it is broken. Unless this is fixed there cannot be a robust theory that will be able to speak about modernity, industrialization, postmodernism, and so on. You may say none of it is relevant. We just want to make sure that people have tramps [free public transport] and enough food to eat. And that's fine. That's a fine perspective to take …

… it's not either or.

… well, sure, it's not either or, but if it's not either or, then you're asking for the low-hanging fruit. I mean, who on the left is going to argue against universal basic services or universal basic income, if it's done in a way that will enhance the welfare state as opposed to a libertarian Friedmanesque (Friedman, 1962) version. So I see it as a default. To me, that's not even an issue, to be honest. To me, the issue goes deeper. If you engage with the German-speaking world and you take somebody like Jürgen Habermas, who is the reference point for German social democracy, whether you want it or not, then you'll see that Habermas (1981) has a theory of action that is very simple. It says the world is getting more and more complex – in that sense he agrees with Hayek and Luhman – and the only way to reduce this complexity is by relying on markets and by relying on law, so essentially money and the legal system. There is nothing else. And then all that can be done is to sometimes push back against the encroachments of all that complexity on the life world. For Habermas this can be done through traditional liberal institutions and the media. And that's a story accepted by and large by social democracy.

I would argue though that this is not true as it completely leaves out the most important mechanism of social coordination and reducing complexity, which is information technology. There is no need to rely on money or law. Once you understand that complexity can be reduced in very different ways, then you understand that all sorts of other things become possible. You don't really need to buy all of the bourgeois liberal political institutions we inherited from the French Revolution whole scale, because you can have people organizing and still have all the complexity that you want and all of the rights that they want, but you can do it outside of the traditional money system with banks and legal system with laws and bureaucracies. And I think that, unless you go and piece by piece analyse and understand what the mental and intellectual building blocks are, we're going to end up reusing and recycling neoliberalism. Because to some extent when it comes to non-communicative action in Habermas, that's what he does. The only way you account for these creative sparks of action, which I mentioned earlier, in mainstream debate is through the concept of entrepreneurship. And then you have to invent all sorts of entrepreneurship. We have moral entrepreneurship, ideas entrepreneurship, cultural entrepreneurship, religion, everything is entrepreneurship now, because we have no way to account for truly new creative non-teleological behaviour in domains that are not the market. The problem with neoliberalism is that everything has to be channelled through the market and therefore it has to become an entrepreneurial venture. And I think it's just dumb. But this will continue spreading unless somebody stands up and says, look, you're basically working with the wrong concept. The Austrian concept of entrepreneurship doesn't even describe entrepreneurship itself, because it cannot tell you about entrepreneurs that suddenly decide to, I don't know, switch from for-profit to non-profit status, pursue social entrepreneurship or completely change their goals or completely reinvent themselves. With entrepreneurship, you're still tied to the idea that these people need to make something and that they're imprisoned by the price system and the only innovations they can introduce is in the techniques of production.

So all I'm saying is that I think it's not either or, on that I agree with you, but I do think that we need to completely rebuild social theory block by block to account for complex behaviour. We need a different complexity, a non-neoliberal complexity favourable to the core leftist ideals and ideas. And some of those ideas have to do with a diversity of lifestyle and diversity of life forms producing fantastic social effects that will be disruptive, progressive, and it will move society forward. The kind of effects that we currently attribute to the market.

Jan Groos: Now you mentioned again that one of the tools that we would need to use, a tool that should be in our toolbox, but is not yet utilized in order to bring about these alternative modes of coordination, would be digital technologies. Can you sketch in more concrete terms how specifically digital technologies can be of use in this task?

Evgeny Morozov: Yeah, but again, you will find it very banal. If one community will be happy to use an abacus and a timetable, and another one would want an AI, I mean, great. All we can do as critical intellectuals is to look at the current tech landscape and see which parts of it make such a project unlikely or not favourable. We can look at them in terms of use, but also, for example, if they allow surveillance, if they require people to pay for them with their data or with money and so on. So you can make a critique based on use and praxis, so to say, or you can bring forward a critique based on what the non-state ownership of these infrastructures, for example in fields like education, healthcare and so on, mean geopolitically in the current economic juncture. You would want your basic communication, education, healthcare, transportation, to be somehow run in a democratic way, where the policy decides on how to offer it, how to structure it, how to reform it, which you would not be able to do if you integrate Palantir [a US data analytics company with strong ties to intelligence services] into your health data and so on. You will not be able then to later kick them out for all sorts of reasons, contractually and infrastructurally. So this is a different side of critique then. It has nothing to do with praxis, because you can even buy into it and say that Google offers you a fantastic tool, like a Google Calendar. You can even accept that argument on the level of use and praxis, but you can then strike it down and strike it out based on the geopolitical meaning of delegating so much power to a foreign company that you cannot control. I think that these are the criteria through which this has to be thought through. But beyond that, I just think you will end up at a level of generality that will tell you that yes, overall, it's better to have infrastructures that are generative, so you can build on top of them in an easier way than infrastructures that are closed. This is the truth we've learned in the last 50 or 60 years. Is it always the case? No, because there are tradeoffs. And some of those tradeoffs may have to do with security, with the fact that you just don't have access to technologies because somebody is not selling them to you, which is now happening in China with microchips. This is a constraint and you have to live with that constraint. So I don't really think that you can arrive at a point beyond that, I don't think you can arrive at a set of more specific normative criteria that you want to have in this tech infrastructure, at least I cannot. Because, ultimately, it has to be

Jan Groos: secondary to a political project. And unless you have a political project, this infrastructure is not going to help.

There has been a time in which there was a conjunction between a large-scale leftist political project and a novel techno-infrastructural approach. When it comes to examples of large-scale techno-political infrastructures from the left which have tried to provide alternatives to both capitalist market economies and hierarchical central planning, the Cybersyn project sticks out in many ways (Medina, 2014). In preparation for our conversation today I listened to all of the six Massey lectures by Stafford Beer on 'Designing freedom' (1973). A lot of what you said in our conversation today resonates with the ideas that we know from the work of Stafford Beer, and I would like to make the link to that body of work and the historical example of Cybersyn. You have worked on the topic extensively in different formats.[2] Could you start by giving an overview of what Project Cybersyn is, and then go into how it is relevant for your thinking about alternatives today?

Evgeny Morozov: It's a good question, but I'm afraid I have to disappoint you.

Jan Groos: [*laughing*] Whaaat?

Evgeny Morozov: [*laughing*]

Well, I don't think that Project Cybersyn itself is necessarily very relevant, because essentially, if you really want to be honest historically, you have to take it for what it was. Cybersyn essentially was a system that would allow a ministry, or a state-run corporation, to run a bunch of companies that were being nationalized in a way that would be scalable. So that's all it was. And it wasn't some great insight that we need to move from central planning to managerialism of the kind I was describing. It was just that the circumstances were like that. They couldn't move to central planning, even if they wanted to, and they couldn't exit the market because of the political conjuncture on the ground in Chile. So they were stuck with these companies buying and selling things on the market, but being state companies that needed to be managed in a way that would soon involve the workers, and nobody really knew how exactly that would happen. So this is Cybersyn. This doesn't mean that the ideas circulating in that milieu don't have anything to recommend to us. I think they do. Not necessarily ideas about cybernetics, but ideas about technological dependence and the way in which technology plays a certain role in the geopolitical order. And this is actually the focus of my more recent work looking at Chile and, to some extent, Brazil of the 60s and 70s. In Stafford Beer himself there are many elements that are interesting and that can and should be integrated with a certain type of socialism. But it's a certain type of socialism that I think itself is in a minority position. And it's a socialism that sees complexity as a good thing and tries to embrace non-neoliberal complexity and live with it and profit from it. But having studied Stafford Beer very closely, having spoken to many of his friends and colleagues and family and having spent a lot of time in his archives, I also don't want to overstate the case. Beer was a management theorist who, by coincidence, ended up working in Allende's Chile, which changed his life. But it was not a conscious effort to think through how to rebuild socialism through cybernetics. It doesn't mean that there weren't other people who have tried to think about this question, and there have been some (Gerovič, 2002; Rindzevičiūtė, 2015). Stafford Beer, however, is essentially a management theorist. His ideas can be applied to other domains though, and this is exactly what happened in Chile. His body of thought can be applied in domains that have nothing to do with corporations. This is, I think, the part of cybernetics that remains relevant.

Jan Groos: Evgeny, at the end, I always ask the question: if you think about the future, what makes you joyful?

Evgeny Morozov: I've listened to your podcast, I should have prepared for this question. What makes me joyful? I mean, ultimately, I think that there are, how should I put it. [*pauses for a significant moment*] Yeah, I don't really know. [*pauses to think*] So, nothing makes me joyful in the very specific sense, because I think optimism is the kind of luxury that we cannot really afford at this point. But let me think about it some more. [*pauses again*] Well, I mean, I don't want to sound like one of those accelerationist guys celebrating the power of technology to solve all these questions, but I do think that if there is a silver lining to the kind of rise of big tech in the last 10, 15 or 20 years, it's that it showed us that so much social coordination is possible in a completely non-market way. And we have not realized that yet. Think about all the tools, all the apps, that all these people in Silicon Valley and elsewhere that are obsessed with productivity, with collaboration and coordination are using. I mean, yes, you might be paying something for them, but what they probably don't realize is that ultimately, they're not coordinating through the price system. I mean, they're using the price system to get access to a non-market system of coordination. So, in a way Silicon Valley has consistently shown us that collaboration and coordination happens outside of the market. And with enough money being poured into it, it can become even deeper and better and faster and more efficient. And, in that sense, that is the best argument against relying on the market to facilitate social coordination a la Hayek that we have seen. And that does make me optimistic, but that requires somebody to see. And if a tree falls in the forest, then there is nobody to see it. So if people will be able to see that element of it, great. But I think, right now, the only thing we have seen in this phenomenon, by and large in the public debate is the opposite, is the idea that the market is so much better than the non-market mechanisms in building these cool things. The point is what these new technologies of coordination allow us to do and what they allow us to do is to completely bypass the market when it comes to coordinating.

Jan Groos: That's so interesting that you frame it in this way now, at the end again. Because leaving aside the too narrow focus within the planning debate, at least this point, that there is potential in these types of non-market coordination, I think this is absolutely part of the revived planning debate. The fact that these technologies provide a potential for some form of alternative coordination definitely features in *Future Histories*, for sure.

Evgeny Morozov: Sure, sure, sure. This question, Jan, gets us to the heart of it. The question then becomes, what do you need this coordination for? And I think that this is a philosophical question. And for a lot of people, including, I would say most of the people involved in the democratic planning debate, this coordination by and large is just a way of fulfilling the need to distribute and allocate goods, because this is the primary focus, right? They're not really stepping into the world of discovery, becoming creativitiy and so forth. Because, ultimately, it's almost like they operate with a Maslow pyramid of some kind, right? Marx makes a similar distinction when he's talking about the realm of necessity and the realm of freedom, right? Even if you stick closely to Marx you have to admit that he slightly neglected the realm of freedom in this thinking. Maybe his idea was some kind of a liberal interpretation of everybody to their own devices. That as long as we coordinate production in the workshop in a democratic way, what you do when you hunt and drink wine and write poetry in the afternoon doesn't matter and we shouldn't think about it. I think that's a mistake. So if there is one big message, I'd like to leave you with, it's that I think it's a mistake because, in a sense, the neoliberals understood that it's that element that accounts for the most exciting parts of modernity. So this is the stuff that really gets people excited about technology, cities, urbanization, modernization, and so on. It's not the mere satisfaction of basic needs. And the neoliberals argue that the market is key to providing this element. So this is one reason why I think the left should engage with planning in the realm of freedom more than it has. And the second reason is that I do think that the realm of freedom, once organized properly, is productive of value, in the non-Marxist meaning of the term, and that value can then feed back to satisfy the needs in the realm of necessities. And that's, to some extent, what Silicon Valley has done. They allowed you to do whatever you want in your everyday life. They get all the data through your devices about what it is that you do, and then they monetize it. And then they do whatever they want with that money. If you really want to have a socialist biopolitics, that's a good candidate. They are appropriating that and making sure that value is generated from that, not just from individual everyday life, but also from collectivity, because we all engage in it collectively. And once analysed collectively, of course, this data has enormous value when it comes to traffic analysis or epidemiological trends and so forth. But that comes from us being in the realm of freedom, by and large, or at least in the realm of social reproduction, if you really want to be middle-groundish about it. So in that sense, I do agree that questions like this have attracted the attention of people on the left. I just think they're asking them in the wrong register.

Jan Groos: But, intuitively, if you go to a person who is now struggling in subsistence and you ask them, is it either the realm of necessity that should be covered first or should we immediately jump into the realm of freedom, I'm pretty sure that they will say please, let's start with the realm of necessity.

Evgeny Morozov: I don't think that that's the correct way to think about it, because I don't think that dichotomy is accurate. You're not going to get very far if you really pose the question this way, because once you start with both of them separated like that, which assumes a division between work and non-work that's very strict, that's separate, where value is produced in the workplace, then of course you're going to end up with the most obvious conclusion. We need to get away from this separation because most of the people on the left who did think about the realm of freedom end up saying that we need to reintroduce the realm of freedom into the realm of necessity. The way Marcuse would, for example, propose that the factory work should be like a playground. I just don't think that this is a helpful way to think about it.

But, of course, I don't think that what I am proposing is the right paradigm, for example, for the Global South. There you still probably need to be building factories and have people working there, you need to industrialize, you need to build your own base, you need to recreate some of the capacity domestically, instead of relying on global supply chains. So the Global South will probably be fine with the older socialist programme. I understand the geopolitical and regional bias of what I'm saying, but I don't think that the fact that there are people who are poor or homeless or who have troubles which could be immediately resolved, should take pressure off us to find holes in legitimation strategies of neoliberals, or contribute to articulating an alternative political project. Because the fact that people are hungry right now, stripped of the ideological context, tells you absolutely nothing – you might as

Jan Groos: well believe that Elon Musk should give them basic income, or some philanthropist should fund something for them. Right? So to me, the presence of problems in the world, that are as such easily fixable, is no reason not to engage with these other questions. I think we both agree on this, but I just wanted to reiterate on it, because one is not the reason not to think about the other.

Jan Groos: Yeah, I absolutely agree with that. Maybe it's that I think about the ability to bring about the new in different ways. Since it's an intrinsic feature I don't see it as that much of a challenge. But I think I get the point you're making. At least I think I get the point you're making in terms of providing …

Evgeny Morozov: … but that was the project for Marx, though. What is Marxism? Marxism is very simple. You have social relations of production that eventually block forces of production from advancing further. It's just a philosophy of the new. There is nothing else in Marx. That's the core idea, that you need to change relations of production so that the forces of production can continue unimpeded. And you can, of course, make all sorts of cases for ecology and whatever, and they're all important points, but ultimately, that's what it is. So the question of the new and its sustained, almost industrial, methodological, theoretical production, it's at the core of the leftist project.

Jan Groos: Yes, but there are a lot of questions that are connected to that. For example, if we need to think about progressivism in a different way. I'm just not sure if we should simply jump into this competition with the neoliberals and accept their premise of markets as the harbingers of the production of the new in the first place …

Evgeny Morozov: … that's where we disagree, I think, because for me it's just undeniable. I also think it's undeniable phenomenologically for the majority of the population. I mean, you just need to open an app store. I mean, don't you

Jan Groos:

Evgeny Morozov:

Jan Groos:

Evgeny Morozov:

see all the apps? How can you possibly deny that that's the production of the new? I mean, that's what people think …

… well, there is a strong argument to make that capitalism is limited in a certain sense to the production of the ever old in new forms. That's an argument that is out there and it has some form of plausibility to it. The way in which markets and capitalism are able to produce the news is a very, very narrow corridor in which we have this accelerated perpetuation of the old, actually, and not really the production of the new. But maybe that's what you're stating as well and we are not apart in this …

… no, no, I believe in productivity improvements. I believe that there are productivity improvements in capitalist firms that are real. They're not fake or inventions. There is no reason for capitalist firms to fake the production of productivity improvements because, if they did, they would just be eaten alive. In that sense, I do believe in competition.

But that's why I mentioned that it's also important to talk about new ways of thinking about progress, because it's not only about productivity improvements when talking about the new. This way of thinking, this logic and narrow framing of the new has brought us into a place where we are aiming for catastrophe …

… but that's a different argument from saying that they're repackaging the old. I just don't think they're repackaging the old, because if they're repackaging the old, they'll just be out of business as individual capitalists. And in that sense, I think if you read somebody like Anwar Shaikh (2016), his view on competition is the same as mine and is the same to some extent as Hayek's. So competition is real and it does produce new things, both on the consumption side and on the production side. You can make all sorts of arguments based on that, of course. That's partly what I'm saying, that there are other ways in which the new is generated, because there are other ways in which we coordinate. And so far, we've put all of our resources, all of our thinking and money and laws into boosting markets as the only infrastructure for doing that. But clearly, that's not the only infrastructure. We need alternatives for all sorts of reasons that, I accept your argument there, have to do with redefining progress and so forth. But to me, to deny that there is something new being produced in the market by both producers and consumers, and that therefore part of the neoliberal argument is correct, is counterproductive I think, because it just rejects our phenomenological everyday experience. And I see no problem in accepting that part of the neoliberal story.

Jan Groos: Well, yes, if you state it this way, then I wouldn't say that there is nothing new being produced. But that actually brings us to a question that I wanted to ask before, but didn't. Maybe you could specify what you mean by 'the new'? Is it just productivity gains? So, if you talk about that which has to be replaced when it comes to this question of the production of 'the new', what is 'the new'? How do you define it?

Evgeny Morozov: Does it need to be defined?

Jan Groos: ... well, it makes a big difference, if ...

Evgeny Morozov: ... I mean, if you look at it in terms of practices, these are practices and ways of being and ways of existing that were not there before when you started. We just need to introduce a temporal element in this and you're going to see practices and ways of doing things that were not there before, ways of doing old things in new ways or ways of doing completely new things.

Jan Groos: But if you define it in this way, then 'the new' is being produced in many different social fields all the time. Why then act as if the market was this magic tool when it comes to producing the new?

Evgeny Morozov: But who's denying that, Jan? You are telling me things that are at the core of my argument and

Jan Groos: I'm trying to build an infrastructure for scaling them up and generating value out of them.

[*laughs*] Yeah, I know, I know, I know. I think it's just that … I think why we land at this position is that I'm not sure if the thing that market competition is able to provide when it comes to building 'the new' is as huge as you put it. I think it should be problematized much more than maybe you would do. But it seems we're circling around in different ways …

Evgeny Morozov: Yeah, but it also depends. I mean, it depends on what your project is. It depends on how you think about neoliberalism. I don't think about this as an economic theory. I think about it as a theory of modernity and a theory of civilization, essentially. A theory of civilization that tells you precisely how to incorporate the new into your life and into the world. If you read Hayek, it's just there stated very clearly. He tells you there are all sorts of effects if you install the cash nexus where you previously had social relations or family ties, but in the long run the pie expands and the pie expands even if certain people end up as losers. And it expands precisely because this new stuff is being produced and is being produced in a sustainable way as far as capitalism is concerned. And this is what market civilization does. It's not about coordinated firms and consumers. It's about bringing novelty into the world. And if you look at the legitimation of neoliberalism, that's the reason why it's of any appeal, unless it's imposed by force. That is the most exciting part of neoliberalism, which is so exciting that social democrats are buying into it. And if you really want to dethrone it, you need to have an alternative account of how society can move forward and structurally, infrastructurally produce the new in a way that scales up. And that's not just about arts and crafts and artisanal people building things, but that there are actually ways to interconnect people in, I don't know, Ecuador with people in Moldova, which is what the market does and you'll have to make sure the changes in the practice in one place are reflected in the life and in the practice of the other place as well.

Ultimately, what I'm saying is that we can have infrastructures that allow people to coordinate, collaborate, produce things, whether these things are effects or emotions or ideas or things that have all of the markings of what neoliberals attribute to market civilization, but without most of the costs. Currently they are not developed, because public policy is such that it doesn't channel resources into the development of these infrastructures. You cannot scale them up properly. Currently your only option is to orient yourself towards the market. And that's why we have all these idealistic people who, beyond protesting, if they really want to do something, what do they do? They form a startup in most cases, and they seek money and they know that this will allow them to scale. If they don't want to be just local operators and if they want to scale, that's what they need to do. Why? Because our entire civilization favours the market as the default and only infrastructure of scaling up this coordination and generating value out of it. But what I'm saying is that you can have a multiplicity of them. That's why in one of my earlier articles in *New Left Review* (Morozov, 2019), I basically said that Hayek has a flawed evolutionary theory and what he says about how people become less altruistic as they move from villages to cities is wrong. Evolutionary theory actually teaches us otherwise and you might as well say that solidarity will be as productive as what Hayek calls discovery, as productive as competition. There is no reason to believe that he's correct on that point and I don't think he is. But it doesn't mean that solidarity is the only thing that can do it. You can maybe list 10 values that will do it. Maybe you can list 20 and maybe you can list infrastructures that will go along with them to enable them and to elicit these behaviours and to elicit these orientations. To me, that seems like the core question of how do you organize modernity. It's not about making sure we have a different system for building apps. It's a way for me to think about how you move society forward and embrace the new in a structured way that bypasses the dichotomy of the market and the state and refuses the idea that the only way to do it in a scaled up way is by relying on the market.

Jan Groos: I absolutely agree. I think it's maybe … maybe you are holding something back that is in the book, because there's something missing. I absolutely agree with everything you just said. But, for example, within capitalism, you do have private property as a form of guiding lens that is able to unify these actions much, as the market as competition does. So you will have a mechanism that is able to provide a form of pre-coordination. And in the way that you describe the alternative, of course, it's right to point out that there needs to be a multiplicity of different approaches that look at different aspects of, for example, the market, but also of different regional contexts, and so on. But then, still, you would have to come up with a mechanism that provides this glue, this form of directionality that is provided in capitalism through private property and markets as competition. You would have to find a different form of mechanism for the production of pre-configuration, so to speak, for the alternative.

Evgeny Morozov: I don't think so. I don't think it's my problem. Because in that sense I depart from describing what so far we have been talking about for the last 10 minutes as a socialism. What I'm describing is a non-capitalism at best. It's not post-capitalism, it's a non-capitalism. And if you want to go really far, you can say that it's possible to have a multiplicity of non-capitalisms. And I don't think that it requires any grounding, for example, in an alternative property regime.

	You might argue that it would require certain rights to preserve those forms of life. You might argue that you would need a right to ignorance of something, for example, because that would be the only way to preserve certain core features. We might argue that you would need some kind of institutional slack so that you don't over-optimize. But to generalize it into a theory or a guiding lens would be to convert it into an -ism, which is not what I'm trying to do. So, at best, my -ism is a non-ism and it's a non-capitalism.
Jan Groos:	Evgeny, thank you so much for being part of *Future Histories*.
Evgeny Morozov:	Sure, my pleasure.

Notes

[1] Find the extended audio version of the conversation here: https://www.futurehistories.today/episoden-blog/s02/e44-evgeny-morozov-on-discovery-beyond-competition/

[2] See for example: https://the-santiago-boys.com/

Bibliography

Beer, S. (1973) 'Designing freedom', 11 July. https://archive.org/details/DesigningFreedom_CBC_Lectures

Buchanan, J.M. (1975) *The Limits of Liberty: Between Anarchy and Leviathan*. Chicago: University of Chicago Press.

Friedman, M. (1962) *Capitalism and Freedom*. Chicago: University of Chicago.

Gerovič, S. (2002) *From Newspeak to Cyberspeak: A History of Soviet Cybernetics*. Cambridge, MA/London: The MIT Press.

Habermas, J. (1981) *Handlungsrationalität und gesellschaftliche Rationalisierung*. Series: Theorie des kommunikativen Handelns / Jürgen Habermas Bd.1. Frankfurt am Main: Suhrkamp.

Hayek, F.A. (1945) 'The use of knowledge in society', *The American Economic Review*, 35(4): 519–530.

Hayek, F.A., Bartley, W.W. and Kresge, S. (1988) *The Collected Works of Friedrich August Hayek*. London/New York: Routledge.

Lange, O. and Taylor, F.M. (1938) *On the Economic Theory of Socialism*. Minneapolis: University of Minnesota Press.

Medina, E. (2014) *Cybernetic Revolutionaries: Technology and Politics in Allende's Chile*. Reprint edition. Cambridge, MA: The MIT Press.

Menger, C. (1981) *Principles of Economics*. New York: New York University Press.

Mises, L. von (1922) *Die Gemeinwirtschaft – Untersuchungen über den Sozialismus*. Jena: Verlag von Gustav Fischer

Morozov, E. (2019) 'Digital socialism? The calculation debate in the age of big data', *New Left Review*, 116/117: 33–67.

Morozov, E. (2021) 'Beyond competition: alternative discovery procedures & the postcapitalist public sphere', 21 April. https://matrix.berkeley.edu/research-article/evgeny-morozov-beyond-competition-alternative-discovery-procedures-the-postcapitalist-public-sphere/

Rindzevičiūtė, E. (2015) 'The future as an intellectual technology in the Soviet Union: from centralised planning to reflexive management', *Cahiers du Monde Russe*, 56(1): 111–134. doi: 10.4000/monderusse.8169.

Schumpeter, J.A. (1976) *Capitalism, Socialism, and Democracy*. 5th edn; with a new introduction by Tom Bottomore. London: Allen and Unwin.

Shaikh, A. (2016) *Capitalism: Competition, Conflict, Crises*. Oxford: Oxford University Press.

Weber, M. (1930) *The Protestant Ethic and the Spirit of Capitalism*. London: Unwin University Books.

PART II

Building Bridges

8

(Re)imagining Housing as an Infrastructure for Social Reproduction

Rabea Berfelde and Philipp Möller

Introduction

In the search for alternatives to capitalist modes of production and the market-based allocation of labour and resources, a debate has emerged that considers the technical possibilities of a new democratic planned economy and that analyses currently practised forms of capitalist planning. In this new planning debate (Jones, 2020), the focus is primarily on the sphere of production and the related negotiation of social (consumption) needs (cf Saros, 2014). How to democratically plan the reproductive sphere, that is social infrastructures such as health, care or housing, has not been a focus of the debate so far.

This chapter takes the 'Expropriate Deutsche Wohnen & Co' ('Deutsche Wohnen & Co Enteignen') campaign, which won a Berlin-wide referendum in September 2021, as an example of planning in relation to housing provision. The campaign proposes to socialize the assets of private landlords who own more than 3,000 flats in the city of Berlin, as it is these financialized housing companies that are driving the current housing crisis in the city. The campaign argues that this change in ownership, achieved through socialization, will allow for a management of the housing stock that is no longer profit-oriented, but rather oriented towards the common good. The chapter analyses the campaign's concept, which argues that changing the ownership of the estimated 270,000 dwellings concerned would allow for a needs-based allocation of housing, a radical democratic planning of investments and a planned, social-ecological management. In this way, we want to expand the new planning debate into the field of social reproduction and link it to a discussion on the reorganisation of public services and social infrastructure.

The first part of the chapter is devoted to developing a basic understanding of the political economy of housing provision and its relationship to state planning. By establishing an understanding of how the state has historically negotiated the contradiction between housing as exchange value and housing as use value, through different welfare regimes, we develop an understanding of planning in the realm of social reproduction. We then use this notion of planning to illustrate how housing provision was organized in the Keynesian welfare state. The German system of social housing provision after the Second World War is analysed to discuss how state intervention in social housing provision worked at the time. Reflecting the historical critique of this technocratic planning regime, which gradually emerged since the 1960s, we illustrate the difference between the housing provision of the Keynesian welfare state and the more utopian, radical democratic vision proposed by the 'Expropriate Deutsche Wohnen & Co' campaign.

In the third part of the chapter we look at the history of the housing crisis in Berlin to contextualize the campaign's proposal to socialize the housing assets of financialized real estate companies. We will see how the neoliberal privatization of entire housing companies enabled the 'financialization of rental housing' (Fields and Uffer, 2016), which is now the dominant cause of the city's ongoing housing crisis. We define this active withdrawal of the state from social housing provision and the state's role in creating a financialized housing market, as a neoliberal and austerity-driven planning regime.

In the last part of the chapter, we look closely at the proposal of 'Expropriate Deutsche Wohnen & Co' to transfer the socialized housing assets to a democratic public body governed by a council structure with tenant participation. We discuss this as a proposal for a radical democratic mode of planning that can enrich the new debate on planned economies by providing a concrete model for radical democratic participation in socialized infrastructures.

The role of state planning: housing between use value and exchange value

Housing plays a contradictory role in capitalist economies. As an exchange value, housing is a central mechanism of capital accumulation, and as a use value it is an indispensable infrastructure for social reproduction (Aalbers and Christophers, 2014; Holm, 2022). In what follows, we will take a closer look at this contradictory relationship and develop an understanding of the role of state planning in mediating between housing as use value and housing as exchange value.

As the source and origin of surplus value, living labour is the fundamental commodity in the capitalist production process. Consequently, capitalist production requires the reproduction of labour power, which Marxist-feminist theories have continually made the starting point of their critical reflections. However, capital's orientations towards accumulation and growth subordinates life-making activities and the satisfaction of basic human needs (Bhattacharya, 2017; 2019; Ferguson, 2020). These 'social reproductive contradictions' (Fraser, 2017) are inherent to the capitalist system as such. However, their particular form is historically contingent on different regimes of capitalist accumulation, as they are negotiated and regulated by the (welfare) state.

This contradictory and dialectical relationship also structures the provision of housing in capitalist economies (Soederberg, 2021, p 27). Housing provision is a 'necessary element in the social reproduction of labour power and hence the reproduction of capitalism itself; workers need houses to live in and capitalists need live workers to exploit' (Berry, 1981, p 3). Housing is where reproductive and care labour – such as childcare, cooking, cleaning and emotional labour – takes place (Madden, 2020; Power and Mee, 2020). Moreover, due to their existential vulnerability, bodies are dependent on infrastructures 'understood complexly as environment, social relations, and networks of support and sustenance' (Butler, 2018, p 133). This is why we can understand housing as an infrastructure of social reproduction (Luke and Kaika, 2019), that is, as a necessary and fundamental condition for the reproduction of labour. That is why 'interventionist states have often made housing provision, whether in the form of subsidized physical property itself or of housing 'benefits' of some kind, part of their redistributive programs' (Aalbers and Christophers, 2014, p 381).

We propose to understand this kind of state intervention in the field of social reproduction as a form of planning. We draw this understanding from the Operaist Marxist critique of the Keynesian welfare state, which is reflected in the concepts of the 'planner state' (Negri, 2005) and the 'social factory' (Tronti, 2019).[1] Both concepts shed light on the role of the state in capitalist planning. It is argued that capital, in the form of management, plans inside the factory to increase labour productivity in industrial production. Outside the factory, in society at large, the welfare state acts as an agent of capitalist planning in the sphere of social reproduction (Negri, 1994, p 121).

What we gain from these two concepts is an understanding that production and reproduction are always embedded in state regulation and planning. Thus, there is always planning, the question is how planning is conducted and for what purpose. With our proposal to understand state intervention in the realm of social reproduction as a form of planning, we are therefore not developing a normative concept of planning, but arguing that we need to discuss qualitative criteria for what kind of planning we want in order to strengthen infrastructures of social reproduction, such as housing.

Technocratic planning: housing provision in the Keynesian welfare state

The 'golden age of social housing provision [...] commenced at the end of the Second World War' (Harloe, 1995, p 10). In the face of massive wartime destruction, the West German welfare state began to invest heavily in housing provision. The policies included a partial and temporary rent freeze in the existing housing stock (Jenkis, 1996, pp 223–227). One can see here how the state sought to reconcile the contradiction between housing as use value and housing as exchange value by reducing profits through rent regulation aimed at ensuring affordability. The far-reaching interventions in market-based pricing were temporary and justified by the housing shortage after the Second World War (Holm and Schreer, 2019, p 9). From 1950 onwards, the Federal government also launched a major housing programme, which provided large sums of funding for the construction of social housing to private, municipal and non-profit housing companies. In return for the use of extensive subsidies and low-interest loans, 'subsidized units were to be let only at rents set by social housing law and reserved for residents eligible according to social-housing income levels' (Schönig, 2020, p 1025). The government stimulated investment in new construction through the subsidy programmes by guaranteeing developers a return on their investment.

Social housing was a central pillar of the Keynesian welfare regime, which ensured the social reproduction of labour through the provision of social housing (Harloe, 1995, p 408). In this sense, Marxist architectural theorists of the time saw the provision of housing as a projection of the needs of industrial production, that is the reproduction of labour power through the provision of infrastructure, onto the urban plan. Modernist urban planning was conceived as part of the Keynesian rationalization of the post-war industrial city and the neutralization of the conflictual potential of labour power (Tafuri, 1976). Social housing provision was state-orchestrated and top-down planned, which is why we characterize this regime as technocratic to distinguish it from the more utopian and radical democratic vision of the 'Expropriate Deutsche Wohnen & Co' campaign. This analysis also explains why the 1960s saw a 'paradigm shift' (Schönig, 2020) towards more market-oriented instruments. The state withdrew from its interventionist role as the housing situation of the middle class and better-off sections of the working class, which were crucial for the Keynesian welfare state, improved.

Neoliberal planning: the genealogy of the housing crisis in Berlin

The paradigm shift towards the neoliberalization of housing intensified with the abolition of the non-profit sector in 1990 (Lay, 2022, p 27ff). As a result, formerly non-profit and municipal housing companies were transformed into more market-oriented actors. Since the mid-1990s, the state has increasingly withdrawn from an active role in social housing provision. In 2001, the state stopped subsidizing social housing altogether (Egner, 2014). Instead of shaping the market as a provider of municipal housing and through public investment in new construction, the state created the conditions for a privatized and financialized rental housing market to unfold. In what follows, we focus on the privatization politics in Berlin as an expression of this neoliberal turn.

The 'Expropriate Deutsche Wohnen & Co' campaign is calling for the socialization of the housing assets of all landlords who own more than 3,000 flats in the city. To understand how the campaign's proposal responds to Berlin's housing crisis, it is necessary to look at the city's specific history of housing privatization, which has led to an extraordinary concentration of capital in the housing market. More than 10 companies each own more than 3,000 apartments in the city – in total they hold 270,000 apartments (Trautvetter, 2022) that would be socialized if the campaign's proposal were to become law.

The story of privatization began in the 1990s, initially affecting parts of the formerly state-owned housing stock in the eastern part of the city, which was part of the former GDR. The privatization of public housing stock and land accelerated after the 'Berliner Bankenskandal' (Berlin banking scandal) in 2001. Risky lending and real estate deals nearly bankrupted the bank and the bailout led to a financial crisis (Bernt, Grell and Holm, 2013, p 128). Politics responded with austerity measures and the decision was taken to privatize the two largest public housing companies, which, at the time, owned around 94,000 flats. This en bloc privatization is an exception in the history of neoliberal privatization compared to other European countries. Privatization in Berlin was not facilitated by an increase in owner-occupation, but entire housing companies were sold to institutional investors (Uffer, 2013). Further privatization on a smaller scale followed. As a result, the stock of public housing halved from 588,563 to 269,627 housing units between 1990 and the low point in 2010 (Lompscher, 2018, p 11). In total, between 1989 and 2017, 21 km^2 of public land, equivalent to the size of the Berlin district of Friedrichshain-Kreuzberg, was privatized (Schüschke, 2020).

Privatization enabled the 'financialization of housing' (Aalbers, 2017) and led to the emergence of 'a new type of landlord, one whose primary "clients" are not tenants but shareholders who expect a return from their investment'

(Kusiak, 2021, p 4). Financial speculation on the built environment is a global phenomenon, but it unfolds differently locally, depending on the specific context of financial market and welfare state deregulation.

In Berlin, rental housing is still the dominant form of tenure, with 84.1 per cent of the population living in rented rather than owner-occupied housing (Investitionsbank Berlin, 2022, p 39). In this case, therefore, the financialization of housing here did not take place through the individual purchase of residential property and subsequent individual household debt, but rather through the financialization of the landlords, that is the real estate corporations. As a result of the financialization of the German rental housing market, public-municipal companies gradually lost relevance and were replaced by institutional investors (Metzger, 2020, p 158). In recent years, financialized housing companies have become a significant driver of rental prices with growing market power (Gabor and Kohl, 2022).

Through this history of privatization and deregulation of Berlin's housing market we can identify a specific form of state intervention that created the possibility of a financialized housing market. This is exemplary of a neoliberal and austerity-driven planning regime that creates the conditions for the contemporary 'hyper-commodification of housing' (Madden and Marcuse, 2016, p 26), where the exchange value of housing is emphasized over its function as an infrastructure for social reproduction. The profit interests of investors and shareholders, rather than the public interest in affordable housing, determine how housing is managed in a financialized market. Despite legal regulations, the allocation and pricing of housing is essentially determined by the market.

The privatization and deregulation policies that have enabled the financialization of real estate companies and their increasing importance in housing markets are embedded in a more general neoliberal rollback of the welfare state. The dismantling of the welfare state goes hand in hand with the increasing disciplining of individuals to take responsibility for their own welfare (Heeg, 2013, p 77).

Radical democratic planning: 'Expropriate Deutsche Wohnen & Co' and housing as social infrastructure

The current debate on planning still lacks a broader discussion of transformation perspectives, that is a discussion of how the current political and legal system can be used by social movements to demand emancipatory planning in both the spheres of production and reproduction. The 'Expropriate Deutsche Wohnen & Co' campaign draws on Article 15 of the German Grundgesetz (Basic Law) to make its demands legally plausible. Article 15 states: 'Land, natural resources and means of production may be transferred to common ownership or other forms of common economy for the purpose of socialization by a law regulating the nature and extent of compensation.'² The legal system secures capital accumulation (Pistor, 2019), but can also be used for progressive purposes, as the campaign's reference to the constitutional norm shows. The campaign thus makes a demand that radically challenges the status quo of ownership in Berlin's housing market, but is able to show that this demand is legally possible, which was central to its success (Kusiak, 2021). Berlin is a federal state, and the German political system allows for popular legislation by referendum at the state level. This allowed the campaign to get the referendum on the ballot and, in September 2021, 59.1 per cent voted in favour of the proposal to socialize financialized housing companies. The successful referendum resulted in a non-binding resolution. Non-binding in this context means that, although the popular demand has been expressed, the power to implement it through legislation still lies with the state. Following the successful referendum, the Berlin government appointed a commission of experts, mainly constitutional lawyers, to examine the constitutionality of a possible socialization and to outline ways of implementing Article 15.

However, the referendum was successful not only because of its concrete demands and legal plausibility, but also because it was supported by a broad political campaign, which in turn was based on the long-standing struggles of tenant initiatives against for-profit housing companies. In particular, since 2010, Berlin has witnessed a new cycle of an urban social movement made up mainly of tenant initiatives fighting in their neighbourhood against rent increases, lack of maintenance and the sale of buildings to real estate speculators (Berfelde, 2019). The campaign emerged from this cycle of urban activism, seeking to bring together local initiatives demanding a change in housing provision, which could be achieved through the socialization of financialized housing companies. The transformative strategy of the campaign thus consists of three elements: (1) the use of a constitutional norm to make its demands legally plausible; (2) the direct democratic element of a referendum; and (3) the connection to an activist base. It remains to be seen to what extent this transformation strategy can be successful and serve as a blueprint for socialization movements in other sectors.

If the demands of the campaign were implemented by law, housing would be institutionalized as social infrastructure in relation to the then socialized stock, as housing would be withdrawn from the market and instead be provided as a common good managed in a radical democratic way. In this respect, the proposal to socialize large housing stocks is related to the debate on the new concept of a post-neoliberal social policy, which seeks to make the universal provision of 'basic services' (The Foundational Economy Collective, 2018) or social infrastructures the core of a new conception of the welfare state. In what follows, we turn to a discussion of qualitative criteria for understanding housing as social infrastructure and discuss the campaign's proposal as an example of a radical democratic mode of planning in respect to housing provision.

Transformation of the ownership structure

What is often implicit in the new debate on planned economies, but not central to the argument, is the fact that new forms of production (and consequently labour relations) and a socially just provision of social goods and services require a change in ownership structures and property relations.

Regarding the change of ownership, the campaign proposes that the flats of the real estate companies should be socialized and transferred to a newly founded institution, a so-called Anstalt öffentlichen Rechts (AöR, institution under public law) (Deutsche Wohnen & Co Enteignen, 2023, p 9). Berlin's AöRs are institutions under public law, owned by the city-state, not profit-oriented and often entrusted with the provision of services of general interest. This form of public ownership would legally institutionalize the long-term management of the housing stock as a public good. Unlike the temporary interventions of market provision in the Keynesian planning regime, decommodification through transfer to public ownership would be permanent, as reprivatization would be legally excluded.

In this chapter's section on the neoliberal planning of the housing market, we saw that under current conditions, state planning merely regulates the conditions under which the housing market can unfold. However, for planned urban development, and democratic control over housing, control over land, and thus the transformation of property relations, is a necessary precondition, precisely because land is a non-replicable resource. In order to reorganize housing as a social infrastructure, public ownership is an essential prerequisite for decoupling the provision of housing from the valorization of private (finance) capital.

Needs-based allocation of housing

Outside the public and non-profit housing stock, housing is currently largely allocated through market mechanisms, which means that tenants must be able to pay the prices, and that the most solvent tenants are selected when housing is allocated. However, socialization would allow for a needs-based and non-discriminatory allocation of housing. The calculation of rents in the socialized housing stock would no longer be based on profit, but on affordability. To this end, the campaign proposes the so-called 'fair rent model', according to which rents should, on average, only account for one third of people's income; for people living on the officially defined poverty line, this would be calculated at €3.70/square metre (Deutsche Wohnen & Co Enteignen, 2022, p 287ff). The purpose of the AöR is to provide decent housing at affordable prices for the general public, thereby institutionalizing housing as a use value through socialization.

In order to ensure a discrimination-sensitive allocation of housing, the campaign suggests working with a weighted lottery procedure. Possible criteria that could be weighted are, for example, 'the experience of racist discrimination, cramped living conditions of families, family or social spatial ties to a district (e.g. avoidance of changing schools/day-care centres, relatives in need of care in the neighbourhood), receipt of transfer payments (Bürgergeld, Grundsicherung, AsylbLG) or a low income' (Deutsche Wohnen & Co Enteignen, 2023, p 16; translation by the authors). A direct allocation of housing to 'hardship cases [...] outside the lottery procedure' should also be made possible (Deutsche Wohnen & Co Enteignen, 2023, p 19). Possible hardship cases could be, for example, imminent homelessness or unhealthy housing conditions, for example caused by mould.

Radical democratic planning

The campaign proposes not only to decommodify housing, but also to democratize it. This is also the central difference between a nationalization and a socialization whereby the latter goes beyond state planning and requires forms of radical democratization. The transformation of the housing stock into an institution under public law would legally allow for radical democratic participation in its management. The campaign proposes the introduction of a council structure (see Figure 8.1) that ensures the participation of tenants at different administrative levels: 'At the lowest level there are the neighbourhood councils, above them the area councils, which send delegates to a general council of all tenants, which in turn delegates representatives from its midst to the administrative board, the highest decision-making body' of the institution under public law (Deutsche Wohnen & Co Enteignen, 2023, p 29; translation by the authors).

The lowest level of the council structure is the neighbourhood council. A neighbourhood council should represent a maximum of 2,000 tenants and the representatives would be directly elected. The neighbourhood council should deal with immediate local issues, such as which shops are located in the neighbourhood and which maintenance and modernization measures are necessary (Deutsche Wohnen & Co Enteignen, 2023, p 30). The question of shops, local amenities, kindergartens, cafés, and so on also shows that the institutionalization of housing as social infrastructure is not only about individual housing, but also about the social and infrastructural networks of the neighbourhood.

The campaign's proposal is that there should be a total of 23 area councils. The task of the area councils is to form a hinge between the local level (that is the neighbourhood council) and the general council, so that a process

Figure 8.1: Illustration of the council structure as proposed by the campaign 'Expropriate Deutsche Wohnen & Co'

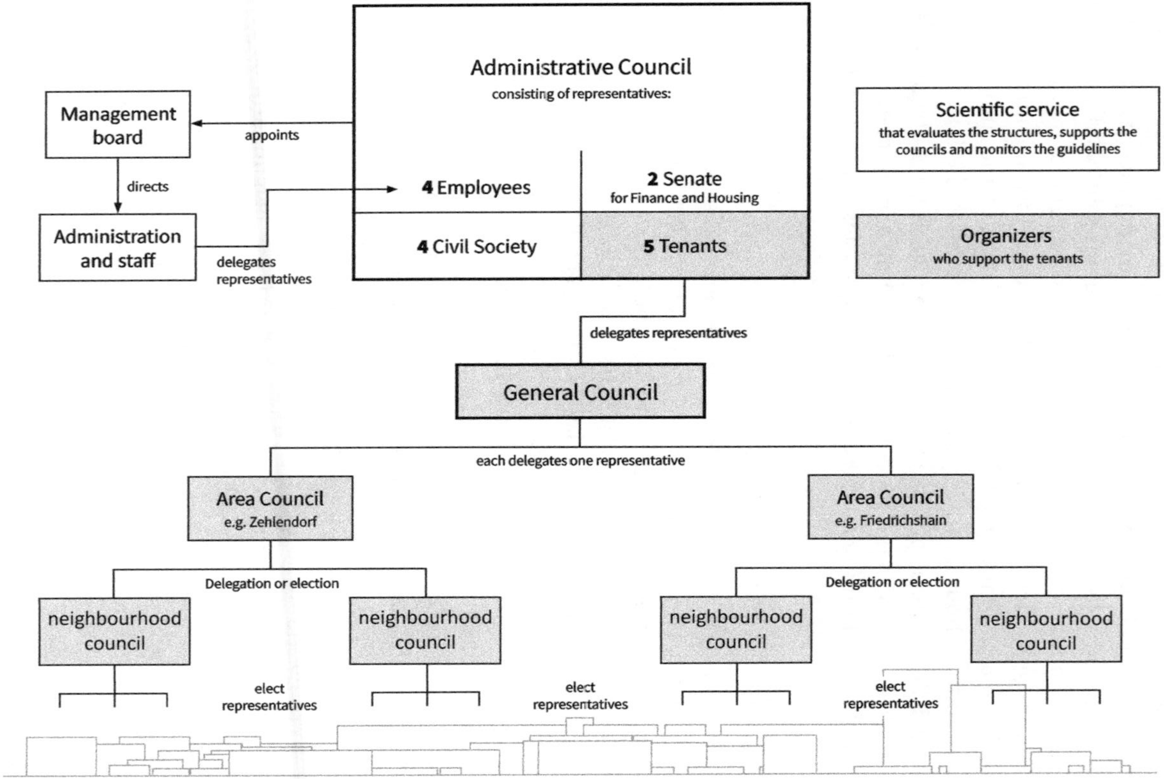

Source: Deutsche Wohnen & Co Enteignen, 2023, p 28; translation by the authors.

of will-formation can take place at the local level and that this collective will can be integrated into the decision-making at the central level, the general council (Deutsche Wohnen & Co Enteignen, 2023, p 31). The general council is composed of representatives from all 23 area councils and should therefore represent the collective interest of all tenants of the AöR. From the level of the general council onwards, delegation is preferred to the election of representatives. This is to ensure a better representation of the collective interests of the tenants. Through the principle of delegation, representatives have the opportunity to review the decisions of the councillors they delegate. This ensures the accountability of the representatives to the delegating council structures (Deutsche Wohnen & Co Enteignen, 2023, p 34). The council structure is thus intended to ensure democratic deliberation between different local levels and a central administrative level. In this way, the collective interest of the tenants can be formed and incorporated into the administrative decisions. The council-democratic administration of housing, which places this social infrastructure under the democratic control of the tenants and the city dwellers, shows a significant difference from the technocratic, top-down planning of housing provision in the Keynesian welfare state.

In the highest council, the administrative council, the general guidelines, such as the guidelines for the allocation of housing, are to be decided. As these guidelines 'affect the entire AöR or even the whole city', they are to be 'decided in a centrally organized way' (Deutsche Wohnen & Co Enteignen, 2023, p 34; translation by the authors). For an example of guidelines that are developed at this level, we can return to how housing allocation works in the AöR. We have seen that the campaign proposes a weighted lottery procedure. The quotas and their respective weighting would be defined in guidelines by the administrative council. This also means that there will be no participation in the actual allocation of flats, only in the discussion of the guidelines, in order to avoid discrimination and homogenization, especially in a city with a tense housing market.

A full-time administration is responsible for the property management as this cannot be carried out by the voluntary members of the councils. The administrative council consists of five seats for delegates of the general council, four seats for representatives of the employees of the AöR, four seats for representatives of civil society (Berliners who are not tenants of the AöR, for example tenants' associations or charities), one representative of the Senate Department for Urban Development and Housing, and one representative of the Senate Department for Finance. The executive board of the AöR is appointed by the administrative council and is bound by its instructions. The representation of the interests of Berlin's civil society is necessary to ensure that not only the interests of tenants living in the socialized housing stock are taken into account (Deutsche Wohnen& Co

Enteignen 2023, p 33). Why this reconciliation of interests is necessary can be seen, for example, in the question of how to deal with surpluses: Should surpluses be used to reduce the rents of the AöR, which might be more in the interest of the tenants living in the socialized housing stock, or should they be invested in the construction of new buildings?

Social-ecological transformation

A sustainable management of housing is a central pillar of a broader socio-ecological transformation, as approximately 30–40 per cent of greenhouse gases emitted annually are generated by the use and construction of buildings (Coulomb and Walker, 2021, 48; Vollmer and Kuhnhenn, 2022, p 2). Under the current housing market conditions, it is often private capital that determines whether and when the building stock is ecologically retrofitted. There is often a contradiction between the social need for affordable housing and a climate-friendly retrofitting of the housing stock, as the costs of energy modernization can be added to the rent. According to German law, landlords are allowed to pass on to the rent a maximum of 8 per cent of the modernization costs spent on an apartment. Therefore, ecological modernization is often used by landlords as a means to increase rents (Vollmer and Kuhnhenn, 2022, p 5). The campaign argues that the AöR should therefore pay the costs of energy modernization out of its revenues and not pass them on to the tenants (Deutsche Wohnen & Co Enteignen, 2023, p 23). In this way, socialization allows for a planned energy refurbishment of buildings in which social and ecological issues are no longer played off against each other due to the profit interests of capital.

Another ecological concern is the increased per capita consumption of living space (Coulomb and Walker, 2021, p 51). Mobility in the rental housing market is limited in that, due to the current housing crisis, there is generally too little supply in the affordable segment and significantly higher prices can be expected for new rentals. With rent control, the AöR contributes to more mobility and facilitates the exchange of flats (Deutsche Wohnen & Co Enteignen, 2023, p 25). In the long term, however, a redistribution of concrete living space within the housing stock of the AöR would also be possible. For example, when children move out of their parents' home, they could look for a new flat in the housing stock that better meets their new housing needs. This discussion also points to a central task of a planned housing supply, but also of a planned social production and reproduction in a broader sense: The socio-ecological transformation makes it necessary to distinguish between individual and collective needs. Accordingly, it could be an individual need to use more living space than would be appropriate according to the goal of socio-ecologically sustainable management of the housing stock. What is considered appropriate and what is considered a need requires structures for radical democratic negotiation that allow for the formation of collective interests that price in ecological externalities. Planning is thus not a top-down process, but a social and conflictual one. This example also shows that the common good-oriented provision of basic needs supports practices of solidarity. By securing housing as social infrastructure, a concrete reduction of living space is made possible.

As we have seen, the radical democratic planning regime of socialization renegotiates the contradiction between housing as use value and housing as exchange value. On the basis of public ownership, it replaces the market as the instrument for managing and allocating housing. Instead of private profit interests, there is a shift towards a common good orientation. Democratic negotiation with broad tenant participation is the central difference to the technocratic planning regime of the Keynesian welfare state. Understood as an infrastructure for social reproduction, this reorganization of housing opens up new, emancipatory possibilities for solidarity.

Conclusion

The socialization of large housing stocks proposed by 'Expropriate Deutsche Wohnen & Co' shows what a democratically planned and common good-oriented alternative to the financialized housing market could look like. As a proposal for a radical democratic planning of housing supply, the model extends the debate on planned economies to the realm of social reproduction.

We argued that socialization involves a transfer in ownership, which is a necessary condition for a common good-oriented and radical democratic management of housing as a social infrastructure. Through the council system, tenants and the broader urban society would be able to have a say in the administration and management of the housing stock. In both the allocation of housing and the determination of rental prices, market principles would be replaced by a focus on basic needs and affordability. The proposed model of radical democratic participation takes into account the goal of negotiating individual and collective needs in the face of an urgently needed socio-ecological transformation.

The choice of a referendum offers the campaign a possible answer to the question of transformation strategies, which has so far been little addressed in the new planning debate. Should the referendum be implemented by law, the new structures would provide an opportunity to test democratic planning in a real-life example.

The concentration of socialization on a sub-segment of 270,000 units also marks the limits of the proposal. Large parts of the housing market would remain organized in a free market economy. In addition, the AöR would be economically dependent on borrowing from banks for investments as long as it is not fully financed by public funds. Moreover, the implementation of the referendum by the Berlin Senate is still open, which shows the pitfalls in addressing the state in a transformation strategy. To translate the model for housing socialization and the transformation strategy to other contexts, an analysis of the specific legal conditions, the structure of the housing market and the political power relation would be necessary.

Notes

[1] The concept 'social factory' was developed by Marion Tronti specifically in the 1962 essay 'Factory and society' (Tronti, 2019, pp 12–35) and the 1963 essay 'The plan of capital' (Tronti, 2019, pp 36–64).

[2] https://www.gesetze-im-internet.de/gg/art_15.html

Bibliography

Aalbers, M.B. (2017) 'The variegated financialization of housing', *International Journal of Urban and Regional Research*, 41(4): 542–554.

Aalbers, M.B. and Christophers, B. (2014) 'Centring housing in political economy', *Housing, Theory and Society*, 31(4): 373–394.

Berfelde, R. (2019) 'Urban citizenship as cuidadanía. on urban social movements redefining the neighbourhood as an infrastructure of care', *éngagée*, (08): 18–22.

Bernt, M., Grell, B. and Holm, A. (eds) (2013) *The Berlin Reader: A Compendium on Urban Change and Activism*. Bielefeld: transcript (Urban studies).

Berry, M. (1981) 'Posing the housing question in Australia: elements of a theoretical framework for a Marxist analysis of housing', *Antipode*, 13(1): 3–14.

Bhattacharya, T. (2017) 'Introduction. Mapping social reproduction theory', in *Social Reproduction Theory. Remapping Class, Recentering Opression*, London: Pluto Press, pp 1–20.

Bhattacharya, T. (2019) 'From the production of value to the valuing of reproduction', in P. Osborne, E. Alliez, and E.-J. Russell (eds) *Capitalism: Concept, Idea, Image. Aspects of Marx's Capital Today*, London: CRMEP Books, pp 105–120.

Butler, J. (2018) *Notes Toward a Performative Theory of Assembly*. Cambridge, MA: Harvard University Press.

Coulomb, F. and Walker, B. (2021) 'Grüne Wände. Es gibt zu wenige Wohnungen für alle und die existierenden sind klima- und umweltschädlich. Wir müssen umbauen', *Jacobin*, 4: 48–53.

Deutsche Wohnen & Co Enteignen (2022) 'Was Vergesellschaftung kostet – Zahlen und Mythen', in Initiative Deutsche Wohnen & Co enteignen (ed) *Wie Vergesellschaftung gelingt: zum Stand der Debatte*, Berlin: Parthas Verlag, pp 275–291.

Deutsche Wohnen & Co Enteignen (2023) 'Gemeingut Wohnen Eine Anstalt öffentlichen Rechts für Berlins vergesellschaftete Wohnungsbestände'. https://content.dwenteignen.de/uploads/Gemeingut_Wohnen_3a03fa4c87.pdf.

Egner, B. (2014) 'Wohnungspolitik seit 1945, bpb.de'. https://www.bpb.de/shop/zeitschriften/apuz/183442/wohnungspolitik-seit-1945/ [Accessed: 26 June 2022].

Ferguson, S. (2020) *Women and Work. Feminism, Labour and Social Reproduction*. London: Pluto Press.

Fields, D. and Uffer, S. (2016) 'The financialization of rental housing: a comparative analysis of New York City and Berlin', *Urban Studies*, 53(7): 1486–1502.

Foundational Economy Collective (2018) *Foundational Economy. The Infrastructure of Everyday Life*. Manchester: Manchester University Press.

Fraser, N. (2017) 'Crisis of care? On the social-reproductive contradictions of contemporary capitalism', in T. Bhattacharya (ed) *Social Reproduction Theory*, London: Pluto Press, pp 21–36.

Gabor, D. and Kohl, S. (2022) 'The financialization of housing in Europe "My home is an asset class"'. http://extranet.greens-efa-service.eu/public/media/file/1/7461 [Accessed: 10 January 2023].

Harloe, M. (1995) *The People's Home. Social Rented Housing in Europe & America*. Oxford/Cambridge, MA: Blackwell Publishers.

Heeg, S. (2013) 'Wohnungen als Finanzanlage. Auswirkungen von Responsibilisierung und Finanzialisierung im Bereich des Wohnens', *sub \ urban. zeitschrift für kritische stadtforschung*, 1: 75–99.

Holm, A. (2022) *Objekt der Rendite: zur Wohnungsfrage und was Engels noch nicht wissen konnte*. 1. Auflage. Berlin: Dietz Berlin (Analysen).

Holm, A. and Schreer, C. (2019) 'Mietpreis-Exklosion und Wohnungsnotstand: Ursachen und Alternativen', ISW Report Nr 116/177, München.

Investitionsbank Berlin (2022) 'IBB Wohnungsmarktbericht 2021'. https://www.ibb.de/media/dokumente/publikationen/berliner-wohnungsmarkt/wohnungsmarktbericht/ibb-wohnungsmarktbericht-2021.pdf [Accessed: 20 January 2023].

Jenkis, H.W. (ed) (1996) *Kompendium der Wohnungswirtschaft*. 3., überarb. u. erw. Aufl. München: Oldenbourg.

Jones, C. (2020) 'Introduction: the return of economic planning', *South Atlantic Quarterly*, 119(1): 1–10.

Kusiak, J. (2021) 'Trespassing on the law. Critical legal engineering as a strategy for action research', *Area*, 53(4): 1–8.

Lay, C. (2022) *Wohnopoly: wie die Immobilienspekulation das Land spaltet und was wir dagegen tun können*. Frankfurt/Main: Westend.

Lompscher, K. (2018) 'Gemeinwohlorientierter Wohnungsbau und Wohnungsbauförderung in Berlin', *Fachtagung 'Gemeinnütziger Wohnungsbau in Wien und Wohnbauförderung in Berlin im Vergleich, veranstaltet durch das kommunalpolitische forum e.V. (Berlin)*, Berlin.

Luke, N. and Kaika, M. (2019) 'Ripping the heart out of Ancoats: collective action to defend infrastructures of social reproduction against gentrification', *Antipode*, 51(2): 579–600.

Madden, D. (2020) 'Housing and the crisis of social reproduction', *e-flux architecture*. https://www.e-flux.com/architecture/housing/333718/housing-and-the-crisis-of-social-reproduction/.

Madden, D. and Marcuse, P. (2016) *In Defense of Housing*. London/New York: Verso.

Metzger, P.P. (2020) *Die Finanzialisierung der deutschen Ökonomie am Beispiel des Wohnungsmarktes*. Münster: Westfälisches Dampfboot.

Negri, A. (1994) 'Keynes and the capitalist theory of the state', in *Labor of Dionysus. A Critique of the State-Form*, Minneapolis: University of Minnesota Press, pp 23–45.

Negri, A. (2005) 'Crisis of the planner-state: communism and revolutionary organization (1971)', in *Books for Burning: Between Civil War and Democracy in 1970s Italy*, London: Verso, pp 1–50.

Pistor, K. (2019) *The Code of Capital: How the Law Creates Wealth and Inequality*. Princeton: Princeton University Press.

Power, E.R. and Mee, K.J. (2020) 'Housing: an infrastructure of care', *Housing Studies*, 35(3): 484–505.

Saros, D.E. (2014) *Information Technology and Socialist Construction: The End of Capital and the Transition to Socialism*. New York: Routledge, Taylor & Francis Group.

Schönig, B. (2020) 'Paradigm shift in social housing after welfare-state transformation: learning from the German experience', *International Journal of Urban and Regional Research*, 44(6): 1023–1040.

Schüschke, F. (2020) 'Ausverkauft. Die Privatisierung von landeseigenen Grundbesitz in Berlin', *Arch+ Zeitschrift für Architektur und Urbanismus*, 53: 76–85.

Soederberg, S. (2021) *Urban Displacements. Governing Surplus and Survival in Global Capitalism*. New York: Routledge.

Tafuri, M. (1976) *Architecture and Utopia. Design and Capitalist Development*. Cambridge, MA: MIT Press.

Trautvetter, C. (2022) 'Wem gehört Berlin? Wer sollte enteignet werden (und wie)? Input zur Expertenkommission zum Volksentscheid "Vergesellschaftung großer Wohnungsunternehmen"'. https://www.berlin.de/kommission-vergesellschaftung/_assets/trautvetter_folien_oeffentliche-anhoerung_eigentuemerstruktur_2022-06-09.pdf [Accessed: 20 December 2022].

Tronti, M. (2019) *Workers and Capital*. London/New York: Verso.

Uffer, S. (2013) 'The uneven development of Berlin's housing provision. institutional investment and its consequences on the city and its tenants', in M. Bernt, B. Grell and A. Holm (eds) *The Berlin Reader. A Compendium on Urban Change and Activism*, Bielefeld: transcript, pp 155–170.

Vollmer, L. and Kuhnhenn, K. (2022) 'Bausteine für Klimagerechtigkeit. Gerechte Wohnraumverteilung'. Edited by Konzeptwerk Neue Ökonomie. https://konzeptwerk-neue-oekonomie.org/wp-content/uploads/2022/10/Dossier_Gerechte_Wohnraumverteilung_KNOE2022.pdf.

9

Democratic Planning in One Country? From the Anarchy of Public Planning to Negotiated Globalization

Christoph Sorg

A self-governing planned society ultimately requires a self-governing planned world.

(Devine, 1988)

Introduction

There is an unfortunate gap between the current Eurocentric debate on economic planning and the plural Southern histories and presents of planning, which features not only Chile's Cybersyn project, but also Yugoslavian and Arab socialism, the Latin American Pink Tide, varieties of Asian indicative planning, participatory planning in Kerala and visions of a new international economic order, among many others. The experience of colonialism and imperialism has always countered hegemonic discourses of capitalist free markets versus socialist planning, with core states using conscious political power to subsidize and protect strategic industries while prohibiting peripheral states from engaging in similar activities. Despite this rich history and the importance of the inter- and transnational realm to contemporary economies, the debate suffers from methodological nationalism. Most models of democratic planning seem to implicitly or explicitly assume a relatively closed national economy that is mostly self-sufficient and external to any kind of international division of labour.

This chapter departs from the assumption that democratically planned alternatives not only need to replace the destructive anarchy of production (and by extension the world market), but also the anarchy of the interstate system, which is home to the endless accumulation of political power on a world scale. I will first conceptualize planning in capitalism and communism and situate the anarchy of public planning within it. From there I will argue that a trans- and international perspective basically poses two questions, which will be tackled in later sections of this chapter: How can single experiments of 'democratic planning in one country' survive until a counter-hegemonic bloc has emerged that is large enough to subvert the logic of capital at a world scale? And, once a lower stage of world communism has been achieved, how could democratic planning be extended to the world scale in order to achieve a democratic world order, North–South convergence and planetary sustainability? With these issues being largely unexplored in the literature on democratic planning, this chapter will mostly explore questions that a more global perspective poses. So, the reader is encouraged to not interpret trajectories discussed here as a polished blueprint or concrete model, but as food for thought and further debate.

The argument will be that successful projects for democratic planning at the national scale will need to engage in 'delinking', that is a form of planning that privileges citizens' needs over world market imperatives. Successful projects can successively build structures of 'collective self-reliance', which creates space for and collaboration between democratic planning experiments, but also contributes to pushing world capitalism beyond its limits. Once a structural crisis emerges, this critical juncture creates the chance to break with capitalism at the global level also and subsequently create structures for a negotiated globalization. At such a point democratic planning can be substantially deepened within political territories, but there also need to be institutions for such territories to cooperate or engage in exchange. A form of communist commonwealth needs to replace the anarchy of public planning in order to facilitate global cooperation and coordinate a limited number of tasks. These include issues such as peacekeeping, provision of public goods and the coordination of social and ecological standards. Most immediately, a global negotiated coordination body needs to facilitate a global socio-ecological transformation. In the short term, this includes decarbonization funded by the payment of climate debt, thus linking colonial and climate reparations. In the longer term this means coordinating global investment in a way that ensures even development on a world scale.

Islands of conscious state power in a world market and interstate system

I would first like to briefly summarize my understanding of planning, capitalism and communism. There is not enough space here to properly elaborate my theory of planning in capitalism, but I have outlined this in detail elsewhere (Sorg, 2023b; forthcoming).

Following Nancy Fraser's (2014) expanded conception of capitalism, I understand capitalism as an institutionalized social order composed of an economic, social, ecological and political sphere (Sorg, 2023a). The economic sphere links private property of the means of production to generalized commodity production on markets. This institutionalized division of capital from labour ('workplace despotism') and of capitals from each other ('anarchy of production') constitutes capitalism's economic sphere, which is additionally separated from and depends on a social sphere that reproduces households and communities, an ecological sphere of non-human nature that provides free resources and sinks for waste, and a political sphere that stabilizes and subsidizes capital accumulation. The latter is where we can find the national–international interface: the interstate system segments national workforces and thus demarcates the difference between exploited and expropriated workers (Fraser, 2016). The former do not receive back the full value their labour creates, whereas the latter are compensated beneath even the costs of their own reproduction. Such racialized segmentation is profitable for capital as it marks some groups and territories (including the natural resources located therein) for expropriation. But in promising material and ideational 'wages of whiteness' (Roediger, 2007) it also prevents the global working class from coming together as a whole (Virdee, 2019).

Since capitalist totality takes the form of such an interrelated set of institutions/spheres, critiques of and struggles against capitalism have historically formed around individual grievances associated with single institutions, such as democracy at the workplace, the material recognition of care work or the safeguarding of nature. The task for a movement to overcome capitalism is to create explanatory frames that grasp capitalist totality and build alliances between movements against particular grievances. Against this background, democratic planning proposes a solution to competitive commodity production between workplaces, on the one hand, and the separation of the economic and political sphere on the other. In other words, democratic planning tries to create cooperative structures between workplaces and additionally mediate this cooperation with our multiple lived realities as citizens, consumers, marginalized status groups and so on.

Planning is already endemic in capitalism. This planning is neither particularly democratic nor directed at needs, but is instead dominated by the frequently irrational profit motive (for an extended conceptualization of planning in capitalism, see Sorg, forthcoming). With the economic and political being separated into distinct spheres, with their own respective logic of power, economic planning in capitalism takes the dual form of private corporate planning and public planning. Companies are 'islands of conscious power' (D.H. Robertson, quoted in Coase, 1937), where planned collaboration reigns supremely and individual divisions do not trade with each other. This corporate planning is conducted atomistically from other economic actors in the pursuit of profit. Atomistic decision-making in the presence of widespread interdependency creates uncertainty, inefficiency and periodic crises (Dobb, 1960; Devine, 1988).

Public planning aims to reign in such irrational and self-destructive tendencies of markets via regulation, redistribution and public investment, but can ultimately never overcome them in market economies. Public planning in market economies is indirect planning through the market. This includes the construction of public infrastructure, the provision of public goods and foundational research that is not directly profitable for individual firms. It is for this reason that much innovation in capitalism comes from the public sector (Mazzucato, 2013). However, inventions such as computers, digital cameras, typewriters, radio, air mail, virtual reality, microwaves and, arguably, even tampons, come from a particular part of the state, that is the military. Similar to the economic sphere of commodity production, capitalism's political sphere is itself separated into an international state system dominated by the endless accumulation of political power (Harvey, 2003; Arrighi, 2007, p 211ff). This means that public planning is also conducted atomistically in economic and political competition with other political territories. Militaries are pivotal for political competition, as leading powers have historically managed to boost economic growth via military spending ('military Keynesianism') and used arms to expropriate other territories, secure rents and generally shape terms of trade in their favour, which in turn allows for more military spending (Arrighi, 1994). At the same time, strategic industrial policy promises higher profits for the firms located in a particular territory, which equals higher taxation and thus higher public capacity for even more expenditure. Expenditures can also be financed via public debt, so states also compete for mobile capital, even more so in periods for financialization (Arrighi, 2007, p 94).

So, in a similar way that the anarchy of production features atomistic decision-making over investment by highly interdependent companies, the anarchic interstate system features atomistic decision-making by highly interdependent political territories. Public planning is conducted under 'subjective uncertainty' (Dobb, 1960) over the military, economic and ecological policies of competing states. Such uncertainty contributes to world economic and financial instability, arms races and military escalation, international inequality and ecological degradation. Anarchy here means the absence of central rule, not chaos (Arrighi, 1994, p 30), and a variety of institutions have emerged to mitigate interstate uncertainty. In the international realm this includes international organizations such as the United Nations, the World Trade Organization or the International Atomic

Energy Agency. Historically, even more important have been hegemonic orders, under which a particular political formation became dominant via a mixture of coercion and consent. Over time, such hegemonies have tended to innovate world political-economic organization and became more socially inclusive and featured ever larger hegemonic political territories to solve social complexity over time (Silver, 2003). Along these lines a future (post-neoliberal) order might feature multipolar globalization of regional blocs that internalizes social and ecological reproduction costs (Silver and Arrighi, 2011), but without popular intervention from below the future might as well hold new waves of fascism, ecological collapse or nuclear destruction.

Given that capitalism has always been a transnationalizing system and the devastating impact of international pressures on efforts at national economic planning in the early Soviet Union or Chile during Allende's regime, it is quite remarkable that the world market and interstate system feature so little in the older and current debates on planning. The analysis above precipitates two broad questions the new planners will have to find answers to: one relates to transformation and the other to how global planning might actually work. The following two sections will discuss them in turn.

Deglobalization by design, not by disaster

Marxists have historically expected revolution to break out in the most 'advanced' countries, where productive forces are most developed and the process of proletarization has created the social basis for transformation. From a global perspective one might add that attempts at democratic planning in high-income countries would have the highest chances to survive backlash by the world market and interstate system. However, dependency theorists such as Samir Amin have rightly observed that such countries receive 'imperialist rents' (Amin, 2010) derived from unequal international power relations, which makes it possible to provide more social welfare and thus somewhat soothe economic grievances. Along these lines Amin (1990) expects social unrest in underdeveloped countries, where exploitation and suffering is the highest. Christopher Chase-Dunn (1999, p 206ff) notes that, while this might be true, underdeveloped and dependent economies are also most vulnerable to foreign intervention. They thus expect social transformation mainly in the semi-periphery, that is the countries in the middle strata of the global power hierarchy, where relatively high exploitation meets state apparatuses strong enough to shield democratic socialist projects from foreign pressures. Even though the semi-periphery is notoriously hard to measure, it is hard to deny the role of, for instance, Argentina, India, Greece, Tunisia, Egypt, Chile, South Africa, China, Brazil and Turkey for recent and contemporary contentious politics as 'laboratories of contradiction and subversion' (Amar, 2013).

The point of such reflection is not to speculate where revolution will break out in a determinist way, but to situate local strategies for transformation in a global context. Unlike many of his followers, the late Karl Marx himself made clear that he rejected 'a historico-philosophical theory of the general course fatally imposed on all peoples, whatever the historical circumstances in which they find themselves placed' (quoted in Anderson, 2007, p 3). Social bases for protest and relative freedom from foreign intervention differ vastly across the globe and such discrepancy shapes terrains for struggle, but does not determine where the struggles will be successful. Discrepancies in social bases have given rise to peasant-worker alliances experimented with in much of the Global South, where a much smaller share of people had been divorced from their means of subsistence. More importantly for this chapter, foreign pressures might differ in strength, but the general constellation also applies to powerful core states in a globalized world economy. For instance, François Mitterrand's 1981 socialist-communist coalition experienced tremendous backlash when it tried to nationalize industries and banks and intensify dirigist industrial policy (Fourcade-Gourinchas and Babb, 2002, p 565ff). Capital flight and speculation against the franc split the coalition and thereby entailed a turn to neoliberal austerity.

The pandemic, the Suez crisis, the war in Ukraine, trade conflict between the USA and China and the general rise of the BRICS have precipitated discussions about deglobalization, which would increase national or regional sovereignty. While automation has so far not led to reshoring (Butollo, 2021), the perceived vulnerability of global supply chains in the face of geopolitical escalation could potentially entail widespread reshoring, friendshoring or regionalization. While such a development would certainly open space for transformation at the national level, periods of deglobalization and hegemonic decline have historically been associated with military conflict, for example the Thirty Years War, the Napoleonic wars and the two world wars (Arrighi, 1994; 2007). Given the dissemination of nuclear weapons and the dizzyingly long list of nuclear close calls, there is an urgent need for a global peace and demilitarization movement. Either way, any prediction of substantial deglobalization remains speculation at this point and projects for democratic planning will need to engage with substantial foreign pressure in the foreseeable future, especially in more dependent and peripheral states.

A global perspective on democratic planning thus needs to grapple with what may be called the transformation paradox: 'Socialism in one country' is impossible but so is a coordinated parallel world revolution. Social movement studies have very well documented that, while protest has increasingly trans- and internationalized, such processes are still mediated through the pivotal national scale, which is where political opportunities, mobilizing structures and thus most mobilization and claim-making reside (della Porta and Tarrow, 2005). Successful social struggles for democratic planning are therefore most likely at this level. The problem is that any national-level project that goes ahead and pursues post-capitalist transformation against vested interests and the law of value on its own does not only need to fear a capital strike by local businesses refusing to invest, but also capital flight and even sabotage by foreign states and elites. System-wide transnational rebellions have historically seen rulers put aside their disagreement and antagonisms and collaborate to restore social order (Arrighi, 1994, p 42ff) and there is no reason to assume that new attempts at social transformation would differ. Experiments with democratic planning might lose access to international capital and pivotal imports, face resistance by reactionary groups with strong foreign support and, in the worst case, military intervention. Given that popular support for democratic planning depends on subjective improvements in life chances, such backslashes would, over time, erode the social coalition that maintains democratic planning and thus either precipitate failure or authoritarianism.

Against this background democratic planning in one country needs to survive long enough for other states to follow in order to establish international support. In the meantime organized resistance by capital will likely precipitate a 'transition trough' (Wright, 2010), that is a decline in material conditions for the median person due to economic crisis, product shortages and unemployment. There are a series of strategies to smooth such a transition trough: Strong cooperative and social economy sectors less likely to sabotage social transformation, mutual aid and a strong cooperative financial sector to offset capital flight (on the role of democratic finance during a transition trough, see Block, 2019; Sorg, 2023b). However, there is ultimately no way around a confrontation with entrenched interests, which can only be won by strong social power from below and eventually by successful projects for transformation in other countries.

Samir Amin (1987; 1990) has previously suggested the concept of 'delinking' to describe a strategy of development that reorients national development from the priorities of the world market to the needs of a particular population. While this has been mistakenly interpreted as a form of misguided autarky, delinking does not preclude foreign trade, but engages in trade in terms of locally established priorities. The concept was specifically created for what was at the time called the Third World, where capitalism was introduced via colonial violence instead of endogenous enclosures and economic development was deliberately set up to channel economic rents towards colonizing countries. While trade under colonial and imperialist capitalism essentially means monopsony, colonized exporters being dependent on a particular metropole, delinking implies the sovereign right to free trade for all (Bockman, 2015).

Along these lines, Amin (2013, p 144) suggests 'self-reliant modes of development through national plans and by strengthening South–South cooperation'. Such a strategy necessitates conscious social and democratic control over the economy, investment and financial flows, that is democratic planning. However, the scope for such planning would still be extremely limited at this point. Dependence on foreign exchange means goods and services need to be competitive enough on the capitalist world market to pay for exports.

Delinking also implies unilateral sovereign debt cancellation to gain sovereignty over public spending until broader coalitions can collectively leverage their debt to push for a fair sovereign debt restructuring framework and broader financial transformation (Sorg, 2022; 2023b). Throughout the history of capitalism, debt has been a pivotal tool for colonial extraction and control, from the Haitian revolution to the British invasion of Egypt and the Global South debt crisis since the 1970s (Roos, 2019). There is a structural tendency for debt to build up in subordinate economies: Peripheral countries are dependent on access to technology and input imports for development, but can only pay for those with raw materials and other low-value-added products. Attempts at development thus require sovereign debt, the paying back of which depends on the uncertain outcome of development projects (Fischer, 2018). The issue has become particularly important as financialization has generally increased interstate competition for mobile capital (Arrighi, 2007; Krippner, 2011) and sovereign debt has become the primary source for public expenditure (Streeck, 2015; Roos, 2019). Most recently, the pandemic has further exacerbated sovereign indebtedness across the Global South and debt-servicing therefore swallows large segments of public budgets that are, in turn, not available for social spending and socio-ecological investment. Debt audits to cancel illegitimate debt and thus regain relative financial autonomy should therefore be part of any attempt at delinking. Attempts to repudiate debt in Argentina, Ecuador and the cancelled debt audit attempt in Greece have shown the possibility, but also the difficulties of such a strategy (Roos, 2019; Sorg, 2022).

Successful delinking needs to show that change is possible and desirable, but progressive countries are important also because they can provide resources for transnational social movements. While this should not take the form of previous Soviet domination of international communism, the capacity of Bolivia to host the 2010 world summit, which produced the People's Agreement of Cochabamba, reflects the importance of alliances between progressive governments and social movements.

Once enough countries have delinked from the systemic pressures of the world market and interstate system, they may pursue a strategy of 'collective self-reliance' (Lemper, 1977; Amin and Lindbeck, 1981). Structures of economic and technological collaboration facilitate further delinking by other emancipatory projects. The plural but unfortunately (in the Global North) largely forgotten histories of South–East collaboration, UNCTAD and Southern market socialism, may serve as inspiration of what such collective self-reliance could look like (Bockman, 2015). Socialist globalization and multilateralism would replace the bilateral hierarchies established by colonial capitalism.

In the presence of a multitude of social struggles for the material recognition of care work, universal basic services, higher wages, expanded commons, and the internalizing of ecological costs, among many others, projects for delinking and collective self-reliance will successively contribute to a structural crisis of the profitability of global capitalism. Without access to cheap natural resources, ecological sinks, Southern labour remunerated below reproduction costs and general 'imperialist rents' (Hickel, Sullivan and Zoomkawala, 2021), capitalism would enter a deep structural crisis. Such a crisis would radicalize struggles over social transformation, which might open the window for a break with global capitalism, but also for a post-neoliberal (potentially more exploitative and oppressive) regime of accumulation. In order to outline the relevance of a global perspective for post-capitalism in the next section, I will assume the pathway of a successful break.

Negotiated globalization and planning on a world scale

Once delinking and collective self-reliance have produced a counter-hegemonic bloc large enough to challenge the logic of capitalism at a world scale, the said bloc can successfully reshape and democratize institutions of global governance to subvert the systemic logic of capitalism at a world scale. It is at this stage that democratic planning can be vastly expanded within and between political territories. World market and interstate pressures stop to contain democratic planning at the national scale so property relations can more easily be overthrown, workplaces democratized, access to democratically established basic needs provided to everyone and decisions over social surplus made deliberately and democratically instead of leaving them to market forces. We could imagine a plural world in which different countries experiment with forms of negotiated coordination (Devine, 1988), multilevel democratic iterative coordination (Laibman, 2002), participatory economics (Hahnel, 2021), cybernetic socialism (Medina, 2011), democratic central planning (Dapprich, 2022), market socialism (Roemer, 1996; Schweickart, 2011) or come up with new varieties of planning. Not only would planning mechanisms probably differ, but also conceptions of basic needs and workplace democracy, the organization of political communes and the transformation of care work. The abolition of capitalism would also end systemic pressures for racialized expropriation, accumulation by dispossession and the endless accumulation of political and economic power. As a consequence, varieties of socialism would not feature systemic pressure to expand at the expense of outside territories, but could, in principle, learn from other experiments with planning.

Such transformations are necessary but not sufficient for global equality and justice. Even during the Second World War, in 1942, Otto Neurath warned that '"common ownership" in itself is no medicine at all' since '[w]ithout a kind of major international planning it could happen that a great number of local bodies (called "states") would fight one another on the world market as monopolists did before the war' (Neurath and Cohen, 1973, p 434). If market forces rule the economic interaction between varieties of national democratic planning, citizens of countries with pivotal natural resources, superior land and better climate will always enjoy birthright privileges over others. More concretely, and much more immediately important, any form of negotiated globalization needs to tackle the colonial legacy of capitalism's international division of labour and at the same time facilitate collaboration to avert ecological collapse. So, planning needs also to exist above the national level. What could this look like?

We could imagine that democratic planning moves to a regional-continental level parallel to a successive shortening of global supply chains. Circular-local economies would automatically reduce the need for economic exchange between regions to a minimum and thus rule out that any significant market forces emerge, thus prioritizing the mobility of people and ideas over the mobility of commodities and finance. In general, democratic planning needs to internalize ecological costs and long-distance transport of goods and inputs would thus be much less attractive, so we can only speculate what supply chains would look like in such a world. Whatever the answer to this question, however, in the shorter run a significant number of inputs will still be required from other countries. The global trade-to-GDP ratio has risen from 25 per cent in 1970 to above 50 per cent since the 2000s and a UNCTAD (2013) report estimates that 80 per cent of global trade takes place within value chains coordinated by transnational corporations. This means that not only are economies dependent on certain consumption products from abroad, but indeed goods production itself is dependent on inputs from global production networks. The provision of such inputs in the early stages of global communism really depends on the varieties of socialism that have emerged at this stage.

Boswell and Chase-Dunn (2000) have elaborated what a form of global market socialism could look like. They mainly take inspiration from John Roemer's coupon socialism and complement this approach with a more global perspective. Concretely, they (2000, p 184ff) argue that a combination of global democracy and world market socialism necessitates a federal socialist world bank to invest in transnational corporations and encourage investments in the periphery via interest rate manipulation. In addition, significant employee ownership requirements are supposed to ensure that workers in the Global South participate in the wealth they create within global value chains. Maybe most importantly, they propose a world government responsible for 'supporting international peacekeeping activities, providing certain public goods best delivered or coordinated globally, and enforcing global standards for human rights and environmental conditions' (2000, p 191).

Elias-Pinsonnault, Dufour and Tremblay-Pepin (2023) have discussed elements of international exchange present in three models of democratic planning. The proposals essentially provide mechanisms to make prices from other economic systems compatible with the import and export interests of a particular national variety of democratic planning. These mechanisms serve to protect democratic planning from external capitalist pressure and follow what is essentially a socialist version of the comparative advantage principle. They add that multifactorality should feature in decision-making, information on goods and services should be made transparent and trade should be cooperative in order to avoid dependencies and inequality.

Boswell and Chase-Dunn's (2000) global market socialism provides interesting reflections on global democracy, but falls short of the advantages of democratic planning and thus cannot overcome subjective economic uncertainty. The international components of Elias-Pinsonnault, Dufour and Tremblay-Pepin's varieties of democratic planning do abolish subjective economic uncertainty. However, their international components are rudimentary and the models they discuss either do not overcome interstate anarchy in the cases of Hahnel (2021) and Saros (2014) or do so in a problematic, overly centralized and unspecific way in the case of Cockshott and Cottrell (1993). Combining these approaches, the task for a model of negotiated globalization would thus be to link economic cooperation between national varieties of democratic planning to a form of global democracy.

Elias-Pinsonnault, Dufour and Tremblay-Pepin (2023) have discarded Devine's model of negotiated coordination because it does not explicitly elaborate on international trade or collaboration. However, I would argue that it is precisely this model and its combination of market exchange and democratic decision-making over surplus that has significant potential for a form of negotiated globalization at this early stage, in which forms of market exchange likely coexist with expanded forms of democratic planning. Even more so as Devine (1988, p 20f) does reflect on regional inequality at the subnational scale, which provides a fruitful departure point for reflections at the transnational scale. Concretely, he argues that the market success of a particular locality produces a virtuous cycle of attracting more investment and thus again more development, while unsuccessful regions experience the opposite. For Devine, national planning commissions are responsible for (sub-national) regional distribution in order to counter-balance such self-reproducing core-periphery dynamics. The main mechanism is the distribution of funds for investment, the concrete disposition of which is determined locally to ensure full employment and a fair social distribution of labour (Devine 1988, p 212ff).

We can easily imagine similar mechanisms for (transnational) regional or even global institutions. A communist commonwealth (CC) could take the form of an elected representative world government or a democratized United Nations. Notwithstanding the question whether representatives are directly elected, the institution could feature a two-chamber body in order to strike a balance between representation in terms of population size and better representation of smaller populations. The CC would generally be funded via progressive taxation on the multifactorial index used to measure material wealth (instead of GDP per capita) in such a world. Permanent progressive taxation would ensure that core-periphery dynamics could be continuously counter-balanced. The CC's main tasks would be Boswell and Chase-Dunn's peacekeeping, public goods and the enforcement of global social and ecological standards (including equal distribution of planetary natural resources); but we might add coordination of the immediate socio-ecological transformation, reparations and investment redistribution to ensure North–South convergence and generally even development.

The CC would distribute funds among these different tasks. We can imagine a global negotiated coordination body, which channels resources from under- to overdeveloped territories in order to drive North–South convergence and to continuously counter-balance core-periphery dynamics. This would concern material wealth, but also the global social division of labour. In terms of the latter, the body makes sure that, for instance, management and creative tasks (for example, planning and designing smartphones) and unskilled and repetitive tasks (or example assembling smartphones) are not clustered in different regions. The institution could receive an additional one-off climate tax based on historical carbon emission, which would link climate debt to colonial reparations. These resources would be used to fund decarbonization and technology transfer in order to converge resource-intensive and labour-intensive varieties of industrialization (Austin and Sugihara, 2013) within planetary boundaries.

Unlike the World Bank and International Monetary Fund, the governance of such a transnational negotiated coordination body would not be related to financial contribution, but representative of the world population and different regions. A marriage of democracy with technocracy (Braun, 2021), of radical democracy and radical bureaucracy (Morozov, 2019) could take the form of public officials selected by the representative CC. In order to combat the large distance between world government representatives and local citizens, the principle of subsidiarity would ensure that concrete forms of expenditure and as many decisions as possible would be decided at more local levels. Against this background, shorter supply chains are desirable not only ecologically, but because they ensure that far fewer stakeholders need to be assembled to negotiate a transformation of productive capacity.

Shorter supply chains should not precipitate parochial identities and free movement for humans and the successive abolition of borders should be important goals of such transformation. They set the state for a voluntary association of national-level varieties of democratic planning to be transcended towards a form of democratic planning on a world scale. I paint a picture here of communism as a longer (and uneven) process, but not because of a supposed lack of development of the forces of production and reproduction. Instead, I am assuming that only universal access to means of subsistence, equal development and the absence of interstate conflict provide the existential security to collectively unlearn capitalism and the intersectional particularisms and group-based enmity/modes of misrecognition it thrives on. This is in turn indispensable to continuously recreate the broad majorities necessary to successively get rid of more and more of capitalism's birthmarks, which will require compromises. The market may have lost some of its hegemony due to financial crises, climate change and increasing turbulence, but planning remains discredited for many and capitalism's social production of difference (Lowe 1996; Virdee, 2019) and the ideologies of inequality this generates are currently not on their way out.

In the same way that universal access to the basics of life should provide the foundation for an eventual organization of material life from each according to their ability and to each according to their need, the abolition of interstate competition and global inequality makes it easier for us humans to recognize ourselves as a joint but diverse species embedded in broader systems of non-human nature; and to construct new institutions that fit and further encourage this perception.

Bibliography

Amar, P. (2013) *Security Archipelago: Human-Security States, Sexuality Politics, and the End of Neoliberalism.* Durham, NC: Duke University Press.

Amin, S. (1987) 'A note on the concept of delinking', *Review*, 10(3): 435–444.

Amin, S. (1990) *Delinking: Towards a Polycentric World.* London: Zed Books.

Amin, S. (2010) *The Law of Worldwide Value.* New York: Monthly Review Press.

Amin, S. (2013) *The Implosion of Contemporary Capitalism.* New York: Monthly Review Press.

Amin, S. and Lindbeck, A. (1981) 'Some thoughts of self-reliant development, collective self-reliance and the new international economic order', in E. Lundberg and S. Grassman (eds) *The World Economic Order: Past and Prospects,* London: Palgrave Macmillan UK; Imprint Palgrave Macmillan, pp 534–557.

Anderson, K. (2007) *Marx's Late Writings on Russia Re-examined*. https://www.kevin-anderson.com/wp-content/uploads/docs/anderson-article-marx-late-writings-russia-re-examined.pdf

Arrighi, G. (1994) *The Long Twentieth Century: Money, Power, and the Origins of Our Times*. London: Verso.

Arrighi, G. (2007) *Adam Smith in Beijing: Lineages of the Twenty-First Century*. London/ New York: Verso.

Austin, G. and Sugihara, K. (2013) *Labour-Intensive Industrialization in Global History*. London/New York: Routledge.

Block, F. (2019) 'Financial democratization and the transition to socialism', *Politics & Society*, 47(4): 529–556.

Bockman, J. (2015) 'Socialist globalization against capitalist neocolonialism: the economic ideas behind the new international economic order', *Humanity, An International Journal of Human Rights, Humanitarianism, and Development*, 6(1): 109–128.

Boswell, T. and Chase-Dunn, C. (2000) *The Spiral of Capitalism and Socialism: Toward Global Democracy*. Boulder: Lynne Rienner Publishers.

Braun, B. (2021) 'Central bank planning for public purpose', in D. Fassin and M. Fourcade (eds) *Pandemic Exposures: Economy and Society in the Time of Coronavirus*, Chicago: HAU Books, pp 105–121.

Butollo, F. (2021) 'Digitalization and the geographies of production: towards reshoring or global fragmentation?', *Competition & Change*, 25(2): 259–278.

Chase-Dunn, C. (1999) 'Globalization: a world-systems perspective', *Journal of World-Systems Research*: 186–215.

Coase, R. (1937) 'The nature of the firm', *Economica*, 4(16): 386–405.

Cockshott, W.P. and Cottrell, A.F. (1993) *Towards a New Socialism*. Nottingham: Coronet Books.

Dapprich, J.P. (2022) 'Optimal planning with consumer feedback: a simulation of a socialist economy', *Review of Political Economy*: 1–21.

Della Porta, D. and Tarrow, S.G. (eds) (2005) *Transnational Protest and Global Activism*. Lanham, MD: Rowman & Littlefield.

Devine, P. (1988) *Democracy and Economic Planning: The Political Economy of a Self-Governing Society*. Cambridge: Polity Press.

Dobb, M. (1960) *An Essay on Economic Growth and Planning*. London: Routledge & Kegan Paul.

Elias-Pinsonnault, S., Dufour, M. and Tremblay-Pepin, S. (2023). 'An international interface: democratic planning in a global context', *Competition & Change*. 10.1177/10245294231212681.

Fischer, A.M. (2018) 'Debt and development in historical perspective: the external constraints of late industrialisation revisited through South Korea and Brazil', *The World Economy*, 41(12): 3359–3378.

Fourcade-Gourinchas, M. and Babb, S.L. (2002) 'The rebirth of the liberal creed: paths to neoliberalism in four countries', *American Journal of Sociology*, 108(3): 533–579.

Fraser, N. (2014) 'Behind Marx's hidden abode: for an expanded conception of capitalism', *New Left Review*, (86): 55–72.

Fraser, N. (2016) 'Expropriation and exploitation in racialized capitalism: a reply to Michael Dawson', *Critical Historical Studies*, 3(1): 163–178.

Graeber, D. (2011) *Debt: The First 5,000 Years*. Brooklyn, NY: Melville House.

Hahnel, R. (2021) *Democratic Economic Planning*. London: Routledge.

Harvey, D. (2003) *The New Imperialism*. Oxford/New York: Oxford University Press.

Hickel, J., Sullivan, D. and Zoomkawala, H. (2021) 'Plunder in the post-colonial era: quantifying drain from the Global South through unequal exchange, 1960–2018', *New Political Economy*, 26(6): 1030–1047.

Krippner, G.R. (2011) *Capitalizing on Crisis: The Political Origins of the Rise of Finance*. Cambridge, MA/London: Harvard University Press.

Laibman, D. (2002) 'Democratic coordination: towards a working socialism for the new century', *Science & Society*, 66(1): 116–129.

Lemper, A. (1977) 'Collective self-reliance – a development strategy of promise?', *Intereconomics*, 12(5): 115–120.

Lowe, L. (1996) *Immigrant Acts: On Asian American Cultural Politics*. Durham: Duke University Press.

Mazzucato, M. (2013) *The Entrepreneurial State: Debunking Public vs Private Sector Myths*. London: Penguin Books.

Medina, E. (2011) *Cybernetic Revolutionaries: Technology and Politics in Allende's Chile*. Cambridge, MA/London: The MIT Press.

Morozov, E. (2019) 'Digital socialism? The calculation debate in the age of big data', *New Left Review*, 116/117: 33–67.

Neurath, M. and Cohen, R.S. (1973) *Empiricism and Sociology*. Dordrecht: Springer Netherlands.

Roediger, D.R. (2007) *The Wages of Whiteness: Race and the Making of the American Working Class*. London/New York: Verso.

Roemer, J.E. (ed) (1996) *Equal Shares: Making Market Socialism Work*. London: Verso.

Roos, J. (2019) *Why Not Default?: The Political Economy of Sovereign Debt*. Princeton: Princeton University Press.

Saros, D.E. (2014) *Information Technology and Socialist Construction: The End of Capital and the Transition to Socialism*. London/New York: Routledge.

Schweickart, D. (2011) *After Capitalism*. Blue Ridge Summit: Rowman & Littlefield Publishers.

Silver, B.J. (2003) *Forces of Labor: Workers' Movements and Globalization Since 1870*. Cambridge/New York: Cambridge University Press.

Silver, B.J. and Arrighi, G. (2011) 'The end of the long twentieth century', in C. Calhoun and G. Derluguian (eds) *Business as Usual: The Roots of the Global Financial Meltdown*, New York: New York University Press, pp 53–68.

Sorg, C. (2022) *Social Movements and the Politics of Debt: Transnational Resistance against Debt on Three Continents.* Amsterdam: Amsterdam University Press.

Sorg, C. (2023a) 'Failing to plan is planning to fail: toward an expanded notion of democratically planned postcapitalism', *Critical Sociology*, 49(3): 475–493. doi: 10.1177/08969205221081058.

Sorg, C. (2023b) 'Finance as a form of economic planning? On the financialization of planning and its democratization', *Competition and Change*, 27(2): 209–230.

Sorg, C. (forthcoming) *Capitalist Planned Economies?: Theorizing Economic Planning in Market Economies.*

Streeck, W. (2015) 'The rise of the European consolidation state', *MPIfG Discussion Paper*, 15(1).

UNCTAD (2013) '80% of trade takes place in 'value chains' linked to transnational corporations, UNCTAD report says', *UNCTAD*. https://unctad.org/press-material/80-trade-takes-place-value-chains-linked-transnational-corporations-unctad-report#:~:text=Home-,80%25%20of%20trade%20takes%20place%20in%20'value%20chains'%20linked,transnational%20corporations%2C%20UNCTAD%20report%20says&text=%E2%80%8BGlobal%20trade%20is%20increasingly,a%20new%20UNCTAD%20report%20says

Virdee, S. (2019) 'Racialized capitalism: an account of its contested origins and consolidation', *The Sociological Review*, 67(1): 3–27.

Wright, E.O. (2010) *Envisioning Real Utopias.* London: Verso.

10

The Question of Transformation: Approaches to Economic Planning in Existing Policy Proposals

Samuel Decker

Introduction

This chapter presents a model of post-capitalist transformation that links economic planning at the conceptual level with redistribution and socialization policies. In this framework three constitutive characteristics of capitalist production (separation of wage labour and property, of enterprises among themselves and of the totality of enterprises and the state) are related to three levels of transformation beyond capitalism (redistribution, socialization and planning). This analytical framework, is designed to screen political programmes of left parties and election campaigns for aspects involving economic planning. The chapter concludes with a discussion about how a model of post-capitalist transformation and its empirical application can be improved further.

The new debate on economic planning – which this edited volume consolidates and takes to a new level – is one of the most vital and important progressive academic debates of contemporary times (see Morozov, 2019; Jones, 2020; Groos, 2021; Hahnel, 2021; Benanav, 2022; Dapprich, 2022; Laibman, 2022; Laibman and Campbell, 2022; Sorg, 2023a, 2023b; Vettese and Pendergrass, 2022; Groos and Sorg, 2024; Pahl, Scholz-Wäckerle and Schröter, forthcoming). The debate can be understood as an expression of the enormous crisis of contemporary capitalism, in which radical approaches that correspond to the magnitude of the crisis we are facing acquire more and more plausibility.

According to a system put forward by the author with Decker and Sablowski (2017), the present crisis represents the fourth great crisis of capitalism, which began with the 2008 financial crisis and follows the previous great crises that started in 1873, 1929 and 1973, all of which set in motion a decades-long process of economic and political transformation. In Gramsci's terms, these 'organic crises' are defined by the failure of existing institutional frameworks to solve them while still preventing radical political solutions (Candeias, 2013). In 2022 the author proposed the working hypothesis that the outbreak of the COVID-19 pandemic in 2020 and the war between the West and Russia in Ukraine in 2022 may have ushered in a new phase of the prevailing organic crisis that has been unfolding since 2008. This second phase, which is characterized by the mutual reinforcement of its (geo)political, economic, social and ecological dimensions and a general acceleration of the crisis, is marked by the irreversible exceeding of planetary tipping points, the materialization of the climate catastrophe through extreme weather events, crop failures, other climate disasters, increased geopolitical (military) conflicts and bloc-formation processes and increasing migration movements, all of which are connected to the economic crisis of globalization and the political crisis of liberal democracy (Albert, 2020; Alami, Copley and Moraitis, 2023).

Against this background, the new planning debate has been overly tardy demonstrating the foundations of an economically viable and politically feasible systemic alternative that could eventually result in broadly applicable political programmes to adequately address the crisis. If there is a political path towards averting climate catastrophe and progressively resolving the organic crisis of global capitalism, then economic planning approaches must be developed, popularized and linked to existing political approaches and institutions with great speed. In other words, the question of transformation is becoming increasingly more crucial. However, the question as to how a democratic and post-capitalist planning system can actually be established through smaller or larger interventions and ruptures in the coming years, embedded in a broader agenda of macroeconomic transformation, often remains unanswered in the current literature on economic planning (Sorg, 2023b). At the same time, a (rhetorical) agenda of transformation and even planning approaches are progressively being taken over by procapitalist agents and narratives (Brand, Görg and Wissen, 2019).

The aim of this chapter is to address the transformation gap in the economic planning literature on the conceptual level by embedding the approach of economic planning in a theoretical model of post-capitalist transformation, and on the empirical level by systematizing existing (or previous) economic policy approaches regarding their relation to economic planning.

To this end, a nonlinear (dialectical) model of post-capitalist transformation is proposed that combines redistribution, socialization and planning approaches at the conceptual level in the next section (after outlining general criteria for a transformation model). This model can simultaneously be used as an analytical tool to examine existing policy programmes for their transformative potential. In the section that then follows, this analytical framework is applied to systematize various left-wing proposals regarding their relation to economic planning. The chapter concludes with a discussion as to how the model of postcapitalist transformation and its empirical application can be improved further.

A nonlinear model of post-capitalist transformation
General problems of a model of post-capitalist transformation
While the debate on economic planning has fortunately experienced a qualitative development in the sense that basic categories of the various models have been defined and more advanced and complex models have emerged or are being reconsidered (Laibman, 2022; Sorg, 2023b; Heyer in this volume), the academic debate on models of post-capitalist transformation is still at a very early stage. Although some contributions have dealt with the concept of (social–ecological) transformation in the sense of a transformation beyond capitalism (for example, Wright, 2010; Stirling, 2015; Brand, 2016; Reißigs, 2016; Brand, Görg and Wissen, 2019; Klein, 2021), comprehensive and concrete models of explicitly post-capitalist transformation are generally lacking, as are classifications that point out fundamental categories and problems of different models, and relate them to each other. This chapter can provide neither such an overview on a meta level nor a fully developed stand-alone model. Instead this chapter will next describe seven general criteria that an advanced model of post-capitalist transformation should fulfil.

First, any model should be able to distinguish between capitalist and post-capitalist forms of transformation, in addition to explaining how they are interrelated. Second, a transformation model should include economic categories and show how the basic economic characteristics of capitalist economies can be overcome. Third, it must include a theory of change; that is, it must identify the factors and chains of effects through which transformation can be achieved. Related to that (fourth) the model must explain the relationship between gradual and ruptural change as part of the transformation process. Fifth, it should be applicable to empirical economic policy and make examining it possible; therefore, the model must be translatable from the necessarily abstract to the empirical level to enable concrete assessments. Sixth, a transformation model needs to include a clear understanding of the goal of transformation as the outcome of the specific form of post-capitalist transformation. Finally, and probably most challenging, the (hypothetical) process of post-capitalist transformation must be related to the broader process of societal and ecological transformation that is empirically ongoing and expected to unfold during the transformation process in empirical time. In other words, the theory of post-capitalist transformation must be linked with a theory of the multiple crisis, including foreseeable ecological disruptions.

The following introduces the author's own transformation model – which, as mentioned earlier, can only be understood as an initial conceptualization and not as a fully developed model – along with the criteria mentioned earlier.

General characteristics of the present model

First, regarding the distinction between capitalist and post-capitalist forms of transformation, the model draws on the concept of second-order transformation (Decker, 2019; 2020) that departs from Brand's (2016) assumption that transformation (that is, changing patterns of production and investment) is a general characteristic of societies in which the capitalist mode of production dominates. The model conceptualizes the capitalist mode of production based on three interlinked institutional demarcations that need to be transformed to realize a second-order type of transformation, which is supposed to fulfil the second criterion that was outlined previously of a transformation model that is based on clear economic categories.

Regarding the third criterion (theory of change), the model departs from a nonlinear or dialectical understanding of transformation. This means that changes or interventions in the political–economic order lead to dynamic feedback effects, resulting in further changes or the reversal of changes. This implies a certain understanding of the relationship between gradual and ruptural processes of change (fourth criterion), in the sense that gradual processes of change will lead to ruptures at a certain point where previous changes are either reversed or necessitate radical changes in the economic-political order to be stabilized.

The model is supposed to be translatable to the empirical level (fifth criterion) through a clear definition of areas of second-order transformation (see the next subsection) that can be observed in reality; however, the translation from the abstract theoretical to the empirical level remains underdeveloped, as will be presented in the concluding discussion of results. This also applies to the sixth criterion (clear understanding of the transformation goal). The model orients itself among the advanced models of coordinated or iterative negotiation and coordination, in accordance with Devine (2002) and Laibman (2022), without outlining the goal of transformation further. The model does not embed the hypothetical process of post-capitalist transformation in a broader theory of the multiple crisis (seventh criterion).

The model will be further described in the next two subsections by delineating the institutional demarcations the capitalist accumulation system is built on and the corresponding areas of second-order transformation.

Three institutional characteristics of capitalism

The first demarcation runs between property and labour or, more specifically, between the (to a greater or lesser extent) legally institutionalized relations of labour and the ownership of the means of production (Callinicos, 2007). This separation gives rise to the system of wage labour on the one hand, where the societal majority without property (or only with property that cannot be applied as means of production) sells its labour power as a commodity on a market for human labour. The separation of ownership and labour makes it possible to employ human labour in a way that produces use values that can be sold at a higher exchange value than initially invested to produce the use values. In this process, the relations of ownership that are financially represented as a sum of exchange values become capital by 'maintaining and multiplying themselves as an independent social power' (Marx, 2000 [1849], p 282).

The second demarcation runs between the various ownership relations that each independently define a closed system of capital accumulation (Callinicos, 2007). Whereas the separation of labour and ownership creates the *possibility* of absorbing more (exchange) value from the production process than investing in it, the separation between capitals creates *pressure* to absorb as much surplus value from the production process as possible. Capitalism's peculiar character rests upon the inter-capital rivalry for liquidity and sales that activates a competition-based dynamic of capital accumulation on the company level and capital centralization on the intercompany level (ten Brink, 2012, p 99). According to Marx (Marx and Engels, 2005 [1857/1858], p 327, translation by author), 'competition is nothing else than the inner nature of capital, appearing and realized as the interaction of the many capitals against each other, the internal tendency as external necessity [...] Capital exists and can only exist as many capitals'. Just as capital emerges as the unity of the difference between labour and ownership, it unfolds as the unity of the difference between different capitals, which appears as competition.

The internal competition of capital against itself is mediated via markets, especially commodity and capital markets. This shows how the sphere of production (of exchange value) and the sphere of circulation (of exchange value) originate from one another. The overall capitalist context appears as a network of interlinked markets that both enable and enforce the accumulation principle.

The third demarcation runs on a macro level between the different capitals and the network of law-creating and law-enforcing institutions in a certain area of jurisdiction. As with all three demarcations, this form of separation must be understood as a contradictory configuration of unity that is manifested in the form of an institutional separation that gives rise to the specific capitalist forms of the economic and the political in the first place. Whereas the individual capital absorbs (exchange) value in actu from a concrete production process by employing human labour, the capitalist state absorbs (exchange) value ex post from the sum of production processes by taxing labour and capital income and binding capital in the form of government bonds. At the same time, the capitalist state legally constructs and regulates the interlinked system of credit, capital, currency, commodity and labour markets and establishes the foundations for the creation of capital out of credit and the creation of money altogether with its central bank. At the empirical level, the institutional entanglement of the economic and political sphere appears in the concrete form of economic policy (that is, monetary and fiscal policy).

Three interlinked areas of second-order transformation

The three institutional demarcations outlined earlier are related to different conceptual areas of a second-order transformation (Table 10.1). The first demarcation (between labour and ownership) corresponds with the transformation of the relation between labour and capital. Capital exists as the extraction of value out of the production process via employing human labour. The organic relationship between labour and capital can be transformed via disturbing and ultimately disrupting the process of value extraction by capital at the expense of labour. We can distinguish between the ex-ante reduction of value extraction via enforcing wages, labour and production conditions that make production less profitable; and the ex-post appropriation of profit after surplus value has already been extracted. The latter normally takes the form of taxation, where a percentage of capital income or the source of capital income is retained by an authority capable of doing so.

These forms of surplus value reduction or appropriation (for which the term 'redistribution' is used in the following discussion) are highly contradictory as they undermine the process of surplus-value accumulation that they ultimately depend on. Thus, redistribution must be limited – and historically has been limited – to a degree that is bearable for capital. Beyond this threshold the contradiction between the proceeding restriction and appropriation of surplus value and the need to stabilize capital accumulation to enable those forms of redistribution in the future must be resolved towards one of these sides. This means that either the measures of redistribution are reduced to a degree that is compatible with capital accumulation or the process of capital accumulation is disrupted, and the production process is reorganized in non-capitalist ways. In other words, redistribution necessitates and naturally leads to socialization and planning as the other two levels of transformation are needed to resolve the contradictions it creates.

As Patnaik (2010, p 6) asserted, if interventions in the accumulation process are significant, make the system dysfunctional, necessitating either a reduction or withdrawal of such intervention, or a further intensification of intervention to overcome the dysfunction induced by the initial intervention. In the latter case, the progressive intensification of intervention in the system ultimately becomes incompatible with its capitalist integument, and requires its transcendence beyond capitalism.

The second area of second-order transformation is associated with the demarcation between individual capitals, which appears as competition and unfolds in the realm of the market. This relationship – or the constitution of capital in the form of its internal fragmentation – can be transformed by demerging individual capitals from the accumulation nexus and reorganizing production towards the creation of use values. This form of second-order transformation, which is referred to as socialization in the following discussion, logically connects with the contradictions concerning the appropriation of capital revenue created in the course of redistribution. When capital income redistribution completely disrupts the process of capital accumulation in the form of profit participation or taxation, the process of production and use-value creation can only be restabilized via the complete socialization of the respective capital (via employees or representative political agents).

Similar to the process of redistribution, the process of socialization is highly contradictory. While the internal manifestation of capital in the form of surplus value extraction from human labour is replaced with a political unit that organizes production collectively and is use-value oriented, the external manifestation of capital in the form of competition remains in place. Thus, although the relationship between labour and capital as the basis for the extraction of exchange value in one unit of production may have been completely transformed internally, it is expressed as an external necessity to produce exchange values to continue participating in the market. However, the contradiction between labour and capital is transferred from an intra to an intercompany level.

Thus, like redistribution, socialization creates a dialectical dynamic that necessitates either the recapitalization of production or the continuous socialization of the entire system of production as the progressive socialization of production requires and enables the construction of new forms of exchange, which come into conflict with the network of capitalist markets.

The socialization of the entire system of production cannot be carried out through the means of socialization itself but requires planning as the third and final level of second-order transformation. Planning refers to the third demarcation between the totality of capitals (referred to hereafter as capital) and the network of law-creating and law-enforcing institutions in a certain area of jurisdiction (referred to hereafter as state).

The core idea of economic planning is to establish non-market mechanisms to coordinate the production and distribution of use values in certain areas of economic activity. This mechanism involves both political decisions and automated processes to match supply and demand. This leads to a society where production and circulation are coordinated by (partially automatized) systems of societal decision-making, in other words where the demarcation between the political and the economic is dissolved.

Economic planning creates, as does the capitalist economy, a network of contradictions and dilemmas that society must process. For instance, dilemmas emerge between central and decentral as well as technocratic and democratic forms of decision-making and information-processing (Laibmann, 2022; Heyer in this volume). The role of money or a unit of account, the role of the state or a comparable political institution, and the problems of motivation and innovation in a planning system have been central issues in the planning literature (Heyer in this volume). A crucial contradiction that economic planning sets in motion refers to the conflict between one area (or level) of economic activity in which democratic planning has begun to dominate production, and other areas (or levels) of economic activity in which capital accumulation continues to dominate production. It should be made clear that this contradiction already comes into play in the other two areas of second-order transformation (redistribution and socialization), appearing as competition between capitalist states for favourable investment conditions. But it fully develops at the last stage of planning and is represented as a conflict between different political–economic systems. At this level, again, a dialectic dynamic is conceivable in which planning in a certain area or level of economic activity is either scaled back again or, conversely, the area of planned economic activity is expanded.

Integrating redistribution, socialization and planning into a unified scheme of transformation (Table 10.1) allows for the evaluation of the transformative potential of different political programmes discussed later.

Capitalist and post-capitalist forms of planning

Before evaluating whether existing political programmes incorporate economic planning approaches (next section), it is essential to differentiate between capitalist and post-capitalist forms of planning. As many observers have pointed out, capitalism involves economic planning both at the level of individual firms (planning for profit) and at the level of (partly supranational) state systems (planning for overall accumulation) (Sorg, 2023b). Crucially, both levels of planning are dominated by market forces that emerge through the institutional separation of individual capitals, where ex-ante profit-oriented corporate planning is combined with the ex-post valuation of

Table 10.1: An integrated scheme of post-capitalist transformation

Institutional demarcation	Area of second-order transformation	Type of second-order transformation	Contradiction between:
Between labour and ownership	Relationship between labour and capital (income)	**Redistribution**	Appropriating surplus value and making capital accumulation dysfunctional
Between individual capitals	Relationship between capitals	**Socialization**	Use-value oriented production and exchange-value oriented circulation
Between capitals and the state	Relationship between the production and the state system	**Planning**	Planned and capitalist areas or levels of economic activity

commodities on markets (Devine, 2002). The understanding of economic planning as a transformation of the institutional separation of state and capital (and thus of the nature of state and capital itself) that expresses itself in the establishment of non-market mechanisms of economic coordination and decision-making helps to distinguish capitalist forms of planning *through* the market from post-capitalist forms of planning *beyond* the market.

Planning through the market means that state actors implement measures to influence overall accumulation by influencing investment decisions by individual firms (for example, via grants, subsidies, tax credits, low-interest loans, public guarantees, procurements, credit provisions, equity investments or fictional markets) (Bulfone, 2022, p 24). Investment decisions by individual firms can also be influenced through non-coercive negotiation mechanisms (indicative planning), and the articulation of political goals (national economic plans) can also influence the individual firm's investment decisions, which can have a significant impact on private investment decisions, depending on the concrete political context.

A more developed form of capitalist planning not only influences private investment but also conducts public investment (supported by the central bank) that has a significant impact on overall accumulation. Industrial policy combines both – influencing private investment decisions and conducting public investment. Keynesian macroeconomic management also consists of large-scale public investment, which public firms largely undertake.

At this point, the relationship between state and capital is shifting in a structural sense, depending on the degree of public ownership. However, even if firms are publicly owned (or even run by workers), they can still take atomistic ex-ante investment decisions, while the valuation of produced use values continues to occur on markets ex post; thus, market relations and market forces continue to exist. The respective economic order would qualify as post-capitalist depending on the degree of ex-ante coordination of firms' investment decisions. In market socialist models overall ex-ante coordination does not take place, although different models have considered the possibility of influencing private investment decisions through public investment funds or other forms of socialized finance (Roemer, 1996; Schweickhart, 2011; Sorg, 2023b). More advanced models have taken investment decisions out of the hands of individual firms and embedded them in an overall network of democratic decision-making processes/mechanisms (Devine, 2002; Laibmann, 2022). At this point, ex-ante coordination of investment decisions occurs, although firms still interact with one another on a horizontal level through market relations. Market abolitionist models go further by proposing to embed all economic interactions in alternative coordination mechanisms (Cockshott and Cottrell, 1993; Hahnel, 2021; Sutterlütti and Meretz, 2023). Figure 10.1 summarizes the distinctions between the various forms of (post-)capitalist planning.

Economic planning in existing economic policy proposals

Methodological considerations

The theoretical model developed previously can be subject to empirical analysis by building on a mixture of hermeneutic and conceptual methods (discourse analysis and typology). Political programmes articulated in the public discourse can be analysed through the typology of the three areas of second-order transformation, with the specific distinction between capitalist and post-capitalist planning in the third area. In the logic of the nonlinear model of post-capitalist transformation, redistribution and socialization policies are both relevant for economic planning. However, the space constraints of this chapter only permit discussion of socialization and planning approaches and not redistribution policies. The empirical scope of this chapter is limited to the political programmes that political parties (or presidential candidates) have articulated that featured a progressive programme and simultaneously have a certain degree of relevance/visibility in the discourse over the past few years, which is limited to the EU and USA.

Findings

Laiki Enotita (Popular Unity), the left-radical splinter faction of the Greek SYRIZA party, articulated extensive claims in the direction of socialization and planning, though in highly generalized and vague language. The party demanded 'nationalization of the banks and their operation under a regime of social control' and the 'nationalization, reorganization, and relaunching

Figure 10.1: Planning in capitalism and post-capitalism

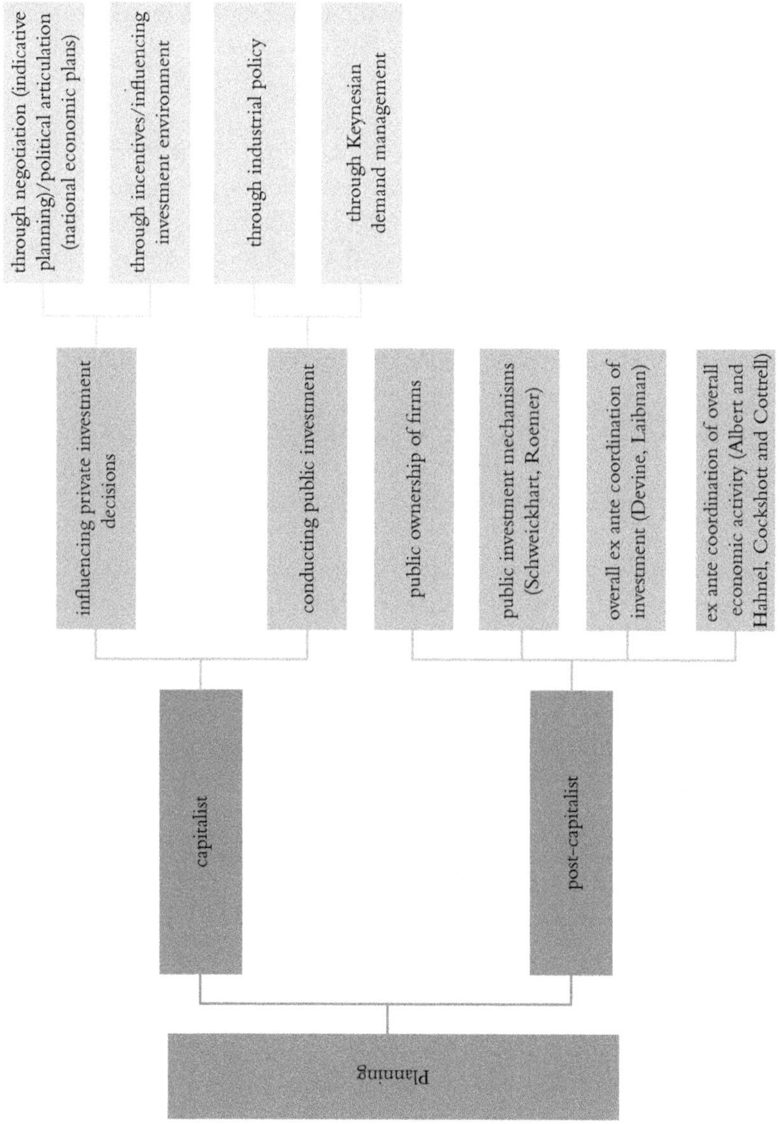

Planning
├── capitalist
│   ├── influencing private investment decisions
│   │   ├── through negotiation (indicative planning/political articulation (national economic plans))
│   │   └── through incentives/influencing investment environment
│   └── conducting public investment
│   ├── through industrial policy
│   └── through Keynesian demand management
└── post-capitalist
    ├── public ownership of firms
    ├── public investment mechanisms (Schweickhart, Roemer)
    ├── overall ex ante coordination of investment (Devine, Laibman)
    └── ex ante coordination of overall economic activity (Albert and Hahnel, Cockshott and Cottrell)

under a regime of workers control/social control of all strategic enterprises, networks, and infrastructure' (Popular Unity, 2015, np), which is a degree of nationalization and socialization that would enter an advanced stage of post-capitalist planning. The SYRIZA 2015 election programme (SYRIZA, 2015) (before the programmatic turnaround of the SYRIZA government with the signing of the third memorandum) contained no demands in this regard (SYRIZA, 2015).

In the UK, the 2019 Labour election manifesto proposed to nationalize the big six energy firms, the National Grid, the water industry, the Royal Mail, railways and the broadband arm of BT Group (Labour Party, 2019, p 16). In addition, it suggested a 'National Transformation Fund of £400 billion' with £250 billion directed to a 'Green Transformation Fund'. A 'National Investment Bank, backed up by a network of Regional Development Banks to provide £250 billion of lending for enterprise, infrastructure and innovation over 10 years' (p 13). These measures would have entailed elements of both capitalist (conducting public investment) and post-capitalist (public ownership of firms) planning, albeit in a premature and incomplete form.

In his 2020 platform for the US presidential election, the independent presidential candidate Bernie Sanders proposed a 'Green New Deal', including various forms of capitalist planning, to 'invest a [...] US$16.3 trillion public investment' to end 'unemployment by creating 20 million jobs needed to solve the climate crisis' (Sanders, 2020). The platform did not specify the degree to which public ownership of firms would have been part of these public investment efforts (in contrast to the Green New Deal approach the Democratic Socialists of America proposed (DSA, 2019; Decker, 2020)). In 2019, Sanders declared that his campaign was working on a plan to require large businesses to regularly contribute a portion of their stocks to an employee-controlled fund that would pay out a regular dividend to the workers (Bruenig, 2019). However, this proposal, which would represent a form of socialization depending on the percentage of stocks transferred to the fund and the degree of workers' control over firms' investment decisions, did not appear in the platform's 2020 demands.

The programme of the left alliance (Nouvelle Union Populaire Écologique et Sociale, NUPES), led by presidential candidate Jean-Luc Mélenchon in the 2022 French legislative elections, proposed to 'launch a massive €200 billion plan for environmentally and socially useful investments' and to 'use this money to invest and re-establish public centres in energy, transport and health in order to re-industrialize the country through sectoral plans' (NUPES, 2022, translation by author). In addition, the election programme contained a full chapter on 'ecological planning', with 27 associated demands. Measures ranged from more administrative forms of environmental planning (particularly in terms of water rationing and distribution) to more far-reaching forms of planning in which the state sets targets for sectors and mediates their transition to meet environmental goals; that is, to 'create a relocation agency under the authority of the Council for Ecological Planning, responsible for identifying the industrial sectors that are essential to national sovereignty and ecological conversion, and for drawing up a relocation plan for each strategic sector or production identified' (NUPES, 2022, translation by author). These demands largely represent forms of capitalist planning and, depending on the extent of public ownership of firms and the accompanying political (rather than market-based) coordination of investment, a post-capitalist form of planning is expected to emerge.

Conclusion

This chapter addressed the transformation gap in the economic planning literature at the conceptual level by embedding the approach of economic planning in a comprehensive theoretical model of post-capitalist transformation and, on the empirical level, by analysing existing (or previous) economic policy approaches regarding their relation to economic planning.

A nonlinear (dialectical) model of post-capitalist transformation that combines approaches of redistribution, socialization and planning at the conceptual level was proposed (after several criteria that transformation models should fulfil were outlined). By articulating the categorical distinction between redistribution, socialization and planning and that between capitalist and post-capitalist forms of planning, it was possible to examine the election programmes of various left parties and presidential candidates in the EU and the USA to assess the extent to which they included socialization and planning policies.

The electoral programmes examined all contained measures for large-scale public investment, some of which involved nationalization or socialization of public infrastructure companies or even key industries. The proposals primarily operated in the field of capitalist planning; according to the systematization presented in the chapter, where the relationship between the totality of capitals and the state begins to shift in keeping with the extent of public control of firms, creating a terrain for post-capitalist transformation. In this sense, Popular Unity (2015), Labour (2019) and NUPES (2022) introduced elements of post-capitalist planning. NUPES (2022) included a stand-alone chapter on ecological planning and proposed far-reaching measures on sectoral transformation beyond market mechanisms. None of the proposals entered the realm of more advanced forms of post-capitalist planning through an overall ex-ante coordination of firms' investment decisions through democratic decision-making processes and technical tools.

Though very limited, the empirical analysis in this chapter could be expanded to a systematic study of all left party programmes in the EU or other regions (including those in Latin America, Africa and Asia). Moreover, to exploit the possibilities of the transformation model presented, an in-depth analysis of redistribution policies might also have to be carried out. In the logic of the model, redistribution policies cannot be considered completely separately from planning policies as they could set in motion a nonlinear transformation dynamic that requires socialization or planning policies to be stabilized.

The transformation model remains underdeveloped and is insufficiently robust to allow for a detailed empirical analysis. In particular, the distinction between socialization and planning policies and between capitalist and post-capitalist planning (the first criterion) requires more concrete definition. Moreover, the interconnection of the three levels of second-order transformation remains primarily conceptual and does not yet allow conclusions to be drawn concerning a potential empirical transformation process. Furthermore, a comprehensive theory of change, a clear definition of the goal of transformation, and a linkage to the empirical analysis of the capitalist and ecological crisis are underdeveloped or missing.

The limitations of both the theoretical model and the empirical analysis highlight the general underdevelopment of the science-based transformation discourse. An overall lack of potentially operational transformation models that can work with the concrete characteristics of capitalism and alternative economic systems remains. Future transformation research should close this gap, focusing in particular on the level of socialization and planning and the connection and transitions between the three levels articulated here. In addition, global relations of dependency and critical developmental perspectives are underrepresented as the transformation scheme predominantly focuses on state–capital relations at the national level. Future research could include the international dimension in an additional category of transformation.

As stated in the introduction to this chapter, as alternative political programmes are gaining momentum amid the multiple crisis of globalized capitalism, it has become increasingly important to scientifically examine alternative policy proposals and contribute to their further development. Far-reaching party programmes that include socialization or even planning policies are usually created ad hoc and under great pressure, are not fully developed and disappear again after political defeat. The task of science is to collect and systematize concrete policies for post-capitalist transformation and embed them in comprehensive transformation models that can guide political strategies for post-capitalist transformation in the long term. The hope is that this chapter has contributed to this goal.

Bibliography

Alami, I., Copley, J. and Moraitis, A. (2023) 'The "wicked trinity" of late capitalism: governing in an era of stagnation, surplus humanity, and environmental breakdown', *Geoforum*, 153. https://www.sciencedirect.com/science/article/pii/S0016718523000179

Albert, M.J. (2020) 'Beyond continuationism: climate change, economic growth and the future of world (dis)order', *Cambridge Review of International Affairs*, 35(6): 868–887.

Benanav, A. (2022) 'Socialist investment, dynamic planning, and the politics of human need', *Rethinking Marxism*, 34(2): 193–204.

Brand, U., Görg, C. and Wissen, M. (2019) 'Overcoming neoliberal globalization: social-ecological transformation from a Polanyian perspective and beyond', *Globalizations*, 17(1): 161–176.

Brand, U. (2016) 'How to get out of the multiple crisis? Contours of a critical theory of social-ecological transformation', *environ values*, 25(5): 503–525.

Brink, Tobias ten (2012) 'Überlegungen zum Verhältnis von Kapitalismus und Staatenkonkurrenz', *Zeitschrift für Außen- und Sicherheitspolitik*, 5: 97–116.

Bruenig, M. (2019) 'Bernie wants power in workers' hands', *Jacobin*, 29 May. https://jacobin.com/2019/05/bernie-sanders-funds-socialism-shares-cooperatives

Bulfone, F. (2022) 'Industrial policy and comparative political economy: a literature review and research agenda', *Competition & Change*, 27(1): 22–43.

Callinicos, A. (2007) 'Does capitalism need the state system?', *Cambridge Review of International Affairs*, 20(4): 533–549.

Candeias, M. (2013) 'Gramscian constellations. hegemony and the realisation of new ways of production and living', *Rosa Luxemburg Foundation*, July 2013, Berlin. https://www.rosalux.de/fileadmin/rls_uploads/pdfs/allg_Texte/Gramscian_Constellations.pdf

Cockshott, W.P. and Cottrell, A. (1993) *Towards a New Socialism*. Nottingham: Spokesman.

Dapprich J.P. (2022) 'Optimal planning with consumer feedback: a simulation of a socialist economy', *Review of Political Economy*, 35: 1–21. doi: 10.1080/09538259.2021.2005367.

Decker, S. (2020) 'On the transformative potential of the "Green New Deal"', *Journal für Entwicklungspolitik*, 36(4): 51–73.

Decker, S. (2019) 'Contours of a critical transformative science', in S. Decker, W. Elsner and S. Flechtner (eds) *Principles and Pluralist Approaches in Teaching Economics. Towards a Transformative Science*, Abingdon/New York: Routledge, pp 287–297.

Decker, S. and Sablowski, T. (2017) 'Die G20 und die Krise des globalen Kapitalismus', *Rosa-Luxemburg-Stiftung*, Studien. https://rosalux.org.br/wp-content/uploads/2017/07/DIE-G20-UND-DIE-KRISE-DES-GLOBALEN-KAPITALISMUS.pdf

Devine, P. (2002) 'Participatory planning through negotiated coordination', *Science & Society*, 66(1): 72–85.

DSA (Democratic Socialists of America) (2019) *An Ecosocialist Green New Deal: Guiding Principles*. https://ecosocialists.dsausa.org/2019/02/28/gnd-principles/

Groos, J. (2021) 'Distributed planned economies in the age of their technical feasibility', *Behemoth* (2).

Groos, J. & Sorg, C. (2024) 'Rethinking economic planning', *Competition & Change*, special issue.

Hahnel, R. (2021) *Democratic Economic Planning*. London: Routledge.

Jones, C. (2020) 'Special issue: the return of economic planning', *South Atlantic Quarterly*, 119(1).

Klein, D. (2021). *Regulation in einer solidarischen Gesellschaft: Wie eine sozialökologische Transformation funktionieren könnte*. Hamburg: VSA.

Labour Party (2019) 'It's time for real change: The Labour Party Manifesto 2019'. http://labour.org.uk/manifesto

Laibman, D. (2022) 'Systemic socialism: a model of the models', *Science & Society*, 86(2): 225–224.

Laibman, D. and Campbell, A. (2022) 'Special issue: (en)visioning socialism IV', *Science & Society*, 86(2): 137–139.

Marx, K. (2000 [1849]) 'Wage labor and capital', in D. McLellan (ed) *Karl Marx: Selected Writings*, Oxford/New York: Oxford University Press.

Marx, K. and Engels, F. (2005 [1857/1858]) *Werke (MEW 42). Second edition*. Berlin: Dietz.

Morozov, E. (2019) 'Digital socialism? The calculation debate in the age of big data', *New Left Review*, 116/117: 33–67.

NUPES (2022) 'Programme partagé de gouvernement de la Nouvelle Union populaire écologique et sociale?'. https://nupes-2022.fr/le-programme/

Pahl, H., Scholz-Wäckerle, M. and Schröter, J. (forthcoming) *Special Issue: Envisioning Post-Capitalist Utopias via Simulation. Review of Evolutionary Political Economy*.

Patnaik, P. (2010) 'Socialism or reformism?', *Social Scientist*, 38(5/6): 3–21.

Popular Unity (2015) 'What does popular unity stand for?', *Jacobin*, 9 August. https://jacobin.com/2015/09/tsipras-popular-unity-syriza-eurozone-snap-elections/

Reißig, R. (2016) 'Transformation in unterschiedlichen Diskursen. Anmerkungen zum ‚Handbuch Transformationsforschung', in M. Brie (ed) *Futuring. Perspektiven der Transformation im Kapitalismus über ihn hinaus*, Wiesbaden: Westphälisches Dampfboot, pp 281–302.

Roemer, J.E. (ed) (1996) *Equal Shares: Making Market Socialism Work*. London: Verso.

Sanders, B. (2020) 'Issues. The Green New Deal'. https://berniesanders.com/issues/green-new-deal/

Schweickart, D. (2011) *After Capitalism*. Blue Ridge Summit: Rowman & Littlefield Publishers.

Sorg, C. (2023a) 'Failing to plan is planning to fail: toward an expanded notion of democratically planned postcapitalism', *Critical Sociology*, 49(3): 475–493. doi: 10.1177/08969205221081058.

Sorg, C. (2023b) 'Finance as a form of economic planning? On the financialization of planning and its democratization', *Competition and Change*, 27(2): 209–230.

Stirling, A. (2015) 'Emancipating transformations. from controlling "the transition" to culturing plural radical progress', in I. Scoones, M. Leach and P. Newell (eds) *The Politics of Green Transformations*, London/New York: Routledge, pp 54–67.

Sutterlütti, S. and Meretz, S. (2023) *Make Capitalism History: A Practical Framework for Utopia and the Transformation of Society*. Cham: Springer International Publishing.

SYRIZA (2015) 'The Thessaloniki Programme'. https://www.syriza.gr/article/SYRIZA---THE-THESSALONIKI-PROGRAMME.html

Vettese, T. and Pendergrass, D. (2022) 'Town, country and wilderness: planning the half-earth', *Architectural Design*, 92(1): 112–119.

Wright, E.O. (2010) *Envisioning Real Utopias*. London: Verso Books.

11

Care Revolution: A Transformation Strategy for a Solidary Society

Gabriele Winker and Matthias Neumann

Introduction

In this chapter we will argue that, in view of the destructive tendencies of the capitalist mode of production, which affect social relationships as well as ecosystems, it is essential to strive for a societal alternative. In view of the political balance of power, we seem to be a long way from such a society. But there is reason for hope that, perceiving the drama of this destructivity, a growing number of people, at first in their personal spheres, will withdraw their consent. A concept of revolutionary realpolitik is required in order to take up these wishes and turn them into political movements. We try to meet this requirement with the transformation strategy of the Care Revolution. Its central starting points are the reduction of gainful working hours, individual and collective security, the socialization of central economic sectors and the support of projects organized as commons. With these measures, a caring economy based on solidarity can be achieved, an area in which alternatives to capitalist development dynamics are tested and enforced. Ultimately, however, an alternative to capitalism at the societal level is required. This we call a solidary society.

Overburdening of human and non-human nature in the capitalist mode of production

Currently, it has become increasingly clear how exhausting it is for care workers, family care workers and people with a high need for care to lead their lives adequately. Care workers in particular work under high pressure to perform in poor working conditions. They are affected by burnout and other mental illnesses significantly more frequently than the average employee.

People doing care work in families are often overburdened when they try to combine increasingly flexible wage work with care work for children and relatives in need of care; as a result, care for oneself is neglected. Children, older relatives in need of care and people who depend on the support of others also suffer from this situation. All of this leads to deep insecurities and shocks, making it difficult for us to relate to one another and thus maintain successful social relationships. It is becoming more and more difficult to preserve the conditions that are still necessary for humans to live together.

By now, it is clear that people suffer not only from the social framework that makes caregiving difficult, but also from the destruction of non-human nature, which is particularly evident in the climate catastrophe: large areas will be lost for the cultivation of food, or will no longer be inhabitable because of temperatures that the human body cannot cope with. Hurricanes are becoming more destructive, and rising sea levels are driving people out of particularly fertile and densely populated coastal areas. Hunger, homelessness and increasing conflicts over resources are forcing more and more people, especially in the Global South, to flee. And there is no reversal of this trend in sight.

The connection between the processes of social and ecological destruction that are outlined here (cf Winker, 2021 in detail) is ultimately created by the capitalist mode of production itself. Both unpaid, family and voluntary, care work as well as ecological cycles count as free resources, which always seem to be available regardless of the extent of their use (Fraser, in this volume). Both processes are prerequisites for the valorization of capital, but they do not take place in the form of commodity production. Capital thus appropriates the results of these processes without having to worry about the conditions for their success.

This 'structural carelessness of capitalism'"[1] (Aulenbacher and Dammayr, 2014) presupposes that ecological processes and unpaid work are positioned outside the economy. Accordingly, unpaid care work is largely invisible. This works because care work in families, in social networks and in voluntary work is still carried out even under the worst conditions, because the life and wellbeing of both the care workers themselves and those close to them depend on it. All this makes it possible to see unpaid labour as an inexhaustible reservoir. In addition, the social infrastructure, which is central to supporting care workers, is primarily a cost factor from the perspective of capital accumulation. Both the scope of the social infrastructure – from maternity units and day-care centres to nursing homes and hospices – and the working conditions of those employed there suffer accordingly from structural underfunding. All of this is true until the point where the exhausted care workers rebel or there is no longer a sufficiently qualified, healthy and motivated workforce available. The parallel to dealing with natural processes is obvious here: the functional conditions of material cycles and ecological networks are also ignored by the mainstream economy as long as they can be used free of charge and capital utilization is not impaired.

This is related to the expansionist drive of the capitalist economic system, which is based on competition-driven growth. In an economy whose purpose is the valorization of capital, there is a systemically necessary ignorance and ruthlessness towards nature and human labour, which leads to their overburdening and destruction. Capital valorization presupposes the creation of a surplus product that can be appropriated by capital as surplus value. This means that more and more substances, more and more lifetime and expressions of life are sucked into the process of capital accumulation. Because the purpose of this process is not to produce more useful things, but to acquire more money, it is fundamentally excessive. There is no 'enough'. Because more efficient competitors threaten to force a company out of the market at any time, capitalist competition establishes a constant compulsion to modernize production processes and expand production. In this way, the growth tendency inscribed in capitalism becomes an immediate compulsion to act.

However, competition implies not only growth, but also cost pressure: it is not only achieved through greater efficiency, but the elements of the production process are made cheaper wherever possible. It does not pay to avoid emissions, and it does not pay to give wage-earners more time for reproductive work by reducing working hours with wage compensation, or to support them with a needs-based social infrastructure. In a society dominated by the valorization of capital, too few resources are always used to care for human and non-human life and the destructive power of this disregard increases every day with the expansion of capitalism into all regions of the world and with technical developments – with regard both to global warming and to the endangerment of social relationships.

As the problem is rooted in capitalism itself, a solution can only be found outside this mode of production. What we need is a societal formation that supports a direct orientation towards human needs and the limits of ecological cycles. This seems infinitely far away, but there is at least some reason for hope, because the number of people who perceive a threat in the continuation of the existing situation is growing, both in terms of the climate catastrophe and the overload and atrophy of social relationships. With regard to the climate catastrophe, this is certainly undisputed. Less obvious is the resistance to the work overload caused by the combination of paid work and care work, which particularly affects those who have taken on large-scale care responsibilities.

Resistance and search for alternatives

We spoke about the overburdening of care workers inherent to the mode of production. The demands in professional and family work are very high, especially for people with young children or adults in need of support. Irrespective of how you distribute the tasks between work and family, self-care and times of leisure are usually neglected. Successful care relationships are therefore difficult to build.

Even attempts at self-optimization usually only open up new time windows in which work that has been left behind can be done. So work without end continues daily, because in a capitalist system gainful employment is usually the only way to feed yourself and your children. This work often takes place under conditions in which competitive and instrumental references to others dominate and mutual empathy can hardly develop.

Nevertheless, many people in different situations in life keep taking steps to improve their living conditions by reducing their workload. Over the years there is, gradually, but consistently, a statistically demonstrable reduction of full-time employment. At the same time, women are reducing household chores, while direct care work for children in couple households is increasing. The focus of this individual action is the goal of gaining significantly more time for what is considered important in one's own life. Involvement in voluntary work and in political initiatives also indicates that many people do not just want to change their living conditions through a career in gainful employment, but also want to be active in a meaningful way. The actions mentioned undermine the invocations for more and more work and willingness to perform.

However, the step of questioning the framework conditions of capitalist society is by no means self-evident for a lot of people who try to improve the conditions of their lives. But, with an understanding of politics that takes people's needs seriously, activists can support this step. This includes voicing the absurdity of current economic activity with clarity: people are called upon to work as much as possible in order to produce as much as possible, even if the workload makes people sick. At the same time, they are encouraged to buy and consume all the manufactured products and services, even if this further damages the ecological system.

In addition, in the minds of many people there is not only an awareness of the suffering caused by existing conditions, but also a positive desire for a different quality of social relationships. This might be transformed into a desire for a change in society. This, however, is rarely linked to the idea of a specific social alternative, or even to its general possibility. To change something here requires taking seriously such suffering and desires, as well as experiences of contradictions and desires, and also developing a transformation strategy that is coherent in itself. The Care Revolution strategy we propose is the subject of the following section.

Care Revolution: a transformative strategy

The concept of revolutionary realpolitik

Even small successes give more people time for political work and strengthen their confidence that joint action can lead to success. It is therefore necessary to combine the struggles for social reforms with advocating a society in which everyone – organized in solidarity – can develop their own skills and democratically determine the future. Such a strategy moves beyond the scope of the current capitalist system. Rosa Luxemburg calls this 'revolutionary realpolitik' because the abstract juxtaposition of reform and revolution did not seem politically appropriate to her. On the 20th anniversary of Karl Marx's death, she wrote that his political conception made it possible for the first time to 'elevate the detailed political work of everyday life to the executive tool of the big idea'[2] (Luxemburg, 1970 [1903], p 373).

Therefore, debate is needed about political objectives that at the same time counteract the destructive tendencies mentioned, lead to an immediate improvement in living conditions and enable trying out alternatives to capitalism on different levels, concerning the purpose of production as well as social relations. This is where the transformation strategy of the Care Revolution comes in. Building on findings from feminist theory and politics, it places the fundamental importance of care work at the centre of society and accordingly advocates shaping all social coexistence based on human needs. Thus, care work, which plays no role in most political strategies or in the prevailing economic theories, and social relationships more generally are chosen as the point of reference for social change. The goal is a society based on human needs that is radically democratic and based on solidarity.

Building blocks of the Care Revolution

In the Care Revolution network (care-revolution.org), since its foundation in 2014, we have opposed profit orientation, competition and the need for economic growth, and we are committed to fundamentally improving the framework conditions for care employees, family care workers and people who have a high need for care. Changes are urgently needed.

Reduction in working hours

First of all, people need significantly more time at their disposal than is currently available, for example to full-time working parents with children. For this reason, a significant reduction in full-time employment, initially to 30 hours per week at most, is essential for everyone so that they can participate in unpaid care work. All employable people will then have, at most, a short full-time job with flexible long-term working time accounts that the employees can control, so that individual time sovereignty will also increase.

This reduction in working hours must be accompanied by wage compensation for lower-earning groups of employees and must be implemented without increasing the intensity of work. In this case both the total volume of gainful employment and production and the demand for goods for individual consumption will decrease. This forces society to engage in debates about the importance of individual economic sectors. For which goods should production be reduced, and to what extent should the health and education systems be expanded at the same time? Such reflections on economic priorities, when implemented – for example through production bans and public investment control – may make a major contribution to actually limiting global warming to below two degrees.

Employment-independent individual and collective insurance

In addition, it is important to ensure an existential security for everyone independent of wage work, for example through the realization of an unconditional basic income. At present, especially with the reduction in state-guaranteed pension payments, the greatest possible extent of gainful employment is becoming a condition for not only securing the current standard of living, but also security in old age. It is also important to expand the public social infrastructure in education, health and nursing, to make it free of charge and to increase its quality by training and hiring more specialist staff. In this context, the working conditions and wages of the mostly female care workers must be significantly improved. The latter also applies especially to the mostly migrant employees in private households. The shift from manufacturing to social infrastructure will also help to slow the pace of global warming.

Democratization through socialization of the means of production

In addition to the shift from individual to collective forms of security, it is important to design the necessary expansion of public infrastructure democratically, since people with care needs must have a say in this area, which deeply affects their own person, on the support they need. Organs of self-administration such as general meetings and councils, for example care or energy councils, as well as plebiscites with the power of decision-making are necessary.

It is a prerequisite for such democratization to stop the trend towards privatization that has prevailed so far and at the same time to promote the socialization of all those institutions and companies that do not allow users and employees to have a central influence on decision-making. This applies to charities and private companies that operate nursing homes or hospitals, as well as to enterprises in energy production or mobility.

Joint organization of work in commons

Community projects in city districts or in villages, which are already trying out new ways of cooperation, are enormously important for the development of a caring economy based on solidarity. They should therefore be supported by state funds. Examples are neighbourhood centres and multigenerational houses, but also facilities such as polyclinics or facilities involved in solidarity agriculture. These projects are already making important experiences with communal ownership and the collective organization of decision-making processes. They make the future more imaginable, are strongly oriented towards ecological goals and sometimes also make ways of living together beyond the core family appear attractive. It is important to us that, regardless of the family form, such communities, whether they comprise three or 30 people, may be seen as commons (Meretz and Sutterütti, in this volume). Whether this is the case does not depend on the number of participants and their family relationships, but on whether the commons criteria – equal decisions about the rules of coexistence, the division of labour and the use of the products of common work – apply or not.

Solidary care economy

If success is achieved in the areas mentioned above, a number of things will change: the living conditions of those people in whose lives care work is of great importance, and also of all people with low incomes, will improve fundamentally. Production in particularly emission-intensive areas will fall significantly. The influence of profit-oriented companies in central economic sectors will decline. Conversely, the employees and users in these areas will decide on the conditions of work and their output themselves. Such changes are particularly important in the areas of care work such as day-care centres, nursing homes or hospitals, but areas such as mobility, agriculture, housing construction or power supply must also be socialized (Berfelde and Möller, in this volume). In this way, a solidary care economy emerges as an area that is organized democratically and can therefore be directly aligned to human needs.

Since families are also relieved of the pressure of the demands of gainful employment, it becomes easier to orient the work done in families directly towards the satisfaction of human needs. In a caring economy based on solidarity, people can experience relationships that are not geared towards competition or the usage of others for one's own interests, but which focus on caring for one another, on solidarity and personal development. In a capitalist environment, however, this area will be constantly contested: it is withdrawn from capital valorization and practices are tested that are dysfunctional in capitalist companies. It is therefore constantly exposed to the risk of a roll back. Conversely, there is an opportunity to put solidarity society on the agenda from here.

Solidary society

Breaking with the division of spheres into paid and unpaid work

Building an alternative to capitalism is a long-term process,[3] because it is not just about the emergence of new social institutions but also about comprehensively breaking down classist, sexist, racist and bodyist norms and values and the actions determined by them. Because these values and norms are structurally secured in capitalist society and are reproduced again and again, they first have to be consciously deconstructed and unlearned. It also takes a lot of time to learn, when satisfying one's own needs, to take seriously the needs of people living far away as well as the needs of future generations, in so far as one's own actions in the present also affect their living conditions.

In order to counter the devaluation and overburdening of unpaid care work and ecological cycles in capitalism, the division of social work into paid and unpaid work must be ended. However, this should not happen by remunerating all work – that is, also work that has not been remunerated up to now – because then family care work would be exposed to even more direct performance checks and attempts to increase its efficiency than has been the case up to now with the call for self-optimization and in view of the omnipresent lack of time.

So the social form of paid work should be pushed back and that of unpaid work should be generalized. However, this does not mean 'idealizing what has been split off as "reproductive" and turning it into the normative'[4] (Hofmeister, Kanning and Mölders, 2019, p 243), for unpaid care work today is purposefully aligned to gainful employment and subject to its requirements and only indirectly considers human needs. However, in a society that does not need money and exchange, and therefore no remuneration, there is the possibility of placing the satisfaction of needs at the centre of the economy. This is valid, because in this society there is much more scope for caring and solidary relationships as well as for the careful handling of human relations with non-human nature, for there is no longer any societal logic that forces cost reductions and short-term overloading of ecosystems.

Society based on solidarity: the goal of the transformation process

In such a solidary society, wages and money, which previously served as a means of determining the individual's share in the social product, lose their function. While in a market society the access to goods and services is regulated by the price of the commodities and the income generated and by the state through transfer payments, the principle of self-selection applies in a society based on solidarity. All people have free access to what they need and what is produced based on the division of labour, because only individuals can know what needs they have and also determine whether a need is satisfied. The allocation of an individual share in the social product – be it through wages or equal income – is not compatible with such a radical need orientation, which takes every single person seriously in their individuality. Nor do we assume that it is necessary. For in a solidary society, material security and status are not related to the accumulation of individual property. Also, by collectively securing livelihoods, the importance of a wealth of things will decrease and instead the wealth of social relationships will gain in importance.

At the same time, it is evident that no one can meet their needs alone; a social division of labour is necessary. In a society based on solidarity, everyone can decide for themselves which activities they carry out and how much time they allow for leisure. The fact that people want to make a contribution is shown by the many experiences that already exist today with family care work and with voluntary or political work, which is also unpaid. Because needs are also satisfied in goal-oriented activity, at work. The variety of possible contributions ensures that everyone will find something they want to do. It is also motivating when the result of one's own work is needed and will be used. From a needs perspective, it makes sense to focus on existing needs. Where is the fun in baking bread rolls nobody needs? People will therefore take into account their knowledge of existing needs when deciding on their own work assignment.

From our point of view, people in a society based on solidarity will be motivated to only take the goods and services that they actually need, even without being forced to do so, and at the same time to contribute their skills and contribute their part to social work. The challenge for such a society is not primarily to solve a problem of motivation, but rather to organize the coordination between contributions and needs in a society in which there is no longer a market or state planning, because the type and quantity of what is produced must correspond to what is needed. A lot of things, especially care work, often cannot be postponed and must be available in the right place at the right time. Additionally, it is precisely here that stable relationships that meet the needs of all those involved are required. But how do people know what is needed and, if a product is scarce, how do they know how much they can take without depriving others?

In a society not founded on markets and compulsion, this coordination must be organized by means of disclosed information and discussions involving all interested parties. Wherever possible, the latter is done through on-site discussions and meetings. At this smaller scale, the people know each other. Directly relating to each other, they can perceive the needs of others, for example in relation to childcare, preventive healthcare or housing, and decide together how these needs can be satisfied. Where there are conflicting interests and conflicts, solutions that do not answer for everyone's wishes may be acceptable; for in conversations the urgency of another person's needs can be experienced.

The principle of notification-based or stigmergic coordination (Sutterlütti and Meretz, 2018, p 175ff.) applies in particular to supra-regional coordination tasks, which are necessary, for example, in the provision of goods and services for long-distance transport, in the production and use of certain machines or the establishment of a special clinic. Information, which is usually computer-aided, allows everyone to find out about requirements, stocks and free capacities. This provides indications of where there are currently surpluses and where bottlenecks are imminent. Building on this knowledge, individuals can decide to step in and work where there is a gap in meeting needs. People may also make suggestions for new products or logistical solutions and implement them together with others.

In all these coordination processes, this, like any other society, benefits from the fact that new needs do not arise every day and people do not want to get involved in a different area every day. Rather, there will be stable supply chains and agreements between individual commons. A farming cooperative and the households or canteens that receive and use this food can exchange ideas directly about production options and needs. Also, people in need of care are not cared for by different people each day, and in a factory it is not reconsidered every day where electricity or screws come from. This mostly makes coordination processes a challenge where extensive changes have to be managed. In such situations, not every distribution problem can always be solved immediately, which can result in shortages. Capitalism solves this by raising prices and thereby excluding poorer people from scarce products. A solidary society will deal with scarcities, quality problems and the inclusion of the limits that the ecosystem sets by democratically made agreements.

But even beyond the coordination of needs and the available volume of working hours, a society based on solidarity will again and again be forced to prioritize, not least because of the destruction of ecosystems that has already taken place, since certain raw materials are not responsibly usable in sufficient quantities or emissions have to be limited. In a society based on solidarity, such fundamental decisions are initially made where people are affected, that is as decentralized as possible. Wherever people work together, in housing projects and families, production facilities, day-care centres or health centres, people are in direct personal contact. These basic units of a solidary society are referred to here as commons. There, people set their rules together and find solutions together, for example when priorities have to be set.

However, this cooperation in commons or in decentralized assemblies does not make meetings and cross-regional decisions between people superfluous who, because of scale, do not know each other. Because there are a variety of problems that require decisions that can be discussed and decided not only in the local community, where the people involved know each other, but at supra-regional levels.

That is why councils, for example care, mobility, energy or nutrition councils at various spatial levels, make sense in a society based on solidarity. Concerning this, it is important in a solidary society not only for councils to be self-governing bodies of producers, but for all groups of participants, including users, to be represented on them. These councils can deal with questions at a supra-regional level, such as what a mobility system without carbon emissions can look like or which measures can be used to appropriately distribute scarce raw materials. It is the task of the councils to prepare social decisions, which can then be confirmed or rejected after broad discussion, for example by votes of the population affected.

The power of the councils is additionally limited by the fact that in a society based on solidarity there is no longer any institution that has the right to force people to act according to a decision. Because if the state as an institution separated from society is dissolved and its useful functions are socialized, there will no longer be an institution that can enforce decisions against individuals. Nevertheless, decisions that are prepared in councils and taken by referendums or plenary assemblies will serve as a guideline for those who have not dealt with the subject in detail. If decisions are made transparently and the benefit of generally applicable rules is seen, they will certainly be supported by people who would not have made them in this way. However, it must be possible to repeatedly discuss regulations and possibly revise them, for a solidary society can only rely on conviction and not on coercion. Social coexistence functioning on this basis is a condition for the existence of this society.

Conclusion

The main features of a society based on solidarity are therefore: all people have free access to what is produced based on the division of labour. At the same time, everyone contributes to the socially necessary labour to the extent that it is appropriate for them. This means that they make their own decisions about their contribution. In addition, the coordination between contributions and needs is realized through open information, notification and discussions with the social participation of all interested people. Societal decisions are either made in a decentralized manner through local debates and decisions, or are prepared nationwide through councils and confirmed by votes.

In this way, caring and solidary relations towards each other are supported by the basic structure of society. Conversely, it can only function based on mutual solidarity. From a care perspective, this is also a core issue because the needs of those who cannot speak for themselves, or only to a limited extent, must be given equal consideration. This may affect small children or some people with severe health restrictions, but also non-human beings. Only in a society in which it is suggested that one's own needs should be satisfied in convergence with the needs of others instead of on their backs do the non-speaking have a chance.

To be dependent on each other, to be vulnerable social beings, is then no longer threatening but can be experienced positively. In addition, in a society based on solidarity, which supports caring relationships and acting in solidarity, one's own potential can also more fully develop due to the free choice of one's own contribution. However, such a relationship towards one another not only requires a different social framework, but also long processes of learning that should be tried out in the rudimentary forms that are currently possible in social movements, communities and producing commons. This is another reason why it is so important to take and practise a caring attitude towards people, but also towards the non-human world.

Notes

[1] Translation by the authors.
[2] Translation by the authors.
[3] In the Care Revolution network, there are different ideas about what an alternative to neoliberal capitalism should look like. Here we present our personal ideas.
[4] Translation by the authors.

Bibliography

Aulenbacher, B. and Dammayr, M. (2014) 'Krisen des Sorgens. Zur herrschaftsförmigen und widerständigen Rationalisierung und Neuverteilung von Sorgearbeit', in B. Aulenbacher and M. Dammayr (eds) *Für sich und andere sorgen. Krise und Zukunft von Care in der modernen Gesellschaft*, Weinheim/Basel: Beltz Verlag, pp 66–77.

Hofmeister, S., Kanning, H. and Mölders, T. (2019) '"Natur" im Konzept Vorsorgendes Wirtschaften. Feministisch-ökologische Perspektiven auf gesellschaftliche Naturverhältnisse', in U. Knobloch (ed) *Ökonomie des Versorgens*, Weinheim/Basel: Beltz Verlag, pp 222–249.

Luxemburg, R. (1970 [1903]) 'Karl Marx', in R. Luxemburg, *Gesammelte Werke 1/2*; Berlin: Karl Dietz Verlag, pp 369–377.

Sutterlütti, S. and Meretz, S. (2018) *Kapitalismus aufheben. Eine Einladung, über Utopie und Transformation neu nachzudenken*. Hamburg: VSA Verlag.

Winker, Gabriele (2021) *Solidarische Care-Ökonomie. Revolutionäre Realpolitik für Care und Klima*. Bielefeld: transcript Verlag.

12

Relational Revolutions

Eva von Redecker in conversation with Jan Groos

Introduction

The following is an edited transcript of an episode of the *Future Histories* podcast, run by Jan Groos.[1] Jan pursues *Future Histories* as a form of research practice and has, since starting the podcast in 2019, recorded a variety of episodes related to the topic of this book. While Eva von Redecker's main research focus is not on questions of democratic planning, she nonetheless engages with the topic frequently. Her work on interstitial revolutions, a temporal understanding of freedom and contemporary anti-capitalist struggles provides important insights for the broader debate about democratic planning.

The extended audio version of the conversation in German can be accessed through the link provided in the endnote.

Eva von Redecker in conversation with Jan Groos

Jan Groos: *Future Histories* engages quite a lot with the question of democratic planning, and my feeling has always been that it is absolutely crucial for the planning debate to occupy two pillars: freedom and security. These two pillars cannot be thought of separately. I can only really have freedom if there is also existential security, for everyone, not just for me. Because if there is no existential security for others, I will always live in fear that those others could endanger my security. Perhaps we can also link this question of security and freedom with the question of democratic planning. I know that you have been dealing with this on an ongoing basis. How can we think about that? What can such a production of freedom and security look like within the framework of democratic planning?

Eva von Redecker: So, of course, it should be ecological and based on solidarity or, as I sometimes say, world-preserving. I am totally in favour of using freedom and security as important basic concepts. The concept of security has been hijacked by the right for much longer than the concept of freedom and I think it's absolutely right to not put up with that and to take these concepts back. In fact, the concept of security has the same problem as the concept of freedom, namely that it has been subordinated to the concept of property in liberal theory. In this derivative way it works for competitive capitalism, otherwise it wouldn't. You can observe this in Jeremy Bentham particularly clearly: he defines security via strongly secured property rights. Security then becomes the idea that I will be able to dispose of a good that already belongs to me in the future as well. That is actually an absurdly small portion of security and not, to use a metaphor, the canteen where I can always be provided for. That's why I think we have to try to think of security differently, namely from the perspective of sharing common goods, from the promise of mutual provision. Such provision will of course require time. If peoples' time is tied up in wage labour, with which they desperately try to provide for themselves by accumulating enough property for their own pension and their own future, then of course it doesn't work. Neither does it work if they have to constantly work against the fear of the future that you have just described so nicely. If others are not safe, then they have a good motivation to attack me and rob me of my stuff. That's the world we live in, and this structural insecurity is something that the capitalist promise of security can't get rid of, except perhaps temporarily through the Leviathan, through punitive institutions. And the failure of law-and-order security gets hidden in racist population politics, which create a white sense of safety by exposing racialized groups to ever greater police brutality. So that is a radical loss of safety for the targeted groups, and a frenzied climate of fear for all. You cannot have real safety without solidarity.

One thing I sometimes ask in debates about material restraint is, 'What would you need to feel safe even though you no longer have a certain thing? What promise, what perspective might make you not need your own car anymore?' The answer might actually be something like occasionally being alone in the train compartment and nobody's bugging you, or something like that. These are often very particular things or particular needs that are guaranteed by property and the security that property provides. In this respect, the democratic aspect of planning would, first of all, be to repeatedly enquire about needs in a way that is actually open to outcomes. I believe that needs also change quite strongly when people have the feeling of living in peace and friendliness. In such a scenario there is certainly a much, much lower need for accumulating things. Provisioning would then look different, because it would be based more strongly on trust in solidarity-based systems (Winker and Neumann, in this volume). In this respect, I would say that separating the question of security from the question of property and a new adjustment to solidarity would be a recipe for success.

Jan Groos: What would this look like in concrete terms? Is there a framework through which you think about democratic planning? Are there certain basic concepts that you have already set out and that need to be worked on? Perhaps you already have concrete proposals for an approach to addressing the question of democratic planning? I would be very interested in that.

Eva von Redecker: I think you always have to consider the level at which we are capable of acting and, depending on that, there are different paths. There is a centralist path, and that would mean that we would have governmental power at least at the national level. If that were the case, I think that even a minimal planning effort in the form of rationing, such as that now being propagated by Ulrike Herrmann (2022), for example, would make a tremendous difference, especially in terms of gaining the trust of the population in relation to justice and equality. If we had simply said during the energy crisis that everyone would get the same number of kilowatt hours for free, roughly enough for a small apartment, and above that it would be really expensive, then that would have already achieved a lot. Then no one who is already struggling would have to worry about their heating costs. So rationing can, I think, change a lot in terms of the overall societal feeling, because you get away from this resentment of always thinking that someone else is somehow doing better. But that would require the will of a government that wants to act and, unfortunately, there isn't one at the national level at the moment. There isn't even a party that has such a programme.

A glimpse of hope is the city of Graz. An example of socialism not in a country, but in a city. In Graz, the mayor is from the KPÖ [Communist Party of Austria], the very social democratic, but still communist, party of Austria. As a communist mayor at the municipal level you can't actually do anything – you can't simply expropriate and socialize, because you don't have the legal basis for that. And what did they do in Graz?

They have socialized their own salaries, that is the mayor herself and all employees of the city administration who are in the KPÖ capped their salaries at €1,900 net. This is still a decent salary, but they would have more otherwise. Everything that is above €1,900 goes into a social fund and so several million accumulate per year. This money is then given away quite unbureaucratically and quickly as an aid measure wherever there is urgent social need. Maybe this is not entirely democratic in the slightly non-procedural form, but it does promote the capacity for democracy to the extent that people can actually experience being helped with their problems individually and quickly. So even where you think socialization is not possible, there are possibilities.

I believe that the path to central planning that imagines to conquer the centre first – be it by election or by revolution – and then to start planning, is hopeless. At this historical moment, a lot depends on how far we manage to set up infrastructures for material solidarity and provisioning within social movements. But the models have to be scalable. It doesn't help to wait until you can implement something on a society-wide basis. We can start now with partial community care or even care for parts of society. But partial need not mean local. That is the great advantage of our real-time information technology.

I think we have to recognize the humble beginnings of planning, or else we have nothing to build upon. Think of forest occupations during which activists create wish lists of things that they need for their activities and then others come and deliver items from the lists. Such structures need to be scaled up, so that they don't just support a specific form of political action, but extend beyond that. It could allow activists to have an existential security beyond a given concrete action in order for them to have time for activism, or facilitate world-preserving work, or help with reproduction and care work for each other, and so on. I think that creating such structures of care should actually be the primary goal for movements at this moment of relative powerlessness on the left. Movements that are working well demonstrate this. Black Lives Matter is a good example. I don't think many people in the German movement contexts are aware of how much reproductive work is done for each other in the movement, among the activists themselves. Some of it is very professionalized. Reproductive work is certainly a very large part of what keeps a movement going. The interesting question would be whether we can also implement this for certain goods that one would otherwise obtain from the productive sector? That's where I currently am in my thinking about ways forward.

So a good way to demonstrate democratic planning would be to introduce it in certain segments of existing movements. With regard to coordination, I think distributed digital systems can certainly help with all the needs that can be fulfilled, irrespective of who provides the service. With these, you can feed in needs — basically the wish list — and then you probably need an assignment system to classify things according to the type of need, the geographical location and so on. A haircut will have to be provided close to your own location; for other services location is not a decisive factor. But it wouldn't have to work in a centralized way, it could work through cybernetic networks, meaning that no one would have control over everything just because they're sitting at a node. The whole system could work completely anonymously, with not only activists connecting to it, but basically everyone. Ideally, something like this would make people suddenly feel safer and give them an experience of non-market, non-state supported care. After all, that's what a democratically planned economy would be, not a state as we currently know it, but a different state. And this is not a decentralized vision. It's a distributed one. Everything is connected, but not to one single lever of control.

Jan Groos: In some cases of commoning you can find very similar structures to the ones you've just described. It reminds me of commons-based approaches such as the one proposed by Meretz and Sutterlütti (in this volume). It also reminds me of the Global Commoning System, which I discussed with Markus Meindl on *Future Histories* (Meindel and Groos, 2022). That's a little bit along the lines of what you described. What I like very much is that this is also very much thought through in a way that has issues of transformation in mind. You don't allow yourself to leap unconditionally into the future, so to speak, but actually try to think it directly coming from the question of transformation, out of the process of construction within the individual movements, which I like very much.

I would be interested in your opinion on a particular problem that is closely intertwined with the issue of freedom. In the planning debate, the approaches differ quite a bit with respect to the question of freedom and voluntariness or, more precisely with respect to the question of whether work should be voluntary. Some form of activity, some form of work is or is not needed to ensure the reproduction of society, and the question naturally arises in the context of democratic planning as to how this is to be implemented. Do you rely on radical voluntariness or is there some other way of addressing that? I would be very interested to hear your thoughts on this. There is also the position that freedom and voluntariness are not the same thing.

Eva von Redecker: I'm sure I'll have to think about it some more, but I am, and this is perhaps surprising in a certain way, more on the side of voluntariness. I'm a big fan of Heide Lutosch (in this volume), whom you've already had as a guest on *Future Histories* (Lutosch and Groos, 2022), and of her critique of the concept of the Friends of The Classless Society (2019). Heide says you must all be nuts, reproductive work is just so exhausting and gruelling and it must be distributed fairly. Everyone has to do their share, I don't want to have to wait until the last dude in the intentional community feels like doing the dishes. From this perspective, it's a privilege in the bad sense to think that from now on you only do what you feel like doing. I think this critique is really important and the text in which she elaborates this is great (Lutosch, in this volume). But a socialist economy nevertheless stands or falls with the slogan 'each according to their abilities, each according to their needs'. And the greatest promise is that fulfilling other peoples' needs within one's abilities does itself turn into a need. We would want to do necessary work. And if we wouldn't, then how would the control function? Models such as timebanks that establish equivalences like 'the more time you invest the more stuff you're allowed to take out', easily degenerate into a different or new kind of terror and also into a kind of pettiness that doesn't make utopia very desirable. I think these models are also pragmatically unrealistic, because the fantasy that you can force people always catches up with them. What I would always ask the advocates of timebank theories and also those for whom work simply has to be compulsory is how they intend to get people to work. You can't force people to do it well and a care job that is done unwillingly and involuntarily is almost worse than if it is not done at all. You can only force people to not be doing anything else during that time, but to think that they would actually do things that they really don't want to do ends up becoming a control fantasy again. That is not realistic planning. Force provokes resistance. I keep having the experience in my collective household that the most urgent jobs are less likely to get done if you put them on a big scary to-do list. I don't think that means that you can just get rid of such ranking and prioritization systems and just wait to see who volunteers in each case. I find the approach of Meretz and Sutterlütti, for instance, interesting (in this volume; 2023), but to simply rely on the fact that some indicator of need, which they call the stigmergic signal, is already sufficient, that is also naive.

I think one way you could link that to my thinking about time is that the work that we commonly call reproductive work, but in which I would also include something like putting out future forest fires, are things that have an incredibly short time horizon. It simply has to be done now, and there is a necessity that arises from the nature of the activity and is to some extent related to it. One definition of reproductive work is 'production of life', 'provision of life's needs', and of course the screw factory that built the screw for this mic stand here is also part of the reproduction of life in the socialist economy. But in case of doubt, one can better endure a supply stop in this screw factory than a power cut in an intensive care unit, a crying child that nobody attends to, or a harvest going to rot. I have the feeling that we need a different way of thinking about the necessity of certain work. So, one of my suggestions would be to say that, to some extent this could be addressed through the immediacy with which the question of life or death arises in the performance of a task, or that this could even be quantified in some way. Based on this, we have to organize society in such a way that there is a great deal of redundancy in the areas where such work arises, for instance in the children's ward and the fire brigade. In other words, a lot of people are working to ensure these needs are met, which is the opposite of how things are now. Firefighting is still ok here, but in the USA they already use prisoners for forced labour. At present, reproductive work in families is unfortunately organized in such a way that there is no safety net at all, which, to be clear, means that one person's time – or at the very best that of two – is totally committed to the needs of another for the rest of their life, or at least for the next 18 years. That someone with this experience of reproductive work in the form of motherhood then says 'it's absurd to say all work is voluntary', seems completely appropriate to me. I'd suggest that what follows for the planning debate is to look at interesting radical feminist proposals, such as Sophie Lewis's (2022), and to say 'well, then we have to organize families in such a way that every mother will have multiple surrogates, and kindergarten teachers, and so on'. We need to make people replaceable first and then see who really does their labour voluntarily. This is roughly the opposite of how we organize our society at the moment. Hospitals are extremely understaffed, although the most urgent work is being done there, and at the universities a lot of people are competing for a few positions and are doing things that could probably also be done tomorrow. And there will be tough democratic debates. Some areas of reproductive work – like cleaning before a visit of the inlaws – to me seem extremely negligible compared to all the labour we need in an ecologically transformed agricultural sector, for instance.

So, those would be some initial considerations. That means, above all, that a reorganization of work areas can have a positive effect on the urgency or necessity of certain work.

	Then you only have to make sure that the required work is being done by any one out of 20 people, and that the same person is not always forced to step in. That is perhaps still not fully voluntary, although one can, of course, then also say that these positions are perhaps taken voluntarily and if no one takes them, then one must ask oneself what is going wrong to make this work so unappealing. Sometimes it is the shadow of past oppression. I definitely will need a few decades without any remainder of patriarchy before I can do housework in the presence of men who do anything less than a full half of it. So, some tasks maybe need to be rationed. And yet the better path always is to investigate how the job could be made more attractive, and made to mean something. Ultimately, I think such mechanisms are a good way to ensure that the work is done.
Jan Groos:	So, if I understand it correctly, this means that there is a core sector that is basically determined by urgency and that this core sector is simply multiply secured by people who volunteer to do it. Everything that lies outside of this sector of urgency is basically not so important that you can't simply see how it unfolds on its own, so to speak. Because one question for 'commonism' (Sutterlütti and Meretz, 2023) is how to create this congruence, so that for all the needs that are there, people can be found whose need it is to satisfy exactly the need of the others. But you're actually shifting that a bit in the direction of, let's look at the basics, so that everything runs well, and from there we can look further. That's how I understand you now.
Eva von Redecker:	I think there is an interesting overlap, because the things that are very urgent are often the ones that have a very unproblematic ecological impact. Another element that I would like to feed into the democratically planned economy of the future, not as the final

criterion, but as a basis for decision-making, is the regeneration time that a good has. That basically goes all the way to geological, ultimately biological material cycles of planet earth. I believe that we need an indicator that shows whether we are using things of which the geological production time is incredibly long, or whose retention time in the earth's ecosystems is incredibly long, for example plastic or carbon dioxide. In such cases, an extra alarm bell is needed so that, in the democratic planning process, the environmental council and the climate research council and other councils look at it and decide whether it can be done at all. Many people are so fixated on this worry about whether everyone will stop working, but there is also the worry that everyone will want to have an electric Porsche or something like that, so there would need to be a mechanism in place to disincentivize such a form of overconsumption, too. This goes as far as saying, no, this is not as important as the pacemaker getting a battery – the latter comes first. 60 per cent of the work that is done now is care work. This is not a side job that women do after work, but actually the majority of the work in the economy. That's why it's so important to first think about how we plan for it. At the same time, we need to avoid the opposite pitfall and forget the role that longer supply chains play in reproduction. Sometimes, especially when white, liberal feminists discuss the topic of reproductive work, it sounds as if reproductive work is only the work that we would also phenomenologically describe as care, that is emotional, affective, physical close-range activity. But that's not the case. Go ahead and try doing some care work without someone building beds and growing potatoes. If you think of an economy from the perspective of reproductive work, you

	naturally also arrive at the necessity of all work, also classical productive work, that is, all the way to industrial supplies. The key is to arrange them according to their usefulness for life and not for profit.
Jan Groos:	Very nice, that's also a good conclusion. At the end, I always ask the question: if you think about the future, what makes you joyful?
Eva von Redecker:	For my new book, I thought a lot about swallows. This unique joy when they arrive. I experience that as a great freedom, to see that another species is alive and comes past, that somehow the reproduction of our lives can fit together. Barn swallows use human buildings. They wouldn't be better off without us. And I learned that they are not quite so much in danger of extinction. I found that so reassuring [*laughs*]. So there probably are still swallows and humans around in the future and I think together we can be able to pull of some kind of economy that is based on solidarity.

Note

[1] This conversation with Eva von Redecker is part of the 'Future Histories LIVE' format, in which selected episodes are recorded live – i.e. in front of an audience. This episode was recorded on January 9, 2023 as part of an event organized by the university group Rethinking Economics Kiel. Find the extended audio version of the conversation in German here: https://www.futurehistories.today/episoden-blog/s02/e38-eva-von-redecker-zu-bleibefreiheit-und-demokratischer-planung/

Bibliography

Friends of The Classless Society (2019) 'Contours of the world commune', *Endnotes* 5. https://endnotes.org.uk/issues/5

Herrmann, U. (2022) *Das Ende des Kapitalismus: warum Wachstum und Klimaschutz nicht vereinbar sind-und wie wir in Zukunft leben werden*. 2. Auflage, Köln: Kiepenheuer & Witsch.

Lewis, S. (2022) *Abolish the Family: A Manifesto for Care and Liberation*. London; Brooklyn: Verso.

Lutosch, H. and Groos, J. (2022) 'S02E32 – Heide Lutosch zu feministischem Utopisieren in der Planungsdebatte', *Future Histories*. https://www.futurehistories.today/episoden-blog/s02/e32-heide-lutosch-zu-feministischem-utopisieren-in-der-planungsdebatte/

Meindel, M. and Groos, J. (2022) 'S02E28 – Marcus Meindel zum Global Commoning System', *Future Histories*. https://www.futurehistories.today/episoden-blog/s02/e28-marcus-meindel-zum-global-commoning-system/

Sutterlütti, S. and Meretz, S. (2023) *Make Capitalism History: A Practical Framework for Utopia and the Transformation of Society*. Cham: Palgrave Macmillan.

PART III

Non-Boundaries

13

Planned Degrowth: Macroeconomic Coordination for Sustainable Degrowth

Elena Hofferberth, Cédric Durand and Matthias Schmelzer

Introduction

While many governments around the world, supported by international organizations, continue to promote economic growth through policies of green investment, decarbonizing industrial policies or through sustainable business practices, more people have started to doubt whether these strategies will be enough. This critique of economic growth is not just increasing within social movements but is supported by more and more within academic research. The popular idea of green growth is increasingly being challenged on empirical grounds (Haberl et al, 2020). Indeed, scientific evidence from recent years shows that, with continued green growth taking place in the high-emitting countries of the Global North, it is extremely unlikely – if not impossible – to reduce greenhouse gas (GHG) emissions at the rate and scale needed to avoid climate collapse.

The framework that has become prominent in recent years to articulate both the analysis that green growth cannot be sustainable and that a different form of organizing society is possible, is 'degrowth'. Degrowth calls for a planned contraction of economic activity aimed at increasing wellbeing and equality. Degrowth argues that, to achieve sustainability, so-called developed countries need to abandon the objective of GDP growth and scale down less necessary and destructive forms of production to reduce energy and material use (Weiss and Cattaneo, 2017; Kallis et al, 2018; Schmelzer, Vetter and Vansintjan, 2022). To avoid major disruptions in such a transition process, the degrowth literature proposes to escape the expansionary and accelerating dynamics of the capitalist economy 'by design, not disaster' (Victor, 2019). Yet, the specifics of this 'design' are rarely precisely delineated. On the one hand, there is a wide acceptance, at the abstract, even definitional, level, that degrowth involves planning or amounts to a planned transition. In fact, degrowth is often defined as a 'planned' social-ecological transformation, in which the reduction of energy and material throughput in the Global North is qualified by terms such as 'managed', 'purposeful', 'intentional', 'deliberate', or 'democratic' (Schmelzer, 2015, p 264; Parrique, 2019, p 224; Hickel, 2020, p 221).

On the other hand, there is strikingly little explicit research into what exactly 'planning for degrowth' could look like. Degrowth scholars have so far largely neglected existing literature on democratic or participatory planning and economic democracy, and related debates, proposals, and models. The potential reasons for why planning has so far largely been neglected in degrowth research are manyfold: the anarchist origins of the movement and a related scepticism of states; the brutal experience of Soviet-style planning and its limits; a tendency to remain wedded to capitalist institutions, including market mechanisms and market instruments in the steady-state economics and, to a lesser extent, the post-Keynesian postgrowth 'new economics of prosperity'; and – in the degrowth current coming from the anthropological critique of growth – a bias toward localism, community, and cultures that stands in a stark contrast to ides of economic planning (Durand, Hofferberth and Schmelzer, 2024).

This gap urgently needs to be addressed. Building on recent arguments that highlight the need to move beyond capitalism to achieve just and sustainable degrowth (Hickel, 2020; Kallis et al, 2020; Schmelzer, Vetter and Vansintjan, 2022), this chapter aims at laying the foundation for a conception of in-kind, non-market-mediated forms of planning through multilevel, fractally integrated and subsidiary democratic institutions. Any social-ecological transformation, we argue, cannot simply rely on cost–benefit-based rationality that underlies market and price mechanism, but must centrally focus on advancing needs-based and limits-based rationalities through social-ecological planning. This allows moving from an economy governed by market exchange, irrational movements of prices, and profit-driven corporations to a more conscious management of production and consumption systems in line with social and ecological needs. Such planning beyond growth, we propose, can be understood as a set of institutions supporting decision-making processes informed by social and bio-physical indicators and driven by deliberately stated social and ecological targets.

So, how could planning beyond growth look like? Here, degrowth does not need to invent the wheel – but can build on ongoing productive debates about ecological planning, participatory economies, and economic democracy. There is a long history of ecological planning in geography, environmental management, and industrial engineering. Most importantly, economic planning has been an important topic in both economics and socialist literature, and is currently seeing a resurgence as an explicitly post-capitalist project (Phillips and Rozworski, 2019; Sorg, 2023). However, most of these planning discussions, as well as related debates on digitalization platform communism, have largely neglected ecological questions, the issue of growth or degrowth, and limits in general (Hahnel, 2021; Cockshott, Dapprich and Cottrell, 2022; Tremblay-Pepin and Legault, 2022). Notable exceptions exist in the eco-socialist tradition (Löwy, 2007; Adaman and Devine, 2017) and in recent efforts to revive democratic socialist planning in response to present ecological crises (Harnecker and Bartolome, 2019; Dyer-Witheford, 2022; Vettese and Pendergrass, 2022).

The chapter starts by framing the questions, challenges and requirements that arise for planning in the context of degrowth, thus laying the ground for future research in this area. We then advance a bridging framework from the current economic institutional setting towards planning beyond growth by sketching a possible design for democratic planning processes within ecological limits.

The degrowth–planning nexus

Degrowth stands for a new post-capitalist economy. This new economy is thought of as diverse, social-ecological, democratic, and participatory, cooperative, needs-oriented, open but regionally anchored, and oriented towards overcoming the distinction between production and reproduction. While in capitalist growth economies, economic activities are mediated through capitalist market processes and are thus not only highly hierarchical but also immensely irrational, degrowth aims putting the economy at the centre of the realm of conscious, political and democratic decisions. This means putting the economy in the hands of people and involving more and more people in key decisions – such as the producers in a factory, the neighbours of a farm, the users of a community-owned power plant, or the care recipients in retirement homes deciding what is produced, how to relate to the environment and other economic agents, which services are needed, and how work is organized. Seeing economic decisions as political problems also implies overcoming the idea of there being a universal yardstick to measure all activities, whether that is GDP, money, or any other indicator, or of delegating decisions about sustainable and just production to algorithms (even though they might be useful as a tool). Overall, one can think of ecological planning for degrowth as the democratic deliberation of both ecological limits and social needs, or of planning what in heterodox economic thought has become known as 'the doughnut' (Raworth, 2017). This means that society at large – based on scientific evidence and democratic debate – takes the decisions of how not to transgress planetary boundaries and about how to organize the process of social provisioning.

Achieving these goals is a difficult task. The planetary boundaries framework and the theory of human needs are pertinent concepts to approach this challenge. The former defines nine boundaries associated with key Earth-system processes that make up the 'safe operating space' and, if exceeded, will take the planet beyond the relatively stable conditions of the Holocene in which human societies have evolved (Rockström et al, 2009a, p 472). While the metaphors of 'limits' and 'planetary boundaries' have been highly effective in public debates, these concepts must be used with caution. There is no definite boundary between sustainability and collapse, but rather numerous interrelated thresholds. Ecological degradation can be viewed as 'one single catastrophe, which unceasingly piles rubble on top of rubble' (Benjamin, 1940). Indeed, the initiators of the *boundaries* approach advance that 'the thresholds in key Earth System processes exist irrespective of peoples' preferences, values, or compromises based on political and socioeconomic feasibility' but also recognize that 'normative judgments influence the definition and position of planetary boundaries' (Rockström et al, 2009b, p 5). These judgements are decisive for planetary survival and justice because vulnerabilities to environmental change are distributed highly unevenly across the ecological and social space and intersect in complex ways with inequities of class, race and gender. And the notion of limits mobilizes the Malthusian ideology of scarcity at the expense of the manifold pathways of possible developments that do not transgress planetary boundaries (Kallis, 2019). All this shows that, while science must inform the definition of boundaries, those must be deliberated and evaluated through a *political* process, involving democratic decisions and conscious planning, to become effective in society.

The theory of human needs identifies a set of universal basic needs, the satisfaction of which is essential for human wellbeing. The material and institutional means of satisfying these needs – the need satisfiers – vary according to context, time, and space and cannot be reduced to bio-physical parameters (Doyal and Gough, 1991; Gough, 2020; Keucheyan, 2019). Raworth (2017) links the theory of human needs to the planetary boundaries approach and includes considerations of equity and justice. Her 'safe and just space' framework visualizes sustainability in terms of a doughnut-shaped space – showing the conditions of people meeting their multiple needs (the inner boundary), while not transgressing planetary boundaries (the outer boundary). While scholars, such as Raworth (2017) and Brand et al (2021), acknowledge that this task requires political intervention in the economic realm, the concrete deliberation processes and the concrete mechanisms for implementation tend to be sidelined. We argue that pluralistic, democratic ecological planning based on normative judgment and procedural robustness could fill this gap.

Key goals of planning beyond growth

To advance such a deliberation of limits and need satisfiers, we propose to understand the economy as a process of social provisioning: the material and institutional matrix that structures the production–consumption framework. As highlighted by O'Neill et al (2018), provisioning systems mediate between biophysical processes and social outcomes. These systems are composed of technological devices and infrastructures, as well as institutions that shape human production and consumption at various levels. These include markets, communities, and the legal framework, which are themselves the result of the complex interplay of multiple factors. Of course, provisioning systems are shaped by and largely deployed according to the overall systems' provisioning logic. Democratic economic planning could therefore help to change the provisioning logic from a primacy of growth and profit to wellbeing within planetary boundaries (Fine, Bayliss and Robertson, 2018). Such a mechanism for a more conscious macro-management of the economy aiming at deliberately setting and implementing ecological limits and priorities in terms of need satisfaction should be articulated with four key goals (see Figure 13.1).

Figure 13.1: A visualization of the goals of planning provisioning systems within the doughnut

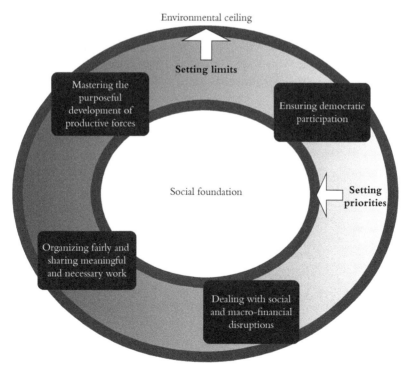

Setting and enforcing limits and priorities

Implementing absolute limits on GHG emissions, resource extraction, energy use and biodiversity loss is a defining feature of degrowth and sets it apart from other sustainability strategies. All of these require some form of deliberation and planning to deal with the complexity of setting and implementing limits at a global scale and breaking them down to regional and local levels, as well as to various economic sectors and need satisfiers. While currently predominantly built within an economic growth framework, post-growth integrated assessment models could play a key role in helping societies to democratically decide among the various future pathways possible (Hickel et al, 2021). The implementation of caps makes decisions concerning the best allocation of remaining resource funds necessary, including priority-setting concerning the types of goods and services to be provided, and the organization of the associated production and distribution channels. For example, considering the need for mobility requires decisions on the comparative significance of public and private transportation, the role of air, land, rail and water transportation, the type of engines used, and how individuals and organizations will be able access to them. Ecological planning would make it possible to organize the use of societal resources in ways to overcome ecological injustice and the appalling coexistence of poverty and wasteful luxury lifestyles (cf Piketty, 2014; Oswald et al, 2021). At the same time, it would permit the expression of individual tastes and unique lifestyles within the boundaries established collectively, and – liberated from the inequalities, alienation and coercions of capitalist markets – enable new forms of flourishing (Soper, 2020). Finally, there should be some type of North–South industrial convergence linked to reparations, which would lead to a partial deindustrialization in the Global North and (re)industrialization in the Global South, with the aim of overcoming uneven (ecological) exchange and global hierarchies (Ajl, 2021; Sorg, 2023).

Ensuring democratic participation

We have highlighted the necessity of democratically deliberating vital economic, ecological and social decisions. Consciously designed planning processes make it possible to meet this ambition. To enable democratic and participatory decision-making, planning beyond growth should involve not just experts, producers and those whose needs are to be satisfied, but also a wider group of stakeholders concerned by the decisions, including people in distant parts of the world, future generations and even ecosystems themselves. To represent the diverse positions in the process of planning, multiple groups of interest, sectors and organizations at different political and geographic scales should be adequately involved. To allow for the broadest and fairest participation, planning institutions should be designed to explicitly tackle existing inequalities and alleviate disadvantages to participation, for example due to race, gender or class (Asara, Profumi and Kallis, 2013; Bourg, 2017; Descola, 2018; Schmelzer, Vetter and Vansintjan, 2022). The planning process can take place in parallel and, to an extent, independently of the state apparatus, involving many autonomous bottom-up projects from commons to cooperatives, while being ultimately approved by some societal institution (such as currently the legal system). Planning can be employed to operationalize key material and socio-economic variables but it does not encompass all socio-economic activity, leaving room for the ongoing development of production and consumption regulated by market, commons-oriented, and statist modes of coordination.

Mastering the purposeful development of productive forces

A degrowth transformation means the simultaneous and selective expansion and downscaling of distinct sectors, technologies, and resource-uses. Expansion may encompass renewable energies and care activities. Downscaling concerns globalized, profit-oriented, fossil fuel-based industrial economic sectors and activities that do not serve the common good and cannot be sustainably or democratically restructured. Social activity that does not advance human wellbeing, such as the arms industry, advertising, lobbying, fast fashion, border security, and large parts of the financial industry, will have to be scaled down. Instead of relying on the market and hoping that green alternatives will eventually outcompete these harmful activities, degrowth proposes a wide range of political measures that aim at actively curbing and downscaling them. These include policies such as resource moratoria, ecological tax reform, just transitions, and even expropriations, and they will have to result in processes of deaccumulation. All of this requires planning. And it requires a radical change in the form and direction of the future development of society's productive forces, including different technical models and changed ownership structures: as long as the primacy of economic efficiency – rather than criteria of sustainability and usefulness– dominates design processes and investments in technical infrastructures, this transformation will not succeed. One attempt to develop a concept of technology for the degrowth debate is the design of 'convivial technology'. The concept of convivial technology includes five central values for technological development in the sense of a degrowth perspective: connectedness, accessibility, adaptability, bio-interaction, and appropriateness (Vetter, 2018; Schmelzer Vetter and Vansintjan, 2022). These dimensions could be central for determining democratically and planning accordingly the future development of productive forces. Such a perspective should be articulated with an effective ability to command the necessary resources and tools to restructure the economy according to the socio-ecological objectives (Zoellick and Bisht, 2018).

Organizing and fairly sharing meaningful and necessary work

Aligning economic activity with social-ecological targets also includes the way in which work is organized. Work is an important focal point within the degrowth debate, encompassing proposals such as access for all to good, non-alienated, and meaningful work, a greater valuation of reproductive and care work and the adequate distribution of this work, working time reduction without lower pay groups losing income, collective self-determination in the workplace, and the strengthening of workers' rights and autonomy. Degrowth thus aims at fundamentally transforming work – by phasing out unnecessary and destructive work, automating as much as possible those necessary activities that cannot be made empowering, making those activities that sustain social life as pleasurable as possible, and giving those that do the work autonomy in their workplaces, thus continually transferring economic activities to a logic beyond the imperatives of accumulation. Again, ecological planning is key – it could support workers' self-organization and a more equitable distribution of work in society. A critical appraisal of existing work patterns can provide a basis for the desirable division of labour by recognizing the necessity and desirability of activities in relation to both ecological limits and social needs. This would ensure that the amount and type of work deemed socially desirable and ecologically viable can be matched to the capabilities and preferences of individuals. An important element would be the inclusion of both hitherto monetized work as well as work provided 'for free' within households and communities (Barca, 2019; cf Dengler and Lang, 2021). Here, the reduction of working hours is not only a goal in and of itself – enlarging the realm of freedom – but is also a lever to ensure a balanced distribution of work in an economy that abandons growth even as productivity continues to increase (Jackson, 2009). The radical reduction in working time can be understood as the redistribution of the surplus value that results from increases in productivity from capital to labour – in the form of free time (Gorz, 1985).

Dealing with social and macro-financial disruptions

The significant structural changes necessary to stay below 1.5 degrees of global heating while also promoting global wellbeing require a rapid and far-ranging transformation that could potentially cause disruptions. The termination of polluting activities presents multiple difficulties and must take into account the potential repercussions of involuntary unemployment and other social effects on local populations and societies. Asset stranding is another challenge. Reducing the extraction and utilization of resources, particularly of fossil fuels, necessitates the early closure of existing infrastructures and production plants and the write-off of related assets. The magnitude of the asset values at stake presents a significant threat to economic and financial stability (Carney, 2015; Mercure et al, 2018; Daumas and Salin, 2021; Pisani-Ferry, 2021; Semieniuk et al, 2021). In order for material degrowth to be successful, planning processes must be connected to monetary, fiscal, and financial policies. It is essential that the monetary and credit systems are modified to meet the requirements of investing in cleaner production and divesting from and dismantling dirty activities (Antal and van den Bergh, 2013; Farley et al, 2013). Rather than pricing financial assets in a risk-based manner, credit policies and innovative monetary policies could be effective tools to pursue qualitative developmental objectives while managing price dynamics (Monnet, 2018; Kedward, Gabor and Ryan-Collins, 2022; Olk, Schneider and Hickel, 2022).

Planning provisioning systems within ecological limits

So how could planning institutions look like that are able to achieve strong sustainability, that are based on a pluralistic and democratic deliberation of limits and needs and that enable the participatory management of provisioning systems? This study considers several pertinent bodies of literature in order to elucidate this question, namely, the literature on socialist and capitalist planning experiences, war economies, post-capitalist models of democratic planning, and the recent resurgence of interest in planning, as well as frameworks developed within ecological economics and political ecology that centre issues of biophysical limits and the scale of economic activities (Leontief, 1976; Mandel, 1986; Monnet, 2018; Brand et al, 2021; Sapir, 2022; Tremblay-Pepin, 2022). Acknowledging these crucial sources of knowledge, we put forward a minimal proposal to advance the dialogue between and about planning and degrowth, putting the safe and just space perspective at the core of the former, while inviting the latter to engage positively in macro-institutional design.

The framework aims at the reorganization of existing provisioning systems in accordance with pre-defined boundaries. It is proposed not as an ideal model, but rather as a source of inspiration for academics, campaigners and policy makers to serve as a starting point for discussion and adaptation to specific contexts. It can be seen as a bridging framework that facilitates the social-ecological transformation by leveraging existing institutions (including markets, firms, community networks, public institutions and state apparatus) and enabling the emergence and strengthening of alternatives. Therefore, this thought exercise is situated in the present historical moment, in that it seeks to repurpose and recombine existing institutions and tools rather than imagining completely novel institutional structures. We assume that a social-ecological transformation towards staying within the safe and equitable space would likely have to eventually overcome the accumulation dynamics central to capitalism. While not being a prerequisite to engage with ecological planning, we expect this to be a consequence of ecologically sound planning.

The proposed architecture identifies distinct levels of planning, where the planning apparatus can be conceived as a multiscalar stack (Bratton, 2016) that provides a canvas upon which autonomous and diversified social relationships flourish. The application of the subsidiarity principle ensures the greatest possible autonomy at the lowest level. For matters that require coordination with other entities, deliberation and enforcement must take place at a higher level. Decisions taken at a higher level then reimpose on the lower levels, for example, resource limits and social goals. Although this process is in some sense 'top-down', the autonomy of the higher levels is only relative. This is due to the inputs from the lower level, as well as a wide range of decisions that are made by individuals and local structures. This constitutes a strong bottom-up element of the framework. In this way, planning is conceived as an iterative process, combining and implementing decisions from the different levels. Overall, we appreciate that social transformation is an open-ended process, and that any institutional framework will benefit from the unmatched creativity and unsurpassable pluriversality (Escobar, 2020) of real-world practical institutional making.

The *fractal architecture* of such multilevel planning is illustrated in Figure 13.2. The various areas indicate different interdependent but relatively autonomous levels of planning. This entails the design and implementation of rules governing the provisioning systems from the top to the local and sectoral levels, as well as the decentralized, grounded unfolding at local levels, within city councils, businesses, collectives, social housing associations, or agricultural production units. The bottom-up shading of each square illustrates the transformation of the disorderly inputs into an orderly plan. The two white squares at each planning level depict the deliberative and executive planning bodies and their associated administrative apparatus.

The *elaborative body* corresponds to the institutional process that deliberates the limits and objectives of provisioning systems. *Pluralistic inputs* from scientific communities, citizens, social movements, and government bodies, including *information and knowledge* from subordinated levels, are deliberated and integrated to elaborate a plan for the socially and environmentally viable provisioning at that level. This is what we understand as qualitative aggregation and integration through deliberation. The democratic quality and density of the process is essential to confirm the legitimacy of the plan and guarantee its implementation over the required timeframe, thus upholding commitments to long-term objectives despite any potential changes in conditions. It must therefore incorporate both representation and

Figure 13.2: A fractal architecture of multilevel ecological planning beyond growth

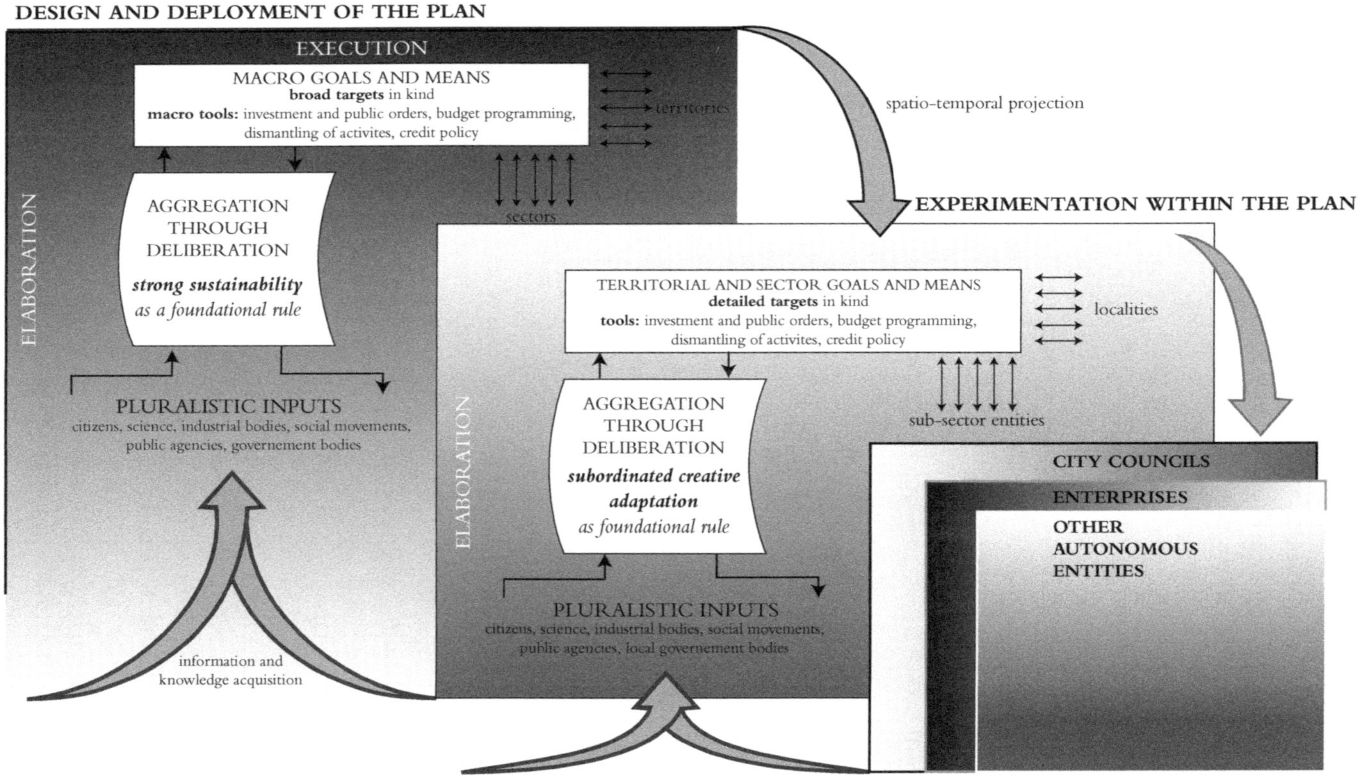

DESIGN AND DEPLOYMENT OF THE PLAN

EXECUTION

MACRO GOALS AND MEANS
broad targets in kind
macro tools: investment and public orders, budget programming, dismantling of activities, credit policy

sectors • territories • spatio-temporal projection

AGGREGATION THROUGH DELIBERATION
strong sustainability as a foundational rule

PLURALISTIC INPUTS
citizens, science, industrial bodies, social movements, public agencies, governement bodies

ELABORATION

information and knowledge acquisition

EXPERIMENTATION WITHIN THE PLAN

TERRITORIAL AND SECTOR GOALS AND MEANS
detailed targets in kind
tools: investment and public orders, budget programming, dismantling of activites, credit policy

sub-sector entities • localities

AGGREGATION THROUGH DELIBERATION
subordinated creative adaptation as foundational rule

PLURALISTIC INPUTS
citizens, science, industrial bodies, social movements, public agencies, local governement bodies

ELABORATION

CITY COUNCILS
ENTERPRISES
OTHER AUTONOMOUS ENTITIES

Source: Durand, Hofferberth and Schmelzer, 2024

participation with an appropriate marshalling of skills. Experiences of direct citizen participation, for instance the citizens assemblies set up for the climate emergency in various countries or the citizen assembly summoned in France after the 2018 *gilets jaunes* uprising, demonstrate that attempts to construct a microcosmic representation of the people through quotas, random selection and a comprehensive process of expert participation can provide a sound basis for deliberation (Pech, 2021). As rightly stressed by Leontief: 'A plan is not a forecast. The whole idea of planning assumes the possibility of choice among alternative feasible scenarios' (1976, p 8). The primary responsibilities of the deliberative body are to combine and integrate different perspectives through deliberation, to initiate a discussion with the executive body to develop potential social, ecological, and economic trajectories, and finally to deliberate and select among them. This higher-level process of formulation is predicated on the principles of strong sustainability as a foundational rule. At the lower level, adhering to the constraints set at the higher level is the fundamental principle that facilitates subordinate creativity and adaptation (Özkaynak, Devine and Rigby 2004; Dietz and Neumayer 2007).

The *executive body* is accountable towards the deliberative body and responsible for mobilizing public administration resources to create plans and select suitable tools for their implementation. It further monitors the achievement of pre-determined goals, as well as making interventions to address unexpected occurrences. This body is equipped with a comprehensive in-kind accounting system that combines both quantitative and qualitative elements, such as carbon quotas, biodiversity goals, restrictions on soil artificialization, and specific indicators related to housing, energy, transportation, education and healthcare. To facilitate the collection of data and providing clear pathways to ensure that sourcing and distribution practices are aligned with the overarching goal of planning, the ecological statistical apparatus (in-kind measures and targets) could be linked to private central planning systems. Examples of such systems can be seen in businesses like IKEA, which have centralized supply chain planning, that integrates operational, tactical, and strategic management processes to anticipate and organize the sourcing and distribution of products in the short and long term (Jonsson, Rudberg and Holmberg, 2013). The Cybersyn Chilean project, advanced during Salvador Allende's term as president, proposed the use of cybernetic loops to connect producers and consumers directly and enable the instantaneous sharing of feedback, data and metrics. This would increase efficiency and allow the executive body to better manage economic and material resources through a variety of policy tools, such as public investment, industrial policy, public budgeting, credit policy and expert appointment policy (Medina, 2011; Vettese and Pendergrass, 2022).

The *spatio-temporal projection* of the plan by the executive body is both material (resource allocation) and semiotic (communication of signs and meanings) and exerts an effective constraint vis-à-vis the subordinated levels (Bensussan, Durand and Rikap, 2022). Though the plan contains certain restrictions, it is still adjustable to accommodate the unpredictable nature of real-life circumstances. Moreover, while it may suggest certain activities, it does not necessarily require those activities; instead, subordinate levels are actively encouraged to be creative and explore new possibilities. This provides an opportunity for an autonomous process of self-planning to occur. Applying the principle of subsidiarity facilitates the greatest possible autonomy at the lowest level of organization and the coordination at higher levels, where needed. The subordinated level's relative autonomy suggests there are restrictions on the capability of the higher-level planning process. This opens up space to address the intricate nature of reality and preserves the variety of socio-economic practices, thus reducing the risk associated with a technical monoculture and top-down structure. Furthermore, it allows people to make sense of their individual activities and subjective investment, and to meaningfully affect the labour process (Clot, 2014).

Conclusion: Mediating limits and needs beyond growth requires planning

Planning and degrowth, so the core argument of this chapter, are key perspectives for any sustainable future, rendering their productive combination a critical avenue forward both in research and politics. We propose to base the discussion on the degrowth–planning nexus on two of the most influential frameworks in sustainability studies: planetary boundaries and the just and safe space framework. We argue that both ecological limits and social priorities cannot simply be defined scientifically, but must be consciously deliberated and planned. Mediating both ecological boundaries and human wellbeing requires pluralistic and democratic planning processes of provisioning systems to enable the management of the economy according to deliberately set limits and priorities. To advance such a framework for planning beyond growth, we focus on four goals: enabling democratic participation, mastering the purposeful development of productive forces, arranging and equitably sharing meaningful and necessary work, and securing adequate coordination to address potential social and macro-financial disruptions.

Furthermore, to bridge the gap between degrowth and planning, we propose a design for planning processes beyond growth. Our design posits a multiscalar stack of autonomous and diversified social relationships, which are based on the principle of subsidiarity. This bridging framework focuses on how to repurpose and recombine existing institutions as a means of providing provisioning systems within a safe and just operating space. In terms of next steps, many questions need to be tackled – including the specific processes of this bridging framework, and how it links to other models. Politically speaking, this could inspire debates about how to mobilize the space for planning there is in capitalism – through instruments such as indicative planning, industrial policy, capital controls, socialized investment and so on (on this see Criscuolo, 2022; Weber et al, 2022; Goar, 2023) – in order to put us on a path beyond it: as forms of 'non-reformist reforms' (Gorz, 1967; 1968), aiming for socio-ecological transformation by using the degrowth-oriented radical reforms to create path dependencies that eventually will sublate capitalist growth imperatives. We hope that our institutional outline will lead to a critical discourse and further research into the relationship between degrowth and planning.

Acknowledgements

We particularly thank the editors of this book, Jan Gross and Christoph Sorg, as well as all co-authors and commentators in our preparatory workshop. For additional critical comments, questions and suggestions on an early version of the paper we would also like to thank Jeff Althouse, Louison Cahen-Fourot, Pierre Charbonnier, Simon Grothe, Razmig Keucheyan, Lorenz Keyßer, Lukas Müller-Wünsch, Christopher Olk, Thea Riofrancos, Mohamed Sir, and Julia Steinberger.

Bibliography

Adaman, F. and Devine, P. (2017) 'Democracy, participation and social planning', in Clive L. Spash (ed) *Routledge Handbook of Ecological Economics*. Abingdon: Routledge.

Ajl, M. (2021) *A People's Green New Deal*. London: Pluto Press.

Antal, M. and van den Bergh, J.C.J.M. (2013) 'Macroeconomics, financial crisis and the environment: Strategies for a sustainability transition', *Environmental Innovation and Societal Transitions*, 6: 47–66. doi: 10.1016/j.eist.2013.01.002.

Asara, V., Profumi, E. and Kallis, G. (2013) 'Degrowth, democracy and autonomy', *Environmental Values*, 22(2): 217–239.

Barca, S. (2019) 'The labor(s) of degrowth', *Capitalism Nature Socialism*, 30(2): 207–216. doi: 10.1080/10455752.2017.1373300.

Benjamin, W. (1940) 'On the concept of history'. https://www.marxists.org/reference/archive/benjamin/1940/history.htm

Bensussan, H., Durand, C. and Rikap, C. (2022) 'Corporate planning: from Industrial Capitalism to Intellectual Monopoly Capitalism'. SASE Conference, Amsterdam, July 2022.

Bourg, D. (ed) (2017) *Inventer la démocratie du XXIe siecle: l'assemblée citoyenne du futur*. Paris/Boulogne-Billancourt: Éditions Les Liens qui liberent; Fondation pour la nature et l'homme.

Brand, U., Muraca, B., Pineault, É. et al (2021) 'From planetary to societal boundaries: an argument for collectively defined self-limitation', *Sustainability: Science, Practice and Policy*, 17(1): 265–292. doi: 10.1080/15487733.2021.1940754.

Bratton, B.H. (2016) The *Stack: On Software* and *Sovereignty*. Cambridge, MA: The MIT Press.

Carney, M. (2015) 'Breaking the tragedy of the horizon–climate change and financial stability', Speech given at Lloyd's of London, 29 September. https://www.bis.org/review/r151009a.pdf

Clot, Y. (2014) *Travail et pouvoir d'agir*. Paris: Presses universitaires de France.

Cockshott, W.P., Dapprich, J.P. and Cottrell, A. (2022) *Economic Planning in an Age of Climate Crisis*. Independently published.

Criscuolo, C., Gonne, N., Kitazawa, K., and Lalanne, G. (2022) 'Are industrial policy instruments effective?', OECD Science, Technology and Industry Policy Papers. https://www.oecd-ilibrary.org/content/paper/57b3dae2-en

Daumas, L. and Salin, M. (2021) 'A "climate bad bank" to navigate stranded assets? Exploring an emerging policy proposal'. https://ec.europa.eu/economy_finance/arc2021/documents/posters/A_climate_bad_bank_to_navigate_stranded_assets_Exploring_an_emerging_policy_proposal_paper.pdf

Dengler, C. and Lang, M. (2021) 'Commoning care: feminist degrowth visions for a socio-ecological transformation', *Feminist Economics*, 28(1): 1–28. doi: 10.1080/13545701.2021.1942511.

Descola, P. (2018) 'Chapitre 1. Humain, trop humain?', in *Penser l'Anthropocène*, Paris: Presses de Sciences, pp 19–35. doi: 10.3917/scpo.beaur.2018.01.0019.

Dietz, S. and Neumayer, E. (2007) 'Weak and strong sustainability in the SEEA: Concepts and measurement', Special issue on environmental accounting: Introducing the System of Integrated Environmental and Economic Accounting 2003, *Ecological Economics*, 61(4): 617–626. doi: 10.1016/j.ecolecon.2006.09.007.

Doyal, L. and Gough, I. (1991) *A Theory of Human Need*. Basingstoke: Macmillan Education.

Durand, C., Hofferberth, E. and Schmelzer, M. (2024) 'Planning beyond growth. The case for economic democracy within limits', *Journal of Cleaner Production*, 437: 140351. https://www.sciencedirect.com/science/article/pii/S0959652623045092

Dyer-Witheford, N. (2022) 'Biocommie: power and catastrophe', PPPR. https://projectpppr.org/populisms/biocommie-power-and-catastrophe

Escobar, A. (2020) *Pluriversal Politics: The Real and the Possible*. Durham, NC Duke University Press. doi: 10.2307/j.ctv11315v0.

Farley, J., Burke, M., Flomenhoft, G. et al (2013) 'Monetary and fiscal policies for a finite planet', *Sustainability*, 5(6): 2802–2826. doi: 10.3390/su5062802.

Fine, B., Bayliss, K. and Robertson, M. (2018) 'The systems of provision approach to understanding consumption', in E. Evans and D. Southerton (eds) *The SAGE Handbook of Consumer Culture*, London: Sage Publications, pp 27–42.

Goar, M. (2023) 'Emmanuel Macron dessine les contours de son "écologie à la française": inciter sans contraindre', *Le Monde.fr*, 26 September.

Gorz, A. (1967) *Strategy for Labor. A Radical Proposal*. Boston, MA: Beacon Press.

Gorz, A. (1968) 'Reform and revolution', *The Socialist Register*, 5: 101–143.

Gorz, A. (1985) *Paths to Paradise: On the Liberation from Work*. London: Pluto Press.

Gough, I. (2020) 'Defining floors and ceilings: the contribution of human needs theory', *Sustainability: Science, Practice and Policy*, 16(1): 208–219: doi: 10.1080/15487733.2020.1814033.

Haberl, H., Wiedenhofer, D., Virág, D. et al (2020) 'A systematic review of the evidence on decoupling of GDP, resource use and GHG emissions, part II: synthesizing the insights', *Environmental Research Letters*, 15(6): 065003. doi: 10.1088/1748-9326/ab842a.

Hahnel, R. (2021) *Democratic Economic Planning*. London: Routledge.

Harnecker, M. and Bartolome, J. (2019) *Planning from Below: A Decentralized Participatory Planning Proposal*. New York: NYU Press.

Hickel, J. (2020) *Less is More: How Degrowth Will Save the World*. London: William Heinemann.

Hickel, J., Brockway, P., Kallis, G. et al (2021) 'Urgent need for post-growth climate mitigation scenarios', *Nature Energy*, 6: 766–768. doi: 10.1038/s41560-021-00884-9.

Jackson, T. (2009) *Prosperity Without Growth: Economics for a Finite Planet*. London: Earthscan.

Jonsson, P., Rudberg, M. and Holmberg, S. (2013) 'Centralised supply chain planning at IKEA', *Supply Chain Management: An International Journal*, 18(3): 337–350. doi: 10.1108/SCM-05-2012-0158.

Kallis, G. (2019) *Limits: Why Malthus Was Wrong and Why Environmentalists Should Care*. Stanford: Stanford University Press.

Kallis, G., Kostakis, V., Lange, S. et al (2018) 'Research on degrowth', Annual *Review of Environment and Resources*, 43: 291–316.

Kallis, G., Paulson, S., D'Alisa, G. et al (2020) *The Case for Degrowth*. Cambridge/Medford, MA: Polity.

Kedward, K., Gabor, D. and Ryan-Collins, J. (2022) 'Aligning finance with the green transition: From a risk-based to an allocative green credit policy regime', *SSRN Electronic Journal*. doi: 10.2139/ssrn.4198146.

Keucheyan, R. (2019) *Les Besoins Artificiels: Comment Sortir Du Consumérisme*. Paris: Zones.

Leontief, W. (1976) 'National economic planning: methods and problems', *Challenge*, 19(3): 6–11.

Löwy, M. (2007) 'Eco-socialism and democratic planning', *Socialist Register*: 294–309.

Mandel, E. (1986) 'In defence of socialist planning', *New Left Review*, 159(1): 5–22.

Medina, E. (2011) *Cybernetic Revolutionaries: Technology and Politics in Allende's Chile*. Cambridge, MA: MIT Press.

Mercure, J.F.A., Pollitt, H., Viñuales, J.E. et al (2018) 'Macroeconomic impact of stranded fossil fuel assets', *Nature Climate Change*, 8(7): 588–596. doi: 10.1038/s41558-018-0182-1.

Monnet, E. (2018) *Controlling Credit: Central Banking and the Planned Economy in Postwar France, 1948–1973 (Studies in Macroeconomic History)*. Cambridge: Cambridge University Press. doi: 10.1017/9781108 227322.

Olk, C., Schneider, C. and Hickel, J. (2022) 'How to pay for saving the world: modern monetary theory for a degrowth transition', *SSRN Electronic Journal*. doi: 10.2139/ssrn.4172005.

O'Neill, D.W., Fanning, A.L., Lamb, W.F. et al (2018) 'A good life for all within planetary boundaries', *Nature Sustainability*, 88(95): 88–95.

Oswald, Y., Steinberger, J.K., Ivanova, D. et al (2021) 'Global redistribution of income and household energy footprints: a computational thought experiment', *Global Sustainability*, 4: 1–13. doi: 10.1017/sus.2021.1.

Özkaynak, B., Devine, P. and Rigby, D. (2004) 'Operationalising strong sustainability: definitions, methodologies and outcomes', *Environmental Values*, 13(3): 279–303.

Parrique, T. (2019) *The Political Economy of Degrowth*. Auvergne: Université Clermont Auvergne. https://tel.archives-ouvertes.fr/tel-02499463/document.

Pech, T. (2021) *Le Parlement des citoyens: La convention citoyenne pour le climat*. Paris: Seuil.

Phillips, L. and Rozworski, M. (2019) *People's Republic of Wal-Mart: How the World's Biggest Corporations are Laying the Foundation for Socialism*. London/New York: Verso.

Piketty, T. (2014) *Capital in the Twenty-First Century*. Cambridge, MA: Harvard University Press.

Pisani-Ferry, J. (2021) *Climate Policy is Macroeconomic Policy, and the Implications Will be Significant*. PB21-20, Peterson Institute for International Economics. https://ideas.repec.org/p/iie/pbrief/pb21-20.html

Raworth, K. (2017) *Doughnut Economics: Seven Ways to Think like a 21st-Century Economist*. London: Random House Business Books.

Rockström, J., Steffen, W., Noone, K. et al (2009a) 'A safe operating space for humanity: identifying and quantifying planetary boundaries that must not be transgressed could help prevent human activities from causing unacceptable environmental change, argue Johan Rockstrom and colleagues', *Nature (London)*, 461(7263): 472–475.

Rockström, J., Steffen, W., Noone, K. et al (2009b) 'Planetary boundaries', *Ecology and Society*, 14(2). http://www.jstor.org/stable/26268316

Sapir, J. (2022) *Le grand retour de la planification?* Collection Le Cercle Aristote. Paris: Jean-Cyrille Godefroy.

Schmelzer, M. (2015) 'The growth paradigm: history, hegemony, and the contested making of economic growthmanship', *Ecological Economics*, 118: 262–271.

Schmelzer, M., Vetter, A. and Vansintjan, A. (2022) *The Future is Degrowth: A Guide to a World Beyond Capitalism*. London: Verso.

Semieniuk, G., Campiglio, E., Mercure, J.-F. et al (2021) 'Low-carbon transition risks for finance', Wiley Interdisciplinary Reviews. Climate change, 12(1): n/a. doi: 10.1002/wcc.678.

Soper, K. (2020) *Post-Growth Living: For an Alternative Hedonism*. London: Verso Books.

Sorg, C. (2023) 'Failing to plan is planning to fail: toward an expanded notion of democratically planned postcapitalism', *Critical Sociology*, 49(3): 475–493. doi: 10.1177/08969205221081058.

Tremblay-Pepin, S. (2022) 'Five criteria to evaluate democratic economic planning models', *Review of Radical Political Economics*, 54(3): 265–280. doi: 10.1177/04866134221093747.

Tremblay-Pepin, S. and Legault, F. (2022) *A Brief Sketch of Three Models of Democratic Economic Planning*. https://innovationsocialeusp.ca/wp-content/uploads/2021/04/Note-2-Legault-and-Tremblay-Pepin-Democratic-Planning.pdf

Vetter, A. (2018) 'The matrix of convivial technology – assessing technologies for degrowth', *Journal of Cleaner Production*, 197: 1778–1786. doi: 10.1016/j.jclepro.2017.02.195.

Vettese, T. and Pendergrass, D. (2022) *Half-Earth Socialism: A Plan to Save the Future from Extinction, Climate Change and Pandemics*. London: Verso Books.

Victor, P.A. (2019) *Managing Without Growth: Slower by Design, Not Disaster* (2nd edn). Cheltenham: Edward Elgar.

Weber, I. M., Jauregui, J. L., Teixeira, L., and Nassif Pires, L. (2022) 'Inflation in times of overlapping emergencies: systematically significant prices from an input-output perspective', UMassAmherst Economics Department Working Paper Series, 340. https://doi.org/10.7275/0C5B-6A92

Weiss, M. and Cattaneo, C. (2017) 'Degrowth – taking stock and reviewing an emerging academic paradigm', *Ecological Economics*, 137: 220–230. doi: 10.1016/j.ecolecon.2017.01.014.

Zoellick, J.C. and Bisht, A. (2018) 'It's not (all) about efficiency: Powering and organizing technology from a degrowth perspective', *Journal of Cleaner Production*, 197: 1787–1799. doi: 10.1016/j.jclepro.2017.03.234.

14

Post-Sovereign Planning? Nature, Culture and Care in the New Socialist Calculation Debate

Samia Zahra Mohammed

Introduction[1]

Current crises such as the climate catastrophe and the global rise of fascism, as well as the issue of how to overcome them in an emancipatory way, are reviving the debate on alternative economic models and questioning the effectiveness and sustainability of the competition- and profit-oriented mode of production. In addition to critique a growing interest and commitment to thinking about concrete proposals for a different, better future for all has emerged. So it is that the debate on various concepts of economic planning that have fallen into disrepute since the socialist projects of the 20th century is currently experiencing a revival. There are indeed, strong reasons for this revival. Not only does the market as a form of economic mediation usually fail to find answers to existential global threats, but the current economic system can also be seen as acting in more than a market-like way in that it already produces extensive planning infrastructure with the help of modern information technologies. Examples of this are large companies such as Walmart and Amazon, which are highly dependent on planning to maximize their own profits, but do so undemocratically (cf Phillips and Rozworski, 2019).

The debate, which is becoming steadily more differentiated, is increasingly politicizing the original feasibility dispute between liberals and socialists that took place a century ago, which this volume especially demonstrates. Certain foci and dominant motifs can still be discerned in the more recent planning debate, which revolves around issues concerning technical feasibility (Cockshott and Cottrell, 1993; Campbell, 2002; Dapprich, 2020), the reorganization of what is now referred to as the productive sphere (Saros, 2014; Srnicek and Williams, 2016; Benanav, 2020), the abolition of the current property order (Phillips and Rozworski, 2019) and the better, more efficient handling of nature (Malm, 2021). Decidedly feminist (radical) democratic theoretical interventions, however, have been relatively rare so far, although they hold particular promise for connection and discussion in the planning debates.

Based on this promise, this chapter argues that a democratic theoretically informed and feminist intervention into the socialist calculation debate (SCD) is almost inevitable, especially if its focal points and associated gaps in dominant strands are examined. To demonstrate this, this chapter continues by reconstructing the author's understanding of the current state of the debate as leaning towards the attainment of collective sovereignty over the economy and non-human nature. Next, the gaps and problems that are associated with this reading of the debate are presented along with an explanation concerning the ambivalence of the mostly Promethean claims that many proposals put forward for a planned economy. For doing so, several lines of critical political theory (property critique, feminist theory and radical democratic theory) are introduced. The chapter then argues that the idea of a democratically planned economy, despite criticism from the aforementioned perspectives in critical political theory, can serve as a decisive pathfinder in realizing a different economy that is not required to meet the goal of being a completely harmonious end of history to consider better economic and political conditions and a more substantial understanding of freedom and democracy.

Democratic socialist planning as a Promethean project

After decades of neoliberal hegemony and capitalist realism, demands for a completely different economy have been growing louder in recent years. The SCD, as a discussion that is becoming more present today and as an archive of the history of ideas, aims in precisely this direction. This also seems to correspond to a change in the status of utopia in critical theory formation. While Marx and Engels (1977, p 491ff) and the older Frankfurt School had (justified) reservations concerning utopian thinking, a growing number of contemporary critical–theoretical and progressive contributions put forward not only a principled, for instance an ideology critical or deconstructive, critique, but also propose concrete, more elaborated visions of another imaginable world. Many socialist contributions in the renewed debate on planned economies fall into this category. Well-known criticisms against utopias should continue to be taken seriously and reflected upon – for example to prevent theory from prescribing a certain practice or the rise of theoretical conceptions of the future that have no material basis and no subsequent practical social equivalent – but the current calculation debate has the potential to awaken and bundle theoretical and practical utopian energies due to its concrete utopianism and by taking up the task of thinking through the conditions and infrastructure of a free and equal society, starting from the present.

What exactly do advocates of a democratically planned economy want today? What key organizational principles do they embrace, and what problems do they claim their proposed solutions address? In view of the previously mentioned differentiation of the debate, the partial response is that what they want varies and is not uniform. Nevertheless some widely shared goals, assumptions and motives are evident, and naming them can help facilitate a substantive discussion about objectives, potentials and possible gaps in the ongoing 'socialist calculation debate 2.0' (Daum and Nuss, 2021, p 16). This chapter will primarily focus on a strand of the debate that can be identified as overarchingly Promethean.[2] For pragmatic reasons as well as in systematic terms this focus seems justifiable since a Promethean undertone – not in a pure form but regarding key motives – has a powerful presence in old and new calculation debates. The idea of a democratically organized planned economy and Prometheanism have some structural similarities in that the aim is to bring the economy, and thus the sphere in which human 'metabolism with nature' falls, under conscious collective control and shape it according to human needs, essentially giving 'all power to the people' (Garreaud and Brock, 2021). In certain respects, a democratically organized planned economy can appear at first glance to be *the* Promethean project par excellence – whereas this must not to be taken for granted and should instead be considered as an open question.

Many contemporary contributions to the debate have initially been motivated by the observation of massive technological progress, especially the Promethean ones, which tend to take an affirmative stance towards such progress. Especially in comparison to the original debate over a century ago, (information) technology now has a decisive role, with the advanced development of productive power being interpreted as an opportunity to realize a socialist project not as an economy of scarcity but one of abundance and reduced workloads. In addition, economic calculation can be completely re-evaluated against the background of today's computing capacities. Economic calculation, which was once considered the Achilles heel of socialism, and used as such by liberals like Hayek or Mises to argue against non-market projects, is now largely seen by socialist advocates as feasible under democratic socialist circumstances that abandon the market as a coordination mechanism.

The feasibility of a planned economy and the associated gains in coordination capacities have a central role in the current debate, which touches on long-standing controversies not only between socialist and liberal positions, but also among socialists. The differentiation between primary and secondary uncertainty in economic and social systems, for example, is a decisive factor in favour of consciously planned coordination:

> A fundamental idea of Marx's critique of political economy is not only that capitalist production is an end in itself, that capital accumulation is its all-determining driving force, but also that it is private production: societal labour, which is interdependent on all sides, takes place in the form of independent private labour, whose interrelation is mediated ex post by value. [...] In addition to a necessary, objective uncertainty, which arises from the spontaneity or natural conditions essential to man, there exists in capitalism a non-necessary, subjective uncertainty, which arises from its economic structure, in which, with all-round interdependence, action is taken independently of one another. (Heyer, 2021, translation by the author)

This secondary uncertainty in capitalist market economies results in instability, polarization, susceptibility to crises and societal and individual alienation and implies the absence of conscious democratic control of the overall economic context. Planned economies usually claim to make the democratic negotiation and legitimation of interdependent economic activities possible in the first place with the help of conscious ex-ante coordination as they are transferred from competition to a process of coordination and communication (Heyer, 2021; Heyer, in this volume). A democratic–socialist planned economy alone can then be understood as the enabler of a conscious shaping of the collective (re)production of humanity.

In connection with the coordinative possibilities of planning, as already mentioned, today's planned economy proposals continue to push centrally for the socialization of the means of production to bring the economy under shared control and to put an end to unequal dependency relationships between labour and capital. Today, however, a further justification for planned economy instruments is seeing it as a way of better and more justly addressing the climate crisis, which at present is primarily induced by capitalism. The type of solutions the discourse on planned economy proposes focuses particularly on the possibilities that the social appropriation of the means of production and the instrument of planning offer for a sustainable and just distribution of scarce and finite resources that is needs oriented rather than profit oriented.

Another goal is the transformation of labour, which has emerged as one of the most controversial issues. The common starting point is that labour can no longer be exploited in visions of democratic socialism since the socialization of the means of production entails that surplus value is no longer skimmed off. In addition, numerous proposals have argued that the overall workload would decrease if technology and automation were finally used in the interests of the people, which becomes possible as soon as the dictate of profit maximization is lifted (Srnicek and Williams 2016; Phillips and Rozworski, 2019; Benanav, 2020; Dapprich, 2020). Furthermore, reduced workloads under socialist conditions would no longer lead to not having enough to eat; thus, at least an end to drudgery becomes imaginable. However, there is a great deal of disagreement on the issue of whether remaining workloads should be taken on voluntarily or rather be distributed through incentive and reward systems or even compulsion.

What's missing? Nature, culture and care

In many respects the central concerns of the current SCD make a more egalitarian and better future seem imaginable. Socialized means of production, more autonomous forms of work and a decreased overall workload through the democratized use of technology, needs-oriented production, genuine democratic participation and a less wasteful use of finite resources are essential characteristics of the society that many contemporary planned economy proposals hold out as a future prospect. Compared with the status quo, this already sounds almost utopian and is undoubtedly an important aspect of imagining a different and better future for all. But is something missing? Society and the economy may already be oriented towards need satisfaction instead of profit maximization in such imaginaries – but who will provide care on a smaller scale in a liberated society – still the nuclear family? What will it take to care for the nature that has already succumbed to the Capitalocene and how do we shape the social relationship to include everything more-than-human in a democratic socialist way without continuing to succumb to instrumentally accessing resources with humans one-sidedly processing nature? And will people still relate to one another as individualized consumers or in a new way once competition and exploitation are replaced by needs-oriented, egalitarian production processes? The importance of these questions tends to be underemphasized in current discussions around planning.

With good reason, one could insist that concrete proposals for the organization of a liberated society should have something to offer concerning these issues if they want to propose comprehensive imaginaries of a better future. The concern of this chapter, therefore, is to solidarily criticize gaps of the contemporary debate and highlight the potential of including the aforementioned issues more properly. A feminist (Lutosch, in this volume), democratic theoretical and ecological (Hofferberth, Durand and Schmelzer, in this volume) critique, especially of the strongly Promethean impulses within the new calculation debate, should thus represent a means for informing and understanding it in certain respects more intensively than before as not primarily a technical feasibility discussion but as a genuinely political one.

As already described, the contemporary debate on planned economy largely presents itself as an attempt to address the ecological issues of our time, giving it particularly urgent justification. Climate justice activists have long recognized that the climate crisis cannot be adequately tackled under capitalist conditions, which is why they have been calling for a system change. The idea of democratically planned socialism can serve as a model for thinking about concrete alternatives that take ecological issues seriously and have the coordinative capacity to address them effectively, while at the same time situating them within a more general and necessarily radical democratic change of the entire economic system.

Capitalocene is a well-known, although not entirely uncontroversial (Haraway, 2016, p 47ff) term in eco-socialist discourse that is used to describe the prevailing societal relationship to nature (Moore, 2017). Its implications are generally compatible with planned economy proposals, if only because resource consumption under capitalism is primarily characterized by unequal property relations and the compulsion to maximize profits, which already makes it impossible to systematically provide well for all people and the planet. The sustainable coordination of resource consumption is thus an important concern of planned economy proposals (Phillips and Rozworski, 2019; Dapprich, 2020).

However, this critique is by no means a guarantee that thinking about societal nature relations in the new calculation debate actually refrains from a strong claim to dominion. Phillips and Rozworski's book, *The People's Republic of Walmart: How the World's Biggest Corporations Are Laying the Foundation for Socialism* (2019) can serve as a paradigmatic example – and certainly one of the most explicit examples in this respect – of a way of thinking about the climate catastrophe, but wanting to solve it in the register of continued dominion over nature. For such proposals do not aim to overcome or even reduce mastery over nature but rather wish to create a 'good Anthropocene' through conscious economic planning (p 233ff). They are heavily concerned with overcoming the specifically capitalist manifestation of the Anthropocene to enable the participation of all people by sharing prosperity collectively – in a sense, universalizing the existing Capitalocene into an actual Anthropocene, which has not yet been reached and is only achievable under socialist circumstances. Thus, a reading of a planned economy as the continued dominion of everything that is external to the human being can be conceived. The understandable goal of democratized possibilities of shaping the world is then confused with total control and taking the differentially distributed responsibility of agents with different degrees of agency seriously within mutual dependency structures is mistaken for a right to dominion.

Elements of coexistence with and dependence on what is generally referred to as nature are usually not included in Promethean perspectives, or they are merely thematized as material for the ongoing realization of human freedom (as in Srnicek and Williams, 2016, p 82). The one-sided hierarchical shaping of nature by humans, in other words anthropocentrism *and* the Anthropocene, is advocated and seen as the basis of prosperity. The anthropocentric assumption of human sovereignty over one's environment as the basis and also the goal of a socialist planned economy is too rarely thematized as incomplete or illusionary, although the realization of socialism aims precisely at finding a way to effectively meet human needs, implicitly navigating dependencies and conditionalities as the *other* of sovereignty. This apparent contradiction remains unresolved and the maintenance of the fiction of sovereignty, which is expressed in the largely uncritical affirmation of (technical) progress, modernity and the Anthropocene, goes hand in hand with repressions that threaten to let various relations of domination remain out of sight (Horkheimer and Adorno, 2002, p 4f).

The continued dominion over nature or its simple subsumption under economic or democratic issues, as expressed in drafts of planned economies (especially Phillips and Rozworski, 2019, p 241; also Dapprich, 2020, p 112ff), is also reflected in an adherence to – or rather a fading out – of the property form. Property *relations* themselves are extensively discussed as an issue that must be overturned because it concerns nothing less than the socialization of the means of production and thus the abolition of class antagonism. Moreover, the proposal to replace market mechanisms with planning mechanisms can also curtail vast overproduction. The planned organization of production would be geared to the general satisfaction of needs and the actual use of goods, which already mitigates the exclusionary gesture of the liberal property ideology that must counterintuitively rely on the exclusion of others from use – as Loick (2023), for example convincingly demonstrated in his examination of Locke's (1980) justification of property. This would come to an end in a socialist polity.

The sole focus on overturning property relations and ending overproduction nevertheless fails to recognize the far greater – also, but not only ecological – effects of property as a social relation. The goal of socialist planned economies is to break with the *unequal* and *unsustainable* exploitation of nature, while assuming that it is possible and unproblematic to appropriate nature in general *as property* – even if in collectivized form – to dispose of it unilaterally and to have the right to destroy it, which is inherent in the modern concept of property and does not seem to be questioned (Redecker, 2020, p 24).

The ignorance concerning the property form also establishes a connection between an adherence to primarily instrumental, subjugating accesses to and conceptions of nature and the tendency to dismiss relations that go beyond directly economic considerations more broadly. This is reflected and repeated on numerous levels: on the level of the already-mentioned relationship to nature and how they extend into or are always already part of the social; on the level of different modes of interpersonal relations that are rarely thought through systematically (this happens more in discussions on the periphery of the calculation debate; see for example Sutterlüti and Meretz, 2023; Sutterlüti and Meretz, in this volume); on the level of labour relations beyond their formal organizability; or on the level of analysing the status quo. The focus here clearly remains on the development of productive forces as an indicator of the possibility of socialism. Technical progress, especially with regard to automation potential and computing capacities, is often cited as the reason to consider a renewed engagement with planned economy as meaningful (for instance Morozov, 2019). A possible objection is that it is not at all clear whether technologies developed under current circumstances and for capitalist purposes can be fully rededicated, if understood as inherently political and thus highly dependent on their respective context of origin (Friends of the Classless Society, 2019).

Despite all the shared tendencies and motives in many planning drafts, a particularly controversial point concerning the distribution of remaining work burdens in the envisaged liberated society has emerged, ranging from an insistence on compulsory work for all capable members of society to arguing for complete voluntarism. A shared feature of these two strands – and the proposals that are positioned within this continuum – is a peculiar and alarming disregard for the reproductive in an analytical distinction from the productive sphere (Lutosch, 2022; Lutosch in this volume). Moreover, historically, the consideration of reproductive labour, which is still primarily carried out by women, represents one of the biggest gaps in (at least not explicitly feminist) Marxist discussions, something feminist socialists have long criticized (Federici, 1975; Kollontai, 2023 [2018]; Hester and Srnicek, 2023); therefore, the gap is not necessarily surprising but no less worthy of criticism.

The emphasis on collective sovereignty and control in the planning debate, which is a central motif in the Promethean strand, can be cited as a shared frame of reference and reason for the voids that have been suggested as examples that are systematically connected, particularly in terms of adherence to a dualistic instrumental relationship to nature. Furthermore, the gap that exists regarding the inclusion of reproductive work in such logics and the commonalities concerning productive labour is a central feature. The attainment of collective – human – sovereignty alone becomes the supposed guarantor of emancipation from natural constraints through the conscious control of the economy.

Post-sovereign planning?

Why should and can the idea of democratic socialist economic planning even be held onto? To what extent can it develop utopian potential despite the objections mentioned previously and thus point beyond not only what already exists but beyond the contradictions and blind spots of utopian concepts in its own name?

First of all, comparison with the current neoliberal–capitalist economic system remains an important motive. This system itself makes it systematically impossible to produce gentler, less domineering relationships with nature. Moreover, it does not provide an answer to a rethinking of the economy from a reproductive perspective that would lie beyond further valorization and ergo commodification, not to mention the realization of democracy as a collective life form that also permeates our mutual relations and is accessible in an egalitarian way. So, the destructiveness, hostility to care and lack of democratization of the capitalist present alone makes it appealing to consider conceivable alternatives, and a democratic planned economy is particularly intriguing, even if its concrete proposals for implementation are not devoid of blind spots. However, the potential of the planning idea seems to point beyond these in certain respects. While the critique of the persistently domineering reference to nature in many of today's proposals in SCD shows that cross-species interdependence is partially recognized, but still unilaterally dissolved in favour of human rule, further reflection on this could push for a stronger mediation and, in particular, democratization of interdependent relationships – because a socialist planned economy at least makes them visible in the first place.

It is not an easy task to translate this attempted shift in perspective into more concrete measures as the goal of democratizing interdependence, as well as taking permanent, perhaps even irreducible conflictuality seriously while holding on to the possibility of a better and freer future, are easier to formulate as abstract goals. However, the thematic areas and motifs focused on here can be used to hint at possible directions for thinking more tangibly to fill the voids of the Promethean perspectives – and also suggest that socialist planning is not necessarily dependent on a strong Prometheanism but is even partially hindered by it.

Starting with the very diagnosis that motivates today's revived SCD – namely (information) technological progress and the already existing forms of economic planning within private corporations – an analysis that is too narrowly economistic needs to be questioned in favour of the inclusion of other social conditions that go beyond economic factors. First, as already mentioned previously, the genuinely political nature of said technology must be taken seriously for a proper examination of the potentiality of socialist futures for contemporary society. In concrete terms, this raises the question of how far planning technologies that are currently used quasiautocratically within corporations and only serve the purpose of profit maximization can possibly demonstrate that a democratic form of planning is also feasible. Second, for an adequate diagnosis of the state of revolutionary potentialities beyond the development of productive forces, there are other factors that require separate examination to determine the extent to which they actually point beyond capitalist society – such as current modes of relation in a broader sense, such as family and work relations or degrees of political organization. Through this, existing forms of living, working and sustaining oneself that already attempt to counter exploitation, alienation and competition can be analysed for their potential to link the abstract calculation debate back to concrete social practice and thus prevent utopianism in a flawed sense (Redecker, 2014).

This also builds a bridge to thinking beyond the property form as a necessary supplement to property critique is in a constructive, world-building endeavour that could possibly learn and benefit from existing practices. The abolition of the property form seems to rely on a cultivation and mutual guarantee of other forms of safety because, at present, the desire for – and even the aggressive defence of – property seems to respond above all to the (exceedingly exclusive, distrustful) need for security. Socialist planned economies can gain capacities to reframe and guarantee *real* safety, for example by reducing secondary uncertainty so that others no longer appear as a threat to that safety, as there will be enough for all.

This importance of centring social relations to exceed mere economic considerations becomes most apparent when examining the reproductive sphere that is so painfully absent from the current SCD. Centring of usually feminized (unpaid) care work can implicitly inform (and, admittedly, complicate) the debate about the voluntariness of remaining workloads, which is one of the biggest discussions within the debate. The case of caring – especially when carried out within close relationships, usually without an explicit mandate – provides an argument against the organization of societally necessary work on the basis of mere voluntariness, which is not mediated by forms of mutual obligation or commitment. Such *non-organization* runs the risk of perpetuating inequalities and power relations that exist in contemporary society as a socialist society cannot emerge out of a vacuum but will be built by already subjectivized individuals and groups. Thus, it is quite conceivable that women will continue to take on large portions of reproductive work when it might otherwise not be performed at all. This involves the danger of concealing the continuing unequal distribution of work because its very distribution is not made the subject of collective decisions. On the other hand, from a feminist perspective, the matter is not as clear-cut as it may first appear through the lens of this argument. This is because collective responsibility, and consequent deprivatization, of working conditions becomes more likely when individualized obligations are dismantled (which raises follow-up questions about sanctioning mechanisms, performance measurement and performance-based distribution) and work must instead be made attractive to take on. The complexity of this issue shows how care and reproduction must be included in considerations about socialist economic planning from the start rather than being added during the process. This also implies a demystification and finally an abolition of the production–reproduction dichotomy to allow examination of production as well as formerly domestic activities for socialization and automation potentials. Feminist proposals for a democratic socialist planned economy could then instead divide necessary work according to which work can best be done where, how and with which skills. In this instance economic planning and division of labour issues overlap with those of urban planning, architecture and housing concepts. Only in this way will it be possible to actually redesign care work beyond a symbolic upgrading because 'the biggest problem with housework, as [Angela] Davis saw it, wasn't that it was devalued, hidden or even gendered, but that it sucked' (Lewis, 2023). For the potentially less bad or even fulfilling parts of care work to emerge as such, the conditions under which it is performed must first be fundamentally changed and therefore equally considered when pondering the organization and distribution of remaining necessary work.

Planned economic forms of organization offer a good foundation for this. However, the concern for the lives and needs of others is currently an incidental byproduct of economic activity when it coincides with profitability – which is also one of the central criticisms of the market form in the historical planning debate – or takes place under (self-)exploitative conditions. In contrast, reproduction moves to the centre in planned economy proposals so that the economy as a whole aims to include it and can thus possibly even be understood as caring in itself. This potentially caring impetus of a planned economy can be striven for precisely through the aforementioned *reduction* of secondary uncertainty that is a specific trait of capitalist market economies and a huge driver of its crisis-ridden nature as well as the *redistribution* of today differentially distributed irreducible forms of uncertainty.

A reorientation of the economy so that it no longer exploits reproduction merely as a background condition also links the discussion back to a new thinking and doing of societal relations to nature – and is perhaps even a prerequisite for it. A caring, non-dominating relation to cross-species structures and interdependent webs of life seems necessary to carry out the reconstructive work and repair that will still have emerged from the Capitalocene as repairable, and to break with a merely dominating gesture towards all that is more-than-human (Redecker, 2020). For this to happen, however, there must first be (together with the material revolution of production relations) a turning away from the conception of nature as a mere resource whose scarcity human beings manage. Instead, a caring but not maternalistic attitude within human–nature relationships has the potential to take nature seriously, including its own logic, agency, unavailability, contradictions and contingency, without romanticizing it as a homogeneous counterpart to society. The last-mentioned impulse is again partially prevented by ideas from today's planning debate, which in their certainly exaggerated modernism at least points to the fact that a liberating and liberated economy must distance itself from the attempt to return to supposedly natural (ergo 'better') conditions. The mediation of these poles could yield an idea of shared freedom to be striven for in a socialist planned economy, which is 'synthetic' (Srnicek and Williams, 2016, p 82) in the sense that it is collectively produced and guaranteed, but not Promethean, as it is not realized as the opposite or entail mastery but is realized *through* caring relations.

Conclusion

This chapter endeavoured to show that the resumed and ongoing debate on democratic socialist economic planning in its current form has some notable voids, especially from a critical theoretical and feminist questioning of some of the implications of the Promethean perspective. The review of this criticism, motivated by the conviction that the project of democratic economic planning should urgently be pursued, considers the possibility of uncovering the potentials of this idea more thoroughly and rigorously. Thus, this chapter attempted to show the significance of generating initial visions of a democratic-socialist planned economy from the currently marginalized arenas of the relationship to nature, social relations and reproductive labour, pointing out that the potential for this lies in the very idea of democratic economic planning as an emancipatory project that pushes for a better but permanently unreconciled future (whereas the idea itself always remains relegated to its own forms of concretization). On this basis, it was argued that post-sovereign planning, in particular, lives up to the potentials of the democratic socialist idea of a planned economy. It can more consequently put an end to notions of dominion over nature and within the social realm, and in doing so advocate for a redistribution of certain irreducible dependencies. The critique of sovereignty was not at all understood as a weakening but rather as an intensification of the strong democratic claim that planned economy proposals entail. This makes it possible to take seriously the contingency of every form of political and economic organization, and radically conceives to a form of democratic society that could possibly do justice to the claim of seeing in the Other not the limitations of, but the condition of, one another's freedom.

Notes

[1] This chapter is partially based on passages and arguments developed in *Zukunft jenseits des Marktes. Demokratie und gesellschaftliche Naturverhältnisse in sozialistischen Utopien*

[*Future Beyond the Market. Democracy and Human-Nature Relations in Socialist Utopias*] (Mohammed, 2023).

[2] In Greek mythology Prometheus is a god of fire. He stole fire from the Olympian gods and gave it to humanity, making him emblematic of enlightenment, breaking with unjust rule, and the acquisition of knowledge through science and secularism. This narrative is referred to when policies or perspectives are described as Promethean. The *Accelerationist Manifesto* interprets Prometheanism as a project (and enabling condition) for achieving (collective) sovereignty over society and nature. Promethean politics endorses socialist projects seeking to overcome capitalism but not the achievements associated and often conflated with it, such as social complexity, technology and the gains in individual and collective freedom it has made possible, and that generally adopts an affirmative relationship to modernity, rationality and progress (Mackay and Avanessian, 2014; Srnicek and Williams, 2017).

Bibliography

Benanav, A. (2020) *Automation and the Future of Work*. London/New York: Verso.

Campbell, A. (2002) 'Democratic planned socialism: feasible economic procedures', *Science & Society*, 66(1): 29–42. https://guilfordjournals.com/doi/10.1521/siso.66.1.29.21009

Cockshott, W.P. and Cottrell, A. (1993) *Towards a New Socialism*. Nottingham: Spokesman.

Dapprich, J.P. (2020) *Rationality and Distribution in the Socialist Economy*. Glasgow: University of Glasgow.

Daum, T. and Nuss, S. (eds) (2021) *Die unsichtbare Hand des Plans: Koordination und Kalkül im digitalen Kapitalismus*. Berlin: Dietz.

Federici, S. (1975) *Wages Against Housework*. Bristol: Falling Wall Press and the Power of Women Collective.

Friends of The Classless Society (2019) 'Contours of the world commune', *Endnotes* 5. https://endnotes.org.uk/issues/5

Garreaud, Á and Brock, N. (2021) 'Alle Macht den Menschen', *iungle.world*. https://jungle.world/artikel/2021/45/alle-macht-den-menschen

Haraway, D.J. (2016) *Staying with the Trouble: Making Kin in the Chthuluzän*. Durham, NC/London: Duke University Press.

Heyer, J. (2021) 'Demokratie und Planung', *ak analyse und kritik*. https://www.akweb.de/gesellschaft/planwirtschaftdebatte-pat-devine-und-david-laibman-ueber-demokratie-und-planung/

Hester, H. and Srnicek, N. (2023) *After Work. A History of the Home and the Fight for Free Time*. London/New York: Verso.

Horkheimer, M. and Adorno, T.W. (2002) *Dialectic of Enlightenment: Philosophical Fragments*. Stanford: Stanford University Press.

Kollontai, A. (2023 [1918]) 'Familie und der kommunistische Staat', in Kitchen Politics (eds) *Die Neuordnung der Küchen. Materialistisch-feministische Entwürfe eines besseren Zusammenlebens*, Münster: edition assemblage, pp 47–65.

Lewis, S. (2023) 'I'll do the dishes: mothers' work', *London Review of Books*, 45(9). https://www.lrb.co.uk/the-paper/v45/n09/sophie-lewis/i-ll-do-the-dishes?s=09

Locke, J. (1980) *Second Treatise of Government*. Edited, with an Introduction, by C. B. Macpherson. Indianapolis/Cambridge: Hackett Publishing.

Loick, D. (2023) *The Abuse of Property*. Cambridge, MA: MIT Press.

Lutosch, H. (2022) *Wenn das Baby schreit, dann möchte man doch hingehen*. https://communaut.org/de/wenn-das-baby-schreit-dann-moechte-man-doch-hingehen

Mackay, R. and Avanessian, A. (eds) (2014) *#Accelerate# the Accelerationist Reader*. Berlin: Merve.

Malm, A. (2021) 'Planning the planet: geoengineering our way out of and back into a planned economy', in H. Jean Buck, A. Malm and J.P Sapinski (eds) *Has It Come to This? The Promises and Perils of Geoengineering on the Brink*, New Brunswick, NJ: Rutgers University Press, pp 143–162.

Marx, K. and Engels, F. (1977) 'Manifest der Kommunistischen Partei', in *Karl Marx Friedrich Engels. Werke Band 4,* Hrsg. Institut für Marxismus-Leninismus beim ZK der KPdSU, Berlin: Dietz, pp 459–493.

Mohammed, S. (2023) *Zukunft jenseits des Marktes. Demokratie und gesellschaftliche Naturverhältnisse in sozialistischen Utopien*. Baden-Baden: Nomos.

Moore, J.W. (2017) 'The Capitalocene, Part I: on the nature and origins of our ecological crisis', *The Journal of Peasant Studies*, 44(3): 594–630.

Morozov, E. (2019) 'Digital socialism? The calculation debate in the age of big data', *New Left Review*, 116/117: 33–67.

Phillips, L. and Rozworski, M. (2019) *The People's Republic of Walmart: How the World's Biggest Corporations Are Laying the Foundation for Socialism*. London/New York: Verso.

Redecker, E. von (2014) 'Topischer Sozialismus: Zur Exodus-Konzeption bei Gustav Landauer und Martin Buber', *WestEnd – Neue Zeitschrift für Sozialforschung*, (1): 93–108.

Redecker, E. von. (2020) *Revolution für das Leben. Philosophie der neuen Protestformen*. Frankfurt/M.: Fischer.

Saros, D.E. (2014) *Information Technology and Socialist Construction: The End of Capital and the Transition to Socialism*. New York: Routledge.

Srnicek, N. and Williams, A. (2017) *Accelerate Manifesto. For an Accelerationist Politics*. Buenos Aires: Gato Negro Ediciones.

Srnicek, N. and Williams, A. (2016) *Inventing the Future: Postcapitalism and a World Without Work*. London/New York: Verso.

Sutterlüti, S. and Meretz, S. (2023) *Make Capitalism History: A Practical Framework for Utopia and the Transformation of Society*. London: Palgrave Macmillan.

15

Democratizing the Forces of Re/Production: AI Planning as a Sensing Device for a Degrowth Economy

Simon Schaupp

Introduction

The ecological crisis is omnipresent. Catastrophic climate change and the sixth mass extinction are threatening life as we know it on the planet. Yet national and international political institutions appear to be structurally incapable of effectively addressing the causes of this destruction (Wainwright and Mann, 2019). For example, fossil fuel subsidies have continued to grow globally, surging higher than US$1 trillion in 2022 (IEA, 2023). In the absence of any political or economic change of course, efforts to achieve sustainability instead hold out hope for various technical remedies for the ecological crisis such as renewable energy technologies, carbon sequestration or geoengineering. Degrowth scholars have heavily criticized this type of techno-solutionism (for example, Latouche, 2009; Hickel, 2020; Saito, 2022; Schmelzer, Vetter and Vansintjan, 2022; Hofferberth, Durand and Schmelzer, in this volume), based on various objections. First, critics of techno-solutionism have highlighted the lack of any extant large-scale forms of carbon sequestration and the potentially disastrous side-effects of geoengineering. Second, they emphasize that even if a complete shift towards renewable energy – of which there is currently no sign – could ultimately be achieved, such measures would hardly be sufficient to mitigate the climate crisis as they are premised on a model of economic growth that is necessarily coupled with resource and energy throughput. In fact, meta-studies have not found any evidence that an absolute decoupling of economic growth from environmental destruction is possible (Hickel and Kallis, 2020). As a result, the proponents of degrowth have argued for deindustrialization and economic localization, emphasizing practices known as commoning. The stance of degrowth regarding technology has largely been ambivalent; some researchers have identified the technologies of industrialism as the source of the present ecological crisis, while others have argued that digital technologies – and especially artificial intelligence (AI) – might become important tools for a post-growth economy. However, the dominant stance across the degrowth literature is one of techno-pessimism (for an overview, see Vetter, 2018).

This chapter, which aims to discuss the role of technology for degrowth by exploring the Marxian concept of productive forces, argues against a technological determinism present in degrowth as well as in ecomodernism. Instead, it advances an interpretation of productive forces as the totality of what human beings are capable of. This definition makes *potentiality* a core feature of the concept of productive forces, shifting the focus away from a narrow understanding of the prevailing technological state of the art. This emphasis on potential is better suited for ecological politics than a gloss of the term that stresses the use of current technology. Furthermore, emphasising potentiality enables the systematic identification of the political and not merely technical nature of society's productive forces. This perspective allows for a more precise critique of environmentally destructive technologies while avoiding technological fetishism, turning technology itself into the subject behind the crisis.

Building on ecological and feminist Marxist literature, environmental destruction may be attributed to the separation between the spheres of production and reproduction. Technological means that are suitable for a socio-ecological transition must therefore be able to transcend this separation by becoming *forces of re/production*. This possibility is evaluated in what follows with regard to AI-based planning. This chapter argues that such planning can become a *sensing device* that serves to reconnect production with its social and ecological foundation, addressing a notable gap in the degrowth literature. For example, Hofferberth, Durand and Schmelzer (in this volume) note that almost all concepts of degrowth imply some type of economic planning but often fail to describe the concrete ways in which planning is to be realized. This omission cannot be left unresolved as it affects the fundamental coherence of the concept of *planned* transition, which distinguishes degrowth from recession (that is, degrowth by design rather than degrowth by disaster). Therefore, the question of the feasibility of degrowth is also – and maybe even primarily – a question of the feasibility of democratic economic planning. This chapter provides some basic evaluation of this feasibility by reviewing various approaches to digital democratic planning (DDP) and participatory integrative planning (PIP). It also aspires to resolve some of the disagreements between the techno-optimistic and techno-pessimistic camps in the ecological crisis debate.

Forces of production

Discussion of the concept of forces of production immediately confronts the contradictions that have historically characterized these forces. One version has understood these contradictions as a source of progress, whereas a second has considered them as a source of destruction. Generally found in an orthodox reading of Marx, the first version is derived principally from a passage in *The Poverty of Philosophy*, where Marx (1847 [1955]) wrote: 'The hand-mill gives you society with the feudal lord; the steam-mill, society with the industrial capitalist' (p 166). This axiom implies a techno-determinist understanding of history as driven by the development of the means of production. In this understanding, '[a]t a certain stage in their development, the material productive forces of society come into conflict with the existing relations of production' (Engels, 1859, p 263). Such passages have been mobilized to support the perspective that technological development is the primary or objective cause of social progress and revolutionary transformations. However, technological determinism is in itself not confined to Marxism but is also to be found in the mainstream messianic belief that the future will deliver technologies capable of effectively removing CO_2 from the atmosphere and generating environmentally neutral energy. Such beliefs exceed even the stereotype of Marxist teleology in their rigidity (for a critical review, see Parrique et al, 2019).

The second version's understanding of the inherent contradictions of the forces of production has taken the opposite view. Environmentalist and feminist scholars have often argued that the forces of production are, in fact, forces of destruction, given that their development destroys the very possibility of life on earth (for example, Mellor, 1992; Caffentzis and Federici, 2014; Barca, 2020). Saito's (2022) recent argument that Marx's theory of productive forces should be abandoned and that an eco-socialist development of technology would have to 'start from scratch in many cases' (p 158) is exemplary of this perspective.

Yet both these opposing approaches to understanding productive forces have shared what might be termed a concretist interpretation of the concept, which equates the forces of production with the totality of presently available technology or means of production. Marx's writing, however, allows for an exceedingly different reading on this point. While Marx did indeed *analytically* differentiate between the means of production and the relations of production, these terms were always empirically intertwined. Thus, the means of production do not realize all of what is technically possible but only what is necessary for increasing profits. In *The Poverty of Philosophy* of 1847, which is the text most commonly referenced as proof of his technological determinism, Marx (1847 [1955]) wrote that 'the productive forces have been developed by virtue of [the] system of class antagonisms' (p 132). In other words, technology is itself to be considered a product of social relations, and the primary cause of progress is social struggle rather than technological development. While Marx's earlier writings did admittedly lend themselves to certain techno-determinist interpretations, Marx later explicitly distanced himself from this perspective. However, Soviet leaders from Lenin and Bukharin to Stalin promoted a deterministic understanding of productive forces, defining it as the core of Marxian historical materialism (Mau, 2023, pp 48–51). This interpretation directly contributed to the careless productivism of the Soviet Union, which prized technological progress at whatever human or environmental cost.

Importantly, for Marx, productive forces are not actually tangible objects. Just as value as such is never visible but nevertheless regulates the capitalist mode of production (Pitts, 2020), productive forces need not appear in pure form to be historically significant as they are always mediated by the prevailing relations of production. As soon as they materialize in the actual production process, they are amalgamated with the relations of production. Thus, a profit-oriented economy not only yields questionable products but also specific production processes that are both inefficient and destructive. The tension between productive forces and the relations of production can be found in these very processes. Yet, conceptually, if productive forces are simply equated with the empirical deployment of technology, the social irrationality of capitalist production is rendered as a property of the productive forces, naturalizing their capitalist form (Lohoff, 1987).

Such a conflation of the productive forces with the actually existing means of production has been implicitly presented in parts of the cybersocialist literature that has assumed digitalization will lead directly to post-capitalism (Mason, 2016) or fully automated luxury communism (Bastani, 2019). However, it is also observable in much of the degrowth critiques of industrialism that have ascribed the irrationality of contemporary production for exchange, and the subsumption of concrete material production to the productive forces themselves under an abstract logic of exchange value. This perspective erases the possible organization of productive forces beyond capitalism, reducing degrowth to localist folk politics (Srnicek and Williams, 2015). In response, Hofferberth, Durand and Schmelzer (in this volume) suggest that degrowth might engage explicitly with economic planning issues, including the role of digital technologies. However, this proposal does not systematically confront the potentials and problems of various existing approaches to DDP. This chapter addresses these points in what follows.

Digital democratic planning

A central idea of DDP is to replace the market in some respects (or in its totality) with AI-based coordination and follows from a critique of the market as the central mode of resource allocation. According to this critique, markets regulate production through prices, which do not reflect needs but rather solvent demand. Markets therefore produce undersupply for those in need but without money, and an environmentally destructive oversupply for those with money. In terms of production, markets rely on competition and subsequently require all enterprises to engage in continuous cost-cutting that comes at the expense of workers and the environment (O'Connor, 1997; Fraser, 2022). Furthermore, the system of carbon prices and emissions trading has been criticized for not providing adequate steering mechanisms (for example, Buller, 2022).

DDP therefore suggests alternative modes of resource allocation that combine production directly with consumption, rather than profit. These models have also promised a systematic accounting of ecological factors (Vettese and Pendergrass, 2022). Most proposals have heavily referenced current logistical systems such as those used by Walmart (Phillips and Rozworski, 2019), Amazon (Saros, 2014) or certain service platforms (Muldoon, 2022). These approaches contend that algorithmic management would not be used as a system of surveillance but rather as a feedback infrastructure (Saros, 2014; Morozov, 2019; Jochum and Schaupp, 2022). Drawing on ideas of cybernetic management, digital feedback is supposed to enable decentralized, self-organized planning concerning both the labour process and economic coordination.

In many instances, such cybernetic modes of control are already employed in contemporary algorithmic management. Labour processes are tracked, and the data are fed back to the workers, who are tasked with optimizing their own labour activity. Often the entire firm's resources are managed based on real-time data establishing an adaptable self-organizing system (Schaupp, 2022). In the DDP literature, such digital infrastructure and indices are contended to enable a continuous optimization process that steers production towards ever-more desirable outcomes. Even a cursory evaluation of the potential of such digital infrastructure as a facet of economic planning – given its evident global applicability in technical terms – suggests a real precondition for addressing the present ecological crisis (Vettese and Pendergrass, 2022). Moreover, digital infrastructure has demonstrated the potential for decentralization and self-organization instead of centralized planning (Saros, 2014; Schaupp, 2017; Morozov, 2019; Muldoon, 2022). In this regard DDP partially concedes a point that has been raised historically by liberals, that socialism was always bound to fail given that, in the absence of a market-mediated price system, it could never adequately match supply with demand (Hayek, 1945). DDP builds on a response by Lange (1967), who argued that computers might be able to solve the essential economic questions more efficiently, yielding superior results to anything markets produce.

In this regard most of the arguments the DDP perspective has presented have not been as contrary to neoclassical economic theories as they claim to be. Both the principles of matching supply and demand and (non-)market design are quite compatible with the conception of markets in general equilibrium theory. There, the market is an equation, with one side expressing demand and the other supply. The building blocks of the market are market participants with individual preferences who engage in voluntary exchange by contract (Stojanović, 2022). Digital socialism tries to emulate such markets by replacing money with digital information, which inadvertently overlaps with Hayek's (1945) abstract understanding of markets as information-processing machines. This overlap replicates the idea that capitalism can be understood as a mode of allocating commodities through the market. Marx (1867 [1976]) criticized this idea as commodity fetishism, because it presupposes the commodity form as a natural given and veils the relationship between capital and labour in the realm of production. Instead, for him, production and circulation of commodities formed an inseparable unity at whose heart lies the capitalist labour process. As Postone (1995) argued, reducing capitalism to the market is not only inherent to neoclassical thought but also to the Soviet misinterpretation of Marx. Thus, Soviet Marxism reduced the contradiction between the forces and relations of production to the opposition between planned production in individual enterprises on one side and an anarchic market on the other. Capitalism was thus reduced to the sphere of circulation. In contrast, the sphere of production appeared as a sphere of rational organization, and socialism became the generalization of the rationality of production in individual enterprises to society as a whole. This was a utopia of socialist society merged with the vision of a total social factory – or, as in Lenin's (1918) famous injunction, it was an effort to 'organize the whole economy on the lines of the postal service'.

Neglecting the organization of production contributed to an authoritarian system of work with disastrous consequences for the Soviet Union. Digital socialism runs the risk of repeating this mistake by focussing only on the sphere of circulation. Thus, for example, the utopia of *The People's Republic of Walmart* (Phillips and Rozworski, 2019) appears to be an echo of Lenin's (1918) idea of modelling socialist government on the existing German postal service. While Philipps and Rozworski (2019) did acknowledge the undemocratic nature of companies like Walmart, the problem of neglecting the sphere of production remains obvious. The fact that Walmart, Amazon or the various platform companies – like the postal service – hardly produce anything underscores this problem.

The practical implications of this neglect can be put in more concrete terms by considering the massive conflicts evolving around precisely those technologies of algorithmic management envisaged as the backbone of DDP. At the turn of the millennium the legal scholar Lawrence Lessig (1999) coined the phrase 'code is law' to emphasize the political nature of algorithms as they structure our actions. In the course of the increasing diffusion of digital devices into all areas of life, these 'laws' have long ceased to apply only in cyberspace, as Lessig assumed would happen. They have spread to all fields of society and are particularly ubiquitous in the world of work. As algorithms increasingly assume the functions of management, the conflicts inherent in the world of work also increasingly involve these algorithms. To make their work easier, workers engage in various forms of technopolitics from below (Schaupp, 2021), including the manipulation of algorithms to decelerate work or even sabotage digital systems.

There is no reason to assume that algorithms will stop being contested once they are in the service of DDP. On the contrary, if they become the central instruments in the allocation of goods and services, they will literally – more than ever before – become laws. This means that measurement itself – as in labour credits (as in Cockshott and Cottrell, 1993; Saros, 2014) or net social benefit (Albert, 2004) – will be contested terrain. Reducing planning to a task of algorithmic optimization conceals this political dimension, excluding democratic deliberation (Benanav, 2020). Other approaches to the planning debate exist, however, that emphasize democracy in the world of work.

Participatory integrative planning

While the discussion around the possibilities of digital economic planning has received more attention lately, there is also an older debate on democratic economic planning that does not refer to technological possibilities. The focus of this discourse has been on institutions that would allow for a participatory design of the entire economy, including both the organization of work and resource allocation (for example, Albert, 2004; Devine, 2020; Sutterlütti and Meretz, 2023). Such approaches might be summarized as Participatory Integrative Planning (PIP). The neglect of work that is typical of digital planning does not apply to this strand of the debate. Instead, PIP approaches address one of the key issues in the debate regarding sustainable work. The sustainable work approach acknowledges that strengthening workplace codetermination, in contrast to mere profit orientation, is a necessary but not sufficient step towards a socio-ecological transformation. It is not sufficient because the outcomes of workplace codetermination regularly conflict with the interests of external stakeholders, especially with regard to the environmental effects of production (Jochum et al, 2019). PIP might offer a way out of this dilemma by articulating concrete suggestions regarding the combination of democracy at the workplace level with societal economic democracy.

Beyond questions of democracy, PIP is also potentially a means for overcoming the separation of the spheres of production and reproduction. Several scholars have identified this separation as the central structural cause of the ecological crisis (O'Connor, 1997; Biesecker and Hofmeister, 2010; Barca, 2020). The sphere of reproduction encompasses all types of work necessary to maintaining life. It may be understood in a broad sense as inclusive of the various types of work that are necessary for reproducing human labour (for instance child-rearing, education and care of the elderly and disabled) and various types of ecological maintenance and reparation work such as foresting, recycling, or indeed some forms of agriculture. Some scholars have also included the building and maintenance of communal infrastructure, such as railways, roads, electricity systems and the like, in this category. The commonality of these various types of reproduction work is that they are necessary preconditions for production; however, they are not included in the sphere of production in the sense that the enterprises that appropriate them do not organize and pay for them. In most cases they are organized and paid for by state institutions or delegated to unpaid housework. This leads to the fundamental structural undermining of reproductive labour that has been identified as a central cause for recurring environmental crises and crises of care.

Combining democracy at the workplace level with society-wide economic democracy could offer a way of reconnecting production and reproduction as it would conjoin the democratic deliberations within and outside the workplace. However, none of the major PIP approaches has systematically addressed the realm of reproduction. Various feminist theorists (Ratta, 2020; Chowdhury, 2021; Lutosch, 2022) have focussed on the neglect of care work in the planning debate. The almost exclusive focus on productive work is already problematized by the fact that in most societies care work constitutes the majority of all work. In Germany, for example care work accounts for 64 per cent of all social work; 8 per cent of this work is paid and 56 percent remains unpaid (Winker, 2015, p 24). More importantly, the focus on productive work repeats the crisis-prone separation of production and reproduction. While productive work is at the centre of PIP, care work has been treated as if it follows a completely different logic that cannot be planned because it is too intimate. This assumption repeats the patriarchal myth that care work is not actually work but an act of love, which functions as a legitimation for the social subordination of female work and has therefore long been attacked by feminist politics, as exemplified by the prominent wages against housework campaign (Federici, 1975). Lutosch (2022) argued that the neglect of care work exposes an underlying problem of the planning debate, namely a decidedly masculine ideal of autonomy. Thus, concepts as distinct as those developed by Saros (2014) and Sutterlütti and Meretz (2023) share the norm of an able-bodied young male who does not have any care responsibilities. According to Lutosch (2022) this is attributable to an individualistic idea of autonomy that is implicit in the idea of the individual articulation of needs (Saros, 2014) or the idea of absolute voluntariness in the choice of work (Sutterlütti and Meretz, 2023). Both approaches have classified interferences in these individual spheres as authoritarian or even violent. Against this approach, Lutosch (2022) argued for an alternative notion of autonomy that acknowledges the fundamental dependence of all human beings on one another.

Human beings are not only mutually dependent but also depend on non-human nature for survival. This dependency has been addressed more systematically in recent planning debates than questions of care (see especially Vettese and Pendergrass, 2022). As described earlier, however, the environmental dimension of the economy has merely been discussed as a problem of resource allocation and not as a problem of work. This framing is inadequate in so far as a degrowth society would have to devote a considerable share of its labour to reparations in the face of ecological crises. Its economic planning, as Dyer-Witheford (in this volume) emphasized, would have to focus on disaster relief. This includes, but is not limited to, building infrastructure for protection against the effects of climate change as manifested in floods, heatwaves, wildfires and superstorms; relocating people from areas that have become uninhabitable and mediating the social conflicts that result from mass migration; massively expanding the healthcare sector to treat diseases and to prevent further pandemics; transforming and repairing damaged ecosystems, for instance in vast reforestation campaigns; and expanding human labour in agriculture, which will decrease productivity by interrupting unsustainable practices and in response to the loss of biodiversity, especially among pollinator insects. Many other profoundly labour-intensive tasks would emerge, not least research into projected environmental risks and the democratic deliberation surrounding adequate forms of adaptation. Thus, in a degrowth economy, the bias of PIP towards productive work might need to be reversed because the majority of social labour would have to be invested in reproductive work. Planning this kind of work, however, would require overcoming the localism inherent to many degrowth visions and developing comprehensive means of coordination.

Forces of re/production

The localism inherent to some approaches in degrowth and PIP is inadequate to the scale of the global ecological crises now confronting humanity. Neither mitigation nor adaptation to global events can be organized locally. Instead, such activities require scalable coordination devices, including institutionalized forms of collaboration and global data-processing infrastructure. An important example of such a global device whose importance would even increase in a degrowth society is climate science. Edwards's (2010) ground-breaking history of climate science refers to it as a vast machine. This vastness is necessary given the inherently global existence of the climate. Consequently, weather and climate data must be collected from as many places on earth as possible, and these heterogeneous data must then be converted into uniform datasets. This process necessitates networked infrastructure composed of people, artefacts and institutions that generate and process specific knowledge concerning the human and natural world. Such infrastructure would include internationally connected weather observatories and their technical equipment – not just satellites but also social networks such as the World Meteorological Organization with the World Weather Watch and organizations like the Intergovernmental Panel on Climate Change. Similar devices would allow for the understanding of ecological crises like mass extinctions.

All aspects of the vast machine (Edwards, 2010) are the result of the development of productive forces, recalling what Marx (1858 [2005]) described in *Grundrisse* as 'immediate productive forces'; that is, what lies beyond technology, namely social knowledge and forms of collaboration. It is, in other words, the development of the productive forces that enable our knowledge of various ecological crises (see Bratton, 2016, on the political centrality of digital sensing). Because this knowledge is essential for planning a degrowth economy, productive force development cannot be abolished per se. Instead, a viable criterion for assessing technologies would be the question of *whether they can be turned into forces of re/production* – or that which facilitates a reconciliation of production and reproduction. Some technologies clearly do not qualify, as in those that rely on massive inputs of combustible fossil fuels.

The status of digital technologies, however, is not as clear. Contrary to popular metaphors like the cloud, digital technology relies on an immense amount of energy, raw materials like rare earth minerals and colossal quantities of water for cooling data centres (Crawford, 2021). Therefore, the digitalization of everything constitutes an ecological problem in itself. However, it is reasonable to assume that preserving a certain degree of digital infrastructure without catastrophic environmental consequences would be possible. In any case such an infrastructure is essential for reconnecting production and reproduction. Through surveying social needs, it would allow for production planning in a way that directly responds to such needs and would replace profit incentives. Such a development would make it possible to eliminate a large proportion of environmentally harmful production, while upholding a relatively high standard of living. Furthermore, production could be consciously coupled with its ecological basis by drawing on earth science models. Thus, the democratic deliberation of various economic options would always entail projections of the ecological effects that would accompany any proposed options (Jochum and Schaupp, 2022). This also means that the ecological dimension does not appear as a scientifically declared limit but rather as socially deliberated boundaries (see also Brand et al, 2021).

To return to the centrality of potential in understanding productive forces, such an approach entails building upon the existing technological and social potentials brought forward by the development of the forces of re/production, though it is not immediately reliant on the prevailing technology of the present. As noted by Adorno (2006) an insistence on the difference between the concretely possible and the present state of things must be kept in mind. The ambivalences thereby entailed can be surmised by recalling the history of climate science. Edwards (2010) reconstructed the components of the vast machine as having developed under the conditions of the Cold War, and as an outgrowth of military technology and the wider (post)colonial conjuncture. Yet climate science projects a future beyond these deeply problematic origins by enabling new forms of understanding of the disasters that have befallen the natural environment.

Conclusion

The inability of political institutions to effectively act in the face of the contemporary climate crisis has been attributed to the dependence of the capitalist economy on growth. Yet the absence of economic growth has historically always meant crises in the form of recession, which, in the recent period, has been accompanied by austerity aimed at the most vulnerable populations (for instance Mattei, 2022). If it is to be meaningfully distinguished from a recession, an economy of degrowth must be based on planning. However, when applied globally, this principle contradicts the localism and techno-scepticism of a large portion of the degrowth literature. This chapter has used a critical interpretation of the concept of productive forces to evaluate the role that AI technologies might play in democratic economic planning for a degrowth economy, arguing against equating productive forces with currently existing technology and instead understanding them as the totality of humanity's capabilities. The critical potential of the term rests on an understanding of the difference between the prevailing ethos of the present and potential future developments.

To build on such an understanding, technologies must be assessed considering their potential to become forces of re/production; that is, their capacity for bridging the separation between production and reproduction that is at the heart of the ecological crisis. In this sense digital planning technologies – like those present in the vast machine (Edwards, 2010) of climate science – could be developed into a global sensing device for coordinating production. This would reconnect production to its ecological basis by providing data-based projections of the ecological effects of a variety of economic possibilities. The emphasis on various options precludes a technocratic approach that veils the political character of economic decision-making by presenting it as a necessary result of scientific insights. In contrast, the ecological dimension of production would be made accessible to political deliberation instead of being left to market forces that appear to take on a life of their own.

The non-techno-determinist approach to the concept of productive forces presented here suggests that a transition to a democratically planned ecological economy would occur neither as a result of technological development – as some digital planning approaches imply – nor as a result of scientific arguments – as some degrowth approaches imply. If it is to come into being, it will instead be the result of social conflict. Consequently, the approach suggested here cannot be restricted to the issue of technological possibilities but must also include political factors and especially analyses of ongoing social struggles. This does not mean merely posing the question of what is politically realistic but is rather an inquiry informed by the identification of political potential. As Nowak (2021) argued, such an approach could find inspiration in various forms of labour unrest. Following Barca (2020), labour unrest in the sphere of reproductive work would be of particular interest as it rebels immediately against the capitalist erosion of the reproduction of life. Another source of inspiration could be the climate movement, which is not only the largest global social movement of our time but also one that increasingly exposes the inadequacy of markets and the private management of natural resources in response to the ecological problem. Some of its most prominent actors have suggested a political form of climate assemblies to develop transition plans towards a sustainable economy (Schaupp, Petermann and Haab, 2024). In addressing issues of production by including workers from firms affected by transition plans, this might also widen the focus beyond allocation. It also promises to transcend the politics of the workplace as found in classical socialist visions of workers' councils by way of its inclusion of external stakeholders. This emphasis on social struggles could likewise aid in overcoming the technocratic implications of some approaches now found in the planning debate and in some degrowth currents.

Bibliography

Adorno, T.W. (2006) *Zur Lehre von Der Geschichte Und von Der Freiheit*. Frankfurt a.M.: Suhrkamp.

Albert, M. (2004) *Parecon: Life After Capitalism*. London: Verso.

Barca, S. (2020) *Forces of Reproduction: Notes for a Counter-Hegemonic Anthropocene*. Cambridge: Cambridge University Press. https://www.cambridge.org/core/elements/forces-of-reproduction/BE9B0DBDC89593F3284FE3F51D3B0418

Bastani, A. (2019) *Fully Automated Luxury Communism*. London: Verso Books.

Benanav, A. (2020) 'How to make a pencil', *Logic Magazine*, (12): 195–214.

Biesecker, A. and Hofmeister, S. (2010) 'Focus: (Re)productivity: sustainable relations both between society and nature and between the genders', *Ecological Economics*, 69(8): 1703–1711. doi: 10.1016/j.ecolecon.2010.03.025.

Brand, U., Muraca, B., Pineault, É. et al (2021) 'From planetary to societal boundaries: an argument for collectively defined self-limitation', *Sustainability: Science, Practice and Policy*, 17(1): 264–291.

Bratton, B. (2016) *The Stack: On Software and Sovereignty*. Cambridge, MA: MIT Press.

Buller, A (2022) *The Value of a Whale: On the Illusions of Green Capitalism*. Manchester: Manchester University Press.

Caffentzis, G. and Federici, S. (2014) 'Commons against and beyond capitalism', *Community Development Journal*, 49(suppl_1): i92–i105.

Chowdhury, S. (2021) *The Organisation of Social Reproduction in a Postcapitalist Participatory Economy*. méta Working Paper 12EN2021. https://metacpc.org/wp-content/uploads/2022/05/12EN-mWP-Chowdhury-Production-1.pdf

Cockshott, W.P. and Cottrell, A. (1993) *Towards a New Socialism*. London: Spokesman Books.

Crawford, K. (2021) *Atlas of AI: Power, Politics, and the Planetary Costs of Artificial Intelligence*. New Haven: Yale University Press.

Devine, P. (2020) *Democracy and Economic Planning: The Political Economy of a Self-Governing Society*. New York: Routledge. doi: 10.4324/9780429033117.

Edwards, P.N. (2010) *A Vast Machine – Computer Models, Climate Data, and the Politics of Global Warming*. Cambridge, MA: MIT Press.

Engels, F. (1859) *MECW, Vol. 16, Karl Marx, A Contribution to the Critique of Political Economy*. Moscow: Progress.

Federici, S. (1975) *Wages against Housework*. Bristol: Falling Wall Press.

Fraser, N. (2022) *Cannibal Capitalism: How Our System Is Devouring Democracy, Care, and the Planet – and What We Can Do About It*. London: Verso.

Hayek, F.A. (1945) 'The use of knowledge in society', *The American Economic Review*, 35(4): 519–530.

Hickel, J. (2020) *Less Is More: How Degrowth Will Save the World*. New York: Random House.

Hickel, J. and Kallis, G. (2020) 'Is green growth possible?', *New Political Economy*, 25(4): 469–486. doi: 10.1080/13563467.2019.1598964.

IEA (2023) 'Fossil fuels consumption subsidies 2022 – analysis'. https://www.iea.org/reports/fossil-fuels-consumption-subsidies-2022

Jochum, G. and Schaupp, S. (2022) 'Forces and relations of control', in J. Muldoon (ed) *Marx and the Robots. Networked Production, AI and Human Labour*, London: Pluto, pp 255–268.

Jochum, G., Barth, T., Brandl, S. et al (2019) *Sustainable Work. The Social-Ecological Transformation of the Working Society*. Working Group 'Sustainable work' of the German Committee Future Earth. https://www.dkn-fut ure-earth.org/imperia/md/assets/dkn/files/dkn_working_paper_2019_jochum_engl_v2__1.pdf

Lange, O. (1967) 'The computer and the market', in F.A. Hayek and G.R. Stigler (eds) *Socialism, Capitalism and Economic Growth: Essays Presented to Maurice Dobb*, Cambridge: Cambridge University Press, pp 158–161.

Latouche, S. (2009) *Farewell to Growth*. Cambridge: Polity.

Lenin, V.I. (1918) *Collected Works, Volume 25, The State and Revolution*. Moscow: Progress. https://www.marxists.org/archive/lenin/works/1917/staterev/ch03.htm#s3

Lessig, L. (1999) *Code: And Other Laws Of Cyberspace*. New York: Basic Books.

Lohoff, E. (1987) 'Technik als Fetisch-Begriff. Über den Zusammenhang von alter Arbeiterbewegung und neuer Produktivkraftkritik', *Marxistische Kritik*, (3): 30–52.

Lutosch, H. (2022) *Wenn das Baby schreit, dann möchte man doch hingehen*. https://communaut.org/de/wenn-das-baby-schreit-dann-moechte-man-doch-hingehen

Marx, K. (1847 [1955]) *The Poverty of Philosophy, MECW, Vol. 6*. Moscow: Progress.

Marx, K. (1858 [2005]) *Grundrisse: Foundations of the Critique of Political Economy*. London: Penguin.

Marx, K. (1867 [1976]) *Capital, Volume I*. London: Penguin.

Mason, P. (2016) *PostCapitalism: A Guide to Our Future*. London: Penguin.

Mattei, C.E. (2022) *The Capital Order: How Economists Invented Austerity and Paved the Way to Fascism*. Chicago: University of Chicago Pr.

Mau, S. (2023) *Mute Compulsion: A Marxist Theory of the Economic Power of Capital*. London/Brooklyn: Verso Books.

Mellor, M. (1992) 'Eco-feminism and eco-socialism: Dilemmas of essentialism and materialism'; *Capitalism Nature Socialism*, 3(2): 43–62. doi: 10.1080/10455759209358486.

Morozov, E. (2019) 'Digital socialism? The calculation debate in the age of big data', *New Left Review*, (116): 33–67.

Muldoon, J. (2022) *Platform Socialism: How to Reclaim Our Digital Future from Big Tech*. London: Pluto Press.

Nowak, J. (2021) 'Global economic planning as a challenge for the labour movement', *Tempo Social*, 33(2): 37–56.

O'Connor, J. (1997) *Natural Causes: Essays in Ecological Marxism*. New York: Guilford Publications.

Parrique, T., Barth, J., Briens, F., Kerschner, C. and Kraus-Polk, A. (2019) *Decoupling Debunked. Evidence and Arguments Against Green Growth as a Sole Strategy for Sustainability*. Brussels: European Environmental Bureau.

Phillips, L. and Rozworski, M. (2019) *People's Republic of Wal-Mart: How the World's Biggest Corporations Are Laying the Foundation for Socialism.* London: Verso.
Pitts, F.H. (2020) *Value.* Cambridge/Medford, MA: Polity.
Postone, M. (1995) *Time, Labor, and Social Domination: A Reinterpretation of Marx's Critical Theory.* Cambridge: Cambridge University Press.
Ratta, D.D. (2020) 'Digital socialism beyond the digital social: confronting communicative capitalism with ethics of care', *tripleC: Communication, Capitalism & Critique*, 18(1): 101–115. doi: 10.31269/triplec.v18i1.1145.
Saito, K. (2022) *Marx in the Anthropocene: Towards the Idea of Degrowth Communism.* Cambridge: Cambridge University Press.
Saros, D.E. (2014) *Information Technology and Socialist Construction: The End of Capital and the Transition to Socialism.* London: Routledge. doi: 10.4324/9781315814001.
Schaupp, S. (2017) 'Vergessene Horizonte. Der kybernetische Kapitalismus und seine Alternativen', in P. Buckermann, A. Koppenburger and S. Schaupp (eds) *Kybernetik, Kapitalismus, Revolutionen. Emanzipatorische Perspektiven Im Technologischen Wandel*, Münster: Unrast, pp 51–73.
Schaupp, S. (2021) 'Technopolitics from below. A framework for the analysis of digital politics of production', *NanoEthics*, 15(1): 71–86.
Schaupp, S. (2022) 'Cybernetic proletarianization: spirals of devaluation and conflict in digitalized production', *Capital & Class*, 46(1): 11–31.
Schaupp, S., Petermann, L. and Haab, B. (2024) 'Climate youth to power: coalition strategy as social movement response to youth power deficits', *Swiss Journal of Sociology* (forthcoming).
Schmelzer, M., Vetter, A. and Vansintjan, A. (2022) *The Future Is Degrowth: A Guide to a World Beyond Capitalism.* London: Verso.
Srnicek, N. and Williams, A. (2015) *Inventing the Future: Postcapitalism and a World Without Work.* London: Verso.
Stojanović, P. (2022) 'Von Ökonomiekritik zum Primat sozialer Kämpfe in modernen Planungsdebatten: Eine Kritik ausgewählter technikzentrierter Rezeptionen der Sozialistischen Kalkulationsdebatte', *Momentum Quarterly – Zeitschrift für sozialen Fortschritt*, 11(1): 37–55.
Sutterlütti, S. and Meretz, S. (2023) *Make Capitalism History: A Practical Framework for Utopia and the Transformation of Society.* London: Palgrave Macmillan.
Vetter, A. (2018) 'The matrix of convivial technology – assessing technologies for degrowth', *Journal of Cleaner Production*, 197(2): 1778–1786. doi: 10.1016/j.jclepro.2017.02.195.
Vettese, T. and Pendergrass, D. (2022) *Half-Earth Socialism: A Plan to Save the Future from Extinction, Climate Change and Pandemics.* London: Verso.
Wainwright, J. and Mann, G. (2019) *Climate Leviathan: A Political Theory of Our Planetary Future.* London: Verso Books.
Winker, G. (2015) *Care Revolution: Schritte in Eine Solidarische Gesellschaft.* Bielefeld: transcript.

16

Embracing the Small Stuff: Caring for Children in a Liberated Society

Heide Lutosch

Capricious

It is hard to grasp, hard to describe. There is something different about care, something disruptive and annoying that does not fit the picture. The roll-up-your-sleeves certainty that everything must be completely different in a liberated society starts to falter when considering how people should care for others in a better future. Sure, this work must become more visible and more recognized – and, above all, it should be divided more fairly between women and men. But otherwise? Would it not perhaps be better to leave everything as it is? Or at least proceed with caution?

Vague discomfort is best brought into view where it is strongest and, surprisingly, this is the case in an area that is considered the most beautiful and satisfying of care work in today's society: caring for children.

Despite (or precisely because of) the silent doubt alluded to in the opening paragraph there is practically no left-wing utopian model that does not emphasize the necessity to 'collectivize' or 'socialize' care work. In substance, this refers to the radical deprivatization of the challenges of, for example, being elderly or sick. Everybody agrees that no woman should have to give up her own life to prevent an aged father from vegetating in a nursing home, stripped to the bare essentials due to cost cuts. Surely the idea of society completely supporting, encouraging and appreciating, for instance people suffering from chronic illnesses, so that they no longer have to expend a vast amount of energy hiding issues that put their performance in doubt, also sounds desirable. But friendly round-the-clock creches for newborns? Intergenerational housing units for 250 adults and minors? Boarding schools created by the Association of Free People for kindergarteners?

Help – that can't be!

Exactly these unpleasant images of collectivized childhoods account for the fact that the urgency loses momentum, and the designs become vague, when it comes to the question if carework can be democratized, collectivized, and planned at a level of society. For what would be more self-evident, more natural, more irrefutable than two people who have conceived children together also wanting to raise them together? Would anything else not be brutal and artificial? Have not enough studies shown the devastating effects on children's development when they grow up without parents? What would have become of oneself – without one's own mother, without a father? And is forced separation from one's own children not almost always a nightmare for parents, too?

All this is true and must take precedence when considering how to raise children in a liberated society. Children need a few permanent adult caregivers who live in their immediate vicinity and are willing to enter into a lasting, caring and emotionally and physically close relationship with them. Especially in the beginning of a child's life, these adults must be exceptionally attentive to needs that are expressed non-verbally. Some needs are *general* and concern matters such as nutrition, cleanliness, sleep and physical and emotional contact, while others are more *individual*. For example, while one baby needs twilight and silence for concentrated nursing, another prefers the mother sitting relaxed at the kitchen table and chatting with guests or roommates. Some infants relax and revel in kicking their bare legs while being changed but others scream furiously if the temperature is not right or a specific melody is not playing. Some can only fall asleep on their stomachs against the belly of a very specific person, and another has to be stroked carefully with the index finger over the area between its forehead and the bridge of its nose to fall asleep. One craves physical contact immediately after waking, another needs to listen to the soothing voice of a close caregiver first for at least five minutes.

Children are capricious and making the whole matter even more complicated is that their specific likes and dislikes, preferred rituals and aids, fears and limitations change every few months, if not every few weeks in early childhood. Furthermore, during this phase of development children are particularly fussy, become easily unsettled, and are particularly quick-tempered. But even toddlers and school-aged children – not to mention teenagers – are rarely happy when they have to adjust too much and subordinate themselves too much. Of course, growing out of infantile narcissism is desirable and necessary, just as a certain degree of socialization is unavoidable but cannot be accomplished through the *negation* of individual boundaries and needs, which on the contrary must be *strengthened*. There should be consensus on this, especially among people who ponder the possibilities of a needs-oriented and domination-free society! Only half-heartedly acknowledging the capriciousness of human beings in childhood or ignoring it altogether is like wanting to caulk a newly built house and courageously going into action with cookie dough and a spatula instead of inquiring about what materials and tools are best.

This lack of recognition of the most fundamental characteristics and needs of children can nevertheless be observed time and again, especially in left-wing circles, for example in how the topic of childcare is dealt with. Fortunately, it has now been agreed that people with young children (who cannot be left alone all day) should still be able to participate in group meetings, plenaries, closed-door conferences and workshops. At least for the duration of the event, childcare should be the responsibility of the entire group and not just the parents. Therefore, either an appeal is issued to everyone to 'feel responsible', or someone from (or even outside) the group is designated to take care of the children present for the duration of the event.

Regardless of the theory, it almost always fails in practice. Despite great effort and collective demonstrations of good will, the mother (and it is almost always the mother) ends up standing in the doorway rocking the infant while simultaneously trying to remain engaged and being constantly ready to leave the room if the baby becomes too loud. Even if help is hired, for example a student to walk the infant around the block between nursing sessions, the infant might just become hungry early. And the three-year-old toddler who refuses to be entertained by a well-meaning comrade will end up sitting on her mother's lap, talking loudly to herself and scribbling on the position paper her mother would actually like to discuss. This tragically doubly reindividualizes the problem of childcare, since the mother is ultimately considered to be solely responsible for the child, who is often perceived as being 'a bit difficult at times', who 'does not like to be handed off' or who is 'in a mommy phase'. Although subconsciously baulking at this interpretation, the mother tends to associate her child's difficulties with herself. Moreover, she is disappointed that she missed more than half of the weekend seminar and has hardly been able to contribute to the discussion. Above all, however, she feels deeply exhausted due to coping with four factors: first, concentrating under adverse conditions, second, ensuring that her child feels comfortable and safe, third, guaranteeing that the child does not disturb the group and fourth, pretending that everything is fine. After all, she brought the whole situation upon herself, or did someone force her to have a child? Sometimes, during the feedback session, the group becomes aware of the mother's frustration due to these complex internal and external demands – and everyone vows to make more of an effort next time, to act more responsibly and to spread the care work across more shoulders instead of leaving the mother to cope alone. However, the mother has long since decided never to subject herself to such a weekend again and will simply stay at home with the child next time. In the long run, this exposes her to being accused of 'withdrawing more and more into her nuclear family'.

Why is so little attention paid to the simple impossibility of children being separated from their closest caregivers and handed over to strangers in the practical situation described previously? Why is the strong attachment of young children to their immediate caregivers not recognized in theoretical considerations of care work in a non-capitalist society as the quasi-material prerequisite that it is? Perhaps recognizing this would result in the task of seeking new, more collective forms of care to lose some of its noble connotations and become not only trickier but also more trivial.

Family sucks

When considering alternative models of society, there is another reason the extreme individualism of children and young people is so readily denied a place at the table concerning objective problems: Whenever it is acknowledged, the nuclear family triumphantly appears on the scene, either as an institution that is actually 'good', but that has been 'corrupted' by capitalism or is at least a lesser evil. Wanting to bid farewell to the patriarchal structures and general stuffiness of the nuclear family does not hinder anyone from ruefully conceding that the cohabitation of two adults connected by a close emotional bond with their 'own' children is the best way of life after all for giving children their much-needed protection, peace and highly individualized support. One minute the radical deprivatization of care work is on the agenda and the next it is back to the family, which is, according to Lewis (2022), basically nothing more than 'the name we use for the fact that care is privatized in our society' (p 4).

This, then, is the complicated and paradoxical task that is faced when honestly considering whether and how the raising of children could be organized and shaped differently in a liberated society: to find a form in which their uncollectivizablility can be collectivized, a form that is not private and yet makes safety possible.

Or has the challenge been defined incorrectly? Why do we need to 'collectivize'? What were the reasons again for wanting to remove raising children from the private sphere? Are the problems that arise from, in and despite the family not manageable in comparison to, 'the fate worse than forced time with family, namely not having a family' (Lewis, 2022, p 78)? In bourgeois society, the fate of not having a family as a child amounts to being shunted back and forth between different care institutions, foster families and pedagogical approaches (Fingscheidt, 2019). For adults it may mean being abandoned in the event of serious illness or during religious holidays. Are the transgressions of the nuclear family not forgiven and forgotten as soon as such fates – or images of children's kibbutzim, children's barracks or children's communes – come to mind?

That may be the case, but it is cynical. 'Things could be worse' is not an argument against what is bad. Not letting the construct of the 'lesser evil' convincingly steer the conversation away from the necessity of generating alternative social designs has always been a challenge of critical thinking about the future, which is particularly difficult pertaining to the family. As an institution to which people have delegated almost everything that has to do with their corporeality (sleeping, eating, crying, menstruating, being sick, having sex and dying) and which is therefore closely intertwined with social practices, the family represents the epitome of social constructs that appear natural and thus unchangeable: without an alternative. On the other hand, imagining the family away is nothing less than imagining a basic condition of one's own existence away, as Sophie Lewis (2002) astutely remarks: 'it is difficult, perhaps impossible, right now, to imagine not being manufactured through the private nuclear household' (p 2).

Because of all this, it is difficult to recognize the suffering that is produced in and by the family. The promises of family – namely care, comfort, belonging, peace and attention – are in fact so essential that also conceiving of the family as an institution that provides those services and attributes sparsely and selectively at best and then systematically denies them in the long run seems almost impossible. This is not to deny that many parents possess enough empathy to recognize and meet the delicate and unique needs of their children described above. However, when one caregiver is responsible for the baby almost around the clock and the other works outside the home at least nine hours a day on workdays, they may fall desperately short of meeting their own needs, including good nutrition and sufficient sleep, which becomes further exacerbated if both caregivers work at least a combined 60 hours a week. The resulting deficiency in the 'emotional hothouse' (Benjamin, 1988, p 96) of the parent–child relationship (which is also architecturally isolated) almost inevitably leads to love becoming possessive and care transgressing boundaries: soon, it becomes utterly unclear who is caring for whom. Feelings of guilt on all sides are inevitable and worsen the strain, not to mention feelings of anger and negligence. When siblings are introduced into the family, competition also becomes a factor. Under the conditions of scarcity described earlier, functioning, performance and good behaviour become weapons in the struggle to receive the sporadic attention of permanently overburdened parents – weapons that are demonstratively laid down at the beginning of puberty. The competition with siblings sometimes turn into a battle against the adults, with lack itself becoming weaponized: silence, withdrawal of love, passivity, closed doors. The hurt resulting from coming up short often re-emerges in the adult children's relationship with their elderly parents, though it is often strenuously held in check and glossed over. However, the addictive search for the promised yet never redeemed comfort and attention not only characterizes every trip back to the parental home, but also the romantic relationships of grown children. The once very material lack of time, sleep, money and space becomes an emotional wound that begins to fester when adult children become parents themselves, having to manage the strenuous balancing act between wage labour and childcare as an isolated couple in a home rigidly sealed off from the outside world.

Furthermore, the encroaching love of the adults affected by scarcity often bears almost invisible despotic traits. At first glance, children in liberal families get to do more than ever in the history of humankind, for example beginning with 'baby-led weaning', which involves letting infants choose from among a variety of age-appropriate finger foods, bypassing purees and mashed food. Later they are not prevented from interrupting all non-work conversations and adult activities any time, even in the evening, robbing parents of the last remnant of their own social life due to endless bedtime rituals. If a child becomes ill, this pattern of children being allowed to interrupt the rhythm of family life with their apparent needs turns out to be rather compensatory and superficial. Although a child's illness may be harmless and temporary, it always seriously disturbs the shaky system. In winter, daycare centres are full of miserable, coughing, exhausted children who are dropped off there by their equally exhausted parents with feelings of guilt: 'I'm sorry, but I NEED to go to work!'[1]

The deep irrelevance of children's boundaries and needs in the concept of the nuclear family becomes apparent whenever parents' romantic relationships end. That is to say: it *does not* become apparent because what is more self-evident than the immediate physical and emotional dissolution of the once so unquestioned family unit? Even parents' failed romantic relationship takes precedence over the needs of the children, who are expected to move back and forth between two households with their belongings from now on, usually on a weekly basis, apparently because everyone agrees that it would be too much of an imposition for their parents to continue to encounter one another daily as adults, perhaps even as friends.

The fact that the will of the children – when push comes to shove – has to bow to that of the adults is not limited to the situation following a separation. Parents also automatically determine the place of residence, not to mention all school matters. And when it comes to the child's leisure activities, clothes and playmates, even the most liberal parents do not resist reigning in and straightening out a bit. Childhood and adolescence are life circumstances in which democratic rights do not exist and participation boils down to either a 'yes or yes' or the profoundly paternalistic 'I know what's good for you'.

Objections immediately arise, even in leftist circles, and are difficult to refute. Do parents not *really* know what is best for their children? Are children not overburdened beyond measure if they are allowed to independently decide everything? Do they not need 'boundaries'? Yes, of course: the ability of children to assess the consequences of their own actions is a gradual process. If left to their own devices they would gorge on sweets unhampered, blissfully unaware of tooth decay and the threat of obesity. But as far as the second-most popular argument against the participation of children (bedtime), the matter is less clear cut. Putting seven-year-olds to bed by 8 pm at the latest is not a basic anthropological constant but occurs because they must be up early and out the door to get to school on time. Moreover, their exhausted mothers do not want to be deprived of having the luxury of listening undisturbed to a podcast on the expansion of the future while cleaning the kitchen and doing the laundry in the evening before hastily going to bed to be reasonably prepared when all the stress starts again a six short hours later.

As despotic as they have to be (under the given social conditions) on the inside, on the outside mothers and fathers often fight passionately for the needs of their children – at least regarding a daycare slot, good schools, support, appreciation and favourable starting conditions for working life – which are a scarcity in a society that merely regards children as future members of the workforce who require varying degrees of training, not to mention as future pension fund contributors of tomorrow. Parents, however, do not recognize their children as the members of a strongly discriminated against social group that they are – in terms of rights, participation and opportunities for expressing their needs and shaping the public space – but perceive them as 'private pleasure'. They are so strongly taken in by the brutal and direct competition described previously that the idea of joining forces to form a lobby for the needs of *all* children does not seem obvious to them. Or where is the influential and powerful parent organization blocking roads and organizing a general strike to put an end once and for all to the fact that a child under 15 years of age is injured or killed in a traffic accident every 24 minutes in Germany (Statistisches Bundesamt, 2022)?

All told, the privatized form of raising children called the nuclear family holds much unnecessary suffering for adults and children: guilt, being overworked, emotional shortcomings, paternalism, and internal and external competition. The fact that, especially for women, caring for and committing oneself to cherished children almost always becomes a prison seems just as natural in the setting of the nuclear family as the fact that the wellbeing of children and parents is often categorically mutually exclusive. However, all this is neither 'completely normal' nor 'totally dysfunctional', but systematically caused by the fundamental structure of isolation and deficiency inscribed in the bourgeois capitalist nuclear family. In brief, 'family is a miserable way to organize care' (Lewis, 2022, p 11). Yet nowhere can the passionate clinging to structures of unfreedom be observed more strongly than in relation to the nuclear family. 'Sure, it may be a disciplinary, scarcity-based trauma-machine: but it's MY disciplinary, scarcity-based trauma-machine' (Lewis, 2022, p 4).

Surprisingly, even people who advocate a needs-based, domination-free society have been strangely unreflective concerning their adherence to the anything-but-needs-based, anything-but-domination-free institution of the family. Paraphrasing the famous saying, 'it is easier to imagine the end of the world than the end of capitalism', Sophie Lewis (2022) bitingly observed, 'It may be easier to imagine the end of capitalism […] than the end of the family' (p 6). A core truth of this lack of imagination is that abolishing the family without abolishing capitalism would not be realistic and not even desirable. And to take the wind right out of the sails of the (mostly male) comrades who love the family, this means no more and no less than the unnecessary suffering caused by the family, in the family and in spite of the family is one of the best reasons to abolish capitalism.

Freedom and care

Among the challenges involved in building childcare that is devoid of domination in a post-capitalist society are gaining a clear view of the capriciousness, delicacy and uncollectivizablility of children, as well as affirming and acknowledging it without delegating the difficult and tedious task of raising children back to the nuclear family. Clearly framing the whole issue as revolving around the distribution of work is insufficient. As far as caring for children is concerned, there is no supra-societal list of fixed tasks that simply need to be planned, distributed, automated and digitalized differently. Instead it is a matter of taking a close look at the relationship between children and adults and 'reinventing' it (Foucault, 2008, p 94; Groos, in this volume) – under the conditions of freedom from domination and orientation to needs. Because forms of work and relationships and organizational and ethical questions are intermingled in the care field (not exclusively but perhaps more intensively than in other social fields), this inventive activity requires a certain readiness for daring to be concrete – not for the pleasure of picturing and writing things down but because sometimes a precise draft is necessary to recognize the obstacles.

In this sense and considering the problem described earlier, children need more than two parents. Even three would not be enough. So let us tentatively assume four adults who should be connected to each other in a friendly way and ideally have known one another for a long time. The focus would be on stability and avoiding complications – which is why romantic love between parents would be the exception rather than the rule. Understanding that sexual attraction can develop much better in the long run in child-free areas, it would be better if everything involving sex occurred outside the parental community. Biological paternity would be considered as unimportant as the month in which people are born – people are aware of when but attach no importance to this knowledge. The biological mother would only have a special role at the beginning. During pregnancy, birth, in the puerperium and breastfeeding, she would have three adults around her to support her in eating well, getting enough sleep and remaining something like a person in the physically and emotionally exceptional situation between conception and weaning. Whether she wants to be part of the parenting quartet after birth at all would be her own decision since bottle-feeding babies would no longer be considered inferior to breastfeeding.

As parenthood will no longer be tied to one's ability to give birth or procreate this would make it possible for anyone from 17 to 67 years of age to take on the parenting roles. Having more shoulders to share the responsibility would make compatibility more realistic. There would be no need to be 'done' with everything before 'having' children, since searching for one's ideal career path, maintaining a colourful love life and travel would still be possible. The terrible dictum that 'many things are no longer possible' when taking on responsibility for children would belong to the past.

It would also be nice that people could raise children in several runs and in different constellations, which would mean, among other things, that the needs of a five-year-old would no longer be the sole concern of adults with a child that age at home. A 40-year-old might think, 'Our kid is already 10, but who knows? Maybe in 20 years I'll have another preschooler?' Concerns about issues such as having a network of car-free paths and squares that runs through entire cities offering opportunities for roaming, playing, hopping and climbing – relegating the sad invention of the fenced-in playground to museums – would then take on continued relevance for many more adults. Moreover, when societal conditions permit the elimination of competition between parents because good schools and paediatricians are ubiquitous, the group of parents (then much larger, of course) could finally become true advocates for children's needs – *all* children, across society. Furthermore, if the four-parent model would eliminate the notorious lack of time, energy, money, nerves, love and serenity involved in raising children, then the needs of children and adults would be much less mutually exclusive. Children could be allowed to stay up late without their parents being threatened with a permanent loss of personhood. The parents, conversely, would now also have the space to perceive children's needs that are not directly their own, making them strong on the level of society as a whole.

Parenthood with four parents includes architectural prerequisites that society would have to desire and implement. If children need their closest caregivers in close spatial proximity, then constructing larger, more flexible dwellings would be unavoidable as would layouts that permit easily adapting to the changing needs for proximity or distance among children and adults. In the event that not all four parents want to live together, other variations of spatial proximity would be required – for example in the same house, on the same block or certainly within walking distance.

Other material requirements would include kindergartens that really *are* gardens or at least *have* them, and schools that function without permanent parental cooperation and protect the comprehensive right to participate among even the youngest learners from the very beginning. Likewise, every conceivable support for children with disabilities and chronic illnesses would be in place. According to society's self-understanding such children belong to their parents – just like everyone else – but would also be (more so than everyone else) the children of all people. Being a child of all people implies that such children are to be treated with special warmth and esteem and showered with care and encouragement.

The same mixture of radical change in the basic collective attitude and social provision of resources would also affect the relationship with young people. Although the war that teens wage with their parents in the pressure cooker of the nuclear family seems almost unavoidable, even healthy, the suffering it causes is anything but natural or inevitable. Dependency–autonomy conflicts will not disappear in a liberated society, but all agree that many adolescents can consider the home too confining; they want to go out into the world, be on their own, form loving, caring friendships with their peers and (damn it) explore their sexuality without their parents and siblings within earshot. Therefore, young people would generally move out of their homes at 16, into shared flats with other adolescents, with other families, into multigenerational homes, to caravan parks – always with the option of returning to the protected space of their parents' home without shame, if necessary. All young people would have to learn how to treat minor injuries and harmless illnesses such as respiratory infections and gastrointestinal flu in the year prior to moving out and also complete a six-month intensive housework course that includes topics like cleaning, laundry, waste disposal, food handling, cooking, baking and fixing things. This course would also have the extremely desirable side-effect of establishing certain levels of cleanliness and best practices as an undisputed standard throughout society in the long run. This is already the case with driving, where multiple driving styles exist but looking in the rearview mirror before turning is undebatable.

Another positive side-effect of mandatory housework courses is that housework would (once again) be considered an activity that must be learned, returning a bit of dignity to such efforts. However, the only way to truly make it 'visible' as *work* is *counting* it as work without any ifs and/or buts.

A society in which democratic planning replaces capitalist market mechanisms will have to relate needs to natural resources, raw materials, intermediate products, machines and labour capacities in some way. It should be self-evident that the basic needs of all people are provided for in such a society – regardless of how much they work. Whether access to certain additional consumer goods should be linked to individual work performance is not the subject of discussion here – nor is the issue of whether the strict calculation of working hours is necessary or useful; however, a culture of timekeeping would likely be established one way or another. Knowledge about how much time certain tasks take would probably be too valuable to withhold from any kind of democratic economic planning. Also, to provide a reference value for how much every able-bodied adult should work to achieve a certain overall social standard of living, or to determine what amount of work is feasible, bearable or desirable in the long run, all working people would need to keep a record of their working hours. Anyone who has ever worked themselves half to death in a friendly startup without a timeclock knows that a clear definition of the number of weekly working hours is always better protection against exploitation and self-exploitation than the diffuse moral expectation of 'commitment' and 'team thinking'. To live up to its name a liberated society would regard care work as *work* without restriction, consequently counting every hour spent that incurs the 'expenditure of human brains, muscles, nerves, hands, etc' (Marx, 1976, p 134) when caring for children as working time – regardless of whether it takes place in a kindergarten or the immediate home environment.

Thus, the following suggestion is proposed with deep solemnity. How radically society's attitudes would be required to change can only be recognized when concretely spelled out:

In the first year of life a child needs a close caregiver in its immediate proximity 24 hours a day, seven days a week. Very often, about 12 hours a day, the baby is dependent on direct physical contact and must be fed, changed and held, during which the caregiver is unable to attend to anything else. In the four hours when the baby sleeps so soundly (albeit with potential interruptions) housework can be done on the side. The baby sleeps another eight hours during the day, during which the caregiver can rest or sleep but must be present and on call. For this reason such hours will only count as half time.

Caring for a baby therefore requires 20 hours of work per day. In the first year of a child's life, each of the four parents in the model suggested earlier could register five working hours per day, or 35 hours a week. Assuming that the standard work week is 40 hours, each parent would be available for non-care work five hours per week. As the child grows older and gradually settles into kindergarten and later school, the number of work hours solely dedicated to care steadily decreases but certainly not below eight hours a day until the child reaches 12, which means that the four parents of an 11-year-old child would be jointly engaged in 56 hours of childcare per week. Subtracting this from the combined 160 hours per week that the four caregivers would be working leaves 104 hours, or 26 hours per week per person, that each parent could spend doing other work.

This is a rough model that requires refinement, for example concerning how many working hours would be calculated for siblings. The somewhat shocking realization emerging from this calculation is that the labour resources that society must make available would be immense if society seriously agreed to assigning the status of self-purpose to that which is a gratuitously available background condition in capitalism (Fraser and Jaeggi, 2018, pp 47–58). Instead of asking how many hours a day 'parents can be released from duty' without endangering a certain level of productivity, society would have to proceed the other way round; first of all by consistently asking what a domination-free, needs-oriented relationship between parents and children might look like and what material preconditions have to exist.[2]

As just discussed, the privatization of the relationship between parents and children in the nuclear family results in a painful situation of deficiency for everyone involved. Deprivatizing this relationship in a way that allows transforming this lack into abundance requires intense consideration concerning what children actually need. Apart from good schools, a completely new housing architecture and a radically altered urban planning, this is something very emotional, complicated and delicate, namely the recognition and protection of their very individual being, prohibiting any solution that leans toward mass processing and even more expanded outside care.

Collectivizing childcare would rather mean deciding as a society that responsibility for children should no longer be the domain of individual parental couples but society as a whole – not in an idealistic sense but in a thoroughly material one. In the four-parent model, with full-time credit for care work, labour capacities would require large-scale planning.[3] Therefore the question of what caring for children should look like in a liberated society is not only a question of general desires, attitudes, and priorities but also a question of democratic planning. If participants in the planning debate agreed that large amounts of working capacity should be designated to a better form of raising children (which, of course is not currently the case) then several basic assumptions concerning this debate would be implied:

1. The hope that everyone would have to work less: Daily hours spent working would not decrease but increase (especially for men).
2. The notion that care work only involves two problematic issues – the distribution of work (between men and women) and appreciation – but the tasks and methods in this area are otherwise basically unquestionable: However, relations of domination and systematic deficiency are inscribed in care

work, especially in the context of the nuclear family; therefore, care work has to be reinvented.
3. The idea that needs orientation basically means identifying and satisfying individual consumer desires: In fact, it also means analysing the specific characteristics of various forms of need – all the 'small stuff' such as the impossibility of being left alone for even an hour that is associated with the life circumstances of a child, ageing or being sick.
4. The approach that treats the topic of care work as an afterthought to the discussion of democratic planning: In reality, for very material reasons, the care sector in a non-capitalist society must be the beginning and centre of democratic planning.

Caring for children collectively – in the sense outlined in this chapter – would be anything but efficient. It would require a vast amount of labour and resources, and possibly slow down and complicate social decision-making processes through the comprehensive participation of children and young people. But the result would be immensely attractive to all those struggling with the insurmountable task of lovingly raising children without losing themselves, namely a society in which all the small stuff of care work is moved to the foreground of conscious social planning and children are no longer a means to an end but an end in themselves.

Notes

[1] Considering the sick child as the exception that brings down the whole life model is downright crazy, considering that children under two years of age typically have four to ten respiratory infections a year – and up to 13 if interacting with other children. This age group also has one to four gastrointestinal infections per year. Children over the age of two have four to eight respiratory infections and up to two gastrointestinal infections annually (Berufsverband der Kinder- und Jugendärzt*innen, 2014).

[2] Frigga Haug (2008, pp 20–21), while starting with the needs of adults, forgets all about the children. In her 'Four-in-One-Perspective' she proposes that every adult spent four hours a day with productive labour, four hours with 'reproductive and family work', four hours with 'life-long development through learning' and four hours with political activities. However, explicitly holding on to the two-parent family, as Haug does, makes the model unfeasible, for who is supposed to look after the children for the remaining 16 hours? Even if they spent eight hours in a day care centre, they would stay unattended for an additional eight hours – apart from the fact that, in her noble 'new time regime', she also misses out on a lot of nice and small adult stuff, for example intoxication, friendship and sex.

[3] The fact that these could well be lacking elsewhere would perhaps finally be a motivation to reduce the very strenuous and often dull work that occurs in the vicinity of the immediate care activities for children: collectivizing cooking and laundry, digitalizing shopping and automating cleaning. And, in a few decades, people could laugh at the supposedly innovation-friendly era of capitalism, when laundry was still hung up and folded by hand and windows were cleaned with the help of rickety ladders that people regularly fell off and broke their bones.

Bibliography

Benjamin, J. (1988) *The Bonds of Love: Psychoanalysis, Feminism, and the Problem of Domination*. New York: Pantheon Books.

Berufsverband der Kinder- und Jugendärzt*innen (2014) *Wie viele Infekte sind bei kleinen Kindern noch „normal'?* Kinder- & Jugendärzte im Internet, 1 December. https://www.kinderaerzte-im-netz.de/news-archiv/meldung/article/wie-viele-infekte-sind-normal/

Fingscheidt, N. (2019) *System Crasher*. [Film]. Weydemann Bros. Peter Hartwig, Jonas Weydemann and Jakob D. Weydemann (prods). Deutschland.

Foucault, M. (2008) *The Birth of Biopolitics: Lectures at the Collège de France, 1978–79. Lectures at the Collège de France*. Edited by M. Senellart. Basingstoke/New York: Palgrave Macmillan.

Fraser, N. and Jaeggi, R. (2018) *Capitalism: A Conversation in Critical Theory*. Edited by Brian Milstein. Cambridge: Polity Press.

Haug, F. (2008). Die Vier-in-einem-Perspektive: Politik von Frauen für eine neue *Linke*. Hamburg: Argument Verlag.

Lewis, S. (2022) *Abolish the Family: A Manifesto for Care and Liberation*. Brooklyn: Verso.

Marx, K. (1976) *Capital, Volume 1*. London: Penguin.

Statistisches Bundesamt (2022) '22 300 Kinder im Jahr 2021 im Straßenverkehr verunglückt' [Pressemeldung Nr N055], 31 August. https://www.destatis.de/DE/Presse/Pressemitteilungen/2022/08/PD22_N055_46241.html

17

Socialism, Planning and the Relativity of Dirt

Nancy Fraser in conversation with Christoph Sorg

On capitalism and socialism

Sorg: I would first of all like to thank you for contributing to our book, I'm extremely excited to hear your perspectives. Should we talk about your understanding of capitalism and socialism first and then work our way towards planning?

Fraser: Sure. My thinking about socialism starts, first of all, with the idea that we really don't have a clear idea today of what we mean by socialism. And we need one. There's a default. I mean, hardly anyone would hold up the Soviet command economy model as an ideal. And there's a widespread sense that social democracy isn't enough. But what are the other options between those two inadequate answers? It's an old question for the left. It becomes a live question at moments when there is a widespread sense that things can't go on as they are, that capitalism has really hit some kind of a wall. And so we have in the United States this interesting spectacle of people going around and calling themselves socialist or democratic socialist. Some of them are even elected to the US congress or run for president, and yet it's not at all clear what they mean by that label. I think it's a very good sign that they want to use that label. But I also think it's time to get serious and try to figure out what it can mean.

My own efforts in that direction are still, I would say, quite preliminary, exploratory, even primitive. But they start from an interest similar to yours, of wanting to overcome any kind of class reductionism and economism. In recent years I have developed a view of capitalism that aims to be a non-class reductionist, non-economistic view of capitalism and therefore a non-class reductionist, non-economistic critique of capitalism. One that can embrace the concerns of people interested in social reproduction, in ecology, in racial and imperial oppression, in democracy. For me, because I come out of the Marxian tradition of so-called scientific socialism, I don't want to start thinking about socialism as just an ideal. I want to think about it as the negation of capitalism. So that's where I start.

My views about socialism are developed in thinking about what's wrong with capitalism, what its crisis tendencies and contradictions are, what are the forms of conflicts that it generates in a non-accidental way and what it would mean then to develop a socialism that aims at overcoming those contradictions and injustices and that can draw on the energies that are released by the forms of conflict capitalism is currently generating. So the idea is that capitalism is not merely an economic system but an institutionalized social order on par with feudalism. Capitalism creates this strange animal called an economy, which really didn't exist before capitalism, I would say. This is a sphere of self-interested and monetized interaction, of wage labour aimed at producing commodities under the aegis of firms motivated by profit accumulation.

Capitalism brings this economy into a very perverse and contradictory relationship with other fields of social action, other forms of social relations, other social institutions such as families, communities, nature, states and other public powers. The contradictory accumulation of profit requires, in my view, the incorporation of inputs whose reproduction costs are not paid for. These inputs come in the form of nature, in the form of care work or other forms of unwaged social reproductive activity, in the form of public goods, and public powers and capacities that are embodied in the institution we think of as political institutions. Capitalism also requires forms of unfree or dependent labour whose reproduction costs are not paid for, which I think is labour that is generally racialized in one form or another. These forms of labour are spreading, where workers don't even receive the payment for their necessary labour hours, let alone the surplus. Such underwaged labour is today spreading even to populations that were formerly protected from that, in my opinion.

So all of these unpaid or underpaid inputs are, I think, actually essential to the accumulation of profit. So the problems with capitalism are not only the contradiction between capital and labour and its crisis tendencies that can be thought of as internal to the economic portion of capitalist society. But we also have a tendency to erode and destabilize these unremunerated inputs, these non-economic background conditions. This includes a tendency to destabilize ecosystems, a tendency to destabilize political systems and a tendency to destabilize families and communities, who supply the care and social bonds that are necessary for a workforce. In all of these cases, I think capitalism wants to have it both ways. It wants to rely on the availability of these absolutely essential forms of social activity and wealth, but it doesn't want to pay for them. It therefore constantly jeopardizes and destabilizes them. When those tendencies to destabilize pile up and become acutely overt, then we get outbreaks of crises that are not simply economic crises, but that are also political crises, ecological crises, crises of social reproduction and of the racial order, the racial division of labour, so to speak.

So that's an expanded view of what capitalism is, of what's wrong with it, of its built-in injustices, of its built-in crisis tendencies and of the forms of conflicts that it generates around those divisions. There will be struggles over where exactly and how the economy will be separated from but also connected to the state. The same is true for production and reproduction, society and nature, and the colour line. All of these things are objects of struggle, and my hope is that in those various intense struggles which erupt everywhere really, that it might be possible to develop some kind of a broad anti-capitalist front that would include ecologists, feminists, racial justice and anti-imperialist activists, democrats of various stripes and so on. I think that anti-capitalism is the thing that actually connects all of them, or should actually. Capitalism is what connects all the problems. Anti-capitalism is what should be connecting the search for a solution, and that means socialism.

So, this requires an expanded view of socialism. Socialism cannot simply be about reorganizing the system of production, at least in the way that production is currently defined. It can't only be about socializing the ownership of the means of production. It also has to be about the relationship between production and reproduction, between work and the coordinating instances that we think of as the political, the public powers. It also has to be about the geography and scale of social activity. We can't have a system that integrates the world through monetized economic interactions and then divides the world according to nationalities and states. We have to rethink all these questions of scale and relationships. So anyway, I think we have to imagine and reinvent a socialism for our time that can deal not only with the terrible insecurities of livelihood that people face, but also with the social reproduction crisis, with the ecological crisis, with the political crisis. This is a huge job. It is bigger than a lot of socialists of the past have thought. I am heartened to rediscover old friends like Sylvia Pankhurst (1920) who wrote a constitution for British soviets in 1920 saying we can't just have factory councils. We also need to have household soviets, soviets to handle social reproduction. She's on the right track. Kollontai is another one. And if we throw in all the great work that is being done on eco-socialism then we have some resources and ecofeminism, we have some resources to draw in here. But this first point that I'm stressing is how big the task is, how complicated it is.

On transformation

Sorg: When reading your work I have been wondering for a while how the economic, social, ecological and political sphere are connected and what this means for transformation. Some of the advocates of planning criticize market socialists and argue that, basically, if you try to fix the despotism of the workplace without the market economy, the market will push market socialism back into capitalism. In terms of your expanded understanding of capitalism, would it be possible to reorganize some of the spheres while leaving others untouched? Could there be a kind of reductionist socialism that fixes some of capitalism's problems but doesn't fix others?

Fraser: Well, that's an interesting question, a hard question. I'm not sure I can have a definitive answer to it. But I would say that historical attempts to fix the economic problem certainly missed the ecological one and for that matter, the social reproductive one, although maybe less so. I think that the way capitalism has developed these problems became interlocked because they share something of this cannibalizing logic. It's all about free riding on unpaid or underpaid inputs, so to speak. Free riding on forms of social wealth which get translated into value but are not replaced or repaired.

I think you could say that some things are so pressing that if we can't do everything at once, they need to be fixed first. However, there should not be the presumption that the rest will follow automatically. I don't think we can assume that at all. Now, the problem about saying some things are so urgent that they need to be fixed first is urgent for whom? For some people living in floodplains or in the path of wildfires or on low-lying islands or whatever, the ecological is the most pressing. For people whose children are being shot down in the streets by militarily armed police in American cities, the racial justice question is the most pressing. For women who are running from one little job to the next and their children are basically being left uncared for, that's the most pressing. So I don't want to say what's the most pressing.

This is where I think of the idea of a coalition. I think it will be up to the various component social movements in this coalition to make the case for what's pressing for them. I don't want to start out with an expert hegemonizing ranking. I've learned that much from the anti-Leninism of the various new social movements, even if I'm still some kind of a communist. I am open in principle to thinking about what the relations are in terms of these things. But I actually think, as a practical matter, we're in a situation where all of these are very hot button issues and they all have to be attended to. I don't think we can ask people to defer their needs right now if we have a chance of doing this.

Sorg: This reminds me of accounts of the crisis of Fordism, for instance by Giovanni Arrighi (2007), which understand this crisis not merely as an internal contradiction of capitalism, but as being unleashed by the challenge of multiple social movements. So, workers demanding a higher income share, feminists attacking the male breadwinner model, anti-colonial struggles and civil rights struggles challenging the expropriation of the peripheries and of minorities in the core, and the emerging green movement pushing for ecological costs to be internalized. So I was wondering if this is how we might think of these struggles as being interrelated. But then there is also the question whether they recognize each other as being interrelated.

Fraser: I think this is very important. My current work, which is still very much in progress, was inspired by W.E.B. Du Bois's (1998) brilliant account in *Black Reconstruction* about the US having two labour movements in the 19th century, trade unionism and abolition. He writes that the whole history of the country, and possibly of the capitalist world, would have been very different if they had recognized each other as fellow labour movements. That if they had understood that the capitalist world system relied on two genres of labour, which had interimbrecated with one another. That the mill workers in Manchester and in Massachusetts were connected to the slaves who produced the raw cotton, and that the profitable textile industry required both of these things working in tandem, but divided from one another. I think that that's still the case about the racialized division of labour even as some of the boundaries are blurring. But I also think that care work is a third genre of labour and that capitalism depends necessarily on three kinds of labour that it separates and that each of these gives rise to its own movement, which could be thought of as three labour movements but are not mutually recognized as such.

This is one possible way of thinking about this problem of a counter-hegemonic bloc, whether feminism could recognize itself as, at least in part, maybe not 100 per cent, but on some core issues a labour movement, an unrecognized labour movement, one that hasn't even always recognized itself as a labour movement. Whether anti-racism and anti-imperialism could recognize itself as, in some aspects at least, a labour movement. This does go with this idea I see in your question of an expanded notion of what counts as work and of what counts as a worker, and therefore of a global working class. This could be a very hard sell because, for some people, it raises all those flags of class reductionism. Again, I think it could be done in a non-reductionist way, but I'm not going to try to push it on people who are allergic to the idea.

Sorg: So anti-capitalism would be the common denominator?

Fraser: Framing capitalism as the underlying villain of all the various issues which in their specificity and particularity people face and experience differently. Instead of all having to say 'we're workers too', they can then all keep their current identities, but say 'we share a common enemy and we're going to work together to end cannibal capitalism'. Anyway, these are two different ideas for how you could imagine a counter-hegemonic bloc developing. Whether there's any grounds for optimism today, I can't say.

On markets and planning

Sorg: Let's use this expanded perspective on capitalism and socialism to talk about democratic planning, which in your model as I understand it is one element of socialism. Progressives have for a while shied away from planning because of its association with bureaucracy and authoritarianism and retreated to the idea of democracy at the workplace. But a post-capitalist system of democratic workplaces merely competing with each other on markets would reproduce a lot of capitalism's shortcomings. But in reopening the socialist calculation debate I feel the new literature on planning reproduces a lot of the older economism and class-reductionism (in more detail: Sorg, 2022). Social reproduction, racialized expropriation and global inequality are hardly talked about and ecology has only slowly been included as a relevant category. So, I think the new planners have a lot to learn from your expanded notion of socialism.

Fraser: So, let me say first that I am not closely following this new planning debate, but I am really glad that it's happening. I think that planning in some form or another is absolutely essential to a desirable post-capitalist form of society. I am a little impatient with the current fashion for localizing everything, which I find a lot among my anarchist students. They're very intelligent and have sophisticated ideas about what anarchism is. But one thing that they share is somehow that almost everything important can be decided on a very small scale and I think that's just simply false. Whether we want that to be the case or not, we are inheriting a world which has an integrated world economic system. It's in a planetary biosphere that can't possibly be dealt with in its present state in terms of small little things here and there.

So it seems to me that it's time to start thinking again about planning in terms of just how one would coordinate decision-making on a broader scale where we have to really deal with the interacting and unintended consequences of interaction among localities, whether we're talking about farms, whether we're talking about enterprises etc. So that's all well and good.

Sorg: If some of your anarchist students end up reading this chapter and they are sceptical of any system that has some sort of centre and doesn't depart from voluntary association. Given the historical experience with planned economies, that is very understandable. But two of the six models of democratically planned economies in the current debate actually come from a libertarian socialist tradition. The older and more established one is participatory economics, which proposes a version of participatory planning based via consumer and worker councils (Hahnel, 2021). There is a centre but it only exists to provide councils with information so that they can plan based on knowledge of macroeconomic developments.

There's also a more recent libertarian model called commonism. This book actually features a chapter by the two authors that have developed it, Stefan Meretz and Simon Sutterlütti. Their approach basically scales up the commons approach using a polycentric principle called stigmergic mediation and discusses how a kind of voluntary association planning could work based on comments. This might be interesting for the anarchists who want to kind of enter the debate.

Fraser: I'm really glad to hear about that, and I'd love to see those essays, please send them to me at some point, because I'm nearing the end of the semester where I've been team teaching a course on socialism and anarchism with a colleague who is an anarchist, whereas I call myself a socialist. We've been looking at the whole way in which, for much of the 19th century and 18th century, those terms overlapped, how they came apart, etc. So this interests me a great deal. I do appreciate that the historic socialist calculation debates were extremely sophisticated, technically above my pay grade. I never followed them that closely and I suspect there is stuff to be learned there: what 'worked', what didn't, what we can take in the way of positive and negative lessons from that body of work, both theoretical work and the attempt to implement it in practice.

On the other hand, I guess I also want to say – and this is in line with your point – that it was a highly technocratic kind of debate. Whatever the intentions of people were, it was a debate almost begging for the constitution of some kind of technocratic elite. The forms of rationality were so specific, and, yes, economistic. So, we really want to think about the problem of planning and democracy. I'm wondering about the potential of the very interesting forms of experiments that have developed like participatory budgeting and so on. I don't mean at all to suggest that these are adequate, but they do seem to me to open up the question of how expert knowledge can intersect with or be in communication with the knowledge of ordinary people who are on the affected end of the spectrum. So, I would be interested in thinking more about this debate. I remember from my days in the New Left we were always worried about the relation between scientific knowledge and democratic practice, and I think it's time to revive that as well. I'm not offering here any answers exactly to these questions.

Now that's all by way of a preamble.

Sorg: Let's maybe start with your perspective on markets in capitalism, which I find very interesting.

Fraser: I'm a Polanyian on markets. I think that the problem is not markets per se. The problem is the so-called self-regulating market, markets in the wrong things and markets that are unhedged in such a way that they become totalizing and take over as the ultra-coordinating mechanism of society. I'm very open to market socialism of some kind, although not of the Yugoslav idea that we're going to have a lot of democratically, self-owned and self-managed enterprises competing. I think that's the wrong kind of market socialism. The idea of socialism that I'm developing, and I again stress how preliminary my thoughts are, turns on two basic principles.

One follows from the free-riding idea that we've been discussing and that is what I call the pay-as-you-go principle. Too much of socialism historically has been about playing catch-up to capitalism and about forms of primitive accumulation, usually off the backs of the peasantry of the countryside. The goal was to rapidly industrialize via centrally planned industry. We know where that led. So, my idea is that we're at a point where the destruction by capitalism (and also state socialism in many places) is so significant that we are in a reparative mode. Socialism has to be reparative today because it inherits a mountain of unpaid reproduction costs. It does not only have to not generate more of such costs, but it actually has to pay back the ones we inherit. So, this idea of pay-as-you-go, no more free-riding on care work, on the carbon-carrying capacities of the atmosphere, on public powers that we desperately need, and so on. So pay as you go, that's one principle.

The other one has to do with this question about markets. And the little formula that I devised was no markets at the bottom, no markets at the top, maybe markets in between. This is a very crude little formula, but it's meant to be suggestive as an invitation for people to think further. The no markets at the bottom is about basic goods and basic needs. I fully appreciate that what counts as a basic need is subject to historical and social unfolding. Even if we identified some very thin set of needs, we would have to work out democratically what form these needs and their satisfaction have to take in a human society. But whatever we decide are the basic needs, they have to be provided as public goods and not in the form of commodities. In my view, this is a familiar, even a social democratic idea, I would say. Nothing too controversial about it.

The more controversial part is that there should be no markets at the top, which refers to surplus. Enterprises cannot be allowed to control surplus that they generate on a scale that actually usurps the general collective right to control the direction of societal development, that is to allocate. Markets can distribute, in my view. But when we talk about allocating forms of social wealth at a scale that effectively determines the course of societal development, then we are talking about a form of collective right and collective property and collective self-determination, in my view. That's where capitalism really goes wrong. It really goes wrong in so far as it allows the investors, the mega corporations, the profiteers to determine how to allocate the societal surplus that is our collective product and our collective wealth. So, I would say to me that's the most important idea in thinking about what socialism is. Surplus is collective wealth, and its use has to be democratically and collectively decided on somehow. This is where planning comes in, to me, in the most important way.

I don't mind having that middle space in which there can be cooperatives, there can be collectives, there can be small, privately owned businesses of various kinds. They can all flourish and, to a certain degree, even compete with one another, but only up to the point at which they can't be in control of massive flows of wealth. That has to be the collective property of humanity, so to speak.

Sorg: This is a very interesting approach. Your image of having no markets at the top and no markets at the bottom seems to overlap with Pat Devine's (1988; 2002) model of negotiated coordination, which distinguishes between market exchange and market forces. For him market exchange is the use of existing capacity to produce commodities and sell them. This is how I understand what you call distributional markets for personal consumption, which you argue have been historically common and are not particular to capitalism (Fraser and Jaeggi, 2018, p 24ff). Devine also keeps such markets for his model of democratic planning, so in this respect there is competition between companies that are socially owned and democratically governed by a board of multiple stakeholders.

The markets that for Devine really need to be abolished and replaced by democratic planning are what he calls market forces. By this he means private, atomistic investment decisions by competing companies to change the productive capacity of society. This is what [Adam] Smith called the invisible hand, Marx called the anarchy of production, and what you seem to call markets for allocation. You have previously (Fraser and Jaeggi, 2018, p 24ff) argued that what is distinctive about markets in capitalism is that they are used to allocate both the social surplus and the major inputs to commodity production. Devine's (2002) model suggests setting up sectoral democratic bodies to decide over investment. His model also features democratically decided input prices, that is labour, capital, natural resources.

That's striking to me because I think there's a huge overlap. I wonder whether this is because you're both inspired by both Marx and Polanyi. Polanyi is often understood as a social democratic advocate of the welfare state, but I think he was much more of an undogmatic democratic socialist with sympathies for libertarian socialism. His contribution to the socialist calculation debate was only translated into English in 2016 (Bockman, Fischer and Woodruff, 2016).

The model he suggests also combines limited space for market exchange with democratic decision-making over surplus. In his case the main institutions are a congress of sectoral production associations that represent our identity as workers and our interest in the conditions of work, and a political community called commune that relates to our identity as consumers and citizens and thus to our interest in the fulfilment of needs and the broader realities of human life. Polanyi suggests that investments related to the direction of production should be negotiated among production associations and the commune. So, again, here is the idea of democratic negotiation over the allocation of surplus instead of leaving this task to the market. In addition, Polanyi provides an institutional infrastructure that does not link political participation exclusively to workplace organization, and thus seems to be compatible with Pankhurst's social soviets, which you mentioned earlier.

Fraser: I'm aware of this text but haven't read this and I'll look up Pat Devine as well. I'll give you another reference – I don't know if it figures in the circles that you're working in, but I come back again and again to an old text by Diane Elson (1988) called 'market socialism or socialization of the market', published in the *New Left Review* in 1988. By the end of the essay, she's suggesting integrating two streams of information – the information generated by markets and information generated by deliberative assemblies. And she's arguing that neither each by itself is partial and they need to come together. A lot of the essay is about why the information generated by the market is only about individual preferences that are not informed by one another and why we need the deliberative stream of input as well. But she also thinks that the market is essential and deliberation is not enough. So that sounds like something that fits what you're telling me about this.

Sorg: This is all the same discussion about market socialism and democratic planning. Elson mainly responds to an exchange between Alec Nove and Ernest Mandel (1986), but I remember she also references Pat Devine, although without engaging with his work. I have to properly read this paper, thank you very much.

Fraser: For the last years I've focused mainly on developing my view about capitalism and the critique of capitalism and on the practical implications of various social movements today. By contrast, I've done very little on socialism. I am very aware of how primitive it is and that there's a very sophisticated literature out there that I should study more.

Sorg: I'm looking forward to your future work on this and again I think your theoretical work on capitalism really foreshadows some issues currently debated in the literature on planning, which is fascinating.

On the all-affected principle and socialism's mode of recognition

Sorg: Returning to your general ideas about 21st-century socialism, you've already said that free writing needs to be replaced by a pay-as-you-go principle, you have explained your principle of no markets at the top and no markets at the bottom. In your text on 21st-century socialism (Fraser, 2020) you briefly mention an all-subjected principle and in previous work you have also discussed an all-affected principle (for example, Fraser, 2007). I would be interested in your perspective on this matter, because Devine's planning model also suggests an all-affected principle, but does not really elaborate how we decide who is affected.

Fraser: Okay, this gets a little bit technical. That distinction became important to me in a somewhat different context, but it's a relevant context. It had to do with this question of the scale of decision-making. Who should count as part of a demos in any given question. We're assuming that the usual territorial principle, the people who live in a given territory, is not a good enough answer. I wouldn't say it's never the right answer, but it's today used for everything. The question is if there's a problem with education or whatever, what's the right demos to deal with that question in a functionally satisfactory way? An answer that has been very commonly given in the philosophical literature about trying to define the demos is the all-affected principle, the idea that everybody who's affected by the decision should have a say. Now, the problem is that affectedness is a very vague idea and there are some people who are affected really existentially and others, like the butterfly effect, only very indirectly.

So, another idea is the all-subjected principle and that refers to power, to coercive rules. Everybody whose action and lives are regulated by some set of coercively enforceable rules or power relations. That has a little more teeth than affected. It helps you deal with questions like the IMF, the role it plays today, where you're in an indebted state, but you are subject to the coercively enforceable rules of another body whom the territorial principle of representation does not allow you to touch. So all-subjected would say something like global finance is something that needs to be subject to democratic control by a much larger demos than that in any state. There were a lot of interesting discussions. I tried to defend this all-subjective principle in work I was doing about global justice a good 15 or so years ago.

Then David Owen (2014) wrote a very interesting critical response to me in which he showed why you actually needed both. And this suggested some kind of idea of weighted voices. There's all this technical literature, if you think the socialist calculation debate is technical, debates about voting systems are very technical in another way [*laughs*]. So, some people's stake is so much more existential than that of others, that their votes should count more, but the others' vote should count for something. That's the kind of thing that Owen was after, all-subjected is very important, affectedness comes in degrees of importance etc. I'm not sure exactly. I haven't myself tried to connect this discussion in a direct way to my thinking about socialism. But it is relevant because the second we want to insist that socialism has to be democratic and that planning has to be democratic, then we have to face up to these questions about the demos. Is it always everybody or are there contexts in which some subsection of everybody is the appropriate demos and which principle of demarcation do we use for that? Is there a question of weighted voting or weighted voice or one-person-one-vote period etc. But I haven't gone any further with this stuff.

Sorg: It definitely relates to things that are being discussed on a still very early level in the planning debate. If we imagine a self-managed health sector, for instance, who should be included or represented in decision-making about where this sector is heading? Which kind of governance would have made sure that better male contraceptives would have been available way earlier, that we put enough resources into gender-reaffirming procedures, which highly affected a minority of the population and so on. So how would you bring expertise and different lived realities together in a fair and sensible process?

Fraser: And how do you direct research resources, which are presumably not infinite. Today pharmaceutical research is done on diseases in rich parts of the world, where people can pay for drugs as opposed to very common and easily treatable things elsewhere that go untreated. Is it about sheer numbers, about how many are affected? I think the best thing we can say about socialism is not that that word gives us any answers to these questions, but that for the first time it actually puts those questions front and centre and forces societies to think democratically and openly about them instead of having them be decided behind our backs, essentially by investment decisions.

Sorg: I think that nicely transitions into another big question that I had. In some of your older work you distinguish between politics of distribution and recognition (for example, Fraser, 2013). The former relates to exploitation in the economic mode of production and division of labour, the latter is about oppression in culture, basically whose humanity gets fully recognized and whose doesn't. Social inequality always seems to have an element of both. So, while class is mainly about economic inequality, there is also physical violence against the homeless or general prejudice against the poor, which in turn justifies maldistribution. Conversely, while transgender people are not primarily oppressed due to their position in the division of labour, the horrific and often deadly misrecognition they suffer entails economic disadvantages, eg via discrimination in healthcare or restricted access to employment. If not all categories of social inequality are evenly embedded in both the mode of production and mode of recognition, what does this mean for transformation? Does capitalism have a mode of recognition and what does the answer to that question mean for socialism? Are these separate struggles that require solidarity or interrelated ones that require coalition?

Fraser: I've always thought that there are structural bases in capitalism for the forms of misrecognition that we're most familiar with, including heteronormativity, cis-normativity and so on. I think that those things have a lot to do with the structural separation of production and reproduction along gendered lines that has given rise to notions about gender, which are not always exactly the same everywhere, but which do exist in some form everywhere. The notion of what it means to be a man versus a woman and you have to be one or the other and so on. So, like most socialists, I believe that structural transformation goes some way in undercutting the bases of misrecognition. However, that doesn't mean that it solves the problem instantly. There will certainly be ongoing struggles for recognition, even in a society that has it structurally right, so to speak. It's also possible that inadvertently a socialist society will generate its own forms of distributive and recognitive asymmetry along lines that perhaps we can't even imagine now. We can't assume that it's the miraculous end to all bad things. So, I think that we should expect ongoing struggles for recognition. One question is do we want a society in which nearly everyone takes a turn at some of what we consider to be the major forms of social contribution? Everyone does some care work, everyone does some other forms of work, everyone does some political activity. So, you would break the association of a certain kind of activity with a certain kind of person that would lead to one kind of recognition order in socialism. Or do we want a society in which people gravitate to whatever is most pleasurable or meaningful to them and specialize in it and then you could end up with a different kind of recognition order in which there are, quote unquote, different kinds of activity performed by different kinds of persons but all equally valued. These are two different pictures. I personally would prefer the first but it's not the kind of thing I think we can actually really decide on now because we do want a kind of a liberatory socialism in which people make a lot of decisions freely. The person I've been reading lately who has made the deepest impression on me is William Morris. I don't know if you've ever read William Morris, but this is a hell of a read, try *Signs of Change* (Morris, 2018). A lot of it is about work, pleasurable work and free work, what it means for work to be free. So lots of choice and that there's something very appealing about that too. Anyway, I think that a lot of these questions about recognition we can't and shouldn't predetermine now. But again, there should be certain principles that, whatever the differences are, there's a sense of equal respect.

Sorg: In your exchange with Rahel Jaeggi you argued that the different spheres of economy, social reproduction, ecology and politics each have a certain ontology and normativity associated with them. If I understand this correctly and take the example of social reproduction, this sphere has a normativity of care and solidarity, which can conflict with economic pressures for rationalization and thus provide resources for social movements to mobilize. But this normativity may also produce and consolidate regressive gender and sexual norms. Is this a way to think about capitalism's mode of recognition? I was also wondering that, if capitalism does not remunerate most care work, which is an injustice in itself, this makes it easier for sexist discourses to misrecognize the people who are mainly assigned this unpaid or underpaid work. There's also the historical interrelations between the economics of colonialism and slavery and racist discourses that co-develop with them.

Fraser: Yeah, that's true. But I just want to add a point that for me complicates things a little bit. I'm pulled in two directions. One is that socialism must revalue the undervalued forms that are supposedly non-economic. But I'm also struck by the sense that capitalism has created these divisions in the first place. It created the family as the anti-factory and the factory as the anti-family. So, there's a sense in which our whole understanding of care work is as the other of corporate work. My sense is that, therefore, both parts of this binary are mutually co-defined in a way that's quite ideological. Rather than simply revaluing one of them saying 'this means what it means but we're going to give it more remuneration and respect in one way or another', maybe socialism will actually just change the meanings of all of these things and redefine them. Maybe it sounds like an idea we don't know how to give much content to right now, but it's somehow a more radical thought.

On socialist care and the relativity of dirt

Sorg: The chapter by Heide Lutosch in this section of the book provides a feminist perspective on post-capitalist utopias. She warns of a romanticization of care work, where the image is that socialization and automation of non-care work frees us to all do so much care work because that is so rewarding in itself and so on.

Fraser: I'm very sympathetic because I'm of the generation that is so aware of this essentialized romanticized femininity trap. Absolutely, I look forward to reading that piece too. Sounds like you're going to have a great book here.

Sorg: I recognize that tendency in myself, being socialized in a traditionally male way. From such a perspective of trying to unlearn parts of your socialization, spending more time with care work and recognizing that part of yourself can become a very rewarding experience. But, of course, when this perspective gets projected on utopias and to be free equals spending more time caring it silences other experiences with and perspectives on how rewarding care work is.

Fraser: Yeah.

Sorg: I was wondering if you currently have an opinion on remuneration of some kind for housework in order to make sure that people who privately take care of the young, elderly and sick are not financially disadvantaged.

Fraser: Yeah. Well, here one is tempted to revert to the old Marxian idea that first comes socialism, then comes communism. In socialism we're still dealing with scarcity, we're still dealing with the legacy of inequality and all the psychological habits that people bring. So maybe you need accounting in the sense of keeping tabs on making sure people are not free-riding. But if you really want an inspiring picture of what we're trying to get we don't want any overbearing policing of contribution. Even though I'm not a fan of basic income exactly, I always liked Philippe von Parijs's (1991) great essay 'Why surfers should be fed', why we should lighten up on the idea that everyone has to do their bit. At the utopian end, work should be so pleasurable and free that this shouldn't be too much of an issue.

Sorg: I would like to refer to something that again Heide Lutosch (2022) has proposed and Helen Hester and Nick Srnicek (2018) have been working on this as well, being at least open to the possibility of automation and assistive technologies contributing to care work and not suspending any such possibility for unquestioned moral reasons. Particularly when we speak about non-affective care work. I have worked in a hospital for a year basically just carrying people and things; there would have been so much potential for assistive technologies, but automation of care work doesn't seem to be profitable enough under capitalism.

Fraser: Right. Look, who could be against the automation of very onerous and unpleasant tasks. Unless there's something about the technology that requires greenhouse gas emissions or that

	requires lots of human beings doing stultifying assembly line work to produce the robots, we'd have to think it through. If it were a total win, then of course.
Sorg:	Another option to reduce and redistribute the reproductive workload would be socialization of care work, something like expansion of communal care or communal kitchens. Which would of course need to be accompanied by what you called universal care-giving, with men taking on more care work. This in turn relates to new literature on family abolition and ideas for different living arrangements, the idea of larger communities than the nuclear family living together.
Fraser:	Such ideas take us back to this point earlier about whether we want a society in which everyone takes their hand at different things: fishing in the morning and hunting in the afternoon, criticizing at night and so on. It does seem to be that, whatever we mean by caregiving, and I agree it has to be deromanticized and defeminized, whatever we mean by it. It does seem to be a pretty fundamental aspect of human living which should not be hived off into a corner for feminized, racialized low waged people to be concerned with. But I think that I would say that we shouldn't think of caring only in terms of what we do for sick people and old people and children, or even our close friends and partners, but it should be part of for instance overall food production or medical production. Somehow, we have to de-enclave it. It's got to be kind of more pervasive rather than a separate thing.
Sorg:	Hester and Srnicek (2018) also suggest lower domestic standards. They argue that, in the same way that productivity gains in capitalism's economic sphere have historically not reduced working hours but increased consumption, efficiency gains via, for instance, dishwashers or washing machines have not reduced household work but increased domestic standards. So, a post-work perspective on care work would probably renegotiate standards of how creative cooking needs to be, how frequently and properly lawns need to be mowed or how much educational support children need to receive to be successful in their later careers. I read this text with my students in a gender studies class, and I think a lot of the female students read the text and relived their experiences living with activist men who never clean.

Fraser: [*laughs*]

Sorg: So, they were understandably sceptical, but I still think that's an interesting perspective.

Fraser: Well, I have two thoughts. I'm on your side with this. First of all, the great British anthropologist Mary Douglas was briefly my colleague at Northwestern. Her most famous book was *Purity and Danger*, and it was about how different societies draw a line between the sacred and profane, the dirty and the clean. She had a dedication of that book to her husband Jim, who 'more than anyone else has forced me into taking a stand on the relativity of the tolerance for dirt' (Douglas, 2002). That was her dedication.

Both: [*laugh*]

Fraser: I love that. I'm tempted to paraphrase Donald Winnicott: clean enough. He talked about the good enough mother. You can't be too proactive. You'll destroy the child's kind of ability to struggle and grow if you satisfy everything too perfectly. Good enough mothering. Let's talk about clean enough. We don't have to go to these extremes.

Sorg: Good enough sounds great.

So my colleague and co-editor of this book Jan Groos has a really great podcast on questions related to non-capitalist futures called *Future Histories*. The podcast was one of the formats that really helped revive the planning debate in Germany. So, I think it's fitting if I ask you the final question he always asks his guests on the podcast: If you think about the future, what makes you joyful?

Fraser: Look, I'm at a stage of life where I think not having to go to faculty meetings is going to make me very joyful. I see a life ahead of me. I'm very fortunate to have adequate retirement income. I see a life ahead of me with a lot more time to think about these things and to just do so in a more relaxed way. Not to have to be so driven because of the time scarcity I feel under me all the time. Young people give me some hope, the students that I teach and the young people I meet when I travel and lecture. I think we're living in a time of tremendous radicalization, tremendous growth and curiosity and energy. It's too dispersed, it's not coalescing yet, but maybe it will, I'm not sure. There are plenty of things to not be joyful about, too, to be fair, we have to say, all right, thank you so much.

Sorg: Thank you so much for the interview and for taking the time.

Bibliography

Arrighi, G. (2007) *Adam Smith in Beijing: Lineages of the Twenty-First Century*. London/New York: Verso.

Bockman, J., Fischer, A. and Woodruff, D. (2016) '"Socialist Accounting" by Karl Polanyi: with preface "Socialism and the Embedded Economy"', *Theory and Society*, 45(5): 385–427.

Devine, P. (1988) *Democracy and Economic Planning: The Political Economy of a Self-Governing Society*. Cambridge: Polity Press.

Devine, P (2002) 'Participatory planning through negotiated coordination', *Science and Society*, 66(1): 72–93.

Douglas, M. (2002) *Purity and Danger: An Analysis of Concepts of Pollution and Taboo*. Oxford/New York: Routledge.

Du Bois, W.E.B (1998) *Black Reconstruction in America: 1860–1880*. New York: The Free Press.

Elson, D. (1988) 'Market socialism or socialization of the market?', *New Left Review*, 172.

Fraser, N. (2007) 'Special section: transnational public sphere: transnationalizing the public sphere', *Theory, Culture & Society*, 24(4): 7–30.

Fraser, N. (2013) *Fortunes of Feminism: From State-Managed Capitalism to Neoliberal Crisis*. London: Verso.

Fraser, N. (2020) 'What should socialism mean in the twenty-first century?', *Socialist Register* (56).

Fraser, N. and Jaeggi, R. (eds) (2018) *Capitalism: A Conversation in Critical Theory*. Cambridge/Medford, MA: Polity.

Hahnel, R (2021) *Democratic Economic Planning*. London: Routledge.

Hester, H. and Srnicek, N. (2018) 'The crisis of social reproduction and the end of work', in I. Vidal-Folch (ed) *The Age of Perplexity: Rethinking the World We Knew*, Barcelona: Fundacion BBVA.

Lutosch, H. (2022) *Wenn das Baby schreit, dann möchte man doch hingehen*. https://communaut.org/de/wenn-das-baby-schreit-dann-moechte-man-doch-hingehen

Mandel, E. (1986) 'In defence of socialist planning', *New Left Review*, 159(1): 5–22.

Morris, W. (2018) *The Collected Works of William Morris: Signs of Change. Lectures on Socialism*. San Diego: Creative Media Partners.

Owen, D. (2014) 'Dilemmas of inclusion', in K. Nash, and N. Fraser (eds) *Transnationalizing the Public Sphere*, Cambridge/Malden, MA: Polity Press.

Pankhurst, S. (1920) *A Constitution for British Soviets: Points for a Communist Programme*. London: Workers' Dreadnought.

Sorg, C. (2023) 'Failing to plan is planning to fail: toward an expanded notion of democratically planned postcapitalism', *Critical Sociology*, 49(3): 475–493.

van Parijs, P. (1991) 'Why surfers should be fed: the liberal case for an unconditional basic income', *Philosophy and Public Affairs*, 20: 101–131.

Conclusion

Jan Groos and Christoph Sorg

This book has put the idea of democratic planning back on the table. It has argued that if we want to effectively address the many and interrelated crises of our time a fundamental paradigm shift is needed. It is a shift away from blind market forces deciding over how our collective surplus is being used, away from an ever-present imperative of profit-driven market competition, away from capitalism 'cannibalizing' (Fraser, in this volume) on our social relations, our solidarity and the environment. Such a project is decisively constructive in its outlook. While firmly based on the valuable insights coming from in-depth critiques of capitalism, it does not stop at critique. It engages in a *creative construction* driven by the question of how to do things differently in concrete terms and on a scale. It is in this spirit that the authors of this volume have investigated varieties of planning as an essential feature of desirable alternatives to capitalism.

Engaging in such a creative construction of alternatives expands the field of what is considered negotiable, what can and should be placed under collective democratic control. It opens up new spheres for democratic debate, spheres that are currently gated within the confines of private property and control. Such debates should, and hopefully will soon, become a matter of course in any society: democratic debates about how to allocate the collectively produced surplus for societal ends instead of capital accumulation, how to distribute the socially necessary tasks (all of them, not just the sphere of production) that are needed to reproduce our societies in a desirable way, how to repair the social, political and ecological damage that has been inflicted by capitalism over the years.

Contradictions

Creative construction, the book as well as the collective and ongoing task behind the term, is not without contradictions. To a certain extent, this is due to the fact that fundamentally different futures must be developed from within a present that is largely hostile towards such efforts, a present characterized by extensive exhaustion and devastation both within humans and more-than-human nature. This question of the present material basis that inevitably represents the starting point for the endeavour of democratic planning forms a largely implicit, yet all the more important field of tension within the planning debate. We will in the following provide two examples of such tension, one on the micro and one on the macro level.

On a micro level the planning debate is riddled with assumptions about the involved subjects and their presumed state of 'social consciousness', seen either as a quasi-material precondition for the success of a given model or something that will need to be brought about in order to be able to progress into some form of 'higher stage'. Such assumptions about the state of the subjects of democratic (economic) planning lie at the heart of one of the most contested questions within the contemporary planning debate, namely whether there should be an element of material reward for work in order to steer the behaviour of subjects within democratically planned economies (see, for instance, Muldoon and Booth, in this volume). Opponents of such an approach provide strong arguments against the continuation of such (semi-)wage relations. They point out that there is an inherent contradiction between arguing that wage relations are needed due to a supposed lack of 'social consciousness', while at the same time wage relations as a disciplinary tool arguably play a central role in preventing the further development of this very 'social consciousness' (Meretz and Sutterlütti, in this volume). Proponents, in return, will point out that there are, at times, conflicting interests between different layers within planned economies, for example between local interests and society-wide interests. They ask how decisions that have been collectively agreed upon on functionally higher levels of society should be guided and, in cases of irreconcilable interests, also be enforced on a local level, if there are no mechanisms of economic incentivization in place that one can make use of.

On a macro level the question of the material basis of democratic planning crucially relates to the modus operandi of the broader societal context. All the canonical comprehensive models of democratic economic planning (Laurin-Lamothe, Legault and Tremblay-Pepin, in this volume; see also Sorg and Groos, 2025) operate within scenarios that are very orderly and well-structured abstractions, with most of them remaining within the very narrow focus of nation states (Sorg, in this volume). However, as Nick Dyer-Witheford (in this volume) points out, what we will arguably need is a highly flexible and adaptable 'disaster communism' that is able to operate effectively and provide relief within tumultuous scenarios of conflict and civil unrest in times of climate breakdown (Malm and Groos, 2024). This is a scenario that is unfortunately already a reality in parts of the world, and certainly within the realm of possibility for growing parts of the worldwide populus. Any convincing proposal for how to do things differently will therefore have to contain elements of 'disaster communism' that convincingly demonstrates that the proposed alternative is able to make life better, even amid chaos.

The contradictions within creative construction are, however, not exclusively due to imperfect starting conditions. While it is certainly true that starting from such a messy and violent present does not make things easier, we should not believe that alternatives to capitalism could or should be free from conflict and contradiction. On the contrary, such purified idealizations of alternative futures have in the past paved the way for authoritarian exclusion of dissent, and would continue to do so in the present and future. As Mohammed (in this volume) rightly points out, democratic planning is not about overcoming conflict as such, but about the possibility to collectively deliberate and decide over our sometimes conflicting interests and the inherent contradictions that come along with social complexity.

Broadening the debate

This volume has shown that, for all its strengths, there is a dire need to decisively broaden the scope of what has, in the past, been called the socialist calculation debate. While there is merit in situating the ongoing engagement with democratic planning within a broader trajectory of the socialist calculation debate, it nonetheless fundamentally misses the point to frame the central task at hand as a *calculation* problem (Groos, in this volume). The central problems of the planning debate are political in nature, and framing them exclusively as technical problems of calculation and control will, at best, only get you so far and, at worst, provide assistance for technocratic deliria. Creative construction as a collective process of democratic planning fundamentally contrasts with deterministic notions of planning as sovereign control over humans and/or more-than-human nature. This is all the more important since the term 'planning' has, over the years, repeatedly been associated with technocratic tendencies. Unfortunately, such tendencies are currently again trying to legitimize themselves through their own form of greenwashing. However, when it comes to modes of government, creative construction will have to go *beyond* (neo-)liberal government and not *back* to pseudo-sovereignty in the form of an ecological benevolent dictatorship.

For this and many other reasons, the planning debate would do well not to return to fantasies of control over nature as a mode of government (Mohammed, in this volume), but instead take into account that the climate crisis cannot be addressed effectively without a change in the way we *relate* to the more-than-human nature and its reproductive cycles (Redecker, in this volume; Groos, in this volume). In order to do so we will need to develop an expanded notion of 'democratically planned postcapitalism' (Sorg, 2022) that includes ecological relations (Hofferberth, Durand and Schmelzer, in this volume; Schaupp, in this volume), care (Lutosch, in this volume; Winker and Neumann, in this volume), North–South convergence (Sorg, in this volume), and commoning (Sutterlütti and Meretz, in this volume) into the picture. This volume sees itself as a contribution to such efforts. Such an outlook, however, does not at all mean that calculation will not have to play a crucial role as well. On the contrary, there is a very promising convergence taking place between the fields of democratic planning and social ecology in which forms of energy and material flow accounting are introduced as a possible basis for the development of forms of democratic planning *as* socio-metabolic planning (Planning for Entropy, 2022; Beaucaire, Saey-Volckrick and Tremblay-Pepin, 2023; Zeug et al, 2023; Heyer, in this volume).

Relief

While there is a temporal aspect of future possibility involved, a scientific utopian element if you will, creative construction will only succeed in becoming a widespread societal practice if it is able to not only envision desirable futures, but *at the same time* provide tangible relief in the present.

On the theoretical side of things this means that models of democratic planning will have to be decisively processual. The still quite common mode of devising a model that is set in a somewhat distant and undefined future without implementing the way to get there *into the structure of the model itself* is insufficient. Arguably, it is because of the way in which many of the models ignore the question of transformation (Decker, in this volume) that they have to rely on arbitrary assumptions about a supposed state of 'social consciousness' as if it was some form of magic sparkle. One of the important tasks for the new generation of planning researchers is, therefore, to work towards processual models of democratic planning that are able to include their own development into the structure of the model itself, starting from a present in which they will (1) have to be able to navigate potentially tumultuous societal contexts while (2) at the same time provide immediate relief from the pain, stress and destruction inflicted by the multiple crises of our time.

While this might sound like an insurmountable task, there are, on the practical side of things, many elements that show that it is not. Not only are there a plethora of prefigurative practices aimed at immediate relief that will have to form a basis of any creative construction to come, but it is precisely the prospect of democratic planning combined with, unsurprisingly, movement power that shows a viable path for how to sensibly combine present-day transformative battles with a processual approach towards creative construction. The 'Expropriate Deutsche Wohnen & Co' project (Berfelde and Möller, in this volume) provides an instructive and highly tangible example for how bottom-up organizing around questions of existential infrastructures (here the provision of affordable housing) can be successfully combined with an outlook that is decisively oriented around the paradigm of democratic planning. As Berfelde and Möller show (in this volume), it is through democratic planning that our collective wealth becomes security, freedom and relief. A relief that is sorely needed.

It is this offer of security, freedom and relief that sits at the heart of creative construction. It shows, against the hopeless mantra of 'there is no alternative', that things can be fundamentally different.

Bibliography

Beaucaire, K., Saey-Volckrick, J. and Tremblay-Pepin, S. (2023) 'Integration of approaches to social metabolism into democratic economic planning models', *Studies in Political Economy*: 73–92. doi: 10.1080/07078552.2023.2234753.

Malm, M. and Groos, J. (2024) 'S03E23 – Andreas Malm on overshooting into climate breakdown', *Future Histories*. https://www.futurehistories.today/episoden-blog/s03/e23-andreas-malm-on-overshooting-into-climate-breakdown/

Planning for Entropy (2022) 'Democratic economic planning, social metabolism and the environment', *Science & Society*, 86(2): 291–313. doi: 10.1521/siso.2022.86.2.291.

Sorg, C. (2022) 'Failing to plan is planning to fail: toward an expanded notion of democratically planned postcapitalism', *Critical Sociology*, 49(3): 475–493.

Sorg, C. and Groos, J. (2025) 'Rethinking economic planning', *Competition & Change*, special issue. doi: 10.1177/10245294241273954.

Zeug, W., Bezama, A., Thrän, D., Raquel, K. and Gan, K. (2023) 'Holistic and integrated life cycle sustainability assessment: background, methods and results from two case studies'. doi: 10.13140/RG.2.2.21800.75526.

Index

References to figures appear in *italic* type; those in **bold** type refer to tables. References to endnotes show both the page number and the note number (95n1).

A

Aalbers, M.B. 173
abolishing families and capitalism 301
abolishing wage labour 74–78
abolishing the division of labour 78
access to information 88–89
accounting units 62–64
accurate incentive reporting 79–80
activism 234–235
Adaman, F. 21, 24, 39–43, 70, 72–73, 123–124
Adamczak, B. 7, 126
'administration of things' (Engels) 125–126
administrative councils 177–179, *178*
adolescents 299, 303
Adorno, T.W. 289
advanced capitalism 100
Agamben, G. 101
agent-based models 64
Albert, M. 25–29, 78
algorithmic management 283, 285
algorithmic planning 68–70
Allende, Salvador 153, 189, 258
allocating resources 72, 134
alternative social orders 4
Amazon 3, 284
Amin, S. 189, 191–192
anarchic interstate system 188
anarchism 314–315
anarchist gift economies 70–71
anarchy of production 318
Anstalt öffentlichen Rechts (AöR) 176–177
Anthropocene xxi, 270–271
anthropocentrism 271
anti-capitalism 310, 314
Arab socialism 185
Argentina 192
Arrighi, G. 312
artefact of capitalism 95n1
Arthur, C. 78

artificial intelligence (AI) 3, 280, 289
 see also computers; information technology (IT)
arts of government 117, 125, 129, 147–148
asset stranding 254–255
atomistic decision-making 188
Auftragstaktik 107
Aulenbacher, B. 219
Austria 233
Austrian argument on tacit knowledge 24
Austrian concept of entrepreneurship 149–150
authoritarianism 53, 105, 109, 284
automation 190, 325–326
autonomy 73, 78, 91, 287

B

baby caring model 304–305
'baby-led weaning' 299
balanced job complexes (Albert and Hahnel) 28, 43, 78
Barca, S. 290
basic incomes 73, 105, 148, 223
 see also guaranteed income; social dividend; wages
Bastani, A. 106
Beaucaire, K. 127
Beer, S. 152, 153
Benanav, A. 105
Bentham, J. 231
Berfelde, R. 332–333
Berlin 170, 173–177
Berliner Bankenskandal 173
'Beziehungsweisen' 126
Big Pharma 103
Bilderverbot xxii, 4, 7
biocommunism 98–110
 defining 98
 liberal immigration programmes 102
 planning 108–109

rationing 104–105
recomposition of labour 106–108
socialization 103–104
theoretical premises 99–100
biocommunist essential workers 107
biopolitics 99, 100
'biopower' (Foucault) 99, 108
black box 140
Black Lives Matter 235
Black Reconstruction in America (Du Bois) 313
'blueprints of desire' (Adamczak) 7
Bolivia 192
bonuses 121
borders 102
Boswell, T. 194, 195, 196
'boundary model' 108
bourgeois society 297–298, 300–301
Brand, U. 204, 250
Bratton, B. 4
British Soviets 311
Brown, W. 119
Buchanan, J.M. 136
Buck, H.J. 104

C

Callinicos, A. 98
capital
 and commons 104
 extraction of value of production 206
 internal competition 205
 and labour 206
 polycrisis plans 109
capital accumulation 170, 205
capitalism xxi–xxii, 159
 abolishing 301
 allocating forms of social wealth 317
 alternatives to 1–2, 5, 7
 challenging 193
 climate crisis xxii, 289
 competition 220
 creating the economy 309
 critiques 1
 and democratic planning 314
 economic planning 3, 208–209
 expansionist system 220
 framework conditions 93–94
 freedom of choice 91
 household care activities 94–95
 housing 170
 institutional characteristics 205–206
 institutionalized social order 187, 309
 internal and external high profitability 65n16
 and IT 56
 labour as a commodity 170–171
 non-class reductionist, non-economistic critiques 309
 planning 171–172, 187–188, 209–210, *211*
 and post-capitalist forms of transformation 204
 private property 163
 problems with and injustices 310
 profits from worthless activities 90
 property-based material domination 90
 resource consumption 270
 social destruction 219
 sphere of circulation 284
 transnationalizing system 189
 unfree/dependent labour 309–310
 see also post-capitalism planning
capitalist market economies 249, 268
capitalist modes of production 218–220
capitalist totality 187
Capitalocene 269, 270, 275
capital valorization 220, 224
capping salaries 234
carbon capture and sequestration (CCS) 104, 279
carbon emissions 105
caregiving 219, 298–299, 304, 326
Care Revolution 218, 221–224
caring and care work 294–306
 automation 325–326
 care relationships 220–221
 children 295–297
 four-parent model 301–303
 Germany 286
 invisible unpaid work 219
 model for babies 304–305
 overburdening workers 218–220
 parent–child relationships 298–299, 305
 planning debate 286
 post-work perspectives 326–327
 privatized in the family 297
 socialist economic planning 275
 socialization 326
 social subordination of women 286
caring, non-dominating relationships 275–276
cause groups 39
centralized planning bureau 31–32, 44–45
centrally planned economies (CPE) 52–54, 55, 60
central planning 53–55, 234, 258
central state 139
chamber of interests 22–23, 39
Chase-Dunn, C. 189, 194, 195, 196
childcare 295–297, 300–301, 304–306
child-free areas 302
children
 boundaries 299–300
 discriminating against 300
 extreme individualism 297
 illnesses and infections 299, 306n1
 liberal families 299
 and parents' will 299
 permanent adult caregivers 295
 as 'private pleasure' 300

children of all people 303
Chile 3–4, 153, 189
circular-local economies 194
citizen's committees 45
Clausewitz, Carl von 110
clearing prices 57
climate crisis 71, 106, 219, 268, 270, 289
  see also ecological crises
climate justice activists 270
closed national economies 185
Cockshott, W.P. 29–33, 44–47, 53, 60, 70, 195
'code is law' (Lessig) 285
Cold War 139
Cole, G.D.H. 69, 75–76
collective endeavours 84–85
collective insurance 223
'collective morale function' (Laibman) 120, 122, 129
collective ownership 24
collective property and self-determination 317–318
'collective self-reliance' (Lemper) 186, 192–193
collective sovereignty 272
collectivizing childcare 294–297, 301–302, 305–306
Collier, S. 100
colonialism 185, 192
commensurability 57, 70
commodity fetishism 284
'common funds' (Marx) 57
commoning 83, 89, 236, 280
commonism 70, 83–96, 315
  cooperative action 84
  economy and politics/state 91
  framework goals 92–95
  and gender 91
  interpersonal care 89–90
  planning 88–92
  voluntariness 83–84, 91
'commonist' discourses (Dyer-Witheford) 104
common ownership 194
commons
  and capital 104
  cooperation 227–228
  joint organization of work 224
communes 45
'communism' 108
communist commonwealth (CC) 186, 196
communist distributive principles 69, 75, 197
'communist software agents' 3
community projects/production 85, 224
companies 187–188
competition 159–160, 220
complementary holism 43
complexities 142–143, 144–145, 148–150
compulsory work 73, 272

computerized central planning (Cockshott and Cottrell) 29–33, 34, 44–47, 60–61
computers 56, 136–137
  see also artificial intelligence (AI); information technology (IT)
Comte, Auguste 125
conflict loops 93
conspicuous consumption 128
consumer goods 32, 61, 73–74, 76
consumers' councils 27–28, 43
consumer tokens 62, 63
contemporary agent-based models 64
contradictions 12, 329–331
  capitalism 171, 309
  economic planning 208
  forces of production 281
  planning 54, 121
  redistribution 206, 207
contribution to society
  and consumption 80
  decoupling consumption 69
  and ecology 49
  goal-oriented activities 226
  labouring process 74
  wages 47
control and collective sovereignty 272
convivial technology 253–254
cooperation 88–89
cooperatives 89, 187
coordinated negotiation (Devine and Adaman) 21–25, 26, 39–43, 60, 62, 63
coordination 139, 155, 227, 268
COPs (conference of the parties) xxi
corporate planning 187–188
Cottrell, A.F. 29–33, 44–47, 53, 60, 70, 195
council structures 177–179, 178
counter-hegemonic blocs 193, 313
counter-planning 108–109
coupon socialism (Roemer) 194
COVID-19 pandemic xxi, xxii, 100–101, 106, 202
COVID-19 vaccines 103
Cox, S. 105
creative construction 2, 329, 331
creativity 146–147
cybernetic modes of control 283
cybernetic planned economy 61
cybernetic planning system (Platenkamp) 62–63
cybersocialism 70

D

Dale, G. 99
Dammayr, M. 219
Dapprich, J.P. 33, 60, 70
data 87, 258
Daum, T. 267
daycare centres 299
debt audits 192

INDEX

decentral (enterprise) levels 54–55
decentralization 69, 71, 72, 227–228, 283
decision-making 70, 93, 320
Decker, S. 202, 204
decommodification
  housing 177
  production 104
  public ownership 176
deglobalization 189–193
degrowth xxii, 71, 247–260, 279–290
  balanced distribution of work 254
  defining 247–248
  and deindustrialization 280
  democratic economic planning 280–281
  democratic participation 252–253
  development of productive forces 253–254
  GDP growth 247
  global wellbeing 254–255
  limits and priorities 252
  localism 287–288
  planned transition 248, 280
  planning 253, 255–260, *257*, 289
  and reproductive work 287
  social and financial disruptions 254–255
  technology 253
  unnecessary and destructive work 254
'degrowth' ecology (Leonardi) 99
'delinking' (Amin) 186, 191–192
Democracy and Economic Planning (Devine) 21–22
democracy at the workplace 286
democratically planned economy 52–65, 235–236, 267
  classification categories 59
  historical experiences 52–55
  productive lines of conflict 59–64
  socialist calculation debate 55–59
democratic control 80
democratic coordination 72–73
democratic decision-making 72, 210
democratic economic planning 4, 121, 124
  centre decision-making space 47
  degrowth 280–281
  ecological effects 289
  models 127, 330
  provisioning systems 251
democratic notion of autonomy 78
democratic planned economies 119, 169
democratic planning 185–197, 232–233, 329
  basic needs of people 303–304
  centralist path 233
  central planning 2
  closed national economy 185
  cooperative structures 187
  'delinking' 186
  and existing movements 235
  high-income countries 189
  internalizing ecological costs 194
  international exchange 195

  international support 191
  market forces 2, 194, 318
  necessary and feasible 5
  political decisions 4
  regional-continental levels 194
  replacing market society 11
  security and freedom 230–232
  social struggles 190–191
democratic socialist economic planning 268, 272–273, 276
Democratic Socialists of America (DSA) 212
democratization
  economic decision-making 72
  interdependence 273
  planning 3
  socialization of means of production 223
dependency–autonomy conflicts 303
dependency theorists 189
dependent labour 309–310
'Designing freedom' lectures (Beer) 152
Deutsche Wohnen & Co Enteignen *see* 'Expropriate Deutsche Wohnen & Co' campaign
Devine, P.J. 185, 204, 319
  algorithmic approaches 70
  coordinated negotiation model 21–25, *26*, 39–43, 60, 62, 63
  Democracy and Economic Planning 21–22
  labour autonomy 72–74
  market exchange 72, 73, 74, 318
  multicriteria assessment of data 119–120
  participation 123–124
  participatory planned model 68–69, 71–72
  performance benefits 78
  planning model 320
  regional inequality 195–196
  wage labour 75
dialectical model of post-capitalist transformation 202–210, 213
digital democratic planning (DDP) 280–281, 283–285
digital infrastructures 4, 283
digital socialism 284
'Digital socialism?' (Morozov) 133
digital technologies 3, 288–289
direct citizen participation 258
'disaster capitalism' (Klein) 98
'disaster communism' 100, 330–331
disaster relief 287
discovery 138–139, 145
distributed digital systems 235
distribution
  of goods 72
  of goods without wages 74
  and planning 84–85
  and production 86
  productive resources 62
  and recognition 322
  social dividend 74–78

dividend payments 76
Doctorow, C. 106
dominion over nature 271
doubling of cycles 86
doughnut-shaped space 249, 250, *251*
Douglas, M. 327
downscaling 253
Du Bois, W.E.B. 313
Dufour, M. 195
Durand, C. 280, 282
Dyer-Witheford, N. 1, 104, 287, 330–331

E

ecological budgets 71
ecological costs 194
ecological crises xxi, xxii, 56, 70, 270
  see also climate crisis
ecological degradation 250
ecological destruction 219
ecological planning 249, 252, 254
'ecological planning' (NUPES) 212–213
economic calculation 267
economic decisions as political problems 249
economic democracy 286
economic efficiency 253
economic growth 247, 279–280, 289
economic localization 280
economic planning 2–3, 185, 203
  contradictions and dilemmas 208
  corporate and public planning 187–188
  disaster relief 287
  existing economic policies 210–213
  new planning debate 201–202
  non-market mechanisms 208
  state and capital relationship 209–210
economies
  creation of capitalism 309
  environmental dimension 287
eco-socialists xxii, 99, 104
Ecuador 192
Edwards, P.N. 288, 289
elaborative body 256
electoral programmes 210–213
Elias-Pinsonnault, S. 195
Ellman, M. 53
Elson, D. 319
emissions budgets 58–59
empirical economic policies 203
employee ownership 194
employment
  and consumption 73–74
  standard of living 223
  see also labour; wage labour
Engels, F. 125–126, 266
enterprises 35–37, 47–48, 58
entrepreneurship 149–150
environmental constraints 58–59
environmental destruction 280
'environmentality' (Lemke) 127

essential workers 106–108
EU 103
evolutionary theory 162–163
executive bodies 258
'Expropriate Deutsche Wohnen & Co'
  campaign 169, 170, 172, 173, 174–181,
  332–333
expropriation of crisis-critical
  capitalism 103–104
extinctions 108

F

factory work 157
families
  abolishing 301
  as anti-factory 324
  demands with child care 220–221
  promises 298
  social constructs 297–299
federal socialist world bank 194
feminist perspectives
  post-capitalist utopias 324
  socialist economic planning 275
feminist scholars 281
feminized care work 274
financial crises 202
'financialization of housing'
  (Aalbers) 173–174
firefighting 238
flexible wage work 219
  see also wage labour
force provoking resistance 238
forces of production 281–282
forces of re/production 280, 287–289
Fordism 312
fossil fuels 71, 77, 103–104, 279
Foucault, Michel 99, 115, 117–118, 126, 129
'Four-in-One-Perspective' (Haug) 306n2
four-parent model of parenthood 301–303
fractal architecture 256, *257*
framework goals 92–95
France 212, 258
Frankfurt School 266
Fraser, N. 10, 308–327
  capitalism 308–311
  markets and planning 314–320
  mode of recognition 320–324
  no markets at the top and no markets at the
    bottom principle 317, 318, 320
  pay-as-you-go principle 316, 320
  socialism 308–311
  social reproductive contradictions 171
  transformation 311–314
freedom and security 230–232
freedom and voluntariness 236–237
freedom of choice 91
free goods 76
free market competition xxii
Friends of The Classless Society 237

INDEX

full-time employment 221, 222
functional services/activities 39
Future Histories podcasts 133–164, 230–242, 327

G

GDP 194, 247
geoengineering 279
geological production time 241
Germany 148, 170, 175, 286
  Grundgesetz Article 15 174–175
gilets jaunes uprising 258
Global Commoning System 236
global market socialism (Boswell and Chase-Dunn) 194, 195
global networks 88
Global North 247, 252
Global South xxi, 103, 157, 190, 192, 194, 219, 252
global supply chains 157, 190, 194
global trade-to-GDP ratios 194
global warming 101–102
global wellbeing 254–255
golden age of social housing 172
good enough/clean enough (Winnicott) 327
Google 151
Gosplan authoritarianism 2
governance structures 91
governmentality (Foucault) 99, 116, 126–127
'government of things' (Lemke) 117, 125–126
Gramsci, A. 202
Graz, Austria 233–234
Greece 192, 210–212
greenhouse gas (GHG) emissions 247
Green New Deal (Sanders) 107
Groos, J. 133–164, 230–242, 327
Grundrisse (Marx) 288
guaranteed income 73, 78–79
  see also basic incomes
guild socialism 75

H

Habermas, J. 148–149
Hahnel, R. 25–29, 60, 61, 78, 195
Hardt, M. 99
Harloe, M. 172
Haug, F. 306n2
Hayek, F.A. 134, 138
  competition 159–160
  evolutionary theory 162–163
  information problem 118, 120
  market civilization 161
  non-market projects 267
  rational economic order 87–88
  social coordination 154
heating costs 233
hegemonic orders 189
Held, D. 72

Herrmann, U. 233
Hester, H. 325, 326
Heyer, J. 268
historical experiences 52–55, 58
Hofferberth, E. 280, 282
Honduras 102
hospitals 239
household production 86, 89–90, 91–92, 94
housework 303, 325
housing 169–182
  discrimination-sensitive allocation 177
  exchange and use value 170–172
  Keynesian welfare state 172
  needs-based allocation 176–177
  neoliberal planning 173–174
  pricing 174
  radical democratic planning 174–181
  shortages 172
  social-ecological transformation 180–181
humanitarian generosity 103
human needs 220, 287
human wellbeing 253
'hyper-commodification of housing' (Madden and Marcuse) 174

I

IKEA 258
illegal migration 102
'imperialist rents' (Amin) 189
implementation 92
incentives 38, 58–59, 120–121
inclusion 89–90
incomes 75
  see also basic incomes; social dividend; wages
incommensurability problem 70
India 103
indicative planning 209
individual articulation of needs 287
industrialization 157
industrial policies 209
information 56–58, 84–89, 319
informational connections 88
information and knowledge 256
'information problem' (Hayek) 118, 120
information technology (IT) 53, 56, 61
  see also artificial intelligence (AI); computers
infrastructures 162
in-kind, non-market-mediated planning 248
integration through deliberation 256–258
interest groups 39
Intergovernmental Panel on Climate Change 92–93, 288
international exchange 195
International Monetary Fund 196
interpersonal care 89–90
interstate system 186–189
inventions 138
investment decisions 6, 209

339

iteration facilitation boards (IFBs) 27–28, 43–44
'iterative' 35–37, 47–48

J
Jaeggi, R. 323
Jameson, F. 107
joint organization of work 224
just-in-time logistics 100

K
Kantorovich, [initials required] 60–61
Keynesianism 135, 139, 209
Keynesian welfare state 171, 172
kindergartens 303
Klein, N. xxi, 98
knowledge-intensive dimensions 134
Kollontai, A. 311
KPÖ (Communist Party of Austria) 233–234

L
labour
  abolishing division of labour 78
  as a commodity 170–171
  decentralized planning 70–71
  and ownership 205, 206
  prisoners 239
  unfree/dependent 309–310
  voluntary participation 77
  see also employment; wage labour
labour autonomy 68, 72–74, 75
labour control 73
labour cost 57
labour-intensive tasks 106
labour movements 313
Labour Party 212, 213
labour power 73, 171, 172, 205
labour shortages 79
labour solidarity 102
labour theory of value 31, 47
labour time 31
Laibman, D. 62, 119, 204
  classification of models 59
  'collective morale function' 120, 122, 129
  socialist incentive design 58
  social reproduction prices (SRP) 37, 49
  taxonomy of post-capitalist models 35, *36*
  see also multilevel democratic iterative coordination (MDIC)
Laiki Enotita (Popular Unity) 210–212
Lakoff, A. 100
Lange, O. 3, 146, 284
Latin American Pink Tide 185
law-creating and -enforcing institutions 205–206
leftist ideals 150
Le Guin, U.K. 107
Lemke, T. 117, 125–127, 128
Lemper, A. 192

Lenin, V.I. 284
Leonardi, E. 99
Leontief, W. 258
Lessig, L. 285
Lewis, S. 239, 275, 297, 301
liberal immigration programmes 102
liberal parents 299
liberated society 269, 304
libertarian socialism 61
life cycle analysis (LCA) 56–57
life cycle sustainability assessments 57, 58
local authorities 91–92, 94
local decision-making procedures 93
localism 287–288
local plans 59
local production units 53–56
local self-organization 61
logic of value 86
Lutosch, H. 237, 287, 324, 325
Luxemburg, R. 222

M
macroeconomic plans 31, 32, 45
Madden, D 174
Make Capitalism History (Meretz and Sutterlütti) 83
Malm, A. 103
Mandarini, M. 110
Mandel, E. 319
Marcuse, P. 157, 174
market abolitionist models 210
market civilization 161, 162
market competition 137–138
market exchanges 23–25, 39–40, 73
market failures xxii
market forces 23–25, 40, 194, 318
market fundamentalism xxii
markets
  allocating resources 134
  collaboration and coordination 153–154
  consumer goods and costs of production 74
  Hayekian information problem 118
  and neoliberalism 149
  and planning 314–320
  pricing of housing 174
  replacing functions 142–143, 271
  self-regulating 316
  suboptimal 134–135
  unaccounted for costs 140
market socialism 118, 210, 316, 319
market–state relations 118
Marx in the Anthropocene (Saito) xxii
Marxism 3, 99, 158
Marxist architectural theorists 172
Marxist-feminist theories 171
Marx, K.
  anarchy of production 318
  commodity fetishism 284
  'common funds' 57

INDEX

exchange values as capital 205
Grundrisse 288
logic of value 86
The Poverty of Philosophy 281, 282
productive forces 282
realms of necessity and freedom 155
revolutions 190
'socialism' and 'communism' 108
theatre ticket argument 63
utopian thinking 266
Massey lectures (Beer) 152
maximizing cooperation 84
means of production 24, 281–282
measure of enterprise activity 48
mechanism without a spring (Arthur) 78
mediation 84–85
mediation by value 85–88
mediation in kind 85, 87
Meindl, M. 236
Mélenchon, Jean-Luc 212
Menger, C. 146
Meretz, S. 70, 83, 236, 238, 287, 315
Mezzadra, S. 106
migration 101–103
'migration as reparations' (Nevins) 102
military spending 188
Mises, L. von 3, 134, 267
Mitterrand, François 190
mode of recognition 320–324
Moderna, Inc. 103
Möller, P. 332–333
Monbiot, G. 106, 126
monetary incentives 121
moneyless socialist economies 3
more-than-human form of government (Lemke) 127
more-than-human world 90
Morozov, Evgeny 133–164
Morris, W. 323
mothers 239, 296–297, 300
motivation 38, 208, 226
movement between workplaces 77
'multidimensional crises' (Callinicos) 98
multifactorial indicators 121, 128, 196
multilevel democratic iterative coordination (MDIC) 33–38, 47–49, 60, 63–64, 119–123, 129
multilevel planning 120, 256, *257*
multiscalar stacks 256
Musk, E. 158
mutual acceptance of cooperation 89
mutual aid practices 101

N

Nail, T. 102
national economic planning 189
nationalizations 177, 190, 210–213
national planning commissions 22, 195–196
needs-based, domination-free society 301

negotiated coordination bodies 23–24, 40
negotiated coordination (Devine) 21–25, 195, 318
negotiated globalization and planning 193–197
negotiation process 24–25
Negri, A. 99, 171
neoclassical socialism 61
neoliberal austerity 100, 174
neoliberal–capitalist economic systems 273
neoliberal environmentality 127
neoliberal governmentality 116, 118, 127
neoliberal ideology 119
neoliberalism
  death or metamorphosis 109
  as an entrepreneurial venture 149
  the market and the state 140
  market failures xxii
  modernity and civilization theories 161
  price system 139
  socialist calculation debate 145–146
  vision of the market 135–136
neoliberal planning 173–174
Neurath, O. 57, 70, 194
Nevins, J. 102
New Left 316
New Left Review 162
new planning debate 9, 169–170, 176, 181, 202, 314
new socialist calculation debate xxiii
nodes 88–89
no markets at the top and no markets at the bottom principle (Fraser) 317, 318, 320
non-capitalisms 5, 163–164
non-circulating labour money 70
non-coercive negotiation mechanisms 209
nonlinear model of post-capitalist transformation 202–210, 213
non-market based discovery 137
non-market distribution 76–77
non-market, non-state supported care 235–236
non-neoliberal complexity 150
non-techno-determinist approaches 290
'no profit from pandemic' campaign 103
North–South convergence 196, 252, 332
notification-based coordination 227
Nouvelle Union Populaire Écologique et Sociale (NUPES) 212–213
Nove, A. 319
novel techno-infrastructural approaches 152
Nowak, J. 290
nuclear family 297–301
nuclear weapons 190
Nuss, S. 267

O

offshoring refugee camps 102
oikonomia (household production) 90

oil industry 77, 103–104, 279
O'Neill, D.W. 251
Operaist Marxist critiques 171
optimality and self-interest 122
optimal planning 60–61
'organic crises' (Gramsci) 202
organization decision-making process model 48
organization of production 284
organizing modernity 163
organizing work 254
overconsumption 241
overproduction 271
Owen, D. 321
ownership and labour 205
ownership structures 176

P

paid and unpaid work 225
Palantir Technologies Inc. 151
Pankhurst, S. 311, 319
parenthood 301–303
   see also caring and care work
participatory approaches to planning 71–72
participatory economics (Albert and Hahnel) 25–29, *30*, 43–44
participatory integrative planning (PIP) 281, 285–288
participatory planned economy (PPE, Devine) 68–69, 72, 73–76, 79
'Participatory Planning Through Negotiated Coordination' model (Devine) 123–124
paternity 302
Patnaik, P. 207
pay-as-you-go principle (Fraser) 316, 320
Pendergrass, D. 65n11
People's Agreement of Cochabamba 192
People's Republic of Walmart (Phillips and Rozworski) 270, 284
perverse incentives 120–121
Pfizer Inc. 103
Phillips, L. 270, 284
planetary boundaries framework 249–250
planned economies
   computers 136–137
   coordination capacities 267–268
   cybernetic notions 61
   ecological issues 270
   new debate on 176
   problems 52
   reproduction 275
planned housing supply 180–181
planned production 271
'planned' social-ecological transformation
   see degrowth
planned socialism 78, 80, 270
   see also socialism
planned social production and reproduction 180–181

'planner state' (Negri) 171–172
planning 87–88
   adaptive and dynamic process 84–85
   as anti-democratic xxii–xxiii
   arts of government 115–118, 125–128
   capitalism 186–189, 210, *211*
   collection of data 258
   commonism 88–91
   coordination 91–92
   and counter-planning 108–109
   and degrowth 255, 259–260, 289
   ecological limits 255–259
   economic and political 187–188
   and implementation 92
   investment decisions 6
   large tasks 92
   market allocating resources 134
   multiscalar stacks 256
   negotiated globalization 193–197
   participatory approaches 71–72
   realm of freedom 156
   satisfaction of societal needs 87
   as a sensing device 280
   and social goals 54–55
   sovereign control 128
   through the market 209
planning beyond growth 248–249, 251–255
planning commissions 24, 40
planning debate 115
   anthropocentrism 117, 125
   arts of government 117
   collective sovereignty and control 272
   developing modes of (re)production 124–125
   freedom and voluntariness 236–237
   importance 314
   narrow scope 147
   political in nature 331
   'social consciousness' 330
   theoretical strand 124
Planning for Entropy 56
planning literature 69
planning models 38
planning post-capitalist transition 109–110
planning processes 53, 85, 253
planning technologies 273
Platenkamp, T. 58, 60, 62–64
pleasure 254
pluralistic inputs 256
pocket-money wages 69, 75, 79
Polanyi, K. 316, 318–319
Polanyi, M. 24
political competition 188
political economy 116
political programmes 210
'politics of truth' (Foucault) 129
pollution 254
polycrises 98–99, 104–105
Popular Unity 213

INDEX

post-capitalism planning 208–210, *211*
  see also capitalism
post-capitalist models 35, *36*
post-capitalist society 301
post-capitalist transformation 201, 202–204, **209**
post-growth economy 280
Postone, M. 284
post-sovereign planning 272–276
post-work perspectives 326–327
potentiality 280
The Poverty of Philosophy (Marx) 281, 282
praxis
  critiques based on use 150–151
  and socialism 146
prices 40–41, 44, 45–46, 86, 174
'principled optimizing behaviour' 122–123
principle of need 75
prisoners as forced labour 239
private property 163
privatization 173–174, 305
processual models of democratic planning 332–333
producer accounting units 63
producer budgets 59, 63–64
production 62, 86, 280, 285–286, 288, 322–323
production capacity 121
production units (Devine) 22–24, 35–37, 38, 41
productive areas of conflict 59–64
productive forces 280, 281–282, 289–290
productive needs 90–91
productive work 286
productivity improvements 159
profits 5–6, 282, 309–310
progressive taxation 196
Project Cybersyn 3–4, 152–153, 185, 258
projects 46
Promethean perspectives 266–271, 273, 276
property form 274
property ownership 84
protocols 89
provisioning systems 251, *251*
'public luxury, private sufficiency' principle (Monbiot) 106
public planning 188
Purity and Danger (Douglas) 327

Q
qualitative aggregation 256–258
Quesnay, F. 116

R
racialized division of labour 313
racist population politics 232
radical democratic planning 174–181, *178*
radical deprivatization of care work 297
radical feminist proposals 239

radical freedom 84
radical voluntariness 237
rare earth materials 71
rates of return 24, 48
rationalizing political decision-making 125
rationing 104–105, 233
Raworth, K. 249, 250
realistic planning 59, 64
realms of freedom and necessity 155, 156–157
recapitalization of production 207
recessions 289
Redecker, Eva von 230–242
redistribution 105, 206, 208, **209**, 214
referenda 181–182
'reflexive biopolitics' 100
reform socialism 53–54, 57, 123
refuge 101–103
regulation 48, 59
relational materialist approaches 125, 126
relief 332–333
remediating climate change 106
  see also climate crisis; ecological crises
remuneration 44
  see also wages
renewable energy 279
rents 172, 180
reorganization of work areas 239–241
reorganizing work areas 239–241
reparations 252
representative assemblies 22, 41
representative government 22
reproduction
  and capitalist production 170–171
  environmental destruction 280
  planned economy proposals 275
  and production 286, 288, 322–323
  socialist economic planning 275
reproductive work
  and competition 220
  and degrowth economy 287
  distributed fairly 237
  German movement 235
  liberal feminists 241–242
  'production of life' 238–239
  and productive labour 272
  and women 274–275
repudiating debt 192
research resources 322
resource allocation 72, 283, 287
resource distribution 72
resource extraction 255
revolutionary potentialities 273–274
revolutionary realpolitik 218, 221–222
revolutions 189–190
Robertson, D.H. 187
Rockström, J. 250
Roemer, J.E. 194
romanticized femininity trap 324–325

343

romantic love 301–302
Rozworski, M. 270, 284
Russian invasion of Ukraine 103, 202

S

Sablowski, T. 202
'sacrifice value' of tasks 28–29
Saey-Volckrick, J. 127
Saito, K. xxii
sanctuary for migrants 102
Sanders, B. 212
Saros, D.E. 61–63, 195, 287
Saudi Aramco 104
scarce goods 76–77
Schmelzer, M. 280, 282
schools 303
Schumpeterian entrepreneur 138
science 250
Science and Society (journal) 33
science-based transformation discourse 214
second-order transformation (Decker) 204, 206–208, **209**, 214
 see also socialization
Second World War 172
sectoral production associations 319
security 84, 230–232
self-acknowledged motivation 73
self-activation 73, 74, 77
self-determined targets 121
self-government 72
 see also decentralization
self-interest 122
self-management 23
self-optimization 221
self-organization 283
self-referential economic logic of capitalism 90
self-regulating markets 316
'self-reliant modes of development' (Amin) 191–192
semi-autonomous networking 94
semi-periphery countries 189
sensual-vital needs 84, 86, 87, 90–91
separating units of account 62–64
sex 302
Shaikh, A. 159
Signs of Change (Morris) 323
Silicon Valley 154, 156
simplicity 143–144
small-scale activities 24, 41–42
Smith, A. 318
social activities 253
social architecture of capitalism 64
social bases for protest 190
social bodies 42
'social consciousness' 330
social contributions 323
social coordination 140
social costs 57

social destruction 219
social dividend 68–69, 74–78
 see also basic incomes
social division of labour 226
social-ecological targets 254
social-ecological transformation 180–181, 255–256
'social factory' (Tronti) 171
social frameworks 219
social funds 234
social housing 170, 172–173
social indicator measures (Laibman) 37–38, 49
social infrastructure 219
socialism
 'biopower' 108
 complexities 144–145
 computers and the planned economy 136–137
 development of productive forces 272
 as human emancipation 108
 no clear idea of 308–309
 reinventing 311
 reparative mode 316–317
 revaluing non-economic forms 324
 scarcity and inequality 325
 see also planned socialism
'Socialism in one country' transformation paradox 190
socialist accounting 56–57
socialist calculation debate (SCD) 3, 24, 55–58, 124, 135–136, 145–146, 266, 269, 273–274
'socialist calculation debate 2.0' (Daum and Nuss) 267
socialist economic planning 275
socialist economies 33, 121, 237
socialist governmentality 9, 115, 116, 117, 119, 123
socialist incentive design (Laibman) 58
socialist planned economies 271, 274
'socialist rate of return' (Laibman) 121–122
socialist units of account 56
socialization
 and biocommunism 103
 care work 326
 for the common good 181
 housing stocks 173, 176–177, 181–182
 and nationalization 177
 needs-based allocation of housing 176–177
 see also second-order transformation (Decker)
socialized means of production 269
social life 254
social metabolism with nature 128
social movement studies 190
social ownership 42
social provisioning 249–250, 251, 303
social relations 221, 274
social relations of production 158

social reproduction 171–172, 323–324
social reproduction prices (SRP, Laibman) 37, 49
'social reproductive contradictions' (Fraser) 171
social struggles 190–191, 193, 290
social theory 148, 150
social unrest 189
social work 225
societal goals 92
societal information paradox 87–88
societally necessary activities 86
societal mediation 85, 88
societal production system 88, 91–92
societal resources 252
societal structure of mediation 88
socioecological transformation 180–181
sociometabolic planning 125–129
socio-techno-ecological environments 128
'solar communism' 99
solidarity and altruism 138
solidary care economy 224
solidary society 225–228
Sorg, C. 110, 308–327
Sotiris, P. 99
South Africa 103
Southern market socialism 192–193
sovereign debt 192
sovereignty 128, 192
Soviet Marxism 284
Soviet Union 52–53, 134, 189
spatio-temporal projection 258–259
spontaneous volunteering 79
Srnicek, N. 325, 326
standard of living 77
state and capital relationship 209–210
state-owned housing stock 173
state policies 91
status in a community 102
stigmergic mediation 227, 238, 315
strategic plans 31, 46
'structural carelessness of capitalism' (Aulenbacher and Dammayr) 219
structural transformation 323
subject–object separation 90
see also capitalism
subsidiarity 42, 256, 259
supply and demand 70
supply chains 196–197
surpluses 317
surplus value reduction 206
Sutterlütti, S. 70, 83, 236, 238, 287, 315
swallows 242
synthetic indicators 57
SYRIZA party 210–212
system-wide transnational rebellions 191

T

tacit knowledge 24
taxes 42–43, 46

taxonomy of post-capitalist models (Laibman) 36
technocratic utopian visions 125
technological determinism 281–282
technology 6, 134, 253
techno-political infrastructures 152
techno-solutionism 279–280
Terranova, T. 99, 118
theory of action (Habermas) 148–149
theory of change 203, 204
theory of civilization 161
theory of human needs 250
theory of modernity 161
theory of post-capitalist transformation 203
theory of the multiple crisis 203, 204
Third World 191
Thunberg, G. xxii
Ticktin, H. 78
timebank theories 237–238
timetables 142–143
Tooze, A. 98
Toscano, A. 99, 110
Towards a New Socialism (Cockshott and Cottrell) 29
trade offs 151
transformation 190, 202–204, 214, 311–314
transformation of labour 268–269
transgender people 322
'transition trough' (Wright) 191
transnational negotiated coordination bodies 196
transpersonal commoning 89
transpersonal precautionary production of living conditions 90
Tremblay-Pepin, S. 127, 195
Tronti, M. 171
truth-telling 120–121
two-level models 54

U

UK 103, 212
Ukraine 103, 202
UN Conference on Trade & Development (UNCTAD) 192–193, 194
UN Intergovernmental Panel on Climate Change 92–93, 288
UN Paris Agreement xxi
underdeveloped countries 189
underreporting productive capacity 79–80
underwaged labour 309–310
undesirable labour 79
unemployment 64
unequal international power relations 189
unfree labour 309–310
unit of account (UoA) 86
'universal army of labour' (Jameson) 107
universal basic income *see* basic incomes
universal basic services 105–106, 148, 197
unpaid care work 219, 225
unpaid work 1, 219, 225

unprincipled self-interest 123
unreduced data 87
unreliable enterprises 89
urban social movements 175
USA 102, 103, 239, 308
US Center for Disease Control 100
US Federal Emergency Management Administration 100
usefulness 86
utopian decentralized models 68–71
utopian thinking 266–267

V

'vaccine apartheid' 103
valorization of capital 220
Van Parijs, P. 325
Vettese, T. 65n11
vital care systems 101
voluntariness
  commonism 83–84, 91
  feminized care work 274
  planning debate 236–237
voluntarism 79, 272
voluntary work 221

W

wage differentials 77–78
wage labour
  abolishing 74–78
  autonomy 73
  and conspicuous consumption 128
  exploitation 10–11
  flexible work 219
  replacing by social dividend 68, 75, 77
  replacing with guaranteed income 78–79
  separation of ownership and labour 205
  see also employment; labour
wages 40–41, 47, 73, 74–75, 77, 78–79
  see also basic incomes

Walmart 3, 284
'war communism' 99
wasting resources and systemic inertia 53
weather and climate data 288
Weber, M. 146
West German welfare state 172
white liberal feminists 241–242
white sense of safety 232
Winnicott, D. 327
women 274–275
work
  coercing people to 84
  degrowth debate 254
  voluntary 236
work brigades 79
workers
  compensation 28–29
  electing officials 72
  giving their best 122
  performance incentives 78
  social contribution 323
workers' councils 25–27, 44
workloads 221
workplaces 77
World Bank 196
World Meteorological Organization 288
World Trade Organization 103, 188
World Weather Watch 288
worthless activities 90
Wright, E.O. 191
Wright, I. 64
Wróbel, S. 103

Y

Yugoslavian socialism 185

Z

Zizek, S. 103
'zombie neoliberalism' xxii